1970

W9-CJD-372

3 0301 00009941 2

This book may be kept

IMMANUEL KANT

The speculative philosophy, if it ever could claim me, has frightened me away with its empty formulæ; I have found no living fountain and no nourishment on this bleak plain. But the deep and fundamental thoughts of the Ideal philosophy remain an everlasting treasure, and for their sake alone one must deem himself fortunate to have lived at this time. . . . After all, we are both Idealists, and would be ashamed to allow it to be said that things form us and not we things.

Schiller, *in his last letter to W. von Humboldt,*
April 2, 1805.

Immanuel
K A N T

His Life and Doctrine

FRIEDRICH PAULSEN

FREDERICK UNGAR PUBLISHING CO.
NEW YORK

LIBRARY
College of St. Francis
JOLIET, ILL.

Translated
from the Revised German Edition
by
J. E. CREIGHTON and ALBERT LEFEVRE

Copyright © 1963 by Frederick Ungar Publishing Co., Inc.

Printed in the United States of America

Library of Congress Catalog Card No. 63-11843

193.2
P332

TRANSLATORS' PREFACE

This work was written by Professor Paulsen for *Frommann's Klassiker der Philosophie*, and forms the seventh volume of that series. The series, which corresponds in general with *Blackwood's Philosophical Classics*, has been as a whole cordially welcomed in Germany, and Paulsen's *Kant* in particular has met with the warmest reception both from critics and from general readers of Kant's philosophy. It has been pronounced "the crown of the series."

The book possesses several characteristics which seem to make it especially valuable for English readers. In the first place, the author brings together and utilizes the more important results of the detailed investigations which have been carried on in Germany in recent years. Secondly, he has not restricted his account to the critical methodology, but has also treated Kant's philosophy as a whole, and has emphasized the constructive side of his metaphysics. Thus the critical and agnostic elements of Kant's thought are subordinated to a positive and idealistic metaphysic. The author's power of separating what is permanent and essential from what is merely external and accidental is well-known to English readers through Professor Thilby's excellent translations of his *Introduction to Philosophy* and *Ethics*. This gift is nowhere more clearly manifested or its value more evident than in the present exposition of the Kantian system.

The translators have not attempted to give an extensive bibliography of English works on Kant. They have deemed

55582

it sufficient to refer under the appropriate headings to some of the more important English books and articles, and to mention the most available English translations. The author's chronological list of Kant's writings, appended at the end of the volume, has been supplemented by a complete list of English translations. In this connection the translators have made use of the list of English translations of Kant's Works compiled by Professor George M. Duncan of Yale University, and published in the *Kant-Studien* (II., 2 and 3). They are also indebted to him for calling their attention to omissions in the original list and to translations which have appeared since its publication.

JANUARY, 1902.

PREFACE TO THE SECOND EDITION

No essential changes have been made in the second edition. In a few places slight additions have been made, and here and there the expression of the thought has been improved, and the divisions made clear to the eye by means of headings.

The fact that the first edition has been so quickly exhausted I regard with pleasure as new evidence that there is a wide circle of readers who are actively interested in the Kantian philosophy. The new century that stands before the door cannot have any more favorable omen than the fact that it devotes earnest attention to such serious thoughts.

May the two men shown in the accompanying portrait look kindly on the coming century. The one that is just passing would have brought them many severe disappointments. The belief in ideas which they imparted to it has gradually given way to belief in the external forces and material goods that now dominate our life. Nevertheless, as in families the grandson may resemble the grandfather, so it may perhaps happen in history; perhaps the twentieth century will be more like the eighteenth than the nineteenth.

F. PAULSEN.

Steglitz bei Berlin,
March 18, 1899.

PREFACE TO THE FIRST EDITION

THE fact that this book belongs to the series of 'Classical Writers of Philosophy' marks out the task that it is possible for it to undertake. It can only give an exposition of Kant's thoughts in their broad outlines, and not enter upon an exhaustive account of their details. Still less is it possible for it to undertake to solve the thousand questions that have become connected with the system, or to try to take account of the endless and ever-increasing literature that deals with Kant himself. On the other hand, it will have a somewhat different character from the other books that have already appeared in this series. Kant occupies at present a special place in our philosophical literature: he forms the centre of the academic study of philosophy, and is the object of a kind of philological activity, as Aristotle was some decades ago. I have, therefore, thought that I should not restrict myself to a general explanation of the fundamental thoughts of the system, but rather make an attempt at the same time to inform the reader about the Kantian studies of the present time, about the differences of opinion on the chief points, and the sources at our command for a knowledge of these ideas and their development, so far as this was possible within the given limits. I am fully aware that it is a somewhat delicate undertaking to write such a book at a time when every line that Kant left, either in print or in manuscript, is brought under the scrutiny of special investigation. Nevertheless, I could not and would not refuse the task which the editor and the publisher urged upon me with friendly persuasions. And, above all, the task itself attracted me. I cannot count myself as an unconditional adherent of Kant, but I am firmly convinced that the great fundamental thoughts of his philosophy have a mission in pointing the way to a philosophy of the world and of life at the present time; and the earnestness and force that he has devoted to the solution of the deepest and most ultimate problems will render his works for all time both an attractive and worthy object of study.

I have not sought to conceal my conviction that in the system as such there is not a little which is not of permanent value. I have indicated, with the candor due to a man like Kant, the points where he enters on a path that I cannot follow, and which I do not regard as practicable. In this criticism I include not merely the external schematic arrangement, but also the inner form of the system, which is determined by an *a priori* dogmatic mode of thought, which takes its character from mathematics and dominates his epistemology and moral philosophy. It belongs in its presuppositions to the eighteenth century. The nineteenth century has everywhere abandoned these, and adopted in their place the historical and genetic point of view. On the side of its content, I feel much more sympathy with Kant's philosophy. The ethico-metaphysical Idealism, the conception of the relation of the knowing mind to reality, the determination of the significance of the value of knowledge and of will for life and for a theory of the world, — all these have become permanent elements of German philosophy. For the very reason that Kant's philosophy is a living system, I thought that I should not abstain from criticising it. When criticism ceases, it is a sign that a system is dead: to become a matter of history is called death. This time has not yet come for Kant; he still has important things to say, even at the present time. And this is true not merely of his epistemology. I wish especially that the spirit of his practical Idealism, his lofty ideas of human dignity, right, and freedom might again exert an influence in this age of "realism," of belief in might and money. The true German people cannot, without shame, look back from the end of this century to the end of the preceding one, which Schiller celebrated in that proud hymn.

The purpose of the book made it necessary to devote more space to Kant's central doctrines, and merely to outline the less fundamental disciplines. In particular, I have devoted a detailed exposition to the metaphysics, which is usually too much overshadowed by the critical doctrine in the accounts of Kant's philosophy. Kant one time remarked jokingly that it was his fate to have fallen in love with metaphysics, though it was only seldom that he could boast of any favors from her. This is more than a mere jest, however, and in spite of the critique of reason he always remained true to his old love, and the result shows that favors were not entirely wanting on her side. It is true that Kant now and again in the *Critique* adopts the standpoint of the Agnostic. But wherever he expresses himself directly in his own personal thinking, as in the lectures and lecture-notes, we find everywhere the pure Platonist, and he who does not give heed to the Platonist will not understand the critical philosopher. The transcendental Idealism does not exclude the objective, metaphysical Idealism. On the contrary, its vocation is to serve as a basis, on the one hand, for a rationalistic epistemology, and on the other for an idealistic metaphysics. Kant's view of the nature of what is "actually real" remained unaltered throughout his life. Reality is in itself a system of existing thought-essences brought into a unity by teleological relations that are intuitively thought by the Divine intellect, and by this very act of thought posited as real. The method of establishing this view changes, but the view itself undergoes no alteration. In the *Critique of Pure Reason* the negative side, the controverting of a false demonstration, is most prominent. Here Kant's thought has attained the greatest distance from its centre. In the *Critique of Pure Reason*, the reality of the intelligible world continued to be taken for granted as a matter of course, and in the later writings, especially in the two later *Critiques*, it again reappears in a most emphatic fashion as the dominating central point. If one overlooks this and makes Kant either a sceptical agnostic who teaches the unknowableness of things-in-themselves, or a subjective idealist for whom there is no reality in itself at all, he will never be able to make anything of his philosophy. At least he can never present a systematic exposition of it, but only interpret disconnected passages.

I should be glad if this exposition contributed a little to inspire courage in idealistic metaphysics, which in these latter days has begun to venture again into the light, by showing that Kant is no forbidding or threatening name, but a kindly disposed patron.

The purpose of the book answers the question for whom it is written. Above all, it aims to afford guidance to those who wish to read and study Kant himself. Our students nowadays are referred to Kant on all sides, by means of lectures, discussions, and examination requirements. Thus it happens that for many the *Critique of Pure Reason* is the first philosophical book that they seriously attempt to read. It is obvious that the book is not well suited to this purpose. Kant himself would not have recommended it. He did not even write the *Prolegomena* for pupils, but for future teachers of philosophy. In fact, not only are the problems with which the *Critique* deals in themselves the most difficult, but the manner of treatment greatly enhances the difficulty. They presuppose nothing less than an acquaintance with the entire state of philosophy at the time, with dogmatism and scepticism, with Leibniz and Hume. And, in truth, these influences are not merely external to it, but are contained in it as systems of ideas that have been transcended though not yet effaced. That is especially true of Leibniz. The *Critique of Pure Reason* not seldom gives the impression of a palimpsest, over an original half-effaced manuscript. A new work is written, with the effect that its clearness is obscured by the script that lies beneath. Nevertheless, we cannot alter these things. Kant's philosophy is the door to the philosophy of our century, and the door to the Kantian philosophy is the *Critique of Pure Reason.* I have, therefore, taken special pains to explain the historical condition of affairs out of which Kant's philosophy arose with sufficient fulness to render intelligible the problems that he raises. It is certain that with this assistance the door will remain narrow and the path steep ; but even this may have its advantage. An enthusiast in recommending that Greek should be made the beginning of school instruction, advanced the following reasons for his plan : If the nine-year-old boy masters at first the forms of the Greek language, he will proceed smoothly and without difficulty downwards on the path of language study. Thus one could comfort and encourage the reader of the *Critique* by telling him that, when he has worked through and understood it, all other philosophical books would seem easy and afford him no trouble.

So far as possible I refer to Kant's writings according to the titles of sections and the paragraphs. The paging is given from Hartenstein's second edition (8 vols.). More-over, I have been sparing of quotations. I do not believe that on an average one out of a hundred references is looked up. And in the last resort an interpretation of Kant must be based upon his whole system. By using individual passages one can get out of him almost every possible and impossible view.

The portrait that is here given is a reproduction of the Kant-Lessing group from the Friedrich monument by Rauch. The photograph was taken by Herr Niemeyer (Steglitz) from the cast in the Rauch Museum. The head of Kant was originally taken from the bust in possession of the University of Königsberg, modelled from life in 1802, by Hagemann, a pupil of Schadow. It was a happy thought of Rauch to place Kant and Lessing together. Kant himself would scarcely have wished to select any one else as the representative of the readers for whom he wrote. And with the insight of genius the character of the two men is represented: Kant, the teacher, expounding his system with steadfast seriousness and zeal; Lessing, the hearer, listening to the word with quiet attention. And even the slight smile that plays around the refined mouth of the listener, would not have been wanting if he could have read, with his characteristic confidence, the works in which the critical philosopher announced the new doctrine. It is as if the sceptically curved lips would say: "Have we at last, then, the whole and final truth?"

The original of the letter of Kant to his brother which is here reproduced is in the Royal Library at Berlin. It shows the handwriting, and also affords a not uninteresting impression of the man's nature and mode of thought.

FRIEDRICH PAULSEN.

STEGLITZ BEI BERLIN,
    1898.

TABLE OF CONTENTS

IMMANUEL KANT

INTRODUCTION

I. Kant's Significance in the General History of Thought

THERE are three attitudes of the mind towards reality which lay claim to truth, — Religion, Philosophy, and Science. Although sprung from a single root, they become differentiated in the higher stages of mental life, reunite, and again stand opposed to one another in a variety of ways, receiving their characteristic stamp through the manner in which this process takes place. Especially is it true that every philosophy is essentially determined through the attitude which it adopts towards religion and science.

In general, philosophy occupies an intermediate place between science and religion. If one adopts the figure of Bacon which represents the mental world as a ball (*globus intellectualis*), similar to the *globus materialis* by means of which the mediæval cosmology pictured the external world, then one might divide the world into three concentric spheres, corresponding to the three spheres of the cosmos. The outermost sphere of this ball, corresponding to the region of the fixed stars, would represent science ; the inner kernel, corresponding to the earth, would represent religion ; while philosophy finally would occupy the middle or planetary sphere.

Science holds the peripheral position in the mental life. In this field the thinking and calculating understanding gives rise to a system of concepts and formulas by means of which it externally comprehends and rules over nature. Religion forms the inner kernel of our view of the world; its goal is the interpretation of the meaning of things. Science makes the world conceivable, but does not render it intelligible. Conformity to law is not its meaning. All religion claims certainly to possess the meaning of life and of the world, and to reveal this in concrete examples of the good and the perfect. Philosophy occupies an intermediate position between the two, — relating itself on the one hand to science, and on the other to religion. It seeks not only to conceive the world, but also to understand it. The history of philosophy shows that its task consists simply in mediating between science and religion. It seeks to unite knowledge and faith, and in this way to restore the unity of the mental life. It performs this task both for the individual and for society. As in the case of the individual, it mediates between the head and the heart, so in society it prevents science and religion from becoming entirely strange and indifferent to each other, and hinders also the mental life of the people from being split up into a faith-hating science and a science-hating faith or superstition.

It follows from what has been said that the character of a philosophy is essentially determined through the manner in which it performs this historical task. From this standpoint we may distinguish two fundamental forms of philosophy: I shall name them with Kant the *dogmatic* and the *critical*. The essence of dogmatic philosophy consists in the fact that it undertakes to found faith upon knowledge; it seeks to demonstrate what is to be believed. It produces as a variation of itself its own contradictory, that is, the *sceptical* philosophy. For when the latter tests the demonstrations and perceives their inadequacy, it comes at last to discard faith itself as a delusion, and to maintain that knowledge through scientific concepts constitutes the

only form of truth.   The critical philosophy comes forward
in opposition to this.   Its real nature is seen in the fact
that it makes clear the essential difference between the functions of knowing and of believing, between conceiving things
through a system of laws, and understanding their significance; and through a strict division of the field it shows
how an agreement may be reached.   Matters of faith cannot be demonstrated by the understanding, as dogmatism
undertakes to do, because they are not derived from the
understanding.   But just for this reason they cannot be over-
thrown by the understanding, as scepticism tries to show.

I shall indicate the way in which this conceptual schema
is borne out by the historical development.

The original form of positive dogmatism in the Western
world is the *idealistic* philosophy of the Greeks; the original
form of negative dogmatism is found in their *materialistic*
philosophy.   Plato and his successor Aristotle set out from
the fundamental principle that the world is the realization
of ideas.   The cosmic order manifested through mathematically formulated laws is objective reason.   Every living
being is the realization of a purposive idea, while man, as
the highest living creature, as knowing his own end and the
purpose of the universe, is the self-realization of reason.
The real function that philosophy has to perform, then, is
to make known the meaning of the world in the form of a
scientific system.

The same view of the nature of the world and of philosophy is dominant in the systems of the middle ages, which
retained their place as the accepted school-philosophy until
the beginning of the eighteenth century.   It was also an
assumption of the natural theology that after the time of
Locke and Leibniz superseded scholasticism.   The purpose
of this natural theology is to furnish scientific demonstrations of the truth of what is held through faith, at least in
its main principles, or to discover the divine purpose in

nature and in history. Apart from the dependence of
Christian philosophy upon external authority, it is distinguished from Greek philosophy mainly by the fact that it
adopts a teleological philosophy of history, while Greek
speculation limits itself to a teleology of nature.

Along with positive dogmatism, we have, as the obverse,
negative dogmatism. In the ancient world, we meet this
in the Epicurean philosophy, which knows only bodies and
uniform natural laws, and refuses to recognize ideas and
purposes in the real world. Although this point of view
disappears almost completely during the middle ages, it
emerges again as soon as pure scientific thought, which
first showed itself in mathematics and the sciences of nature,
found freer expression. In the second half of the eighteenth
century, this philosophy was at the same time both the pro-
hibited and the prevailing form of thought. This was especially the case in France.

Now, the real purpose of the critical philosophy, the
philosophy of Kant, is to overcome the opposition which
has extended through the entire history of human thought.
Kant undertakes with positive dogmatism to restore the
agreement between faith and knowledge. In the last resort,
however, he establishes this agreement by means of a philosophy of morals, not by means of a philosophy of nature.
In this way, he is able to grant to negative dogmatism its
right to a free, unprejudiced investigation of the entire world
of phenomena.

In his theoretical philosophy, Kant overthrows at one
blow both positive and negative dogmatism. With materialism, he asserts that science leads only to a knowledge of
the uniform connection of things according to law, not to a
recognition of their meaning; it is mechanical, not teleological. A teleology of nature and of history is impossible
from the scientific standpoint, and consequently it is impossible to have a science of natural theology. But a scien-

tific knowledge of the world, which construes all things, from the formation of the cosmos to the origin of life on the earth, and the course of human history, as the necessary effects of given causes, is possible. On the other hand, Kant holds with idealism that there is a meaning in things, and that we can become certain of this meaning. Life has a real significance. With immediate certainty we affirm moral good as the real purpose of life. We do this, not by means of the understanding or scientific thinking, but through the will, or, as Kant says, the practical reason. In the fact that the will, which alone judges things as 'good' or 'bad,' determines morality as that which has absolute worth, we have the point of departure for the interpretation of life. It is through the will, not through the understanding, that we interpret history; such persons and events as, e. g., Jesus and his life and death, are the historical facts of supreme importance. Thus arise all the historical religions. And in the fact that the entire world is referred to this fixed point, the religious view of the world has its origin; nature is interpreted as a means for the fulfilment of that purpose. Faith is convinced that God has made the world in order to realize in it his salvation toward men. All dogmas of every religion are the diverse expressions of the conviction that the world exists for the sake of the good, and that nature and history find their explanation in the purposes of God.

But how now is it possible to bring together in a unitary view of the world these two independent ways of regarding things, — the scientific explanation and the religious interpretation? Kant's answer is, by means of the distinction between a sensible and a super-sensible world. The world which constitutes the object of mathematico-scientific knowledge is not reality as such, but only the appearance of reality to our sensibility. The world of religious conviction, on the contrary, is the supersensuous reality itself. This can never become the object of scientific knowledge, on account of the nature of human cognition, which presupposes perception. Regarding it we can know only that it exists; that is the ultimate point to which knowledge attains. In reflecting critically on its own nature and limits, the understanding recognizes that there is an absolute reality beyond the world of sense. And now the spirit (which is something more than understanding) claims, as a moral being, to be a member of this absolute reality, and defines the nature of this reality through its own essence. This is Kant's doctrine of the primacy of the practical reason over the theoretical.

In this way the critical philosophy solves the old problem of the relation of knowledge and faith. Kant is convinced that by properly fixing the limits of each he has succeeded in furnishing a basis for an honorable and enduring peace between them. Indeed, the significance and vitality of his philosophy will rest principally upon this. Although in the details of this philosophy there may be much that is not agreeable to us, it is its enduring merit to have drawn for the first time, with a firm hand and in clear outline, the dividing line between knowledge and faith. This gives to knowledge what belongs to it, — the entire world of phenomena for free investigation; it conserves, on the other hand, to faith its eternal right to the interpretation of life and of the world from the standpoint of value.

There is indeed no doubt that the great influence which Kant exerted upon his age was due just to the fact that he appeared as a deliverer from unendurable suspense. The old view regarding the claims of the feelings and the understanding on reality had been more and more called in question during the second half of the eighteenth century. Voltaire and Hume had not written in vain. Science seemed to demand the renunciation of the old faith. On the other hand, the heart still clung to it. Pietism had increased the sincerity and earnestness of religion, and given it a new and firm root in the affections of the German people. At this point Kant showed a way of escape from the dilemma. His philosophy made it possible to be at once a candid thinker and an honest man of faith. For that, thousands of hearts have thanked him with passionate devotion. It was a deliverance similar to that which the Reformation had brought to the German spirit a century or two earlier. Indeed, one may in a certain sense regard Kant as the finisher of what Luther had begun. The original purpose of the Reformation was to make faith independent of knowledge, and conscience free from external authority. It was the confusion of religion and science in scholastic philosophy against which Luther first revolted. That faith had been transformed into a philosophical body of doctrines, that *fides* had been changed to *credo*, seemed to him to be the root of all evil. To substitute for belief in a human dogma the immediate certainty of the heart in a gracious God reconciled through Christ, to emphasize the importance of the inner disposition, as opposed to outer acts, was the soul of his work. Kant was the first who definitely destroyed the scholastic philosophy. By banishing religion from the field of science, and science from the sphere of religion, he afforded freedom and independence to both. And at the same time he placed morality on a Protestant basis, — not works, but the disposition of the heart.

To this interpretation and evaluation of the Kantian philosophy there are opposed two other views. Criticism is combated by two forms of dogmatism. Though opposed to each other, they agree in their unfavorable opinion of Kant. Negative dogmatism accuses him of treachery to knowledge; positive dogmatism, of yielding the rights of faith. The latter reproaches him as the destroyer of religion and of the philosophy which was well disposed towards it; the former despises him for his subservience to traditional modes of thought and to the pretended necessities of the heart, — a weakness which at most can be forgiven only in view of his other services.[1]

I shall not further discuss negative dogmatism and the judgment which it passes on Kant. At the present day it plays no great rôle. Materialism does not nowadays speak the final word. The representatives of science for the most part occupy the Kantian position. So much the more frequent and vigorous are the attacks from the other side. Revived scholasticism, in particular, directs its attacks at Kant as the champion of the hostile philosophy. With Thomism, as the fundamental form of constructive idealism, is contrasted criticism, as the type of subjective, false, and destructive idealism. Thus it has been pictured by Otto Willmann in his three-volume *History of Idealism*. He represents the history of philosophy according to the following schema. First, the ascending branch. From Plato to St. Thomas we have the ever richer and fuller unfolding of pure idealism, which posits the ideas as objective, constitutive principles of reality. With Thomas the highest point is reached. Then with Nominalism begins the downward course; the disaster of the Reformation followed, and this in logical train led to the Illumination and the Revolution. In Kant's philosophy the spirit of denial has found its completest expression. It is at the very opposite pole from Thomism. In it false idealism has attained to its final consequence — the reduction of all ideal principles to subjectivism. In this system, the subject, with boundless

---

[1] H. Heine, in his essay on "Religion and Philosophy in Germany," has characterized, or rather caricatured, Kant's relation to religion as follows: After Kant, in the *Critique of Pure Reason*, had destroyed deism, or the old Jehovah himself, the tragedy was followed by a farce. Behind the dreadful critic stands, carrying an umbrella, his old servant Lampe, tears and drops of anguish upon his face. "Then Immanuel Kant has compassion and shows that he is not only a great philosopher, but also a good man, and, half kindly, half ironically, he speaks: 'Old Lampe must have a God or else he cannot be happy, says the practical reason; for my part, the practical reason may, then, guarantee the existence of God.'"

self-conceit, claims to be the bearer of all reality, the creator of both the laws of nature and of morals. The autonomy of reason is the real nerve of Kant's philosophizing. Kant is the absolutely free thinker, "an advocate for the overthrow of faith, morals, and science." "The idea that he is a pure German philosopher is quite preposterous. Kant is a cosmopolite: he follows the English, is an enthusiastic admirer of Rousseau, and raves about the French Revolution. To German honesty (*Treue*) Kant's destructive sophistic is in direct opposition." [1]

There can be no doubt that this condemnatory judgment regarding Kant is a direct consequence of the Catholic principle. The autonomy of reason and the infallibility of the dogma are evidently irreconcilably opposed. It is also a matter of course that for the adherent of the absolute philosophy, sanctioned by the authority of the Pope, there only exist outside his own standpoint various forms of error, over whose differences it is scarcely worth while to linger. *Philosophia cœlestis* has only one opposite, the *philosophia terrena*, unless one should oppose to it a *philosophia infernalis*, which, moreover, also stands in the same relation. Both are sisters born of arrogance and disobedience.

What attitude would Kant have taken towards such criticism? I think he would have accepted unconditionally the characterization *philosophia terrena*. He recognizes that he is a man placed in this world; his standing-place is

---

[1] III., pp. 503, 528. — In an essay on this book by Commer, the editor of the Catholic *Jahrbücher für Philos. und spekul. Theologie* (1896), we find the following statements: There are two species of philosophy, the true and the false — *philosophia cœlestis* and *philosophia terrena*. These correspond to the two kingdoms of reality, as St. Augustine has distinguished them, — the *civitas Dei* and the *civitas terrena*. The one philosophy has its roots in love to God; the other, in self-love. On the one side stands St. Thomas, the representative of divine and true philosophy; and on the other, stand Materialism, Anarchism, Pantheism, Atheism, Agnosticism, and in the midst, Criticism, as the most dangerous foe of God and of religion. — I have made some criticisms of Willmann's book in an essay entitled, "The Most Recent Inquisition on Modern Philosophy," in the *Deutsche Rundschau*, August, 1898.

the earth. It is not strange, then, that the result of an attempt to orient himself in the world should be an earthly and not a heavenly philosophy. To be sure, it will not escape the man who devotes a more careful scrutiny to Kant's thoughts that his standpoint does not at all seek absolute satisfaction in the things of this earth; he rather points everywhere beyond the *mundus sensibilis* to a *mundus intelligibilis*. But his modesty, or rather his critical reflection upon man's position in the world, prevented him from taking this intelligible world as his standpoint and building his system upon it. He sees that he does not enjoy the privilege of dwelling in that world beyond, or of receiving his inspiration from it. So he is compelled to leave the heavenly philosophy to those who are more favorably situated in this respect. There are two considerations which enable him more easily to endure the arrogance of such people. The first is that the alleged heavenly philosophy has as yet accomplished little or nothing for the advancement of human knowledge. It is only since the earthly standpoint has been adopted that the sciences have gained a sure method of advance. The other is that the lauded service of the pretended heavenly philosophy on behalf of religion and idealism becomes very questionable on unprejudiced historical investigation. It seems rather to Kant that the Catholic church and school philosophy, which was derived directly from Thomism, is so far from affording support to religious faith at the end of the eighteenth century that the latter is rather hopelessly compromised, and has been brought into suspicion through its connection with the dead body of Thomism. It is the critical philosophy which has again restored to life the faith of the spirit in itself, and as a result of this has revived faith in spirit in general and its creative power in the world. Only through it has an idealistic philosophy which believes in itself become possible.

Indeed it is a remarkable coincidence that in the same year, 1770, there appeared in Catholic France the *Système de la nature*, in Protestant Germany Kant's treatise *De mundi sensibilis et intelligibilis forma ac principiis* — an end and a beginning: the former work an end, — the final and consistent formulation of the materialistic point of view, to which French thought had long tended under the impulse of the scholastic systems which were protected and fostered in the universities; the latter a beginning, — the first outline of an idealistic philosophy of a new kind, the point of departure, even to our own day, for a long series of idealistic systems. On the other hand also an end, — namely, the definitive end of materialism, if we are to accept the authority of the historian F. A. Lange.

At the same time we will also say what is to be thought of the other boast of the Catholic school-philosophy, that it is the *philosophia perennis*. At the end of last century it was as dead as out-worn system ever was. If that system at present is experiencing a kind of revival in the school of Catholicism, this is due not so much to its own inner vitality as to its supposed fitness to serve an ecclesiastical political system which through the favor of circumstances — *patientia Dei et stultitia hominum*, an old Lutheran would say — has attained again in our time to unexpected power. Moreover, there still remains the question whether continuance of existence is in general something of which a philosophy can boast. Perhaps fruitfulness is a better characteristic, and this the Kantian philosophy shows; it still gives rise to new systems of thought. Thomism, on the contrary, though of course a great achievement for its own time, yields to-day nothing except unfruitful repetitions. It does not set free the spirit, it enslaves it, which of course is just its intention.

But, finally, in regard to the doctrine of the autonomy of reason, with its groundless subjectivism and its immanent tendency to revolution, it is naturally impossible to discuss these matters with those who are not open to conviction. Whoever is determined to subject his reason to ecclesiastical, which now means papist, authority, cannot be hindered. And it would be just as vain to maintain against such a one the right of reason to independent judgment. He would in all circumstances see in this defence arrogance and culpable insubordination. To what purpose has he subjected himself if others may venture to make exceptions and go their own way?

But for those who are not yet so firmly convinced, the remark may be added that the grounding of the certainty of knowledge of morals and of faith upon the inner certainty of the individual is the firmest foundation which is possible in human matters. This is the very foundation that Kant has laid (at least in intention). He thought that he had proved that reason makes explicit its own essence in the laws of nature and of morals, and in rational faith; and that, therefore, so soon as it has knowledge of the real circumstances, it cannot refrain from recognizing this law. Of course, Kant's doctrine is not universally accepted. Nevertheless, in this respect no external authority has an advantage over it, not even that of the chair of Peter. Indeed, one can say that it lies in the nature of reason to react with inner hostility against every external authority that demands absolute subjection in spiritual and moral things. The history of Catholic lands does not permit us to doubt that absolutism brings as its opposite intellectual and even moral and political anarchism.

II. KANT'S POSITION IN THE THOUGHT OF HIS OWN TIME

If we wish to describe Kant's position in a single formula we may say that he is at once the finisher and conqueror of the Illumination.

Kant's early training falls in the period when the two opposing tendencies of pietism and rationalism were influencing the minds of men. The period of his personal activity is the age of the illumination. The spread of his philosophy towards the end of the century coincides with the decline of the illumination and the appearance of the new humanism. By the turn of the century, which Kant as an old man lived to see, the critical philosophy in connection with modern classical literature had victoriously completed the great spiritual revolution in Germany, which ran parallel with the politico-social revolution in France. A new view of the world and a new ideal of culture had gained predominance.

I shall attempt to characterize in a few words the general tendencies and the leaders in this movement.

Pietism and rationalism both begin to find their way into Protestant Germany from the Netherlands and France in the second half of the seventeenth century. Although mutually antagonistic, they coöperate in overturning the theologico-dogmatic mode of thought that had prevailed since the generation in which the reformed doctrines had been fixed.

Pietism is, in its origin, a popular religious movement. Its object is to make Christianity — which in the state churches had degenerated into a subject of dispute for theological scholars, and a tool for obtaining the mastery on the part of the scheming politicians — what it originally sought to be, the great personal concern of the individual. This explains the insistence on conversion. Connection with a church is of no avail; everything depends on the personal turning to God in Christ. There is in this something of the original impulse of the Reformation. The subjective religious life asserts itself against the religion objectified in church doctrine and ordinance, — Luther rebels against Lutheranism.

If pietism is the renewing of the original and most fundamental tendencies of the Reformation, rationalism may be

characterized as the continuance of the Renaissance. Like
the latter, it proceeds from a worldly aristocratic impulse
toward culture; the soil in which it grows is independent
investigation that has been emancipated from authority.
The new sciences, cosmology and physics, united with
mathematics, and also that critical historical investigation
which, since the days of Valla and Erasmus, had rent the
veil which lay over the past, have given to reason confidence
in itself. In the great philosophical systems of Descartes,
Hobbes, Spinoza, and Leibniz, it sets itself the task of constructing on the basis of all the modern sciences a world-
system of a purely rational character. Rationalism, in the
most general sense, is nothing else than the confidence that
reason must succeed, without any other presuppositions than
those which scientific investigation and necessary thinking
afford, in producing an all-embracing system of demonstrable
truths in which God and nature, life and history, will be included without any unexplained remainder.

Pietism and rationalism, in spite of their intrinsic opposition, seem, on their first appearance, to be connected just as
the Reformation and the Renaissance formerly were. They
have a common foe in the dominant system, and a common
characteristic in their endeavor after freedom, after the
realization of the personal life. In the university which
had just been founded at Halle (1694), they met in the
persons of two of their most important representatives,
August Hermann Francke (1662–1727), and Christian
Thomasius (1665–1727). Both had been expelled from the
land of pure Lutheranism, the old conservative Saxony, and
its university at Leipzig, and both found the sphere of their
permanent and wide-reaching influence in the young university of the energetic Prussian State. The theologian and the
jurist were soon joined by a third, the philosopher, Christian Wolff (1679–1754). His importance consists in the fact
that he reduced modern philosophy to an inclusive system

that could be taught and learned in the universities, and
by this means banished the Aristotelian school-philosophy
from the German universities. The modern sciences,
mathematics and mathematical physics, form the basis
of his system. Like Leibniz and Descartes, Hobbes and
Spinoza, Wolff sets out from these sciences, in which he had
already worked as a teacher and writer. From their point
of view he writes his logic and metaphysic, his ethics and
psychology. The motto of his philosophy, "nothing without sufficient reason," denotes its strong rationalistic character; nothing happens and nothing is true without a
sufficient reason.

As the political friendship between the Renaissance
and the Reformation was broken so soon as the common
enemy, scholasticism, had been overcome, so the intrinsic
opposition between pietism and rationalism passed into
open hostility as soon as the old orthodoxy had lost its
dominant position. Even in Halle it came to a bitter fight,
which ended with the well-known disaster, the expulsion of
Wolff (1723). But the joy of his pietistical opponents was
too hasty; the power of the illumination was already too
strong. Persecution heightened Wolff's fame and increased
his influence. In the year 1740, immediately after the accession of Frederick the Great, he was recalled with fullest
honors and held his triumph as victor in Halle.

From the year 1740 we may date the undisputed dominance of the illumination in Germany. It lasted until
about the death of its great representatives on the German
thrones, Friedrich and Joseph. If we wish to define its
character in a formula we may say: It was the period of
the peaceful and universally recognized sway of reason upon
the earth, attained after long combat and final victory. Confidence in reason was universal and unconditioned, — reason
in things and reason in men. Now, reason undertakes to
arrange all things according to their principles. The in-

stitutions and arrangements of life are examined with a
critical glance, and ordered anew according to rational concepts. In like manner, knowledge is rationalized. Reason
explains all things as due to reason. God, the world-reason,
has formed nature in accordance with rational thoughts.
The task of the philosopher is to discover these rational
thoughts in things and to re-think them. The historical
world, too, is explained from rational thoughts and purposes.
Here is human reason itself, which creates its own world.
Language and religion, law and the State, are means invented
by the reason for the attainment of rational ends. And
alongside this rationalistic philosophy of history stands a
rationalistic æsthetic that explains art and poetry from
rational principles, and affords guidance for rational production. Gottsched's critical art of poetry is the type of this
æsthetic. Thus reason has become the all-prevailing principle — both formal and material — of philosophy. All
things are made by reason and are intelligible through
reason.

In the second half of the eighteenth century there appeared, at first imperceptibly, then more openly, a reaction
against the universal sovereignty of reason, which finally led
to the direct opposite of the illumination, — to Romanti-
cism. Among the foreign influences which gave rise to this
movement we may mention in the first place Voltaire,
Rousseau, and the English philosophers. All these stand
on the ground of the illumination, but they undermine its
foundation. Voltaire directs his sarcasm against the perfection of the world as the optimistic rationalism of Leibniz
had represented it. Rousseau champions the cause of the
heart against the head; he emphasizes the importance of
nature, and of the unconscious, as opposed to conscious reason; he praises innocent simplicity and good will above
the arrogance of the culture of the understanding. English
empiricism combats rationalism in epistemology and meta-

physics. When carried to its extreme form by Hume, it denies the possibility of metaphysics or of natural theology in general. It asserts that there is no absolute knowledge of the world, that reality does not manifest itself to human reason. A metaphysical theory of the world, according to the view to which Hume's *Dialogues on Natural Religion* leads, is based rather on the disposition of the heart than upon reason and demonstration. It possesses the subjective necessity of faith, not the objective necessity of knowledge.

Similar transformations in the German world of thought are connected with the names of Winckelmann, Lessing, Hamann, Herder, Goethe, and Schiller. To this group also belongs Kant. These men all grew up in the school of the illumination, but they all transcend the conceptions of the illumination. For they abandon strict rationalism and advance to the historico-genetic standpoint, which asserts that things are not fashioned according to fixed plans, they develop and grow. Neither the great works of art and literature, nor the great historical achievements like language and religion, nor even nature and her products have been contrived as means for the realization of ends. Organic growth became the dominant concept, superseding the notion of mechanical creation. The view of the world which belongs to this type of thought is evolutionary pantheism. This displaced the metaphysic of the illumination, anthropomorphic theism.

A transformation in our attitude towards life, and in our general view of the world always shows itself first in the æsthetic field. We find, therefore, that this is the case here. Klopstock, Winckelmann, and Lessing shake men's faith in the rationalistic æsthetic, and in the art and poetry whose expression it is, or which has been framed according to its rules. Klopstock turns from the French to the English, from art to nature, and from what is foreign to what is domestic

2

and national. Gottsched and the poetry formed after the rules of classic verse are despised. Winckelmann proclaimed the degradation of the court academy art in the midst of its own territory. He accused it of being a product of arbitrary choice, and of pandering to the vulgar taste for what is fashionable and exaggerated. In this he contrasts it with the simplicity and calm nobility of the art of the Greeks. Their works of art are not imitative products, fashioned according to the rules of academic art for the satisfaction of vanity or for the purpose of entertaining the fashionable world, but they have proceeded by uniform development from the national life itself. Lessing, the hero who rejoiced in conflict, begins his great war against everything which is canonical and conventional, against the dogmas of the old æsthetics and poetics, as well as against the dogmas of the orthodox or new-fashioned rational theology. He is the first who sees Spinoza's thoughts shining through Leibniz's system, the first who ventured to follow up Spinoza's thought of the ἕν καὶ πᾶν, the doctrine of the All-One.

When Lessing in the summer of 1780 carried on those conversations with F. H. Jacobi about Spinoza in Gleim's garden-house, he did not know that the work was already thought out which should give the death blow to the metaphysics of the illumination. This work was the *Critique of Pure Reason*. Kant showed that the world is in no respect such a transparent thought-product as the illumination assumed; indeed, that reality in general cannot be apprehended by our thought, that it necessarily transcends the standpoint of knowledge. And from this there followed for him the further consequences that religion cannot be derived from or demonstrated by reason, as the illumination attempted. Its roots lie deeper, they are to be sought in the will. The will, the practical side of our nature, determines the fundamental direction of our view of the world, as it determines the value of human life. Kant himself did not complete the transition from the intellectualistic to the voluntaristic metaphysics and psychology. He still possessed, even to the end, too great confidence in the power of reason. But he started the movement which was fully carried out by Schopenhauer.

Kant's younger countryman, Hamann, the "magician of the North," had many points of contact with him. In Hamann, the pietistic sceptic, the reaction against rationalism is almost transformed into a hostility towards reason. He will allow almost no merit to reason except that it leads men to a knowledge of its inevitable shortcomings. In so far as Hume and Kant (whom he once called the Prussian Hume) effect this, he recognizes in them the true philosophy. He was especially concerned with the problem of the origin of language and poetry, and finds its source, not in the reason, where the philosophers of the illumination had sought it, but in the dispositions and passions through which nature works. Hamann is the prophet of those inclined to mysticism among the devout of both confessions who at the beginning of the nineteenth century introduced the great revival of the emotional religiosity which clings fast to mysteries.

A pupil of Kant and Hamann is Herder, though both of them regard him as influenced by Hume and Rousseau. His importance in the development of the German intellectual life consists in the fact that he destroyed rationalism in the philosophy of history. Language, poetry, religion, are not manufactured products, but natural growths, which are produced by the different peoples with the same inner necessity with which the various regions produce different forms of plant and animal life. With this is connected Herder's fondness for the original form of poetry, the popular ballads. This is genuine poetry, which cannot be said of the manufactured verses of the professors of poetics and their pupils. And the same is true of religion. Religion is originally poetry, the great world-poem which the spirit of the people produces in its struggle with reality, and in which are reflected its own nature and destiny. It is said that religion is the manifestation of God. That is certainly true, but the manifestation of God through human nature, in the same sense that Homer is a manifestation of God, or the Zeus of Phidias, or the Madonna of Raphael. This point of view overthrows the old doctrine of special inspiration. It also destroys rationalistic theology, which explains religion as the invention of priests and religious societies, and seeks to purify it, by critical endeavors, of what is false and unessential. The final postulate of the new point of view is here again pantheistic metaphysics: the entire world is the manifestation of God. Herder too found in Spinoza his philosopher.

Goethe's thought, which was enriched by Herder, moved in the same path. Pantheism, poetically apprehended through feeling, is his faith, — Spinoza's philosophy and Rousseau's sensibility to nature united. His first great poetical works, *Werther*, *Faust*, *Prometheus*, are entirely filled with this spirit. He despised the conventional philosophy and science of the schools; he scorned the understanding which works designedly and according to rule, — *encheiresin naturæ*, so chemistry names it! Feeling and intuition are everything; name and concept are only the external appearance. This is the doctrine that he proclaims with youthful vehemence. But even in the scientific form of his later thought, there remains the opposition to the mechanico-rational view. This shows itself in his color theory, as aversion towards Newton; in his geological and biological views as dislike for the Plutonian hypothesis, and as belief in the gradual growth and development of natural forms. It is the idea of organic development which gave direction to his scientific thinking. Development, organic increase, is also the form of his personal life and practical activity. To both is the idea foreign of producing according to set plan.   In his own person the wonderful richness of his nature unfolded itself in unbroken continuity throughout his long life without the haste and commotion of voluntarily setting about to produce it.   And in the same way his great poetical works took form in an organic way from his own inner experience.   Thus Goethe is in his own person the living refutation of the old, narrow, rationalistic view of the nature of poetry, and of life, and of reality in general.   Schiller also was impregnated with the doctrines of Spinoza and Rousseau before he found his world-formula in the Kantian philosophy; but neither in his practical nor in his theoretical philosophy did the influences of his early mode of thought disappear.

To sum up: In the half-century which followed the death of Christian Wolff a mighty transformation had occurred. The intellectual theology of reason which took the form of anthropomorphic theism had been replaced by a poetic, naturalistic pantheism as the fundamental form of its view of the world.   God is the All-One who manifests his nature both in the world and in the process of organic development. The highest revelation of his nature for us is found in the spiritual life of man in society.   Dogmatic anthropomorphism, such as rational theology tried to construct, is impossible; but a symbolic anthropomorphism may perhaps be allowed.   If the nature of the All-One manifests itself in man, man may represent God after his own image, not with the intention of thereby adequately defining the nature of God, but perhaps with the conviction that what is best and deepest in human nature is not foreign to the nature of God; indeed that it forms the essence of his nature.

To have cleared the ground and pointed the way to these thoughts, which have become dominant in the poetry and philosophy of the German people, is the imperishable service of Kant.

PART I

KANT'S LIFE AND PHILOSOPHICAL DEVELOPMENT

LITERATURE : Information regarding Kant's life is meagre. The main source is a number of biographical sketches that were published immediately after his death by pupils and admirers, and are largely filled with descriptions of Kant when an old man, taken from personal recollection. Thus Jachmann, *Im. Kant in Briefen an einen Freund;* Wasianski, *Kant in s. letzten Lebensjahren;* Rink, *Ansichten aus Kants Leben;* Hasse, *Letzte Aeusserungen Kants.* Something more is contained in Borowski's *Darstellung des Lebens und Charakters Kants* (1804); the first outline was composed as early as 1792 and revised by Kant himself. Then, in addition, there are the letters to and from Kant, the number of which is indeed not very great, on account of Kant's disinclination to write letters; and they give very little information of a personal character. (In Hartenstein's edition of the *Works* the letters are found in viii., pp. 649–815. The number has been greatly increased by Reicke's collection in the new edition published by the Berlin Academy.) Finally, there is the correspondence of his Königsberg acquaintances, especially that of Hamann. From these materials F. W. Schubert has written a connected account of Kant's life and literary activity for the edition of the *Works* edited by Rosenkranz and himself (1842, xi., 2 of the edition). This, without any further investigation, has generally been made the basis of subsequent expositions. R. Reicke has made important additions in *Kantiana, Beiträge zu I. Kants Leben und Schriften* (1860, reprinted mainly from the *N. Preuss. Prov. Blättern*). E. Arnoldt, in his valuable *Studie Kants Jugend* (1882, reprinted from the *Altpreuss. Monatsschrift*), has subjected the tradition to sharper criticism and drawn what could be obtained of value from official documents. In his critical *Exkursen zur Kantforschung* (1894), he has given a very detailed account of Kant's academic activity as a teacher. B. Erdmann, *M. Knutzen und seine Zeit* (1876), is also of importance as giving detailed and full information regarding the intellectual life of Königsberg at the time when Kant received his education there, and especially of the two men to whom he owed most, F. A. Schultz and M. Knutzen. A book in which one breathes the very atmosphere that prevailed in the circle to which Kant belonged in his later life is the autobiography of Kant's friend and younger contemporary, the war counsellor Scheffner (Leipzig, 1823). [The only extensive biography of Kant in English is by J. H. W. Stuckenberg, *The Life of Immanuel Kant*, London, 1882. It is compiled from the German sources mentioned above. Among the many shorter sketches of Kant's life in English, we may refer especially to W. Wallace's *Kant*, in *Blackwood's Philosophical Classics*, Edinburgh, 1882, and E. Caird's *The Critical Philosophy of Kant*, London and New York, 1889. — TRS.]

PART I

KANT'S LIFE AND PHILOSOPHICAL DEVELOPMENT

I. Biographical Sketch

Immanuel Kant was born at Königsberg in Prussia on the 22d of April, 1724, and died at the same place on the 12th of February, 1804.

His life was passed within a narrow circle. He was a German professor of the old style: to work, to teach, to write books, was the sum and substance of his life. Important external events, exciting crises, other than intellectual, in his history there are none. His birthplace, Königsberg, with its university, is the scene of his life and activity. He spent only a few years, as tutor in a country family, outside its walls, and never passed the boundaries of his native province. Prussia at that time, before the annexation of the Vistula province in the first division of Poland, was a German island in the far East. Its relations with the German Baltic countries, with Mitau and Riga, were closer and more intimate than with the West, and Courland and Livonia at that time supplied a considerable portion of the Königsberg student body. Königsberg, the chief city of this region in the second half of the eighteenth century, had a population of about fifty thousand people, living in about six hundred houses, and was therefore a quite important city for those days. Kant himself (in the Preface to the *Anthropology*) boasts that as the centre of the political and intellectual life of the country, as the port and commercial centre of a widely extended inland territory, inhabited by

52582

LIBRARY
College of St. Francis
JOLIET, ILL.

a variety of Eastern peoples, it was favorably situated for obtaining knowledge of the world and of the various races of men.

Like so many of the spiritual leaders of our people, Kant also sprang from the poorer class of citizens. His father, Johann Georg, was a saddler (harness-maker) of small means. Our Immanuel (who owes his name to the Prussian Calendar) was the fourth child of his marriage with Anna Regina Reuter. Five other children were born later. Only three of Kant's sisters and one brother lived to old age. The brother was first a teacher, then a pastor, in Courland. Two sisters lived in obscure circumstances in Königsberg after having been servants in their younger days. An uncle (Richter), who was in somewhat prosperous circumstances, and helped to bear the expense of publishing Kant's first work, was a shoemaker. As Kant never married, his sisters' children became his heirs.[1]

---

[1] In the *Baltische Monatsschrift*, 1893, pp. 535 ff., Diedrichs gives an account of the life of the brother, Johann Heinrich. He was eleven years younger than Immanuel, and was his pupil at the university. He went to Courland as family tutor, became rector at Mitau, and finally pastor at Alt-Rahden, dying there in 1800. The essay affords us interesting information regarding the relation of Kant to his family during their later life. It contains several letters of the brother and his wife to Kant, and also a few letters of the latter to his brother and the children. The cool, business-like tone of the elder brother, who writes only at very long intervals, contrasts strongly with the affectionate tone which the younger employs. Kant interested himself in his sisters, and in the children of his brother and sister, during his life, by rendering them assistance in their poor circumstances, but he maintained little personal communication with them.

I add here a word regarding the alleged immigration of the family from Scotland. I say "alleged," although the assertion is usually made with the utmost confidence. Indeed, we have Kant's own statements for the fact. In a draft of a letter to a Swedish clergyman who had inquired of the famous man concerning his origin, Kant says that his grandfather, along with many others, "at the end of the last and the beginning of the present century (I know not for what cause) emigrated from Scotland to Prussia, and lived as citizens in the Prussian-Lithuanian city of Tilsit" (viii., p. 804, Borowski, p. 21). Also the name appeared to him to indicate this origin. The old mode of spelling 'Cant' is said to have led to the pronunciation 'Zant,' which he disliked, and

Kant is the third great scholar among German philosophers who came from the ranks of the tradespeople. Melanchthon's father was an armorer; Christian Wolff's father was a tanner. These circumstances have not been without permanent influence on the character of German philosophy. The French and English philosophers of the seventeenth and eighteenth centuries are men of the world; they live in society; their writings are the talk of *salons*. The German philosophers are professors, their sphere of activity the university world; the form of their writings is scholastic. A middle-class respectability of thought, and oftentimes a somewhat didactic mode of expression, are their most char

therefore to have been changed by him to Kant. The evidence of the church register at Memel shows that Kant's statements regarding the history of his family are not entitled to unconditional confidence. Kant's grandfather, Hans Kant (also Kand, not Cant), was a harness-maker at Memel, and had three sons, — Adam (1678), Johann Georg (1683), Friedrich (1685), baptized there in the Lutheran Church. The middle one is the philosopher's father (E. Arnoldt, *Kants Jugend*, p. 2). I cannot refrain from the conjecture that in the story of the Scottish origin we are not dealing with any well-authenticated recollection, but with one of those vague family traditions of foreign descent which are found so frequently in Germany, and which one is not bound to believe. I think that it is quite possible that Kant's grandfather was born at Memel. A search of the parts of the register of the Johannis church, which are still in existence back to 1614, which Vicar Gronau kindly undertook, has discovered no positive evidence for this. But the baptismal records of the years 1645–1661 are lacking, and the name of Hans Kant may possibly have appeared in them. Herr P. Lengning, of the Johannis church, rightly points out in a letter that if Hans Kant had really come from Scotland as a grown man, it would be strange that he did not belong to the Reformed Congregation (Dutch and Scottish) at that time in Memel. Of course his marriage with a German might explain the baptism of the children in the Lutheran Church. That we can draw no conclusion regarding foreign descent from the name Kant (Cant is nowhere to be found, although Kandt, Kante, occur in the school certificates of the philosopher) is evident from the fact alone that the Berlin city register contains the name no fewer than fourteen times. What tricks Kant's memory played with him in later years is shown by a communication by Hasse, a colleague of Kant's. He says that Kant had often thanked him for explaining to him the meaning of his name Immanuel (God with us), and told him that since that time he had written the name correctly, although before that he had spelled it Emanuel. This was certainly not the case at any time (*cf.* Vaihinger, *Kantstudien*, ii., p. 377).

acteristic marks. With its popular traits is also closely connected its relation to religion, which it treats as a serious concern. The philosophers of the world, Voltaire or Hume, when they speak of religion, think of something which they know as the object of political speculation by statesmen, of personal calculation on the part of men of the Church, as a subject for witticisms by authors and educated people, — a something also which is of interest to the reflective philosopher as a natural phenomenon appearing among the masses of mankind; but they have scarcely ever been brought into close contact with a man to whom religion was the great interest of life.

Kant, on the other hand, had grown up among such people. His parents belonged to the pietistic movement which was just at that time passing eastwards, and which insisted upon the personal appropriation of religion. To his mother more especially, religion appears to have been a matter of living faith. And her son showed that he retained throughout his life a strong sense of his own real connection with such people. He never lost the lively appreciation of what he owed to his parents. Even when past middle life his thinking often springs from the environment of his youth. He praises the moral atmosphere in which he was reared, the homely discharge of duties, the strict conscientiousness, the deep piety of his parents. In reply to Rink, he once said: "Even if the religious consciousness of that time, and the conceptions of what is called virtue and piety were by no means clear and satisfactory, it yet contained the root of the matter. One may say of pietism what one will; it suffices that the people to whom it was a serious matter were distinguished in a manner deserving of all respect. They possessed the highest good which man can enjoy — that repose, that cheerfulness, that inner peace which is disturbed by no passions. No want or persecution rendered them discontented; no controversy was able to stir them to anger or to enmity. In a word, even the mere on-looker was involuntarily compelled to respect. I still remember how once disputes arose between the harness-making and saddler trades regarding their privileges, during which my father suffered much. But, nevertheless, this quarrel was treated by my parents, even in family conversation, with such forbearance and love towards their opponents, and with so much trust in Providence, that the memory of it, although I was then a boy, has never left me."

He seems to have stood in specially close relations to his mother. He praises her as a woman of great natural ability, of noble heart, and of fervent, though by no means sentimental, religious feeling.

It was through her, as it appears, that a way was opened for him to pursue his studies. She was a faithful hearer and admirer of the preacher and Consistorial Councillor, F. A. Schultz (1692–1763).[1] This excellent man, who had been a student of Francke and Wolff in Halle, and united solid scientific and philosophic attainments with pietistical devoutness, was both a professor in the university, and director of the *Collegium Fridericianum*, a high school established shortly before this time on the Halle model. He was personally acquainted with Kant's parents, and with the talents of the boy, whom the mother, perhaps, brought with her to the devotional hour in his own house, and he advised the son to pursue his studies. And so it happened that in the autumn of 1732, the eight-year old boy was entered at the *Fridericianum*. He attended the institution until he left it for the university (1740). There, in addition to pietistically colored religious instruction, he had an opportunity to acquire, above all, solid training in the Latin language and literature under Heydenreich. In later life Kant wrote and spoke good Latin, and oftentimes quotations from Latin classical writers flow from his pen.

[1] Regarding him, see Erdmann, *Martin Knutzen und seine Zeit*, pp. 22 ff.

In the autumn of 1740 Kant was matriculated in the university of his native city. His mother had not lived to see the day, having died in 1737 at the age of forty years, of a sickness, as is narrated, which was brought on by nursing a friend. Kant began his studies, after the usual fashion, in the philosophical faculty, which then occupied essentially the position that had belonged to it since the middle ages, that of a preparatory institution for the three higher faculties. Its work was to complete the linguistic and literary instruction of the Latin school by means of a course in the general or philosophical sciences, and thus to prepare for the professional studies of one of the higher faculties. Since the Königsberg University, and more specially the philosophical faculty, is the frame in which Kant's entire future life is set, a short description of it may not seem undesirable to the reader. I take it from the history of the Königsberg University published by Arnoldt in 1746. In this the modesty of all the appointments is very manifest. Moreover, one needs only to have seen the old university buildings on the Pregel to be conscious of the difference between a university at that time and in our own day; it is not much more than a shed compared with the university palaces of the present time.

The number of ordinary [regular] professors in the philosophical faculty was eight. In addition, there was an extraordinary professor for each subject. The subjects were the following: (1) Hebrew, (2) Mathematics, (3) Greek, (4) Logic and Metaphysics, (5) Practical Philosophy, (6) Natural Science, (7) Poetics, (8) Oratory and History.[1] According to the ordinance of studies of the year 1735, "Every ordinary professor shall treat the subjects which he professes in such a way as to complete in his public lectures one science each semester; for example, logic in one and metaphysics in another; similarly natural law is

---

[1] II., p. 346.

to be completed in one, ethics in the other half-year. The object of this is that the students, especially those who are poor, may have an opportunity to hear all parts of philosophy in public lectures without payment of fees, and in one or another half-year may hear treated all the fundamental sciences of philosophy." In like manner the Hebrew professor is to treat in summer the historical books of the Old Testament, and in winter the five books of Moses; the Greek professor is annually to give a survey of the entire New Testament, and to conduct his class in such a way that the students themselves shall be required to expound the text. The professor of mathematics is to lecture each year on arithmetic, geometry, trigonometry, and astronomy. The professor of oratory and history had in winter to treat of style in the following way: Two hours were given to expounding an author, a third to lectures on the principles of oratory, and in the fourth the papers prepared by the students were publicly criticised, partly in Latin, partly in German. In summers he had universal history, lecturing in alternate years on the period before Christ and the Christian era. The professor of poetics had to do with respect to the Latin language, what the professor of oratory did with regard to style, and every two years to devote a half-year to German poetry. The professor of physics "must teach either experimental physics in one half-year and theoretical in the other, or, in case he wishes to combine them, conclude his course in one year, since then the professor extraordinary can treat every half-year some part of *physica sacra*. In general, also, professors would do well, after they have completed their lectures, to hold examinations upon them, partly to learn how well their auditors have understood the various points, partly to stimulate their diligence and attention and to discover students of ability and perseverance, or even to hold special *collegia examinatoria*."[1]

[1] I., p. 335.

It is evident, both from the form and the content of the instruction, that the institution was nothing more than a school.[1]

Of Kant's student days at the university little is known with certainty. Among his teachers the still youthful professor extraordinary, Martin Knutzen (1713–51), attracted him most. Knutzen's lectures extended over the entire field of philosophy and included mathematics and natural science.[2] It is reported that Kant also enjoyed personal relations with him and was supplied with books out of his private library. He was indebted to Knutzen not merely for his introduction to the Wolffian philosophy, but also especially for introducing him to the study of mathematics and physics, and for his acquaintance with Newton. It appears that for a long time mathematical, scientific, and cosmological studies formed his main interest. It must not be forgotten, however, that these sciences were then an integral part of the unitary science, philosophy. Perhaps, also, a reaction against the excess of pietistic and dogmatic religious instruction received at school, of which there are other signs too, may have had some part in inclining Kant towards the mathematical

[1] That it was not a higher institution of learning appears also from the following: " All funeral orations and addresses, as well as addresses of congratulation, must be prepared in prose, not run into theology, and be submitted to the censorship of the professor of eloquence, on penalty of twenty marks. Also it is forbidden on the same penalty to use in these any reference to particular family circumstances, or to name persons and describe events of their lives, but all such things shall remain *professori eloquentiæ privative*" (ii., p. 350). The university professors had thus a monopoly in preparing occasional addresses, especially funeral orations with personal references, of course for a fee. In the higher schools, conducting funerals with singing formed a regular part of the teacher's income. The position of the scholar's profession can be readily understood from facts of this kind. The great change, the raising of the academic world to the rank of the nobility, has begun to take place since the end of the eighteenth century under the influence of the great intellectual, political, and social transformation, that affected Germany and France in particular.

[2] Erdmann, in *Martin Knutzen und seine Zeit*, reproduces a syllabus of these lectures.

sciences. In the same way, it was not an accident that among the Latin authors he had a special preference for Lucretius. In addition it is certain that he heard also theological lectures (Dogmatics) from his old patron Schultz. Whether he ever had any thought of entering the clerical profession is doubtful, just as is the story that he made a trial of preaching in a country church. It is reported also that he aided some fellow-students with whom he was friendly in their studies, which afforded much relief to him in his straitened financial circumstances. How long he heard lectures cannot be determined with certainty. It is known, however, that in the summer semester of 1746 he handed to the dean of the philosophical faculty a work entitled, *Thoughts on the True Evaluation of Dynamic Forces*, which had been already printed. This first work, a thorough discussion of the point at issue between Descartes and Leibniz regarding the measure of force, even if it cannot be called a contribution to the subject, bears witness to the extensive and thorough philosophical and scientific studies and also to the independence of judgment of its youthful author. An active self-reliance, almost defiant in tone, and an openly expressed contempt for those who after the manner of gregarious animals followed the authority of great names, proclaimed a man who felt conscious of strength to go his own way.

In the same year, on the 24th of March, 1746, his father died. The son wrote as an entry in the family chronicle which his mother had hitherto kept: " May God, who did not permit him to taste many joys in this life, grant to him in return to be a partaker of everlasting happiness." The church burial register contains as an entry the following brief but significant words: " Private " (*i. e.*, without interment services), " Poor." A similar entry had been made at the time of his mother's death, nine years before.[1]

Poverty had been the companion of Kant's youth. For

[1] Arnoldt, p. 51.

more than a decade it was still to remain his constant attendant. After the university there followed his years as a family tutor, at that time the regular course for one who was without private means. Of this period we have no certain information. It is said that he was first a teacher in a pastor's house (Judschen, near Gumbinnen), and later in the family of a country landholder (Von Hülsen, near Mohrungen). Finally, he entered into relations with the Count Kayserling's family. It is doubtful, however, whether he lived permanently in this house as a tutor. But he stood in specially close relations with the countess, an admirable, finely educated woman. In her house (she lived after 1772 in Königsberg) he continued to be highly regarded. A portrait of the youthful Kant by the Countess's hand has lately been discovered.[1]

In the year 1755 he began his work as private lecturer at the University of Königsberg. After he qualified (*promoviert*) with a treatise entitled *De igne*, and held a disputation over the work, *Principiorum primorum cognitionis metaphysicæ nova dilucidatio* (with which still another disputation over the treatise *Monadologia physica* was connected), he began his lectures in the winter semester of 1755–56 as *magister legens*. For fifteen years he remained in this position. Twice his applications for a vacant professorship were unsuccessful. The second of these applications was addressed to Catherine II.; for Königsberg was, from 1757 to the time of the peace, under the control of the Russian government. The professorship of poetics which became vacant in 1764 and which was offered him from Berlin, he declined. In 1766 he sought and obtained the vacant position of assistant librarian of the castle library, a position which yielded an income of sixty-two thalers.

[1] A reproduction of this, the oldest portrait of Kant, appeared in Vaihinger's *Kantstudien* II., 2, together with an account by E. Fromm of Kant's relations to the Kayserling family. [This portrait was also reproduced in *The Philosophical Review*, VIII. 3.]

Nevertheless, it is not necessary to think of Kant's position during these years as an entirely undesirable one. The position of a *privat docent* was then, in general, freer and more desirable than at present. The professorships were much less official in character than in our time, especially in the philosophical faculty. The salary was small, and there was yet nothing to give to the senior a superior rank, even as a teacher. Nor did the instruction in the philosophical faculty lead up to a state examination, as has been more and more the rule since 1812, when the *examen pro facultate docendi* was introduced. Thus, at that time a professor was nothing more than a teacher who sat in the faculty and received a small salary from the funds of the university. Even the professor ordinarius gave, in addition to the public lectures which were required of him, and for which he received a salary, numerous private lectures in his own auditorium, on all the disciplines which belonged to his chair. The honorarium from this source, which was treated as a purely private affair, usually made up an important part of his income. There was nothing, therefore, to prevent a successful *privat docent* from having more hearers and perhaps a larger income than a professor. Kant's lectures were soon very highly esteemed, and attracted many hearers, not only from among the students, but also from among men of high rank, and he often lectured before the officers of the garrison, even when Königsberg was occupied by the Russian troops.

At the beginning of his academic career, his philosophico-scientific interest, as appears from his lectures and writings, was particularly directed toward the external world. Besides logic and metaphysics, which from the beginning occupied the most prominent position, he treated in his lectures especially of mathematics and natural science. Physical geography, which Kant was the first to introduce into the university courses, soon became a favorite subject. This was much appreciated, even outside the circle of students; and since it brought together what was most interesting and important from the world of nature and man, it was able to offer guidance for the tour for culture which was at that time common, or even to become a substitute for it.[1] As the literary fruit of his cosmological investigations and studies of the natural sciences, he published, in addition to some small essays on physical geography, in the year 1755, a work entitled *Universal History of Nature and Theory of the Heavens*, or an Attempt to Treat of the Formation and Origin of the Entire Structure of the World according to Newtonian Principles. This work is of great significance, standing as it does at the beginning of Kant's activity as an author. It was dedicated to Frederick II., but appeared originally without the name of the author. It was not until later that it received the recognition which it deserved; at first, through the failure of the publisher, it remained almost unnoticed. That Kant attached great importance to it appears from the fact that he twice called attention to its main content by giving summaries of it (1763, 1791). The problem which he set for himself in this work was to explain genetically the structure of the cosmos, and especially of our planetary system, entirely in accordance with physical principles. Newton had regarded the first arrangement of the world system as the direct work of God. But Kant begins where Newton had left off, and shows how through the immanent activity of physical forces, cosmic systems arise and perish in never-ending rotation. The direct interposition of God is here neither necessary nor applicable. It may indeed be rightly questioned whether Kant's attempt is so closely related as is often assumed to the theory which Laplace

[1] P. Lehmann, *Kants Bedeutung als akademischer Lehrer der Erdkunde*, 1886. Arnoldt, *Krit. Exkurse*, pp. 283 ff. G. H. Schöne, "Die Stellung Kants innerhalb der geographischen Wissenschaft," *Altpreuss. Monatsschrift*, xxxv. (1896), pp. 217 ff.

afterwards worked out, that the planetary bodies are broken off from a rotating central body and are arranged through its attraction.[1] Kant stands in close relation to the old cosmogonic theories (Lucretius was an author in whom he had much confidence), but he stood firmly on the Newtonian principle of gravitation and the results of modern astronomy. In general we may say that it is his lively and fertile imagination rather than the exactness of his investigation which is worthy of mention. It ranges hither and thither, even to the fantastic, to discover possible ideas regarding the development of the cosmos and the earth.

What he says in the preface to this work, regarding the relation of natural science to religion is worthy of attention. Religion has no interest in setting limits to the mechanical explanation of natural phenomena. It is just the possibility of a purely mechanical explanation which furnishes the best proof of the original purposive character of the nature of all its elements. On the other hand, he protests against all explanation of particular phenomena from particular purposes of God, — a kind of explanation to which the " easy philosophy that tries to hide its vain uncertainty under a pious air " is prone. This method is fatal to faith, since a later natural explanation helps the naturalist to a triumph. In this passage we have an indication of the view which is systematically worked out by the critical philosophy; natural science and religious faith are completely indifferent to each other and are therefore to be entirely separated. Their intermixture in physico-theology is equally injurious for science and for faith. That this opinion of his aroused anxiety among strict and narrow-minded persons, we may conclude from the behavior of his old teacher and patron, Schultz. Before he would recom-

[1] Eberhard, *Die Kosmogonie Kants* (Munich Dissertation, 1893). Zöllner's work, *Ueber die Natur der Kometen*, pp. 426 ff., gives a panegyric on Kant's services to natural science.

mend Kant for a professorship which the latter desired (it was in 1758), he sent for Kant to come to him and received him with the solemn question, " Do you fear God from your heart ? " Only after having received Kant's frank assurance that he did, would he use his influence in his behalf.

In the sixties a transformation begins to be apparent in Kant's thought, which we may call the Socratic tendency. The inner world, the realm of man and of his moral nature, gains an importance at the cost of the mathematico-scientific, and even of the scholastico-metaphysical. Kant's personal development is connected with the general movement of the time. It is the time in which the German spirit, awakening from its long lethargy, raises itself with astonishing rapidity and energy to the fulness of new life. Lessing had begun the influence. The subtle scholastic disputes of theological and metaphysical dogmatists, like the dead antiquarian scholarship, fall into disrepute. Philosophy endeavors, by throwing aside the rules of scholastic demonstration, and by employing the German language, to exert an influence upon general culture. The public life of the nation begins to take form; besides the sympathy for the modern *belles lettres*, in the age of Frederick and Joseph, a political self-consciousness appears among the better-educated classes. I may mention J. J. Moser in the South, Schlözer and J. Möser in the North. Moreover, new influences from the West begin to be felt. English philosophy and literature attract his attention. Shaftesbury was a familiar author, and in addition he became acquainted with Hume, especially with his essays in the fields of mental and moral sciences. Among French authors we may mention, besides Voltaire, Montesquieu and Rousseau.

To all these influences Kant, who rejoiced in the good fortune of a prolonged youth and long years of development, yielded himself with an open mind. As his biographers show, his personal feeling was most strongly and directly touched by Rousseau. He himself, in a passage which has often been quoted, has spoken of the change in disposition which Rousseau produced in him: " I myself am by inclination an investigator. I feel an absolute thirst for knowledge, and a longing unrest for further information. There was a time when I thought that all this constituted the real worth of mankind, and I despised the rabble who knew nothing. Rousseau has shown me my error. This dazzling advantage vanishes, and I should regard myself as of much less use than the common laborers if I did not believe that this speculation (that of the Socratic-critical philosophy) can give a value to everything else to restore the rights of humanity." [1] Thus it is a new valuation of knowledge for which he here acknowledges his obligations to Rousseau. Science and speculation are not of unconditional worth, they are not absolute ends in themselves, but means to a higher end whose purpose is to serve the moral destiny of mankind. The primacy of the moral over the intellectual, in the evaluation of the individual and in the determination of the purposes of the race, remains hereafter a constant feature of Kant's thought. And this gives philosophy a new significance. For, as practical wisdom (*Weisheitslehre*), its function is to bring sciences into relation to the highest purpose of humanity, and also to warn the individual against the arrogance of mere knowledge. Thus Rousseau, the philosopher of the microcosm, had replaced Newton, the philosopher of the macrocosm (Kant himself parallels the two men in this way).[2] The moral and anthropological interest, rather than cosmological and metaphysical speculation, assumes the central position. On the basis of this anthropocentric direction of thought, the critical philosophy grew up. Its mission is to make an absolute end of cosmological speculation, in order to render the moral the

[1] VIII., p. 642.   [2] VIII., p. 630.

essential element in a philosophy of life and of the world. One of the *Reflections* published by Erdmann (II. 59) clearly shows this tendency: "The *Critique of Pure Reason* is a cure for a disease of the reason which has its root in our nature. This disease is the opposite of the inclination which binds us to our country (*Heimweh*); it is longing to wander beyond our proper sphere and establish relations with other worlds." With this we may connect the question with which the *Natural History of the Heavens* closes: "Perhaps still other members of the planetary system are being transformed to prepare new abodes for us in other heavens. Who knows but that those satellites revolve about Jupiter in order to give us light in the future?"

I shall later treat together the writings of the sixties, in which this tendency first finds expression. Here I wish to place before the reader an excellent picture of the teacher at the height of his strength and influence. It is by Herder, who sat at Kant's feet during 1762–64, and who draws this sketch from memory: "I have had the good fortune to know a philosopher who was my teacher. In the prime of life he possessed the joyous courage of youth, and this also, as I believe, attended him to extreme old age. His open, thoughtful brow was the seat of untroubled cheerfulness and joy, his conversation was full of ideas and most suggestive. He had at his service jest, witticism, and humorous fancy, and his lectures were at once instructive and most entertaining. With the same spirit in which he criticised Leibniz, Wolff, Baumgarten, Crusius, and Hume, he investigated the natural laws of Newton, Kepler, and the physicists. In the same way he took up the writings of Rousseau, which were then first appearing, — the *Émile* and the *Héloïse*, — as well as any new discovery with which he was acquainted in natural science, and estimated their value, always returning to speak of the unbiased knowledge of nature, and the moral worth of man. The history of men, of peoples, and of nature, mathematics, and experience, were the sources from which he enlivened his lectures and conversation. Nothing worth knowing was indifferent to him. No cabal or sect, no prejudice or reverence for a name had the slightest influence with him in opposition to the extension and promotion of truth. He encouraged and gently compelled his hearers to think for themselves; despotism was foreign to his disposition. This man, whom I name with the greatest thankfulness and reverence, is Immanuel Kant; his image stands before me, and is dear to me." [1]

In 1770 Kant received the ordinary professorship in logic and metaphysic. Shortly before this, calls had come to him from Jena and Erlangen. He had long been happy in the high estimate which the government placed upon his services. This appears especially from a Report of 1767, which contains complimentary references to him and a *magister*

[1] *Briefe zur Beförderung der Humanität. Werke*, Ausg. Suphan, xvii., p. 404. *Cf.* the original work of the year 1792, xviii., p. 304. Herder's picture of the youthful Kant of the sixties has, however, a point. He turns it against the Kantians and their arrogant, even despotic dogmatism, from which Kant himself was free: "Never in the three years in which I heard him daily on all the philosophical disciplines have I ever noticed the slightest trace of arrogance in him. To found a sect, to give his name to a company of disciples, was not the end for which he strove. His philosophy aroused independent thought, and I can scarcely imagine anything better adapted and more effective for the purpose than his lectures." He was far from being satisfied with speculation remote from experience, or encouraging pure thinking, but was constantly referring to the necessity of experience, of knowledge of the world by means of natural history and the history of peoples. Even the *Critique of Pure Reason* was written with the purpose of rooting out the thorn thickets of speculation. It certainly could never have entered Kant's head that it would occur to any one "to transplant the thornbush, which he had been compelled to use in hedging-in false speculation, into every good field as a garden product;" or, to change the figure, that "the medicine he had prescribed as a purge would not merely be recommended as the only and everlasting means of nourishment, but that people would have it thrust upon them and be bullied with all kinds of good and evil arts." "Still, did not this take place in the school of Socrates?"—That Herder did not regard the Kant of the System so free from blame as he is here represented appears from the *Metakritik*, published in 1799. The opinions expressed there he had held for a long time.

legens (Reusch). In the previous year the professors had
been severely censured: they took little pains to perform
their duties when they were not emphatically enjoined and
commanded to do so. The king reserved to himself the
right "to make an entirely new arrangement; at all events
to remove the teachers who were of no value to the university, and to place the university on the basis of Halle and
Frankfort and appoint diligent professors."[1] Kant was held
in especially high esteem by the minister, von Zedlitz, who
controlled educational matters from 1771 to 1788. This excellent man, who was fitted for his post in an unusual degree
by the refined and thorough nature of his culture, and his
high appreciation of intellectual and moral excellence, lost no
opportunity of assuring the Königsberg philosopher of his
esteem. When, in 1778, a professorship was vacant in Halle,
by far the most important of the Prussian universities of that
time, he repeatedly urged Kant to accept it, with the respect-
able salary of 800 thalers, and the title of counsellor (*hof-
rath*) if he wished it. Nevertheless, neither such attractions
nor the claims of duty which the minister delicately urged
upon him of not refusing the wider sphere of influence, were
able to draw Kant from his home and his customary place.
"All change makes me anxious," he writes to Herz,[2] "even
when it seems to promise the greatest improvement of
my condition. I believe I must heed this instinct of my
nature if I am to draw a little longer the threads which the
Fates spin very thin and brittle for me." He felt that he
had still a great work to perform, — the reconstruction of
philosophy. In the *Dissertation on the Form and Principles
of the Sensible and Intelligible Worlds*, with which he had
entered upon his professorship in 1770, he had taken the
first step toward this restoration.[3]

---

[1] Arnoldt, *Krit. Exkurse*, p. 547.   [2] VIII., p. 703.

[3] E. Fromm (*Kant und die preuss. Zensur*, 1894, p. 62) has collected the
following information regarding Kant's salary from the records of the privy

In 1781 the *Critique of Pure Reason,* the fulfilment of the promise of the *Dissertation,* finally appeared. It was dedicated to Zedlitz.

The further history of Kant's life is the history of the origin of his works, and of the effect which they exercised upon the time. The eighties are the years of greatest literary activity. In the nineties Kant's strength gradually failed, while at the same time his influence and fame were extended. In all the German universities, Protestant and Catholic alike, the critical philosophy was taught. Adherents from all parts of Germany made their way to the far East to salute the bearer of the new light. One of the first of these was J. G. Fichte.[1] When the Dane Baggesen called him the second Messiah, this did not, to many, appear too much to say in that age given to exaggeration.

From the eighties Kant was by far the most important figure in the Königsberg University. The remote institution had through him for the first time received a European reputation. To describe his immediate surroundings I add here the names of his colleagues in the philosophical

state archives. The salary of his predecessor, the ordinarius in logic and metaphysics, was 166 thlr. 60 gr., — probably also the amount that Kant at first received. In 1786 he received in all, 417 thlr. 36 gr. 4 pf. (salary, 255 thlr. 80 gr. 12 pf.; as senator, 36 thlr. 45 gr. 10 pf.; and in addition, 100 thlr. as senior of the faculty, and 35 thlr. as decan). In 1787, after the endowment of the university had been increased by Frederick William IV., the regular salary had been raised to 342 thlr. 64 gr. 4 pf. In 1789 he received in addition an extraordinary personal allowance of 220 thlr., so that he now received in all, 725 thlr. 60 gr. 9 pf. Of titles and orders, such as are now bestowed on professors as suitable decorations, the biographers of Kant have nothing at all to report. Perhaps Kant regarded these things as a lessening of his independence rather than as adding to the respect of his rank. Did Frederick the Great ever hear anything more of Kant than his name? This cannot be determined. But he regarded the entire world of German scholarship as far beneath him; and so perhaps even the name of the most celebrated of the Prussian professors remained beneath the limen of the royal consciousness.

[1] See the interesting account of the meeting between the two men, in the life of Fichte by his son, I. H. Fichte, II., pp. 129 ff.

faculty. In the year 1789 there were (according to Baczko's
History and Description of Königsberg, p. 431) only six of
them : Reusch in Physics, Kraus, Kant's pupil and friend,
in Practical Philosophy ; Mangelsdorf in Poetry, Oratory, and
History ; the court-preacher Schulz, Kant's pupil and commentator, in Mathematics ; Hasse in Oriental languages ; and
Wald in Greek. In addition to these there was a professor extraordinarius for oratory, and four readers.

I may here say something regarding the external conditions of Kant's life. His household arrangements and
habits were very simple, and entirely subordinated to considerations of bodily and mental hygiene. From his youth
his bodily strength had been frail. He was small of stature
and had a hollow chest cramping his lungs and heart. This
weakness had early drawn his attention to dietetics. By
care and prudence he managed to live, even at an advanced
age, without suffering much disturbance from bodily ailments.
He remained unmarried, but not from principle or from
any hatred to women. In his reflections on the feelings of
the beautiful and the sublime, in particular, he speaks with
regard for women, and draws a pleasing picture of their
character with a touch of the French gallantry that belonged to the time. It is said that he twice thought of
making proposals of marriage, but reflecting over the matter
too long he lost the opportunity. Still, a disinclination,
even in mature age, to assume the responsibilities of family
life may have given the decision. There was nothing moody
and solitary about Kant, as about Schopenhauer. He was
not disinclined to society, and possessed a gift of lively and
pleasing conversation, and moved easily and lightly in the
forms of polite society. He did not choose his society especially from the academic circle, but loved to mingle with
people of the world, with office-holders, merchants, book-
dealers, etc. Not until the eighties did he buy himself a
house, and set up his modest establishment with a man-

servant and cook. (This house stood on Prinzessinnen Street, but gave place in 1893 to a new one.) At dinner he liked to have a few guests with him, and regularly had one or two, generally chosen from among his younger friends and students. Now and again he had a larger company, up to five in number. His day was strictly ordered by rule. He rose at 5 o'clock, worked until his lectures began at 7 or 8, and again from 9 or 10 until dinner-time at one o'clock. He loved to prolong the midday meal — the only one which he took in later life — for two or three hours with pleasant conversation. Then he walked for an hour, and the remainder of the day was given to reading and meditation. At ten o'clock he retired to rest.

Thus one day passed like another. Scarcely any interruptions came to break the uniform regularity of his life. In this age of the illumination, inclined more to work than to holiday, the vacations were very short. Journeys were not made; Kant during the last decade of his life did not go beyond the nearest environs of Königsberg. The outer world of his own experience remained a very restricted one; he knew of foreign cities and lands only from books. The first academic teacher of physical geography never saw a mountain with his own eyes. Indeed, I do not know that he ever saw the sea, which could be reached in a few hours from Königsberg.

For all that, reading had to compensate. As an exact scholar of the old time, books were his world. And here he loved not the abstract, but the concrete. Especially did he value descriptions of travel and works of natural science, which he had sent unbound from the book shop (for a long time he lived with the book-dealer Kanter). His pupil and friend Kraus tells that he liked to have a new book beside him as he wrote, in order to refresh himself by looking into it from time to time when he was weary. In the field of *belles lettres* he was especially fond of witty

and satirical writings, like *Hudibras*, or *Don Quixote*, while
Swift, Lichtenberg, and even Montaigne were among his
favorite authors.[1]   He had a strong dislike both for everything weakly sentimental and extravagant, and for sentimental novels, moving tragedies, etc., as is well known to
readers of his ethical and æsthetic works.

We may add here some remarks regarding Kant's relation
to the public institutions of his time.   His relation to the
state and to political life was determined by the circumstances of his time.   As a whole he stood as a stranger, outside and opposed to the political institutions and events of
his time.   He was too much of a philosopher and a citizen
of the world to cherish any strong feeling of attachment to
or dependence on the state as it was — something that this
state, which only recognized subjects, neither expected nor
demanded.   To the great representative of the illumination
on the Prussian throne he was extremely grateful for maintaining freedom of thought.   He also appreciated and highly
valued the legality of his rule, and the impartial maintenance of justice.   In other respects, he could scarcely be
said to belong to the unqualified admirers of the king.   He
so often and so emphatically expressed his abhorrence of
war, this scourge of mankind, this destroyer of all that is
good, especially of war undertaken without necessity for
political reasons, that one cannot refrain from including the
wars of Frederick the Great in this judgment.   Kant
showed none of the enthusiasm which the deeds of the king,
defending himself against a hostile world, aroused in the
young Goethe.   To be sure, in Frankfort the war was far
enough distant to appeal to the imagination, while in Prussia
one felt too keenly the bitter reality.   Moreover, the nig-
gardliness of Frederick's government towards schools and
universities was the result of the expenditure of all the
country's forces in the war.   Kant repeatedly proclaims

[1] Reicke, *Kantiana*, pp. 14 ff.

with bitterness that the state has money only for the war. In addition, it is doubtless true that our good citizen philosopher had a strong dislike for all court personages. And we may assume that this dislike was not lessened by the French philosophers of the king's court (*e. g.*, de la Mettrie). It cannot be doubted also that Kant's sympathies were not with a monarchial and absolute form of government, but with a democracy, such as had just been established in North America, and as appeared, at the beginning of the Revolution, to be the form of government desired in France. These were the two political movements of his time for which Kant felt the keenest sympathy. Even in the year 1798, when the enthusiasm in Germany for the French Revolution had pretty well gone by in other quarters, he spoke of this event as the hopeful turning-point of the times. And he applied this designation to the Revolution, while condemning the execution of the king in decided, and even in exaggerated terms. In the movement of the states towards a republican form of government he saw the springing up of the seed of everlasting peace.[1]

Even Kant's relation to the church was not a personal one, but rested upon an intellectual appreciation. He understood the historical necessity of the church, and appreciated what it had accomplished in disciplining and moralizing the populace. But he had no personal needs that the church could satisfy, and he took no part in church services. Perhaps the superfluity of church-going which he had been compelled to undergo in his youth may have been of some influence. All sentimental piety was distasteful to him. The affectation of a personal intimacy with the heavenly powers appeared to him as self-praise and vanity, and to be akin to the arrogance with which the favorites of earthly princes look down upon common mortals. For true Christianity he had a strong feeling of

[1] VII., pp. 399 ff.

respect. He also had a high regard for its author, in whom
he recognized the ideal of moral perfection. Moreover, he
preserved throughout his life a high estimate of the value
of the Bible, with which from his youth he had a close
acquaintance. On one of the unbound pages (*Löse Blätter*)
preserved by the Königsberg library [1] stand these words :
"The existence of the Bible, as a book for the people, is the
greatest benefit which the human race has ever experienced.
Every attempt to belittle it, or to do away with it entirely,
as the 'lovers of God and man' do, is a crime against
humanity. And if there are to be miracles, this book, in
which the accounts of miracles occur only incidentally, as
historical confirmation of the doctrines of rational religion,
is itself the greatest miracle. For here we have a system
of religious doctrines and beliefs, that has been built up
without the help of Greek philosophy, by unlearned persons,
and that has, more than any other, exercised an influence
for good upon the hearts and lives of men."

The nineties brought to Kant, who was now growing old,
his first and only conflict. Though externally this was
soon over, it had a strong influence upon his mind. The
successor of Frederick the Great had appointed in Zedlitz's
place a priestly-minded enthusiast, the former preacher
Wöllner, with whom he was connected by a Rosicrucian
mysticism and a common hatred of the illumination. With
the religious edict of July 9, 1788, there began the systematic uprooting of the illumination in Prussia. By
means of the censorship and inquisition, by removals and
punishments, Frederick William II. and Wöllner undertook
to destroy the spirit of their predecessor, a regular régime of
priestly resentment. It was as if long delayed vengeance must
be had for all the injuries which the scoffer on the throne
had done to the "priests" and to the pious in the land.[2]

---

[1] Convolut G. i., ii.

[2] On Wöllner, *cf.* Bailleu in the *Allg. Deutschen Biographie.*

The philosophy of Kant was naturally offensive to the government. He made no secret of his political attitude, especially with reference to the events in France, which then held the attention of the whole world. It was his work entitled *Religion within the Bounds of Pure Reason*, however, which first brought him directly into conflict with the ruling powers. He intended to publish the work in instalments in Biester's *Berliner Monatsschrift*, but the censor condemned the second article. He then had the work appear in book form under the censorship of the philosophical faculty at Jena. In the same year he received a cabinet order dated October 1, 1794, and of the following purport: "Our highest person has been greatly displeased to observe how you misuse your philosophy to undermine and destroy many of the most important and fundamental doctrines of the Holy Scriptures and of Christianity. We demand of you immediately an exact account, and expect that in the future you will give no such cause of offence, but rather that, in accordance with your duty, you will employ your talents and authority so that our paternal purpose may be more and more attained. If you continue to oppose this order, you may certainly expect unpleasant consequences to yourself."

Kant, in replying, first defended himself fully against the charges brought against him. He then emphatically maintained the right of the scholar (as distinguished from the popular teacher) to form independent judgments on religious matters, and to make his opinions known. But in concluding he gave up the exercise of this right for the future. In order to avoid the least suspicion, he thought it safest "hereby as his Majesty's most faithful servant, to declare solemnly that I will entirely refrain in future from all public address on religion, both natural and revealed, either in lectures or in writings."

On a scrap of paper among his remains we have the fol-

lowing reflection on this subject: "Recantation and denial
of one's inner convictions is base, but silence in a case like
the present is a subject's duty. And if all that one says
must be true, it does not follow that it is one's duty to tell
publicly everything which is true." The phrase, "as his
Majesty's most faithful servant," he must have intentionally
added later, so as to bind himself only during the king's
lifetime." [1]

It cannot be denied that more discretion than courage is
manifested in this solemnly imposed duty of silence. The
old man of seventy might have calmly awaited the "unpleasant consequences" threatened by the order. The Berlin
authorities could scarcely have done more than to prohibit
his writings and perhaps to withdraw the increase of his
salary. Nevertheless, Kant was not of the stuff of which
martyrs are made. And he might comfort himself with the
thought that he had already said all that was most essential.
So he chose what was in accord with his nature, silence
and peace. Of course, if he had declared, like the seventy-
year-old Socrates in a similar position, that he had a higher
mission in the world than the professorship which had been
intrusted to him by the royal Prussian Commission, that to
this mission of teaching truth and combating error and lies
he would not and could not become untrue, then a page of

---

[1] Kant himself published these documents, after the death of the king, in
the preface to *Streit der Fakultäten* (vii., p. 323). Frederick William III. dismissed Wöllner and abolished the censorship. *Cf.* W. Dilthey, *Archiv f.
Gesch. d. Philos.* 1890, pp. 418 ff.; E. Fromm, *Kant und d. Preuss Censur*,
1894; the fullest account by E. Arnoldt, with critical and explanatory
remarks, *Altpreuss. Monatsschrift*, vol. 34, pp. 345 ff. From a report of
the secret state archives at Berlin, sent by E. Fromm to the *Kantstudien*,
iii., pp. 142 ff., it appears that the king personally insisted on proceedings
against Kant. In a letter of March 30, 1794, he wrote to Wöllner, who was
proceeding too slowly and gently for him: "At Frankfort there is Steinbart,
who must be driven out; at Königsberg, Hasse, who is a chief radical; of
such things as well as of the disgraceful writings of Kant must there be an
end. . . . There must be an absolute stop put to this disorder before we are
good friends again."

his life history, and a page of the history of German philosophy, would have been more splendidly distinguished than is now the case.[1]

However, in passing judgment on Kant one must not forget that at the time of the conflict he was long past the vigor of his life and strength. From 1789 his letters complain of a decrease of strength. Even before the cabinet order, he had himself excused from war in consideration of his age. In 1793 he refused a request of the book-dealer Spener to reprint, " with some additions referring to present conditions," his earlier essay (*Idea of a Universal History from the Cosmopolitan Standpoint*). In his answer he refers to his advanced age: " In this remnant of a half-life, the old should remember that *non defensoribus istis tempus eget*, and consider their weakness which scarcely leaves anything to be desired except rest and peace." And in a preceding passage: " When the strong in the world are in a state of drunkenness, whether this proceeds from the inspiration of the gods or from a *mufette*, one should advise a pygmy who is anxious to keep a whole skin, not to meddle." [2]

A much more pronounced and sudden diminution of mental force occurred in 1799. He was compelled to give up his lectures. Gradually there came upon him that weakness of old age in which he had to still pass a number of years. He had lost the strength to work, but not the inclination. He still sat always at his desk, his pen passed over the paper, and his thoughts moved weakly and uncertainly in the old grooves, as appears from the manuscript which he has left on the transition from metaphysics to physics. At the beginning of this period we have his letter to Garve, which one cannot read without emotion. Garve, who was suffering with

---

[1] That his too accommodating conduct gave offence even in his own time is shown by Nicolai's opinion. *Cf.* Hettner, *Litteraturgesch.* ii., pp. 2, 30.

[2] VIII., pp. 756 ff., 790.

an incurable and painful disease, shortly before his death dedicated his last work to Kant, and asked the latter's criticism of it. Kant replied immediately (21st Sept. 1798):[1] " I hasten to acknowledge the receipt of your affectionate letter and able book. The most affecting description of your bodily suffering, together with the resolution to rise above it and still to work away cheerfully for the good of the world, arouses in me the greatest admiration. Perhaps the fate which has befallen me might seem to you even more painful. I am incapacitated for intellectual work, though in fairly good bodily health. I have undertaken to complete my account of questions which concern the whole of philosophy, but I never am able to get it done, although I am conscious that it is quite possible of accomplishment: a most tantalizing experience." Nevertheless, he adds, he still has hope that the present disorganization, which began with an attack of catarrh about a year and a half previously, will not be permanent. "The task with which I now busy myself has to do with the transition from the metaphysical basis of the natural sciences to physics. This problem must be solved or otherwise there is a gap in the system of critical philosophy. The demands of reason with regard to these problems are not abated, nor is the consciousness that the thing is possible. But the satisfaction of these demands is most painfully postponed either by the complete paralysis, or at least constantly disturbing inhibitions of my vital force."

On the 12th of February, 1804, a merciful death finally took him, after he had tasted the suffering, sorrow, and loneliness of old age to its dregs. The last word he spoke was in thankfully declining some service: " It is good."

His native state and university held him in high esteem. His memory there — and not merely there — is more cherished than that of any other German philosopher.

[1] Reprinted in A. Stern's *Ueber die Beziehungen Garve's zu Kant*, p. 43.

Over his grave in the Cathedral, on the *Stoa Kantiana*, are the words from the *Critique of Practical Reason* : —

> " The starry heavens above me,
> The moral law within me."

These words describe truly the two poles of his thought : the cosmos, the object most completely known, was that towards which his youthful love was directed ; the moral law, the source of highest and final certainty, was the object of the almost mystical enthusiasm of his old age.

II. KANT'S CHARACTER

In an oft-quoted passage from a letter to Mendelssohn, of April 8, 1766, Kant makes the following remark regarding himself : "However much of a fault it may be not to be able to abandon completely one's deepest convictions, still the fickle habit of mind, which is concerned only with appearances, is that which never will be natural for me, since I have learned during the greatest part of my life to avoid and despise that more than all other things which corrupt the character. The loss of self-respect, which arises from a sincere mind, would be the greatest evil that could ever happen to me, but it is quite certain that it never will happen." He adds: "It is, indeed, true that I think many things with the clearest conviction and to my great satisfaction, which I never have the courage to say ; but I will never say anything which I do not think." [1]

Two characteristics are manifest in this description : Kant ascribes to himself a strong will, but no strong natural disposition. We have here, indeed, the two fundamental traits of his nature. He was not a strong nature, rejoicing in conflict, like Lessing or Basedow, Luther or Bruno. He was a quiet scholar, resolute in elaborating his thoughts, not in realizing external purposes. Noise and

[1] VIII., p. 672.

contention were unpleasant to him; even the controversy of scholars, he hated. What is not agreeable to him he prefers to yield to. A little of the diffidence which belonged to the boy retained its hold upon the man. It is not an accident that we more than once hear from him that he would never say what he did not think, but had not the courage to say all that he thought.

On the other hand, Kant is a man of strong and constant purpose. He is a man who has made himself what he is by his strength of will. He governs his life according to principles, in moral as well as in economic and dietetic respects. He is the complete opposite of Rousseau, to whom he felt himself so irresistibly drawn. Rousseau is weakly, at the mercy of his temperament, a gypsy nature inclined to libertinism and vagrancy. Kant is, to the point of pedantry, a friend to order. Nothing is left to inclination, to the disposition of the moment. Reason is everything, nature nothing, nothing but the substratum for the activity of reason. Kant himself evidently sat as the model for his moral philosophy: the man of rational will, who acts according to principles, is the perfect man. All that takes place through natural genius, as well as the worship of the "beautiful soul" (*schöne Seele*) (whose discoverer was Rousseau), was foreign to him. Perhaps we may say that there is an inner relationship between Kant's ethics and the Prussian nature. The conception of life as service, a disposition to order everything according to rule, a certain disbelief in human nature, and a kind of lack of the natural fulness of life, are traits common to both. It is a highly estimable type of human character which here meets us, but not a lovable one. It has something cold and severe about it that might well degenerate into external performance of duty, and hard doctrinaire morality. The German people may well regard themselves as fortunate that there is room as well for another type of character in their nation; that is, the richer, warmer, more joyous type of the South, such as simultaneously found its embodiment and expression in the life and ideals of Goethe and Schiller.

Kant has been often compared with Socrates. Herder, for example, in the passage already quoted, made this comparison, and it is not without justification. There is a real kinship of character and thought between the two men. In the case of both we may say that independence of disposition was the fundamental trait of their character. With their attention directed exclusively to what they considered essential, to the realization of their personal ideals, they were indifferent to external consequences. The personal mission was dominant; external position and influence were of little importance. This was true even of authorship: Socrates never attempted it, and Kant was nearly sixty years old before he attained influence as an author. And this came almost without his seeking; it is seldom that a book has been written with so little thought of the reader as the *Critique of Pure Reason*.

There is also a close relationship between the two men in the mode and direction of their thought, as well as in their character. This concerns both what they affirm and what they deny. To both is common a peculiarly negative characteristic of thought, which turns itself against pompous erudition, and arrogant speculation in particular, and also loves to assume an ironical tone towards those who boast of possessing greater wisdom. How much there is, not merely in the market-place at Athens, but in the science of the time that is worthless to me! This is the temper in which Socrates attacked the fashionable sciences of the Sophists, and the speculation of the physicists. He had just enough knowledge of these things to be certain of their worthlessness in regard to what is most important: they contributed nothing to the worth or happiness of mankind. Like Socrates, Kant, in his youth, earnestly pursued cos-

mology and metaphysics. Then he followed the example
of Socrates and "founded a negative philosophy in regard to
speculation, maintaining especially the worthlessness of many
of the alleged sciences and the limits of our knowledge." [1]
The true good of life does not consist in knowledge, in
decorating the mind with everything that is brilliant and
pleasing, but in the homely virtues, where the humble man
often surpasses the great and the learned. And Kant does
not fail to employ the Socratic irony against the great men
who love to arouse the astonishment of the masses by their
great wisdom. He directs his attacks both against the
great metaphysicians, who dwell on the high towers of
speculation, "where there is usually a great deal of wind,"
and against the "Cyclops of erudition," who are hardened
with an enormous mass of knowledge, but do not know
how to use it. Kant believes, with Socrates, that wisdom
(*Weisheit*) is more than knowledge, and that it is possible for
it to exist with but little knowledge. What the former does
pre-suppose is insight into the worthlessness of false knowledge. And so Kant concludes that the real task of the
philosopher is to bring us to a consciousness of the false
claims of pretended knowledge. Even the value of astronomy, the favorite study of his youth, he is inclined in
his old age to estimate from this point of view. "The observations and calculations made by astronomy," he writes
in a noteworthy passage of the *Critique of Pure Reason*,
"have taught us much that is admirable, but perhaps its
most important service is that it has revealed to us the
abyss of uncertainty which would never have appeared so
great to the human reason without this knowledge, and
when we reflect on this uncertainty it must produce a great
change in our view of the proper purpose and employment
of the reason." [2]

In the case of both men, positive convictions form the

[1] Erdmann, *Reflexionen*, II., 44.   [2] III., p. 603.

obverse of this negative philosophy. Socrates opposed to the scepticism of the Sophists logic in the form of definitions, morality as an exact knowledge of the good, and religion as faith in the divine. Kant replied to Hume's scepticism with his epistemological rationalism ; he defended the traditional morality against the bold libertinism of the French Revolution, and confronted the raillery of the great thinkers and atheists with the faith of practical reason.

III. KANT AS AN ACADEMIC TEACHER

For more than forty years Kant served his country with great fidelity as a university teacher. In this capacity he exercised an important influence on the leaders of the country. For decades nearly all the office-holders and clergymen, the teachers and the physicians, of old Prussia and the adjoining German territories in the East had come under his instruction. Through his influence, the small and remote university rose for a time to the front rank of German institutions of learning.

His lectures, like Wolff's, embraced the whole field of philosophy in its old sense of the aggregate of the theoretical sciences. The historical sciences alone lay beyond his field. I give here a summary of his subjects, noting in each case the date of the first and last semester when Kant lectured on them :[1] Logic, 54 times (1755–56, 1796) ; Metaphysics, 49 times (1756, 1795–96) ; Moral Philosophy, 28 times (1756–57, 1788–89) ; Natural Law, 12 times (1767, 1788) ; Encyclopædia of Philosophy, 11 times (1767–68, 1787) ; Natural Theology, once (1785–86) ; Pedagogics,

[1] In what follows I thankfully adopt the dates which E. Arnoldt, in his work, *Kritische Exkurse im Gebiet der Kantforschung*, 1894 (reprinted from the *Altpreuss. Monatsschrift*, 1888–1893), has compiled with great diligence and care from all available sources, especially from the proceedings of the Senate, and the announcements of lectures of the Königsberg University. The dates, as Arnoldt remarks, are not entirely complete.

4 times (1776–77, 1786–87); Anthropology, 24 times (1772–73, 1795–96); Physical Geography, 46 times (1756, 1796); Theoretical Physics, 20 times (1755–56, 1787–88); Mathematics, 16 times (1755–56, 1763); Mechanics, twice (1759–60, 1761); Mineralogy, once (1770–71). In addition, there were occasional *privatissime*, and, after his accession to the professorship, regular 'disputations.'

It will be seen that three subjects — logic, metaphysics, and physical geography — are the chief subjects of Kant's lectures throughout his whole life as a teacher. In the first years, as *privat docent*, he lectured on them nearly every semester. After 1770 he alternated, treating of logic in summer and metaphysics in winter, his lectures now being public. To the course of private lectures on physical geography there was added anthropology in 1772, the latter being given in winter and the former in summer. The lectures on mathematics and natural science fall for the most part at the beginning of his career as a teacher: he did not deal with mathematics after 1763, though he lectured on physics five times after he became professor. Ethics continues all through; natural law, anthropology, and pedagogy found a place only after the end of the sixties. Pedagogy was a subject on which the professors of the philosophical faculty were required by a decree from Berlin to give lectures in turn.

The number of subjects at first dealt with in the same semester was very large, — four, five, or six, — four, and sometimes more lectures of an hour being given one after another. For one semester eight courses of lectures were announced, — among them a *disputatorium* and a *repetitorium*, though doubtless not all were given. On the other hand, it is certain that in the winter of 1766–67 Kant gave five private courses, lecturing twenty-six to twenty-eight hours weekly. After 1770 he gave three, and after 1789 only two, private courses, of four hours weekly, in addition to a *repetitorium*.

The number of hearers, which is now and then stated after the middle of the sixties, reaches a maximum of about one hundred in the public lectures of the eighties; in the private lectures, it falls to twenty or less.

We turn now to the form of his instruction. And first a word regarding its external form. We find that Kant employed the two forms of academic instruction, — lectures and class-drill. The latter appear under different names, as, *disputatorium, examinatorium, repetitorium,* even *examinatorio-disputatorium, examinatorio-repetitorium.* These exercises accompanied, from the time he became professor, the public lectures which he gave on logic in summer and on metaphysics in winter, and at first occupied two hours, and later one hour, weekly. Nothing more definite is known regarding the intercourse of the teacher with his students in these hours. Evidently what took place was a modified form of the traditional academic disputation more in harmony with the spirit of the time. The 'disputation' had become gradually obsolete in the eighteenth century. This was the result of the decline of the old Aristotelian scholastic philosophy, and the introduction of the new systems of thought founded upon modern science, of which Wolff's system was the first example. In a notice of his lectures of the year 1758, Kant describes the purpose of the *disputatorium.* He proposes "to treat polemically on these days the propositions advanced at previous meetings. This he regards as the best means for securing a thorough understanding of the subject." [1]

The lectures, so far as the prescribed disciplines were concerned, regularly followed text-books, as was explicitly required by the bureau of education. An order of the minis-

---

[1] II., p. 25. In my *Geschichte des gelehrten Unterrichts* (II., pp. 128 ff.), I give a detailed account of the changes which academic instruction underwent in the eighteenth century. For the further modifications of the nineteenth century, *cf. Ibid.,* II., pp. 253 ff.

ter, von Zedlitz, of the year 1788, reads: "The worst compendium is certainly better than none, and the professors may, if they are wise enough, improve upon the author as much as they can, but lecturing on dictated passages must be absolutely stopped. From this, Professor Kant and his lectures on physical geography are to be excepted, as it is well known that there is yet no suitable text-book in this subject."[1] Among the text-books which Kant used, I may mention Maier's *Theory of Reason* for logic, and Baumgarten's *Metaphysics* for metaphysic. Both of these were used by him from the beginning to the end of his career as a teacher, and both show the marks of use. In his copy, inserted leaves, and even the pages of the book, are written over with numerous remarks which refer to the text, but also show complete independence of it.

Thus in using the text he did not merely read it and make comments upon it, but he employed it only as a starting-point for critical and independent exposition; so that often there remained little or nothing of the thought of the author, except perhaps the general scheme of division. The author of the text, he says in the report of his lectures, "is not to be regarded as fixing the judgment, but only as furnishing the occasion of making independent judgments,—yes, even of opposing him." The lectures on the dogmatic metaphysics of Baumgarten, with its demonstrative method, afforded the author of the *Critique of Pure Reason* abundant opportunity for criticism, which, however, he did not always use to the fullest extent, as published notes show. They also make clear that a text-book under such circumstances must have done more to hinder than to stimulate thought. As Arnoldt has justly remarked, it is difficult to understand how the hearers gained any clear ideas from this mixture of the dogmatic and critical mode of procedure.

The internal form of instruction corresponded with the ex-

[1] Arnoldt, p. 578.

ternal. It was not dogmatic and scholastic, but zetetic and critical: it did not seek to lay down and inculcate ready-made philosophical doctrine, but to afford direction to investigation and independent thought. The following points are to be noticed. The presupposition of this procedure is that philosophy is not a completed system. That was the conviction on which the traditional scholastic instruction proceeded, even in the seventeenth century; it occupied itself with the scholastic tradition of the authorized systems, *i. e.,* with the Aristotelian philosophy as harmonized with the doctrines of the church. Kant from the very beginning opposed this conception with the new view, which he announces as follows: "Philosophy cannot be learned, as mathematics, physics, and history can be learned; but one can learn only to philosophize. One reason why philosophy cannot be learned is that it does not yet exist as a complete and universally recognized science. Every philosophical thinker builds his system upon the ruins of another; never, however, has any system reached the condition where it has become permanent in all its parts. One cannot learn philosophy, then, for the reason that it does not yet exist." But even if it did exist, we could not gain possession of it by learning. A philosophy which is 'learned' would cease to be a philosophy, and would be merely 'historical' knowledge, not philosophy.[1]

It is the age of the illumination which speaks to us in these words. To lead students from a state of pupilage to independent thought was the task that the universities began to set before themselves. It is the *bien raisonner* that the pedagogy of Frederick the Great recommends as the goal for all teachers.

How then shall students learn to philosophize? "Through exercise and independent employment of the reason," Kant answers. The material for the necessary exercises are fur-

[1] II., pp. 313 ff., *Logik*, Introduction, iii. ; Arnoldt, pp. 374 ff.

nished by the facts of nature and history on the one side, and on the other by the attempts which have been already made to interpret these facts philosophically. Kant employs both of these sources in dealing with his students. He made it his business to tell them facts, or to direct them in discovering facts. This is the significance of the two courses of lectures to which he attached so much importance, physical geography and anthropology. The mistake of previous philosophical instruction, as he tells us in the announcement of his lectures (1765), is seen in the fact "that the youth early became versed in logical subtleties without having sufficient historical knowledge." Before the understanding. has been matured through discipline they are prematurely instructed in general concepts. "From this source spring the perennial prejudices of the schools, which are more inflexible and often more absurd than those of common life, and also the precocious loquacity of young thinkers, which is blinder than any other form of self-conceit, and more incurable than ignorance." To obviate this evil, he used to preface his lectures on metaphysics with material taken from empirical psychology and physics. In like manner, in ethics he described what actually happened before undertaking to show what should take place. Finally, there were the lectures, on physical geography. In the first part of these lectures, the present condition of the earth was described, the second dealt with man as a natural being, while the third treated of the constitution of states and societies. In this way the hearers were furnished with a store of interesting and instructive information. In addition, in 1772 a course of lectures of the same general character on anthropology was offered, and thereafter regularly alternated with the course on physical geography. In a letter to Herz in 1773, he speaks as follows regarding the purpose of these lectures, which he intends to make a regular part of the academic discipline: "I am trying to furnish by means of these very interesting facts of observation, as they appear to me, a training for the academic youth in address and readiness, and even in wisdom. This course and that on physical geography are different from all other kinds of instruction, and may be called knowledge of the world."[1]

Kant also employed the history of philosophy as a means in teaching his students to philosophize. He gave historical sketches in the introductions to his lectures, and also took account of the doctrines of his predecessors when treating of particular problems.[2] In the Encyclopædia and also in the Logic, he gave a short summary of the history of philosophy.

It is evident that Kant pointed out the way which higher education has taken since his time. In the greatly broadened gymnasium courses, instruction in the sciences and history have taken the place of the former academic instruction in logic and metaphysics; and in the universities, dogmatic teaching has been perhaps too generally replaced by courses on the history of philosophy.

The aim of Kant's teaching, however, was not to make professional philosophers, but by means of philosophy to form men of independent thought and upright character. Or, as he defined "the chief end of his academic life" in a letter to Herz, it is "to promote right opinions, and to inculcate fixed principles in minds of natural excellence, in order to afford the only proper direction to the development of talent."[3] Kant's students were drawn from all the different departments. Among them were the future pastors, teachers, judges, and physicians. The one thing which they all required was practical wisdom; that is, the capacity to recognize the true value of all knowledge from its relation to human ends. "Science has a real and true value only as an instrument of practical wisdom. As such an instrument it is indeed indispensable."[4] But without practical wis-

---

[1] VIII., p. 696.
[3] VIII., p. 703.
[2] Arnoldt, p. 386.
[4] Logik, Introduction, iii.

dom it is a dangerous possession, and has the tendency to make one conceited, rude, and inhuman. Now it is just the task of the academic teacher of philosophy to guard against this: he is called to undertake the Socratic process of testing (ἐξετάζειν). In one of the 'reflections' published by Erdmann,[1] there is an excellent statement of the matter. As we have already remarked, Kant was fond of calling the boorish scholar a cyclops. He found such cyclops in all four faculties. "The cyclops of literature (the philologian) is the most insolent, but there are cyclops among the theologians, jurists, physicians, and even among the geometers." What constitutes them cyclops is not their strength, but the fact that they have only one eye; they see things only from a single standpoint, that of their specialty. The task of philosophy is to furnish a second eye to the scientifically instructed youth, "which shall cause him also to see his object from the standpoint of other men. On this depends the humanity of science." " For each one, however, the eye must be formed from special material: for the physician, from criticism of our knowledge of nature; for the jurist, from criticism of our knowledge of legal and moral affairs; for the theologian, from that of our metaphysic; and for the geometer, from criticism of our rational knowledge in general. The second eye is thus the self-knowledge of human reason, without which we can have no proper estimate of the extent of our knowledge."

One might say that we have here the idea of academic instruction in philosophy correctly outlined for all time. And the undertaking imposed is not less necessary to-day than it was then, for cyclopism has greatly increased in the century which has since elapsed. Doubtless the undertaking is now even much more difficult. The astounding development of the sciences during the last century makes it impossible for any one person to epitomize their results, as

[1] II., p. 60.

Kant was still able to do. Who would now venture to give lectures on the disciplines which were included in the fields with which he dealt? And the unthankfulness of the task has perhaps also increased: the spirit of specialization is to-day much more opposed to philosophy than it was in the eighteenth century.

IV. KANT AS THINKER AND AUTHOR

The most prominent characteristic of Kant's intelligence was undoubtedly an acute understanding, by means of which he elaborated his own conceptual system with unusual strength and persistence. He rejoiced in definitions, distinctions, and deductions. His understanding was of the juridical type, and he liked to formulate and explain his problems as controverted legal questions. But in addition to his acuteness of understanding, Kant was not lacking in profundity of mind. He had an intelligent sense and a fine appreciation of all deep and ultimate questions regarding the universe and life. In its final form his thought approached the boundaries of mysticism. Man, he taught, possesses a double life, a temporal life of sense as a member of nature, and a transcendent, timeless life as a member of the intelligible world. Finally, Kant was distinguished by his astounding breadth of view and of scientific interest, as well as by his unusual wealth of knowledge from a great variety of fields. He was at home in mathematics and the sciences of nature, and was not unacquainted in the realm of the historical sciences, as is shown by his writings on the philosophy of law and of religion. His exceedingly trustworthy memory enabled him to retain without trouble the results of his reading, which was especially comprehensive in the fields of cosmology and anthropology.

In considering Kant's activity as an author, it is well to remember that this is essentially something which belongs to the period when he was already growing old. He was fifty-seven years of age when the *Critique of Pure Reason* appeared. There is scarcely another case where a philosophical author was so late in reaching the definitive form of his thought, or where a man at such an advanced age first became known as a great thinker and influential writer. If Kant had died at the same age as Spinoza, Descartes, Lessing, or Schiller, his name would scarcely be heard at the present time. One may regard this as a favor of fortune: he was preserved from outliving his fame, as happened to so many of his successors. On the other hand, his works have suffered from the fact that they were not written at the time of his greatest strength and vigor. They show a maturity which approximates to over-ripeness. In more than one sense the precritical writings represent his best performance as an author. This is especially true of the writings of the sixties.

The form of the later works is thoroughly scholastic. In the first place, they are scholastic in the sense of pedantic: Kant thought and wrote in the strict style of the dogmatic philosophy of the schools. He does this consciously and voluntarily. He rejects with scorn the literary popularizing form that had become fashionable in philosophy. This was especially affected in Berlin and Göttingen, and during the last third of the eighteenth century it had gained the upper hand and replaced the old doctrinal form of philosophical writing. Kant himself approximated to this style of thinking and writing during the sixties. After he reached his own systematic standpoint he returned to the strict scholastic form. He praises this form in Wolff and Baumgarten. In addition, it may have been impressed upon him by his prolonged occupation with mathematical studies. It is evident, moreover, that this form corresponded with the natural tendency of his thought. And even the self-consciousness of the scholar, which in Kant's case gradually became very strongly marked, as opposed to the world of the court and of politics, might have had some influence in the same direction. We may imagine him saying: We are reviled as pedants because we do not write like people of the world. Well, let us glory in the reproach by employing the greatest care with regard to the precision and exactness of our thought.[1]

In a still further sense, however, his thinking was scholastic: it was not intuitively contemplative, but logically constructive. The energy of logical thought predominates over the tendency to resign one's self to the perception of things, as we find it, for example, in Schopenhauer. The latter, like the poet, is in a sense passive in the presence of things, in order that they may reveal their secrets to him. Kant brings to his view of things a dominating and imperious *a priori* understanding. This understanding does not wait upon things: things must conform to its concepts. It makes a logical dichotomic or trichotomic division, into which things are compelled to fit without much thought whether the classification is adapted to them or not, or allows the true relations of their members to appear. Thus it may happen that thoughts are obscured and darkened. Or, on the other hand, thoughts may be built up merely for the sake of rounding out the treatment, and thus many parts of a system which appear most stately and magnificent may be like the artificially inserted branches of the fir trees sold at the Christmas fair.

This imperious character of Kant's understanding makes itself evident also in his attitude towards the thoughts of others. He had little patience with other people's thoughts, but interpreted them directly according to his own theo-

[1] Many of his old friends were greatly disappointed at the scholastic and dogmatic mode of thought which prevailed in the *Critique*. Among these were Feder, Mendelssohn, and Herder, whose description of Kant we have already quoted (p. 40), and who praises the Kant of the precritical period at the expense of the critical philosopher.

ries, from this standpoint adopting or rejecting them. It is said that he was not inclined to discuss philosophical matters in private conversation, probably because he was conscious that he had not the capacity to listen, but only to teach. The same is true of his relation to other authors : he was not able to listen. Kant had reflected long and deeply, ever turning his thoughts on this side and on that, but in the philosophical field he had not read widely, and not with proper attention to the texts. He was not lacking in a general knowledge of the history of philosophy, both ancient and modern, and he understood also how to use this knowledge aptly. But he instantly subordinates the doctrines of others to his own purposes, and especially to the purpose of refutation. This is true of his treatment of Leibniz and Wolff, as well as of Hume and Berkeley. Those among his contemporaries who opposed his views, e. g., Feder and Eberhard, had a similar experience. It was vain to expect from Kant any real consideration of the doubts and objections which they raised. He was not able to listen or understand, but felt only the contradiction. Against this he rose with a sharp remonstrance, and then proceeded to set forth his views again as the truth and the only truth. Indeed, he cannot understand why every one does not find these views convincing, and is therefore quick to reproach others with intentional misunderstanding and misrepresentation. In the end, even Kant's disciples, like Fichte and Beck, experienced this kind of treatment. Kant insists strongly on subordination and unconditional acceptance of his views. So long as his disciples confined themselves to appropriating and expounding his system in its original form, as his first and only faithful commentator Schultze did, they had Kant's approbation. But so soon as they began to handle the thoughts more freely and independently, or to transform them in accordance with an internal necessity or the spirit of the system, he reprimanded them sharply. The *Critique* is to be understood according to its letter, not according to a pretended spirit. Indeed, he finally turned away from such disciples as from false friends, with suspicion and dislike, and announced his position in unrelenting public explanations.[1]

In this attitude there is manifest the fixity of thought which often shows itself in old age. One can notice the beginning of this tendency comparatively early in Kant's case. In a letter to Herz of the year 1790,[2] he says apologetically that as he grows older he does not have much success in employing the thoughts of other people in a purely speculative field. "I must give myself up to the movement of my own thoughts, which for some years have followed a kind of beaten track." How exclusively he did this is shown by the inventories, writings, and letters of the last decade of his life. Adickes says of Kant's notes during the nineties: "The thoughts have become fixed firmly in his brain, and are aroused in a purely mechanical way without any really new act of thought taking place. It is just like the case of a music-box: it has been wound up, and so it plays its *repertoire.*" This condition of things was long foreshadowed. The ever renewed confusion of thought with regard to the transcendental deduction and the dialectic, which goes back to the sixties, is the beginning of it. (The *Reflections* and the *Loose Leaves* and even the expositions in the *Critique* give documentary evidence of this process.) Kant's thought became fixed; he ceased to receive any fresh impressions. With great energy and persistence he continued to consider and treat fixed problems according to unchanging methods. But during the last twenty-three years of his life it can

---

[1] VIII., p. 600. On Kant's relation to Beck, *cf.* Dilthey, "Aus den Rostocker Kanthandschriften," *Archiv für Gesch. der Philos.* II., pp. 592 ff., where eight letters of Kant's to Beck are given. His inability to understand another's views is very clearly shown in these letters.

[2] VIII., p. 720.

scarcely be said that any new motives arose to influence his thought.[1]

Finally, we have to make some remarks regarding the literary form of his writings. Kant does not belong to the great writers of the German language. He perhaps might have attained this rank, and his earlier writings are not lacking in artistic merit and attractiveness. In addition to a suggestive and emphatic style, and a happy choice of expressions, he possessed a pleasant and subtle humor, and had command of a store of conceits, often wittily fashioned, and of keen observations. He knew also how to employ effectively many words and phrases which his reading had left in his memory. In the prime of life all these things must have made his lectures very excellent. Among his writings it is especially those of the sixties which show these characteristics, as, *e. g.*, *The Dreams of a Ghost-Seer*. It is true his work is lacking in finish, and this is especially true of the construction of his sentences. Moreover, he himself says that nearly all his works were hastily written. The later writings, especially the principal systematic works, give but little evidence of the excellence of his earlier style. This, however, is more evident in the shorter essays, like the papers in the *Berliner Monatsschrift*, or in minor works like the *Prolegomena*, where the polemic gives a livelier movement to the exposition, or in *Religion within the Bounds of Pure Reason*, where oftentimes a caustic humor breaks through the logical form of the sentences. In the main treatises, on the other hand, a dry style of indefatigable and inexorable didactics everywhere prevails. Only in single passages is the style light-

---

[1] Characteristic of his old age are odd whimsical scientific and medical explanations of certain phenomena, especially of those which he had observed to take place in his own body. He also was fond of putting forward on every occasion strange etymological explanations which he maintained with extreme obstinacy against all contradiction. Compare the accounts by Wasianski and Jachmann. In general he could not endure any contradiction, even in society.

ened a little by figures drawn from legal procedure or from experiences at sea. Here and there at times an appearance of secret waggishness marks the pages, or there is in some interpellation a pathetic digression from the style of the whole, generally dealing with something surprising, while the humor of the sixties appears to have entirely disappeared.

If one is to praise anything in the form of these writings, it must be the three things which we here enumerate: (1) The great and stern earnestness and plain genuineness, which disregards all non-essentials and despises all adornment, in order to bring conviction only through the weight of the thought itself. (2) Great care in systematic completeness. (3) A certain detailed exactness of speech.

Every one, however, has the faults which his virtues entail, and this is true of Kant as a writer. The stern, plain genuineness becomes wearisome uniformity and dulness. What Schopenhauer understood so well, and what Kant himself liked to do in his earlier writings — to give the reader relief from his own thoughts by means of occasional remarks, witty or polemical quotations, or ironical and humorous turns of expression — all this was entirely lacking in the author of the *Critiques*. With his mind directed toward a single purpose, he never relaxed the stern earnestness with which he followed the course of his abstract thoughts. Even the tendency to systematic completeness had its reverse side: it degenerated finally into a mania for a system. The filling up of an *a priori* determined schema became the most important concern, and not infrequently the content had to be forcibly treated in this process. General reflections of a purely logical character were often premised to justify the divisions which had been decided upon, *e. g.*, the Introductions to the Analytic and the Dialectic. All kinds of devices and padding were invented to fill out the vacant places of the *a priori* scheme. Even the *Critique of Pure Reason* suffers from this tendency, but it is found to a much greater extent in the two later *Critiques.*   It might appear that Goethe's lines were made with this reference:

> When you once the wood into a cross have fashioned,
> For a living body 't is most well adapted.

Finally, the "detailed exactitude" not infrequently became a cumbersome diffuseness, as, *e. g.*, in "The Methods for discovering all the pure Concepts of the Understanding, first, second, and third Sections." Or as we have it in the "Transcendental Deduction," with its repetitions and variations of the same thought, and without the '*aliter*' to guide the reader which scholastic philosophy placed before the various forms of demonstration furnished for the same proposition. A new start is constantly made in order to settle some point, but there always remains something unfinished which seems to require a fresh exposition. He who reads through the Transcendental Analytic for the first time will perhaps feel as if he had wandered the whole day through endless sand-hills. He constantly keeps hoping that he has climbed the last barrier and will see his goal before him, but ever new obstacles appear in his path. Even the construction of Kant's sentences adds to the difficulty. They are sometimes enough to reduce the most patient reader to despair, especially in the two later *Critiques.* If one turns to almost any page, one finds sentences of from ten to twenty lines in length. One has scarcely begun to read before explanations, reservations, in brackets and without brackets, in the text and as foot-notes, begin to appear. It seems as if Kant felt compelled at every line to recall the entire *Critique* to the reader's mind, so that he should not forget that here everything is to be understood from the critical and transcendental point of view. The inversion of the Latin construction in German subordinate clauses, the frequent use of the relative pronoun, whose antecedent the reader is left to seek among half a dozen substantives, makes it often necessary for one to read a sentence two or three times in order to understand merely the grammatical construction.

The tendency to 'detailed exactitude,' on the other hand, does not exclude a certain lack of exactness in small matters. He frequently uses expressions which are contrary to his own definition. For example, after proving that space is not a concept, but a perception, he does not refrain for a moment from speaking of the 'concept' of space. Or, after undertaking to show that objects do not enter the mind ready-made from without, but are the products of the synthetic functions of the understanding, he does not hesitate to speak constantly of the objects which are 'given' in perception. He makes much use of indefinite, ambiguous, or equivocal expressions, like 'experience,' 'reason,' 'metaphysic,' 'synthetic,' 'transcendental,' 'refer to an object,' etc. Another defect is the great carelessness in external details; paragraphs and headings are found where they do not belong, and are lacking where they are really required. All these characteristics, greatly increased, appear in the manuscript remains which Kant wrote during the latter years of his life.

I do not say all these things to reproach Kant, or to detract from his reputation. I only wish to prepare the reader, who becomes acquainted with these works for the first time, for their peculiarities, or to deliver him from them. Very well I remember that on first reading the *Critiques* I often came to a stand, disheartened and discouraged. My experience was not unusual. I venture to say that there are not a few persons who, when they first attempt to read the *Critique of Pure Reason*, doubt the possibility of understanding it, and then go on to doubt their own capacity for understanding philosophical books in general. Those who are in such a condition I wish to encourage not to stop for difficulties of this sort, but rather to go on calmly and gain a general view of Kant's work and purpose. If after this one turns to the beginning, many difficulties will have vanished, though many will still remain. At all events, one will see that in spite of such oddities, there is an important meaning in these writings that will reward all the earnest attention which one bestows on them.

V. KANT'S PHILOSOPHICAL DEVELOPMENT [1]

It will not be possible for me to undertake here a detailed treatment of the difficult, and, as the literature shows, the much-discussed problem of the development of Kant's thought. This is neither the place nor the time to renew the investigation that I undertook in the work cited below, and the results of which still appear to me valid with regard to the essential points. Such an undertaking will be fitting only when the new edition of Kant's works has made available the entire mass of notes, letters, and copies of lectures. On the other hand, it is, of course, not possible to pass over the question altogether; for to understand properly the crit-

---

[1] LITERATURE. Investigations of the development of Kant's thought have multiplied during the last decade. The reason of this is that the conception which one has of the critical philosophy is partly determined by one's view of its origin; or at least one may try to support one's interpretation by such an appeal. Kuno Fischer, in his *Geschichte der neueren Philosophie,* undertakes to give a thorough account of the writings of the precritical period. I may mention the following investigations: F. Paulsen, *Versuch einer Entwickelungsgeschichte der Kantischen Erkenntnistheorie* (1875); W. Windelband, "Ueber die verschiedenen Phasen der Kantische Lehre vom Ding-an-Sich" (*Zeitschr. f. wiss. Philos.,* I., pp. 224 ff., 1877); K. Dietrich, *Kant u. Newton* (1876), *Kant u. Rousseau* (1878); G. Thiele, *Die Philosophie Kants nach ihrem system. Zusammenhang u. ihrer logisch-historischen Entwickelung* (1882–87); B. Erdmann, *Reflexionen Kants zur krit. Philosophie,* II., Einleitung (1884); E. v. Hartmann, *Kants Erkenntnistheorie u. Metaphysik in den vier Perioden ihrer Entwickelung* (1894); H.Höffding, " Die Kontinuität im philos. Entwickelungsgange Kants" (*Archiv. f. Gesch. d. Philos.,* 1894, Bd. VII., pp. 173 ff., 376 ff., 449 ff.); E. Adickes, *Kant-Studien* (1895), and the article in the *Kant-Studien* edited by Vaihinger (Bd. I., 1896): "Die bewegenden Kräfte in Kants philosophischer Entwickelung und die beiden Pole seines Systems." [E. Caird, *The Critical Philosophy of Kant,* vol. I., chaps. iii.–v.; J. G. Schurman, "The Genesis of the Critical Philosophy," *Philos. Review,* Nos. 37, 38, 39.]

ical philosophy, a correct conception of its starting-point is of the utmost importance.

When Kant himself speaks of his philosophical development, he recognizes only two periods,—the critical and the precritical, or the period when he was conscious of possessing the principle of true philosophy, and the antecedent period of search and groping. And he uniformly dated the dividing line between these two epochs, the beginning of the critical era, with the conception of the thoughts which he first outlined in the *Dissertation* of the year 1770.

A more careful examination of the writings of the precritical time shows that even within that period noteworthy transformations had taken place. Two epochs are clearly distinguishable. The first has as its literary result the writings of the second half of the fifties, and the second the writings of the first half of the sixties. The first epoch is characterized by the fact that while Kant departed from the current Leibnizo-Wolffian philosophy in natural philosophy and cosmology, where his main interest was manifested in his independent work along the lines of Newton, he yet remained in the field of epistemology and metaphysics in essential accord with the German school philosophy. In the second period, in which his interest in the natural sciences was somewhat less pronounced, he freed himself more and more from the school philosophy, and approximated to the empirical and sceptical mode of thought that just at that time was exerting an influence from England. The third period was characterized by a decided opposition to sensualistic rationalism both in theoretical and in practical philosophy.

If we wish a descriptive name for these periods, we may call the first the dogmatic-rationalistic; the second, the sceptico-empirical; and the third, critico-rationalistic. The last period, then, in a certain sense represents a return to the point of view of the first, while on the other hand, with regard to the total tendency of the thought (the turning away from transcendent speculation, and emphasis upon the practical), it belongs to the second period.

At this point, however, I wish to make a general remark. The changes in Kant's thought, the " transformations " of which he speaks, have to do rather with the form than with the content: they concern his epistemology rather than his metaphysics. His metaphysics (like the fundamental notions of his physics) remained essentially the same through all the other changes of his thought. He is an idealist of the type of Leibniz and Plato. We can trace this theory from the writings of the fifties to the lectures of the nineties. He also continued to use throughout his whole life Baumgarten's *Metaphysics*, which is essentially a scholastic form of monadism, as a text-book for his lectures. That which changes in these transformations of standpoint is chiefly the form of the epistemological foundation of his philosophy, " the method of metaphysics," as he himself says. I shall attempt to show in detail this juxtaposition of the two factors — the constant and the variable — from an examination of the writings.

The works of the first period are entirely devoted to the natural sciences, to cosmology and physical geography, and to the development of the concepts of mathematical physics. The first two more extensive works — the *Thoughts on the True Evaluation of Dynamic Forces* (1746), and the *Natural History of the Heavens* (1755) — are characterized by decided and sometimes bold declarations of the sufficiency and right of independent thought as against the authority of the schools. This is especially marked in the first work. The second rises to bolder cosmological speculations, and ranges to the extreme limits of fantastic hypotheses regarding the cosmic position and the destiny of man.

With regard to the world-view which appears in these writings, there is, as we have already said, one characteristic that is worthy of note. That is the strict application of physical and the rejection of all hyper-physical explanations in that cosmology, together with the assertion which accompanies it that by this means the divine origin of the world is best established. If an ordered world could, or rather must, have arisen from the movements of given elements according to merely natural laws, it is hereby proved that the very "nature of things depends upon and is determined by a significant rational arrangement." Even the nature of "thinking beings" is deduced from the cosmic constitution of the planets which they inhabit. The greater the distance of the planets from the sun, the lighter and finer the material of which they are composed, and also the greater "the excellence of the thinking beings which inhabit them," the swiftness of their ideas, the clearness and liveliness of the concepts which they receive through external impressions, of the faculty which unites those impressions, and their ability to make real use of their ideas; in short, "the whole sphere of their perfection."[1] He brings into connection with this speculation, "which is not far from an ascertained certainty," the doctrine of the immortality of the soul. He thinks of the soul as passing through the various planets with increasing development of the individual. Perhaps, he concludes, it is permitted to the soul, when freed from this coarse earthly matter, "to become acquainted at close quarters with those distant spheres of the universe and the excellence of their disposition, which even from afar so greatly stimulate our curiosity."

Those essays which were occasioned by the Lisbon earthquake of 1755 are more nearly related to natural science. The same is true of a number of short papers on geo-physics, especially of the treatise on *The Theory of the Winds* (1756), in which he was the first to propound the law of periodical winds that was afterwards developed by Dove. The general standpoint which all these writings occupy is the assumption of complete unity in the development of the physical

[1] I., p. 337.

universe, which can and must be explained solely from the effect of physical forces.

The only metaphysico-epistemological work of these years — *New Exposition of the First Principles of Metaphysical Knowledge*, his habilitation essay (1755) — scarcely shows so much independence as we find in the cosmic and geo-physical treatises. It is true that it contains various attacks on the Wolffian philosophy, and here and there shows dependence upon the Leipzig theologian, Crusius, the most prominent opponent of Wolff in the German universities. In general, however, Kant still occupied the standpoint of the Wolffians, and, above all, had not broken with their modes of thought. This is especially evident in the rationalistic tendency to hypostatize things. The "natures of things" are absolutely posited essences. With this view there is connected an idea which is of great and permanent importance for Kant's thought. The final presupposition of the unity of the world in space and time by means of the reciprocity of substances is that "the natures of things" are posited in the being of God with archetypal relations to one another. Reciprocity in nature is the manifestation of this *nexus idealis* of the essences in the divine understanding. When differently applied, this consideration affords a proof for the existence of God: the *commercium substantiarum* shows that these substances have an archetypal unity in one principle which creatively posits their nature. This is the argument of Leibniz, which Lotze has in our day renewed and made the corner-stone of his system. Kant might have been led to this point of view by M. Knutzen's (his teacher's) treatment of the problem of causality. The latter revived the doctrine of monads in the Leibnizian form, that all simple beings are ideating beings, while at the same time he maintained reciprocity (though not holding to an influence or inter-action from accidents).[1] Moreover, this position is implicitly

[1] B. Erdmann, *M. Knutzen*, pp. 84 ff.

contained in the notion of God of the school-metaphysic (*Deus ens perfectissimum seu realissimum*), and Kant had it before him in this form in Baumgarten's work, which also contained in addition the concept of an *influxus idealis*. It is the same notion which forms the basis of Shaftesbury's optimistic and teleological view of the world. Nature represents, in unending gradations of internally harmonious beings, the infinite fulness of reality or perfection in individualized form that is comprised in absolute unity in the nature of God. It is also Spinoza's point of view, the difference being that the latter advances it with a strong polemical emphasis against anthropomorphic theism, and against anthropocentric teleology.

In the works of the second period (1762–66), Kant turns more directly to the problems of metaphysics and epistemology. The first series of these works, which were written during the years 1762–63, group themselves around the principal treatise, *The only Possible Ground of Demonstration for the Existence of God* (1762). With this there are connected the two shorter essays, *An Answer to a Prize Question of the Berlin Academy: An Investigation of the Clearness of the Principles of Natural Theology and Morals* (printed 1764), and *An Attempt to Introduce into Philosophy the Conception of Negative Magnitude* (1763). These were preceded by the short paper on *The False Subtlety of the Four Syllogistic Figures*. At the end of the period we have *The Dreams of a Ghost-Seer Explained through the Dreams of Metaphysics* (1766). The work entitled *Observations on the Feeling of the Beautiful and the Sublime* (1764) belongs to a different field — the moral and anthropological. It is essentially made up of remarks on the moral characteristics of different temperaments, sexes, and nations.[1]

---

[1] Regarding the date of composition, *cf.* B. Erdmann, in the Introduction to his edition of *Reflexionen Kants*, II. pp. xvi. ff. The *Beweisgrund* appeared at Michaelmas 1762. The manuscript of the prize-treatise, according to a

In the *Ground of Demonstration for the Existence of God*, which is put forward as the result of "long reflection," we have a fundamental piece of Kant's metaphysics, the doctrine already referred to in the habilitation essay regarding the nature of God in his relation to the world. The intention is to replace the dominant form of natural theology, especially the current physico-theology, by a more profound view. One may formulate the main points of this conception as follows: The ordinary physico-theology, which ranges through nature to find there evidences of design, is good for nothing. It discourages and disturbs the investigation of nature, since it encourages the "slothful reason," through pretended devotion, to content itself with the purposes which it has discovered, and to abandon the search for causes. Finally, this method is unable to afford any real demonstration of the existence of a highest, all-sufficient being. It can make it only highly probable that an architectonic intelligence was concerned in the formation of the real world. Just as little can the current ontological and cosmological proof demonstrate the existence of God, as Kant shows in a criticism which anticipates all the chief points of his later criticism of the proofs for the existence of God in the *Critique of Pure Reason*. Especially the ontological proof in its old form, which deduces the real existence from the concept of God, is worthless. We find here already the formula "that existence is never a predicate or mark of a thing." This was also familiar to Hume, who tells us that "if one connects the idea of existence with the idea of any object whatsoever, one does not thereby increase the content of the latter."

letter of Kant's to Formey now in the royal library at Berlin, and dated June 28, 1763, had been handed in to the Academy before the 31st December, 1762. It could not, therefore, have been written, as Erdmann supposes, during the first months of 1763. The *Negative Grössen* was handed to the philosophical faculty at Königsberg for censorship June 3, 1763. Erdmann's guess that the third work was partly completed when Kant, at the last moment, decided to compete for the Berlin prize may accordingly be groundless.

As a substitute for this argument, Kant brings forward his own demonstration of God's existence, a kind of inverted form of the ontological proof. He does not argue that from the possibility of an *ens realissimum*, its existence follows; but he reaches existence as the ground of the possibility of the conception. The possible — thus he proceeds in scholastic style of argument — presupposes an existent; this is the necessary being, and this the *ens realissimum*, which has the attributes of consciousness, understanding, and will. The real significance of this proof, however, is found in the thought which we have already repeatedly met with: the real world, with its harmony of many things in a unitary reality, is the actualization of a possible world. This world of "possible things" is the product of the divine intelligence. In this realm the logical and teleological adaptation of the elements to one another is already provided for; and this makes possible the fact that in the real world the elements, acting according to immanent laws, constitute a significant whole. There is thus no necessity for constant acts of special adaptation by means of supernatural influences. Thus the planetary systems, and the earth with its streams and mountains and entire physical constitution, owe their form to the mechanical interplay of their parts working according to universal natural laws, and without any supernatural intervention. Kant indeed hesitated to extend this view so as to apply it to the development of organic forms. Only in this way do we obtain an "all-sufficient" God, who is the ground not only of the actual, but also of the possible, and at the same time obtain a real demonstration of his existence — if, indeed, there can be any demonstration at all.

For it is noteworthy that at this time Kant expresses himself somewhat sceptically regarding the value, necessity, and possibility of such metaphysical attempts. "It is absolutely necessary," so he concludes his essay, "that one should *convince* himself of the existence of God, but not so essential that one should *demonstrate* it." And at the beginning we find for the first time those phrases which afterwards became so common, of "the bottomless abyss of metaphysics." Metaphysics is "a dark ocean without shores or lighthouses," where one may be easily carried out of his course by unperceived currents.

The sceptical tone is still more pronounced in the other writings of this group. The essay written for the prize offered by the Berlin Academy, which received *proxime accessit*, while the prize fell to Mendelssohn, compares the method of philosophy with that of mathematics. The issue of the comparison is very much to the disadvantage of philosophy. Mathematics possesses really adequate definitions, for it produces the object "synthetically" by means of the definition, and, at the same time, it can represent its concepts in perception. Philosophy, on the other hand, — physics, as well as psychology and metaphysics, — has to determine its concepts through analysis, an undertaking which can seldom or never be brought to completion. Moreover, it cannot represent its concepts in a concrete case, but is compelled to think them abstractly. It is therefore a serious and confusing error to suppose that the metaphysician has imitated the methods of the mathematician. This would be permissible only if he had attained an equal clearness and completeness of definition. In the meantime, he has operated with easily attained nominal definitions of 'possibility,' 'reality,' 'body,' and 'spirit,' and really accomplished nothing. "Metaphysics is undoubtedly the most difficult of all human sciences; but it has never as yet been written." [1] Can it be written at all? Kant regards it as possible. Can it become a demonstrative science? He believes that this also is possible, only it must have fixed definitions. And how are these to be attained? We get always

[1] II. p. 291.

the same answer, namely: through the analysis of given, but confusedly given, concepts. If Kant had been an empiricist, he would have answered that the materials from which concepts are formed are not obscurely given concepts, but experiences; and that a demonstrative science of metaphysics is just as little possible as a demonstrative science of facts in general.

The essay on *Negative Magnitude*, which appeared as an independently deduced corollary to the prize treatise, shows how one definite mathematical concept, that of negative magnitude, can be employed in philosophy throughout all its parts. Here also one sees that Kant has abandoned the rationalistic method of equating conceptual and actual reality. No contradiction can obtain between realities, Baumgarten teaches, *ergo omnes realitates sunt in ente compossibiles.* Yes, says Kant, that holds in the realm of concepts. It is different, however, in the world of actual fact. Here it may very well happen that two positive determinations exclude each other, as when they are related as positive and negative magnitudes in mathematics. At the end of the treatise the causal problem is brought forward for the first time. The distinction is made between a logical and a real ground, and then the question is put as follows: I understand very well how a consequence is conditioned by a ground in accordance with the law of identity. But, on the other hand, "how shall I understand the proposition that because something is, something different may be? Or that because something is, something else is destroyed?" How can the existence and particular condition of one element of reality explain why another is or is not? With this question, which is commended to the "thorough-going philosophers who are daily increasing in number," and to "metaphysical intellects of complete insight," Kant ends the treatise, begging the "great minds" to be pleased to aid "the weakness of his insight" with their great wisdom. It is Hume's problem, and also the problem of the critical philosophy which is here formulated. The relation of cause and effect is not a logical relation; the effect cannot be derived from the cause by means of a logical process. In what then does this relation consist, and upon what does it rest? Hume answers that it rests upon experience, and consists in the observed sequence of cause and effect which is assumed to be uniform. Kant does not furnish any answer. Did he possess one?

The ironical and sceptical tone toward metaphysicians and their renowned philosophy which breaks out here reaches its height in *The Dreams of a Ghost-Seer Explained through the Dreams of Metaphysics*, — metaphysics a vision and an interpreter of vision suitable to explain the fantastic dreams of one who sees spirits. The work was occasioned by the sensational performances of the Swede Swedenborg, who not only had the gift of spatial and temporal clairvoyance, but also possessed the privilege of associating with departed spirits. Kant had been persuaded, by many inquiries from "over-curious and idle friends" to investigate these matters.[1] His interest in the subject went so far that he had the works of the visionary (*Arcana cœlestia*, 8 vols. quarto) sent over from London; and besides seven pounds sterling, they cost him the trouble of reading them.

This very remarkable work, half jest and half earnest, and written with a happy humor, outlines in its first part a metaphysical pneumatology. The spirits of immaterial beings on the one hand stand in relation to bodies, and on the other belong to a *mundus intelligibilis*, in which they are related to one another in a hyperphysical way, according to pneumatic laws that are not subject to the conditions of space and time. This spiritology, which is put forward as if seriously — and which indeed is not intended to be entirely without seriousness — evidently foreshadows the later doctrine of the double

[1] Information on this point is given in a letter to Frl. v. Knolbach of the year 1763; *cf.* also Kuno Fischer, *Gesch. d. n. Philos.* I. p. 272.

world to which man belongs: the *mundus sensibilis* as an empirical being, and the *mundus intelligibilis* as a purely rational being. There follows next an amusing exposition, from the naturalistic and sceptical standpoint, of spiritistic phenomena, the metaphysical possibility of which is explained with equal lucidity. They are imaginative products of a diseased brain that under abnormal conditions are projected outwards as physical phenomena. In the second part, the report of Swedenborg's visions of this world and of the other is used to confirm or to throw derision on that fantastic metaphysics which is so clever at demonstrating its possibility.[1] Then follow the concluding words in a serious vein: The lesson of all this is that philosophy ought to be on its guard against all speculations of this sort which transcend experience. Whether there are such powers as Swedenborg believed himself to possess, whether spirits can think and act without any connection with a body, cannot in the least be determined by reason. Experience is the only source of our knowledge of reality. "The fundamental concepts of things as causes which exist as forces and activities are entirely arbitrary, and unless they can be derived from experience they can neither be proved nor refuted." And in this connection we find an answer to the question thrown out at the end of the essay on negative magnitude. "It is impossible," we are here told, "to understand through reason how anything can be a cause, or possess a force, but these relations can be learned only from experience." For those alleged powers of the soul which the spiritism of Swedenborg assumes we have not the common consent of experience, but only the im-

---

[1] In a letter written at this time (VIII., p. 672), to M. Mendelssohn, who was surprised at the tone of the work, Kan speaks of "the absurd frame of mind" in which it was composed. He could not keep from having "a little faith in stories of this sort, or from speculating a little on the possibility of their correctness in spite of the absurdities narrated, and the fantastic and unmeaning conceptions which resulted from any attempt to explain them." Thus, in order to satirize others, he first satirized himself.

pressions which individuals claim to have, and which, for that very reason, are not capable of serving "as the basis of any law of experience whatsoever regarding which the understanding could pass judgment." Therefore it is advisable — not to show that they are impossible — but to let them alone. The place of metaphysical demonstrations and alleged empirical confirmations of the immortality of the soul is filled by "moral faith, the simplicity of which can free one from many subtleties of reasoning, and which alone is suitable to man in every condition, since it directly reveals to him in morality the true purpose of his life."

This was the form of Kant's philosophy at the end of the second epoch. He had lost all faith in the demonstrations furnished by current metaphysical systems, whether they bore the name of Wolff or of Crusius. Even his faith in the possibility of metaphysics, in the old sense of an *a priori* science that interprets reality in terms of logical concepts, is badly shattered. But he does not renounce metaphysics in general; "as the science of the limits of human reason" it remains a necessary undertaking.[1] In this form it would constitute that to which one can really apply the name philosophy (*Weisheit*), *i. e.*, the capacity " of choosing, among many problems that offer themselves, those which man is called upon to solve." [2]

What brought about Kant's estrangement from the old dogmatic school metaphysics ? This has been explained by pointing to the influence of English thought, particularly to that of Hume. There is no doubt that through the prominence of English modes of thought on the continent, espe-

---

[1] II., p. 375.

[2] *Cf.* Kant's letters to Lambert and to Mendelssohn (VIII., pp. 655, 672). He speaks in these letters of the reform of metaphysics as the problem that most nearly concerned him. He believes that he is in possession of a new method which will free the science from the delusions of knowledge and put it on a sound basis. This discovery will be of the greatest importance for the true and permanent well-being of the human race,

cially under the rising influence of Voltaire, the intellectual atmosphere of Germany had been changed since the middle of the century, and that this change was not without its effect on Kant. That he read and esteemed highly English authors, especially the writers on moral philosophy, we know both from the characterization that we quoted above from Herder, and especially from the program of his lectures of the year 1765-66.[1] To this was added the influence of Rousseau, who, as we have already mentioned, had great weight, especially in putting an end to Kant's over-estimation of things intellectual, and teaching him that wise simplicity and a good heart are more than all metaphysics and natural theology. On the other hand, one may assume that the estrangement from the school metaphysics was essentially a development from within. If he shows in the *Only Possible Ground of Demonstration for the Existence of God* how far the current proofs of God's existence are from a real demonstration, or in *The Dreams of a Ghost-Seer* the absurdities of pneumatology, the science of spirits, he would scarcely need any impetus from without to lead him to see these things. Baumgarten's *Metaphysics*, with its demonstrations carried through exactly a thousand paragraphs, must have made a somewhat strange impression on Kant as a student of Newton, a mathematician and physicist, as soon as he directed his attention carefully to the form of the proofs. Propositions regarding God, the world, the soul, and everything in general were there deduced from purely self-made definitions. Where now do these concepts derive their justification? They are not mathematical concepts that create their objects by means of definitions; they are not physical concepts which depend upon experience. Whence, then, do they derive their validity? The problem is in truth so obvious that it did not need to be forced upon him from any external source. The very fact that he comes

[1] II., pp. 313 ff.

so near to certain thoughts of Hume, and yet remains at the same time so far removed from the latter's general standpoint, is evidence that he did not receive the impetus to his work from the English writers, and especially from Hume's epistemological investigations. In particular, he holds fast, in spite of everything, to the rationalistic assumption that concepts are given, though obscurely, and that by means of analysis they can be brought to perfect clearness, and that then in this way something like a demonstrative procedure in metaphysics is not in itself impossible.[1]

The *third* and *last* epoch, that of *Criticism*, was inaugurated by the *Dissertation* which Kant wrote on assuming the ordinary professorship in 1770, in fulfilment of the academic requirement of public 'disputation.' Its content is described by the title, *Concerning the Form and Principles of the Sensible and Intelligible World*. In the letter accompanying the copy sent to Lambert, he expresses his certainty that in this work he has reached his definitive standpoint. "About a year ago, I reached a point of view that, as I flatter myself, I do not require ever to change, though of course it needs to be extended. By means of this, all kinds of metaphysical questions can be tested, and, so far as they are answerable, can be decided."[2] Eleven years later, in a letter to M. Herz, his respondent in the 'disputation,' he connected the *Critique of Pure Reason*, which was just appearing, with the *Dissertation* in the following way : "This book contains the issue of the numerous investigations that arose from the conceptions which we discussed together under the title of *Mundi sensibilis et intelligibilis*."[3]

---

[1] In an article on " Kant und Hume um 1762," (*Arch. f. Gesch d. Philos.*, I. 62 ff.), Erdmann has shown that there is no hint in Herder's description of his Königsberg years of any influence of Hume's empiricism, and that Kant's formulation of his problem, however near it often seems to approach to Hume, is yet independent of Hume's influence.

[2] VIII., p. 662.

[3] VIII., p. 309.

It is not easy to over-estimate the importance of the *Dissertation* for a comprehension of the *Critique of Pure Reason.* It shows what the new conception originally had in view, and something of the impetus of the discovery still attaches to it. In the *Critique* the thought is in a certain sense indirect and weakened. Here, we have the new philosophy in its youthful form. It is the long-sought new method of metaphysics, the transcendental method.

Through the entire treatise, the point of departure for the great and decided transformation in the mode of thought is the distinction between sensible and intellectual knowledge, and, corresponding to this, that between a sensible and an intelligible, a phenomenal and a real world. From this there follows the possibility of an *a priori* knowledge of both worlds by means of formal principles of knowledge that are native to the mind. It is, if one wishes, a decisive eruption of the Platonism in Kant's thought, the restoration of realistic rationalism. The reality given to sense is only phenomenal. Opposed to this, stands the truly real world of ideas, the *mundus intelligibilis*, attained through reason. Or, to employ the old expressions, we have the world of *phenomena* and the world of *noumena ;* the former knowable through pure forms of perception, the latter by means of pure concepts *a priori.*

The sense world is in space and time. These are the universal forms of the phenomenal world, because, and in so far as, they constitute the universal forms of our sense perception. It is just this that explains why the knowledge of spatial and temporal relations, as they are deduced in the mathematical sciences by means of pure reason, are at the same time valid of all objects in space and time. The ideality of space and time is accordingly the condition of the objective validity of mathematics, and the latter is thus safeguarded from all kinds of sceptical attacks on the part of metaphysicians.

Alongside mathematics as the form of knowledge of the sensible world, stands metaphysics as the form of knowledge of the intelligible world.   Through the complete separation of the two worlds, validity in its own domain is secured also for the latter.   As mathematics rules over the phenomenal world by means of the pure forms of perception, so metaphysics embraces the intelligible world in its pure concepts of the understanding.   And the latter is now secured against the secret attacks of sensuous thought, against the demands that its objects should be represented as perceptible objects in space and time, through which metaphysics, and especially natural theology, have hitherto been disturbed and polluted.   God and the soul stand entirely outside of space and time.

Looked at more closely, the epistemological foundation of metaphysics has now the following form: In addition to its formal logical application, the understanding has also a *usus realis* (a transcendental use, as Kant afterwards says).   By means of this latter employment, it creates concepts and axioms, and these have absolute validity, because in their production they are not polluted in any way by the subjective moment of sensibility.   The objective form-principle of the intelligible world is the original connection of all things in God, — the *ens realissimum*.   The intelligible things are posited in the unity of the *perfectio noumenon*, — the all of reality.   It is the old thought which we everywhere met in the precritical writings, — God the unitary ground of all that is possible, and therefore of the real.   These inner relations of all things to their unitary ground (*nexus idealis*, pre-established harmony of essences) are represented in the phenomenal world as universal reciprocity.   Thus space is phenomenal omnipresence, and time phenomenal eternity.   Moreover, the human understanding has no perceptive knowledge of the intelligible world: God alone possesses an intuitive understanding; he has a perception of the intelligible things. We can know, then, only by means of general concepts *in abstracto*, not by means of individual perceptions *in concreto*.

These are the outlines of the new system of philosophy in its original form. If we wish to reduce it to a formula, we may say that it is made up of three parts, — one the presupposition, and the other two, logical deductions from this. The presupposition is the ideality of space and time. The deductions are: (1) the possibility of *a priori* knowledge of the phenomenal world through the mathematical sciences, and (2) the possibility of knowledge of an intelligible world which is free from the conditions of sensibility by means of pure concepts in their transcendental employment; *i. e.*, the possibility of metaphysics.

With but one alteration, — to be sure, an important one, — this is the final form of the critical philosophy. The *Critique of Pure Reason* made no alteration in the first two doctrines; on the other hand, it deviated in the third position, though here too only on one point. The belief in the existence of an intelligible reality which is free from the limits of space and time is retained, and also the view that man is able to enter into most intimate relations with this world through his reason. Only one thing is given up, — the speculative knowledge of the intelligible world. In the *Critique of Pure Reason*, the pure concepts of the understanding have objective validity solely in their application to the phenomenal world, just as the mathematical concepts have. In place of the transcendent metaphysics, we have on the one hand the phenomenal ontology of the Analytic, and on the other the faith of practical reason.

As for the other points, Kant was right when he connected closely the *Critique of Pure Reason* with the *Dissertation*. In a letter to Herz, of the year 1771, he describes it as "the text on which something further is to be said in the following work," and regrets "that this work must so quickly undergo the fate of all human undertakings, viz. to be forgotten." As a matter of fact, many misinterpretations of the critical philosophy would have been impossible if this work had been kept in mind, perhaps if it had been printed as an introduction by the editors of the *Critique of Pure Reason*. I would recommend this still at the present day. And to this should be added the principal passages from the other letters to Herz, especially the important letter of the 21st February, 1772. This letter shows Kant occupied with the very problem from which the variations of the *Critique* from the *Dissertation* proceed. This problem asks how pure concepts of the understanding can yield knowledge of a world of objects. He finds that the relation to an object is intelligible in the case of knowledge from experience. Here the idea depends upon an affection through the object, and is therefore related to this as effect to cause. The objective validity of ideas is also intelligible in cases where the understanding creates its object, as in mathematics or ethics, or in the case of God's thinking, which creatively produces its objects. But where this is not so, as in the relation of the human understanding to the real world, how can we comprehend the fact "that the understanding undertakes to form concepts of things entirely *a priori*, with which the real things are to agree? How is it able to lay down real principles regarding their possibility, which experience must actually prove true, and which nevertheless are independent of experience? Kant does not here give any answer. He simply rejects the answer given by the old rationalists, — mentioning Plato, Malebranche, and Crusius. They all seek to effect the harmony of our rational knowledge with absolute reality through the medium of the highest metaphysical principle, God. That was also the means to which the *Dissertation* seemed to appeal.[1] But, on the other hand, it contained more than one hint of the

[1] §§ 9, 22, Schol.

solution by means of the transcendental method that was afterwards employed in the *Critique*. At any rate, the problem is prepared in this work, or rather it is implicit, though not explicitly present. Caird rightly calls attention to the fact that the *Dissertation* also regards sense knowledge as phenomenal, and conceptual knowledge as real. And, on the other hand, it too emphasizes the proposition that it is only in the intuitive understanding of God that this knowledge is actually realized, while in us it remains abstract and therefore unrealized.[1]

The question arises regarding the source from which the impetus came that led to the transformation of the views of 1770.

In my work on the development of the Kantian epistemology, I traced this to the influence of David Hume. I was not led to this position through any inclination to seek out external influences. I am certainly not of the opinion that thoughts flow into the mind of an independent thinker from any external source. And Kant was surely an independent thinker, not to say an imperious and strong-willed man. We may add to this the fact that he was now forty-five years of age, — a period of life when even ordinary minds do not so easily adopt the opinions of others. Moreover, I have not held that Hume influenced Kant by giving to

---

[1] One's estimate of the *Dissertation* depends directly upon one's conception of the critical philosophy. Erdmann and Windelband do not regard it as the beginning of the critical philosophy, which they rather date from the appearance of the problems of the Analytic and their rationalistico-phenomenalistic solution (after 1772). It is certainly true that one may say that the result of the Analytic leads to a point of view that is so widely different from that of the *Dissertation* that it can no longer be regarded as the exposition of the same thoughts. But one must immediately add that the Analytic never entirely permeated Kant's thought, not even in the *Critique of Pure Reason*. The Æsthetic, with its *mundus sensibilis* and *intelligibilis*, and the Dialectic, with the *ens realissimum* and the intelligible character, are likewise there, and represent, alongside the epistemology, Kant's metaphysics, which reappears in the two later *Critiques*, in a more independent and emphatic form, as the real form of his philosophy.

him a positive theory, but rather as furnishing an incentive to turn towards his original position. In Hume's "scepticism," Kant perceived where empiricism, to which he had in a certain sense approximated, logically led. The rationalism of the *Dissertation* is the reaction against the "scepticism" of the *Dreams*. I have attempted this construction, then, not from any general enthusiasm for "influences," but simply because Kant himself connects causally the origin of his philosophy with Hume's scepticism. If those passages did not occur in the *Prolegomena*, and in the *Critique of Pure Reason*, I should no more maintain that it is necessary to assume Hume's influence at this time to render Kant's development intelligible than at the beginning of the sixties. One may indeed say that in 1766 only one step was necessary to bring Kant to the view of the ideality of space and time, and consequently of the physical universe, a view that since the days of Plato was not unknown in philosophy. Even at this time he had the two worlds, the world in space and time, and the non-spatial, timeless world, each with its own laws. But for the latter, in which he nevertheless believed, he could find no principle of construction. It required only the epistemological reflection that the spatial and temporal world is a representation in our sensibility, and the actually real world is thought by means of pure concepts of the understanding, to give us the *Dissertation*. To account for this turn in Kant's thought, it is certainly not necessary to appeal to external influences, neither to Leibniz's *New Essays* (published in 1765), to which Windelband refers, nor to Hume's criticism of the notion of causality. The little essay on the nature of space of the year 1768 shows how Kant's own thought was revolving about this problem.[1] Moreover, even in the old metaphysic this change of view was foreshadowed. The *mundus sensibilis* and *mundus intelligibilis*, the former

[1] II., pp. 385 ff.

being in sense as (confused) knowledge, the latter existing in the absolute knowledge of God; the extended world
as the *phenomenon substantiatum*, the world of monads
as the true knowledge of reality, — all this, one could
find in Baumgarten's *Metaphysics* (§§ 869, 70). Of course,
there is the difference that the phenomenal character of
the physical world was not taken with entire seriousness
in Baumgarten, just as it was not in Kant's precritical
writings.

B. Erdmann has, however, called attention to another
point from which the impetus to the distinction of the
sensible and the intelligible world may have proceeded.
This is the antinomies.[1] He has rendered it certain that
these were very real influences in Kant's thinking. The
antithetical and sceptical mode of procedure that is developed in the Dialectic to a technique had long been employed
by Kant, and already appears very clearly marked in the
Dreams. He frequently says that the appearance of the
conflict of reason with itself in metaphysics was a source
of wonder and stimulus to him (*cf.* especially *Prolegomena*,
pp. 50 ff.). Now the ideality of space and time, according
to the *Critique*, is at once the explanation of that strange
appearance, and the key to its solution. The contradiction
always rests on the fact that appearances are taken for
things-in-themselves; or, in other words, that phenomena
are intellectualized. Thus the matter is set forth in the
Critique, and even in the *Dissertation* we find the same doctrine announced. The contradictions disappear as soon as
the distinction is made between the phenomenal and the
intellectual world, and all propositions are assigned to the
sphere to which they belong. This is especially manifest in
the case of the antinomy of freedom and necessity. As

[1] *Cf.* the Introduction to Erdmann's edition of the *Prolegomena*, pp.
lxxxiii ff., and especially the Introduction to *Reflexionen Kants zur Kr.
d. r. V.*, pp. xxiv. ff.

phenomena, actions are conditioned; as manifestations of an intelligible nature, they are free.

Kant himself has repeatedly referred to this point as that from which the development of his thought proceeded. Thus in his latest reference in a letter to Garve in 1798, he says very definitely: "The point from which I set out was not the existence of God, or immortality [as Garve had assumed], but the antinomies of pure reason: the world has a beginning; it has no beginning — up to the fourth [third]: man possesses freedom; he is not free, but everything takes place in him with necessity. It was these things which first aroused me from my dogmatic slumber and drove me to a criticism of reason in order to take away the reproach of an apparent conflict of reason with itself." With this a passage from the sketch on *The Progress of Metaphysics* [1] is in agreement, where the doctrine of the ideality of space and time, and the concept of freedom are described as the two corner-stones of the system. We also find in a rough draft of this work: "The origin of the critical philosophy is found in the moral responsibility of actions." [2]   For purely theoretical philosophy, the *Critique*, with its distinction of phenomenon and thing-in-itself would be really of no importance. On the other hand, it is the freedom demanded by the moral law "that summons reason to metaphysics and destroys the entire mechanism of nature." We may therefore conclude that the possibility of finding a place for freedom alongside nature, which is ruled by causal laws, was the search which gave direction to the new development of Kant's thought. This was the very doctrine on account of

---

[1] VIII., p. 573.

[2] Published in the *Lose Blätter*, I., pp. 223 ff., edited by R. Reicke. The whole sketch deserves to be read. *Cf.* also the preface to the *Kr. d. pr. V.* and the "Critical Explanation of the Analytic:" "The notion of freedom is a stumbling-block for all empiricists, but also the key to the highest practical principles for all critical moralists, who by its aid gain the insight that they must necessarily proceed rationally."

which Kant's philosophy gained its first adherents: Fichte and Schiller were attracted to transcendental idealism by the escape which it offered from the oppressive thought of the all-dominating sway of the law of mechanical causality.

With this we might regard the matter as closed if it were not for those passages in which Kant himself most expressly describes the stimulus to the critical investigation of the possibility of knowledge *a priori* as coming from Hume. It was the remembrance of David Hume, he himself says in the *Prolegomena*, at a time also not too remote from the occurrences to have a definite recollection of them, and Hume's treatment of causality, that furnished the occasion. It is not possible to understand by means of pure reason why the existence of B necessarily follows from that of A. "It was just this that many years ago aroused me from my dogmatic slumber, and gave an entirely new direction to my investigations in the field of speculative reason. I was far from admitting his results," etc. In like manner, he tells us in the *Critique of Practical Reason* that the critical epistemology had been called out by Hume's empiricism, which leads to the most extreme scepticism, not only in metaphysics, but also in physics, and even in mathematics, with the object of warding off "this terrible overthrow" of all the sciences.[1]

These passages, which leave nothing to be desired in the way of clearness, cannot be explained away. One must therefore find some place for Hume's influence. Erdmann, rightly refusing to recognize the influence of the sixties, and not even allowing that of the years 1769–70, places it after 1772, about 1774. He holds that Kant at this time learned from Hume that the pure concepts of the understanding have only an immanent use, and do not possess validity with reference to things-in-themselves. It seems to me that this date is not altogether consistent with Kant's statements. For (1) these all have reference to the time of the origin of

[1] V., pp. 54 ff.

criticism. This, however, falls in the year in which the *Dissertation* was thought out (1769–70). Kant has no recollection of a deeper impression in the seventies, from which criticism really takes its rise. For him the critical philosophy always has its origin about twelve years before the appearance of the *Critique of Pure Reason*.[1] And because (2) his statements regarding Hume's influence do not agree with this interpretation. After 1772, according to this interpretation, Kant should have adopted Hume's conclusions, in limiting all knowledge to experience. But he everywhere says the opposite. Hume gave him an obstacle (*Anstoss*) in the literal sense of the word; he set him a problem but did not furnish its solution. On the contrary, Kant rejects Hume's empirical and sceptical 'solution; the critical philosophy is the only possible refuge from empiricism which results in complete scepticism.

There remains, then, the task of uniting both of Kant's expressions regarding the point of departure in the development of his thought. It seems to me that this is not at all impossible. We cannot indeed always speak of progress in a straight line in the development of Kant's thought. A great multitude of metaphysical, epistemological, and ethical problems had occupied him for a long time, and each year his lectures

---

[1] I should like to take this opportunity to utter a warning against constructing too numerous "stages of development." Vaihinger gives six of these. All that we are concerned with is to describe the main alterations in Kant's thought, not to specify the yearly and daily variations, that doubtless also occurred. Kant himself recognized no essential change of standpoint after 1770, although not inconsiderable changes in his combination of elements occurred up to the nineties. But they bring no alteration with regard to the fundamental principle: with the distinction between the sensible and intelligible world we have the key to the main entrance of the critical philosophy. Perhaps it might be possible to construe our three stages of development as *a priori* necessary according to the Kantio-Hegelian formula of thesis, antithesis, and synthesis. For every one, the point of departure is the tradition of the school. The thinker who is seeking an independent position moves in the opposite direction from this. After he has attained the extreme point of opposition, there is a tendency to feel again more strongly the truth of the tradition and to seek for a reconciliation of the new and the old.

gave him new occasion to reconsider them all. If we suppose that in reflecting on the "antinomies" the thought first came to him that the ideality of space and time was the key to their solution, the answer to Hume's scepticism connects itself with this, it appears to me, without difficulty. We may assume that Kant knew of Hume's theory of causality before 1769. He would scarcely have left unread the volume of essays by the Scottish author whom he esteemed so highly, that appeared in a German translation as early as 1756. If any one wishes he may suppose that he had again taken up the work at this time. At all events, it was at this time that the full significance of Hume's problem and the possibility of solving it first came home to him. He saw that it was just this that Hume declared impossible which he had himself so long sought — the possibility of a firmly grounded metaphysic. And this was the very thing that he now had at hand in "the method of metaphysics." Pure knowledge of the phenomenal world as given in the mathematical sciences was guaranteed against sceptical attacks by means of the assumption of the pure forms of sensibility. And, in like manner, a pure knowledge of the intelligible world is made possible by means of the *a priori* concepts of the understanding. Mathematics and metaphysics, the two sciences that Hume attacked, are both placed in security by means of the same hypothesis that solves the puzzle of the antinomies.

That was the great discovery of 1770, which made necessary a new review of all the philosophical sciences. It is true that it soon appeared that the position of metaphysics was not so simple as that of mathematics. Knowledge of the intelligible world through pure concepts of the understanding was rather a postulate than an epistemologically established solution of the problem. Hume's problem might have continued subsequently to influence Kant to look for such a justification, until at length, in the transcendental deduction of the categories, which was already foreshadowed in the deduction of mathematics in the *Dissertation*, he became convinced that he was in possession of a satisfactory solution. In his remembrance, however, the two moments are so closely associated that sometimes the one and sometimes the other element is most prominent, according to the nature of the occasion. The elements of the new development of thought had been all present; the new doctrine of the ideality of space and time had proved itself the key to all the difficulties with which he had hitherto struggled.

I hasten on now to the end of the sketch of Kant's literary activity.

After the silent decade of incubation, as one may call the seventies, there followed in the eighties his most zealous and fruitful decade of authorship. The principal works of the new philosophy appeared in close succession. After the *Critique of Pure Reason*, the basal work, which appeared in 1781, there soon followed the *Prolegomena*, also written under the influence of the first conception. In 1785 and 1786 there appeared the first applications to the two main fields of philosophy, — moral philosophy and philosophy of nature. The title of the first was the *Fundamental Principles of the Metaphysic of Morals* (1785); that of the latter, *Metaphysical Elements of Natural Science* (1786). Then followed two works founded on the model of the *Critique of Pure Reason*. These are the *Critique of Practical Reason* (1788), containing the principles of moral philosophy and moral theology, and the *Critique of Judgment* (1790), containing the principles of æsthetics, and, along with certain somewhat arbitrary conceptions, a part of a philosophy of nature, — a natural teleology. With these works a complete exposition is given of the principles of the new philosophy.

Between these principal works, of which we shall later treat in detail, a number of smaller treatises was written, some of which are not without significance. In the *Berliner Monatsschrift*, the organ of free thought edited by Biester, the secretary of the minister, von Zedlitz, there appeared two short papers on the philosophy of history. The first, a very interesting study entitled *Idea of a Universal History from the Cosmopolitan Standpoint* (1784), assumes as the goal of historical development the common recognition of an international law that will do away with war and the use of force, and interprets historical development as an approximation toward this goal. The second, *The Presumptive Beginning of Human History* (1786), is a finely conceived attempt at a philosophical interpretation of the biblical account of the original history of man. In both these works, the way is prepared for Fichte's *a priori* construction of history. Between these falls the "Review of Herder's Ideas toward a History of Humanity" (in the Jena *Litteratur Zeitung*), which aroused the author's anger. Two other short essays are: "What is Illumination?" and "What does it Signify to Orient oneself in Thought?" (*Berliner Monatsschrift*, 1784–86). These contain a vigorous appreciation and defence of the right of free thought and free investigation, — the former with praise of Frederick the Great; the latter with a warning against the tendency to sentimentalism (*Schwärmerei*) then becoming prevalent. We may also mention the little tract *On Sentimentalism and its Remedy* (1790), and recommend it to those who try to make Kant a spiritist.

Then follows in the nineties the decade of declining strength. In the first place, we may mention two treatises, called out by special occasions in the early nineties, that are not without importance for the proper understanding of the critical philosophy. In reply to Professor Eberhard, of Halle, who edited a philosophical journal devoted to combating the Kantian philosophy from the standpoint of the Leibnizo-Wolffian school, Kant wrote the treatise, *On a Dis-*

covery, by means of which all New Critiques of Pure Reason are to be Replaced by an Older One (1790).   A second essay, first published from the remains, treats the prize subject for 1791 set by the Berlin Academy (though the time was extended until 1795): "What real Progress has Metaphysics made in Germany since the days of Leibniz and Wolff?" This is made up of sketches that for the most part apparently belong to the year 1793.   Reicke's *Loose Leaves* also contains much that belongs in the same connection, which makes it possible to fix a date for it.

In their main content the works of the nineties belong to the philosophy of religion, and of law and conduct.   *Religion within the Bounds of Pure Reason* (1793) was preceded by *On the Failure of all Philosophical Attempts at a Theodicy* (1791).   This shows how futile and presumptuous it is to attempt a philosophical theodicy, and to profess to be able to demonstrate from rational grounds that the lot of individuals, and of humanity as a whole, is good and beneficent.   The faith of pious and wise simplicity is more modest in acknowledging that God's ways are unsearchable.   He quotes the Book of Job with a fine discrimination.   A short essay, "On the End of All Things" (*Berliner Monatsschrift*, 1794), forms the epilogue to this.   The treatise "On the Common Saying, That may be Correct in Theory, but does not hold in Practice" (*Berl. Monatsschr.*, 1793), introduces the works on the philosophy of law and conduct.   The essay *On Everlasting Peace* (1795) was followed by *The Metaphysical Principles of the Philosophy of Right*, and the *Doctrine of Virtue* (1797), which in the second edition were combined into *The Metaphysic of Morals*.   With this are connected two short essays, *On the Alleged Right to Lie from Altruistic Motives* (1797), and *On Bookmaking.   Two Letters to Fr. Nicolai* (1798).

The conclusion is made by a collection of essays that appeared under the title, *The Controversy of Faculties* (1798).

The works also embrace editions of some of his lectures: *Anthropology, from a Pragmatical Point of View* (1798); *Logic* (1800, edited by Jäsche); *Physical Geography* (1802, ed. by Rink); *Pedagogy* (1803, ed. by Rink).[1]

Among the lectures subsequently published from notes, the *Metaphysics*, edited by Pölitz (1821), is important, and has long been under-estimated.

Of importance are also the recent publications from Kant's remains. They afford noteworthy information both regarding the history of the development of his thought and also regarding his mode of work. These are: *The Reflections of Kant on The Critical Philosophy*, which we have already frequently quoted, taken by B. Erdmann from Kant's copy of Baumgarten's *Metaphysics* ("On Anthropology," 1882; "On the Critique of Pure Reason," 1884); and the *Loose Leaves from Kant's Remains*, published by R. Reicke, in the *Altpreussische Monatsschrift*, and later separately (2 vols., 1889–95).

---

[1] On the circumstance of the publication of the lectures, and the lack of discrimination shown in their editing, *cf.* B. Erdmann, in the Preface to the *Reflexionen zur Anthropologie*.

PART II

THE PHILOSOPHICAL SYSTEM

The very wisdom and order which man discovers in visible nature are rather imposed upon nature by man than derived from it by him. For he could not become aware of them, if he were not able to relate them to something that he has in himself. Without a standard there can be no measurement. Heaven and earth are for man merely a confirmation of a form of knowledge, of which he is conscious, and from which he gains the skill and courage to master, and of himself to judge, everything. And amid the grandeur of creation he is and feels himself greater than all that environs him; and he yearns after something other.

MATTHIAS CLAUDIUS.

LITERATURE : Obviously, mention cannot be made here of the end-less multitude of large and small treatises on the philosophical system of Kant. For this purpose I may refer to Ueberweg-Heinze, *Grund-riss der Geschichte der Philosophie* (III. 8th edition, 1896), where nearly all the modern literature is mentioned. For the older Kantian litera-ture, E. Adickes has published an extremely careful bibliography in *The Philosophical Review*, edited by J. G. Schurman and J. E. Creighton, 1893–96. The editions of Kant's works are first given, and then the writings which deal with Kant, up to the year 1804, are treated and characterized in over three thousand numbers. We thus have the written exposition of the whole Kantian movement up to the time of his death. In connection with the editions of Kant's works, I may mention that there is an edition in preparation which is to contain everything that Kant has left us both in print and in manuscript; it is being edited under the auspices of the Berlin Academy. The most available edition at present is Hartenstein's sec-ond edition in eight volumes, which is careful and complete (Leipzig, 1867); the references in the present volume are to it. Besides that, the edition by Rosenkranz and Schubert (twelve volumes, Leipzig, 1838) is still much used. The main works are also to be found in careful editions by K. Kehrbach in *Reclam's Universalbibliotek*. The *Kr. d. r. V.*, the *Prolegomena*, and the *Kr. d. Urt.* are well edited by B. Erdmann, and the *Kr. d. r. V.* by Adickes. [English Transla-tions: *Critique of Pure Reason*, by F. Max Müller, New York and London, 2d edition, 1896 ; trans. also by J. M. D. Meiklejohn (Bohn's Library), London, 1855. The *Æsthetic* and the *Analytic* were trans-lated from the 2d edition by J. H. Stirling: *Text-Book to Kant*, Edin-burgh, 1881. *Critique of Judgment*, by J. H. Bernard, London and New York, 1892. *Prolegomena*, by J. P. Mahaffy and J. H. Bernard, London and New York, 1889; trans. also by E. B. Bax (Bohn's Library. This volume includes a trans. of the *Metaphysical Elements of Natural Science*), London, 1883. The *Dissertation* by W. J. Eckoff, New York, 1899.]

Expositions of the Kantian system are to be found in all histo-ries of philosophy; the most exhaustive is in two volumes of Kuno Fischer's *Geschichte der neueren Philosophie*, 4th edition, 1898. [Kuno Fischer's small volume entitled *A Critique of Kant* has been trans-lated by W. S. Hough (London, 1888).] I call attention also to the expositions contained in Falckenberg's [trans. by A. C. Armstrong, Jr., New York, 1893], Windelband's [trans. by J. H. Tufts, New

York and London, 1901], and Höffding's [trans. by B. E. Meyer, London and New York, 1900] histories of modern philosophy; and, further, to Riehl's *Geschichte und Methode des philosophischen Kritizismus*, and to Lange's *Geschichte des Materialismus* [trans. by E. C. Thomas, London, 1892]. Of special works on Kant, I may mention : E. Caird, *The Critical Philosophy of Kant*, 2d edition, 2 vols., 1889; H. Cohen, *Kants Theorie der Erfahrung*, 2d edition, 1885; *Kants Begründung der Ethik*, 1877, and *Kants Begründung der Æsthetik*, 1889 ; J. Volkelt, *Immanuel Kants Erkenntnistheorie, nach ihren Grundprinzipien analysiert*, 1879 ; B. Erdmann, *Kants Kritizismus* in the 1st and 2d editions of the *Kr. d. r. V.*, 1878; E. Laas, *Kants Analogien der Erfahrung*, 1876; E. v. Hartmann, *Kants Erkenntnistheorie und Metaphysik*, 1894. Of the expositions intended for a larger circle of readers, I may name : K. Lasswitz, *Die Lehre Kants von der Idealität von Raum und Zeit im Zusammenhang mit seiner Kritik des Erkennens*, 1883; M. Kronenberg, *Kant, sein Leben und seine Lehre*, 1897. Other works will be mentioned later as occasion arises. It may be added, simply by way of observation, that, after articles on Kant for the last thirty years have filled all philosophical journals, we have now in Vaihinger's *Kantstudien* (since 1896) a periodical devoted exclusively to Kantian philology. [Among English works on Kant's system, the reader may be referred to the following in addition to Caird's exposition mentioned above : Watson, J., *Kant and his English Critics*, New York, 1881; Adamson, R., *On the Philosophy of Kant*, Edinburgh, 1879 ; Seth, A., *The Development from Kant to Hegel*, London, 1882; Mahaffy and Bernard, *Kant's Critical Philosophy for English Readers* (Vol. I., *The Critique of Pure Reason* explained and defended; Vol. II., *The Prolegomena* translated with notes and appendices), London, 1889; also to the following articles in *The Philosophical Review*: Schurman, J. G., "Kant's Critical Problem," Vol. II., pp. 129 ff ; "Kant's Theory of the A Priori Forms of Sense," Vol. VIII., pp. 1 ff., 113 ff. ; "Kant's Theory of the A Priori Elements of Understanding as Conditions of Experience," Vol. VIII., pp. 225 ff., 337 ff., 449 ff. ; Fullerton, G. S., "The Kantian Doctrine of Space," Vol. X., pp. 113 ff., 229 ff.]

PART II

THE PHILOSOPHICAL SYSTEM

CONCEPTION AND DIVISION OF PHILOSOPHY

WHEN we collect and compare Kant's scattered and not altogether consistent utterances upon this problem, we get the following schema.[1]

There are three great fields of scientific knowledge: Philosophy, Mathematics, and the Empirical Sciences. They are distinguished by their methods: Philosophy is pure rational knowledge arising out of concepts; mathematics is pure rational knowledge arising out of the construction of concepts. In contradistinction from these two rationalistic sciences, stand the empirical sciences, which derive their concepts from experience, and establish their propositions by inductive proofs, as, for example, chemistry or empirical anthropology. In this connection, however, it is to be remarked that, in accordance with Kant's view of the essence of science, to which he always adheres, only that whose certainty is apodictic can *properly* be called science. "Knowledge, which can attain mere empirical certainty, is only science improperly so-called."[2] Accordingly, philosophy and science, in the proper sense of the latter term, coincide.

Philosophy, further, has two chief divisions: Transcendental philosophy and metaphysics. Transcendental phi-

---

[1] The chief passages relating to this point are: *Kr. d. r. V.*, Doctrine of Method, chapters 1 and 3, and also the 6th section of the Introduction; the Prefaces to the *Grundlegung zur Metaph. der Sitten* and to the *Metaph. Anfangsgründe der Naturwissenschaft*; *Kr. d. U.*, Introduction; *Logik*, Introduction III. *Cf.* also Erdmann, *Reflexionen*, II., pp. 20 ff.

[2] *Metaph. Anfangsgr.*, Preface.

losophy is the discipline which investigates the possibility, sources, and limits of pure rational knowledge. Its problem is that of a propædeutic for the system of pure rational knowledge, or, in other words, for metaphysics. It coincides in a measure with the science which is now called epistemology; with this limitation, however, that its subject-matter is not the theory of knowledge in general, but only the investigation of *a priori* knowledge. The *Critique of Pure Reason* carries out this investigation, although it does not deal with all the details, but only with the principles.

In contrast with the formal discipline of transcendental philosophy, metaphysics is the sum-total of the rational knowledge of objects. It also falls into two branches: The metaphysic of nature, and the metaphysic of morals, or natural philosophy and moral philosophy. This corresponds with the great division of the objective world into the spheres of nature and of freedom. The physical and the moral world constitute as it were the two hemispheres of the *globus intellectualis*. This is a classification, which, moreover, is closely related to another distinction, namely, that between the *mundus sensibilis* and the *mundus intelligibilis*. In the former realm, natural laws are dealt with by means of which the phenomenal world is constructed *a priori;* in the latter, there is involved a practical legislation according to ideas of freedom for rational beings; but these ideas of freedom, nevertheless, can be regarded also as natural laws of the moral world.

We should thus have a classification of philosophy which is related to the traditional Greek division of the subject into logic, physics, and ethics. Logic is the theory of the form of knowing. And here also, two separate disciplines emerge: common logic, and transcendental logic. Physics, or rational physiology (the theory of nature), is the pure rational science of the phenomenal world. It embraces two chief disciplines: the rational theory of bodies, and rational psychology. Ethics, finally, is the pure rational science of the moral world. It is subdivided into the doctrine of Right or Law, and the doctrine of Virtue.

The elaboration of the system fell short of this schema. For the theoretical philosophy, the *Critique of Pure Reason*, which was originally intended only as a propædeutic for metaphysics, remained the chief work. The system of metaphysics was never written. Kant completed only the *Metaphysical Elements of Natural Science*, and labored while his strength was failing upon a further work, *Transition from the Metaphysical Elements of Natural Science to Physics*. On the other hand, the rational psychology remained altogether untouched, as well as the ontology, cosmology, and theology, — a serious omission, the cause of which, however, it is not difficult to understand. Some things that ought to have had their place in the omitted treatises are taken up in the second part of the *Critique of Judgment*. As far as form goes, the system of the practical philosophy is more complete. The *Critique of Practical Reason* is a kind of preliminary investigation in this field, but it is brought to a point in the *Metaphysic of Morals* as the accomplishment of the system. As far as content, however, is concerned, the latter is of trivial importance. So that in this sphere also, the *Critique*, together with the *Fundamental Principles*, is, as a matter of fact, the main work. Thus in all respects the 'doctrinal' construction fell far short of the 'critical' foundation. Nevertheless, the sole reason for this was not simply that the strength necessary for the completion of the task failed the rapidly aging philosopher.

Besides the determination of the scientific problem of philosophy, Kant defines also its general problem for humanity. This distinction comes to expression in the differentiation between the " cosmical conception " of philosophy and its " scholastic conception." From this point of view, he defines philosophy as the " science of the relation of all cognition to the essential aims of human reason (*teleologia rationis humanæ*)." In this sense, the philosopher is "not a theorist who occupies himself with conceptions, but a law-giver, legislating for human reason;" his completed manifestation is the ideal of the sage. The proper task of the sage is the knowledge of the highest ends, or of the true nature of mankind, and at the same time the manifestation of this in his own person. It was in accordance with this that the ancients formed their notion of the philosopher. And, therefore, philosophy was for them "the theory of the highest good, so far as reason endeavors to reduce it to a science;" and Kant adds, it would be well for us to leave the term with its ancient significance. It is on this account that the organization of scientific work arises as a special task for philosophers. The mathematician, the physicist, the logician, are mere theorists or technical investigators. A philosopher, in the above sense, as well as the ideal teacher, would be one "who presupposes all these, and uses them as instruments, in order to advance the essential aims of human reason."

Obviously, this consideration carries with it a lessening of the respect felt for the philosopher as a theorist of reason. The philosopher was recognized heretofore as a "cosmic sage," who by means of speculation brings to light all secrets of God and of the world. The critical philosophy deprives him of this position. It destroys the hope of a speculative solution of the riddle of the world. In place of this, it gives to him the position of a legislator in the kingdom of ends, and thereby renders subordinate for him all scientific investigation, which has the task of ministering to humanity under the guidance of philosophy in the realization of its destiny.[1]

---

[1] *Cf.: Kr. d. r. V.*, section on "The Architectonic of Pure Reason," and the *Kr. d. pr. V.*, bk. ii. chap. i. ; also the *Reflexionen*, II., pp. 29 ff. Kant is fond of having the critical philosopher play the rôle of law-giver and also

that of police (No. 128), or of governor (No. 161).   In the last passage, he says : " That reason stands in need of training ; that. if in its natural state it is allowed to spread out its branches, it brings forth leaves without fruits. That hence a master of training (not a training-master) is necessary to govern it.   That without such training it does not harmonize with religion and morality, but gives its own decisions as supreme, and, since it has not knowledge of its own nature, it leads astray the healthy and experienced understanding."   See above, " Kant as an Academic Teacher " (pp. 63 ff).

FIRST BOOK

THE THEORETICAL PHILOSOPHY

A FEW years after the appearance of the *Critique of Pure Reason*, K. L. Reinhold made the following remark in his *Letters upon the Kantian Philosophy*:[1] "The *Critique of Pure Reason* has been proclaimed by the dogmatists as the attempt of a sceptic who undermines the certainty of all knowledge; — by the sceptics, as a piece of arrogant presumption that undertakes to erect a new form of dogmatism upon the ruins of previous systems; — by the supernaturalists, as a subtly plotted artifice to displace the historical foundations of religion, and to establish naturalism without polemic; — by the naturalists, as a new prop for the dying philosophy of faith; — by the materialists, as an idealistic contradiction of the reality of matter; — by the spiritualists, as an unjustifiable limitation of all reality to the corporeal world, concealed under the name of the domain of experience; — by the eclectics, as the establishment of a new sect, that for self-sufficiency and intolerance never had its equal, and that threatened to force the slavish yoke of a system upon the neck of German philosophy, which had shortly before become free; — by the popular philosophers, finally, it has been sometimes called a laughable endeavor, in the midst of our illumined and cultured period, to displace healthy human understanding by means of scholastic terminologies and subtleties derived from the philosophical world.   At other times, however, they have regarded it as a peculiar stumbling-block, which had made impassable the path to popular philosophy, lately become smooth through

[1] Page 105.

so many easily intelligible writings; and as a rock upon which not only the understanding of hopeful youths, but also the philosophical reputation of celebrated men, had been already shattered."

In a measure, this characterization of the reception which the critical philosophy experienced on its first appearance is applicable also to that which it still meets with even at present. In spite of the zealous efforts of the last decades, the interpreters even to-day have by no means come to an agreement in regard to the fundamental character of the critical philosophy. The cause of this obviously lies in the manifold aspects which it presents, resulting from the different importance that may be attributed to each individual factor, and, further, the various ways in which these factors may be combined. In order to aid the orientation of the reader, I will here at the outset sketch its characteristic features, and briefly indicate the main forms of interpretation.

Kant's theoretical philosophy contains five moments which emerge as so many standpoints from which it may be viewed. They are as follows: —

(1) The epistemological idealism (phenomenalism): the objects of our knowledge are phenomena, not things-in-themselves. Antithesis: the naïve realism which views the objects of our representation as things-in-themselves.

(2) The formal rationalism: there is knowledge *a priori*, knowledge of objects through pure reason, and this alone is scientific knowledge in the proper sense. Antithesis: the sensualistic empiricism, or scepticism, which rejects all knowledge except that which comes from experience; *i. e.*, from a mere summation of perceptions.

(3) Positivism, or the critical limitation: the concepts of our understanding have objective validity in application to phenomena, or for the sphere of possible experience; not, however, beyond the bounds of experience. Antithesis: the

metaphysical dogmatism which makes the supersensuous the proper object of rational knowledge.

(4) Metaphysical idealism: things-in-themselves are intelligible essences (monads), which are embraced in the unity of the most real being: they form an ideal reality, the natural law of which is the teleological reference to the highest good. Antithesis: the atheistic materialism which regards the corporeal world as the absolute reality, and mechanism as its absolute law.

(5) The primacy of the practical reason: our philosophical view is not brought to a close by the theoretical, but by the practical reason, resting in a pure, practical, rational faith. Antithesis: the intellectualistic doctrine which regards nothing as true and real except that which the understanding can theoretically demonstrate and construe.

There is no doubt whatever that all of these five moments or aspects are to be found in the theoretical philosophy of Kant. Doubt arises only in regard to the question how their relation to each other and their significance for the system as a whole are to be determined. Especially do the first three cause difficulties in this connection. We have here three conceptions, three methods of interpretation of the critical philosophy, standing opposed to each other. Each assumes that the particular *demonstrandum* is contained in only one of the three aspects, while the other two are viewed as related to it merely as logical grounds or consequences.

The first places the goal of the demonstration in the idealistic or phenomenalistic element. According to it, the thesis of the critical philosophy lies in the proposition that our knowledge can never be applicable to reality itself. This view corresponds with the impression which the *Critique of Pure Reason* made on its first appearance, and it is one which may even now easily be obtained from a first reading. Its first effect is the destruction of naïve realism. The first reviews of the work by Garve-Feder and Mendelssohn, who called Kant the complete iconoclast,[1] proceeded from this impression. Schopenhauer, too (in his "Criticism of the Kantian Philosophy," appended to the first volume of the *World as Will and Idea*), closely approximates this notion. It leads to the classification of Kant with Berkeley. The rationalistic moment is either overlooked, or is regarded as the *a priori* ground of demonstration for the idealism. We cannot know things-in-themselves, because the subjective forms of intelligence, space, time, and the categories, are not applicable to things-in-themselves. The critical limitation appears as a self-evident consequence; the fact that we cannot know things through pure reason, through pure logical speculation, scarcely needs any proof.

Related to this interpretation is the one which transfers the chief purpose of the *Critique* to the third moment, namely, the critical limitation. This makes Hume Kant's precursor and nearest kinsman. In accordance with this view, the peculiar dogma of the *Critique* would be the proposition that empirical knowledge alone is possible, and that transcendent metaphysic is impossible. The chief representative of this interpretation is at present Benno Erdmann. He has attempted in numerous writings to establish the contention that the main purpose of the *Critique* is to demonstrate that the objective validity of the categories does not transcend the limits of possible experience.

A third view sees the goal of the argumentation of the *Critique* in the second moment, namely, the formal rationalism. This places Kant in direct opposition to empiricism, and particularly to Hume, without, of course, failing to recognize that there is a real relation between the two. According to this, the primary aim of the critical philosophy is to establish the possibility of universally valid and necessary knowledge in the sciences, particularly

---

[1] *Den alles Zermalmenden.* — Preface to the *Morgenstunden*, 1786.

in the mathematical sciences of nature. To this is added a second purpose, which, regarded from an absolute point of view, is of still greater importance: namely, the establishment of the possibility of metaphysical idealism as a system of philosophy. Consequently, the phenomenalistic element appears as a logical ground for the two other aspects. The critical limitation, however, follows as a necessary consequence, since scientific knowledge goes only so far as we can create the objects themselves. We can, however, of course, create only phenomena, not things themselves. The subjective forms of perception and thought accordingly, so far from being a hindrance to objective knowledge, are the condition of its possibility.

This last view I regard as the correct one. It was the view which I maintained in my *History of the Development of the Kantian Epistemology*, and I am still convinced of its truth. Among the younger investigators, E. Adickes especially presents this theory in a very clear and forcible manner. I should like to say a few words more in defining the standpoint, and to set it forth in opposition to the two rival interpretations. It seems to me that to understand the *Critique* it is of the utmost importance to become acquainted at the very outset with these different possible ways of interpreting it. In this connection emphasis should be laid on the fact that it is not at all necessary to discuss either what may be for us the most important element of the Kantian philosophy, or in what way it has historically had the most important influence. Nor need we enter into the question upon what aspect Kant himself finally laid the greatest stress. We are concerned only with the problem: What according to unbiased philological investigation appears as the actual goal of the argumentation of the critical philosophy, especially of the *Critique of Pure Reason?*

According to the phenomenalistic and positivistic view,

this goal is the proposition that knowledge of things-in-themselves (transcendent metaphysic) is for us impossible. " Kant's greatest service," Schopenhauer begins by saying, " is the differentiation of phenomenon from thing-in-itself, upon the basis of the consideration that the intellect stands between us and things, and that therefore what they are in themselves cannot be known by it." The demonstration of the " dream-like creation of the entire world " is the soul of the Kantian philosophy. According to Erdmann, Kant's real purpose is to " fix the limits of our knowledge in opposition to dogmatism, and in conjunction with the empirical scepticism of Hume." Erdmann characterizes it as a misunderstanding of the chief aim of the *Critique*, if one supposes that it does not deal with the proof "that transcendent knowledge is for us impossible, but with the demonstration how *a priori* knowledge, and therefore metaphysics as science, is possible." [1]

In opposition to this, I am of the opinion that the fundamental character, not only of the system as a whole, but also of the *Critique of Pure Reason*, is positive : Kant's effort is to construct, not to tear down, or at most to tear down only for the purpose of making room for the necessary reconstruction. What he wants to construct is twofold : (1) a positive epistemology, namely, a rationalistic theory of the sciences ; (2) a positive metaphysic, namely, an idealistic philosophical view. In regard to the former, he wants to show that physics as a real science, *i. e.*, as a system of universal and necessary propositions, is possible : he wishes to make the mathematical sciences of nature secure against all attacks of empirical and sceptical subtleties (like Hume's) by basing them upon the sure foundations of the original possession of the intelligence in its immanent forms and functions. He proposes to attain this end by showing how we first create the objects of knowledge through our

[1] See especially *Kants Kritizismus*, pp. 13 ff., 177 ff., 245 ff.

intellectual functions. As mathematics creates its objects by means of construction, so physics likewise in a certain manner creates its object, nature, by means of the function of the understanding, and in so far as it does this, it can yield *a priori* knowledge of nature. In regard to the second purpose, he wishes to render idealistic metaphysic definitely secure against all doubt. But this purpose can by no means be carried out without destructive criticism, inasmuch as he found already in existence a bad and unstable structure, to wit, the old dogmatic metaphysics. The purpose, however, of the demolition of this metaphysics is not the annihilation of the supersensuous world, but, on the contrary, the definite establishment of belief in it and of the fact that we belong to it. What Kant says in the Preface to the second edition of the *Critique of Pure Reason* is really his final and deepest conviction: " I had to destroy (sham) knowledge to make room for (rational) faith." As long as this field continues to be occupied by sophistical reasonings, doubt also continues, and faith cannot come to fruition. If attempts to prove the existence of God and the immortality of the soul cease, the moral certainty of the truth and reality of these things will be absolutely established.

I am well aware that passages which lend themselves to the idealistic, positivistic interpretation are not wanting in Kant's writings. In this field, however, conclusions cannot be drawn on the basis of citations; the verdict must be determined from the whole character and tendency of Kant's work. And, on this account, I maintain that it is not at all possible to construe the *Critique of Pure Reason* as a demonstration of the contention that we do not know things as they are in themselves, although this is certainly contained in it, or on the other hand, that beyond the limits of possible experience knowledge is not possible; but that it is possible to construe it as a demonstration for the proposition that there is rational knowledge of reality, knowledge in the proper sense, though, to be sure, only of objects of possible experience. The three main divisions of the work, the Æsthetic, Analytic, and Dialectic, are based upon this argumentation. The Æsthetic shows that there is rational knowledge, in that phenomena, through their inclusion in space and time, are subjected to geometry and arithmetic. The Analytic shows that there is rational knowledge, in that phenomena, through arrangement in the orderly coherence of nature, are subjected to the laws of the understanding which the formal and transcendental logic sets forth. The Dialectic shows that there are necessary ideas of reason, which contain regulative principles for the use of the understanding, and finally lead us to view reality as a whole connected by ideas of purpose. These ideas do not indeed furnish knowledge in the proper sense, but only principles through which we with subjective necessity determine reality in its relation to us. And the moral philosophy also is projected according to the same schema. Just as understanding and reason prescribe *a priori* laws for nature, the practical reason likewise prescribes laws for the will in the realm of freedom.

To show this in detail will be the task of the following exposition. I merely remark in this connection that an agreement with Erdmann's view would be easier if he did not conceive the " critical limitation " in such a negative way. Certainly it is essentially such, but it is not peculiarly concerned with the erection of a barrier, but with the marking out of a field for reason, where fruitful positive work is possible. This delineation will serve at the same time as a protecting boundary against trespassing on the domain of the Dialectic, which Kant loves to describe as the vast plains of the ocean, where there are only banks of cloud and ice, but no land on which to alight. A limitation, from its very nature, cannot be a ' chief end,' but only a means for the security of a threatened territory. One who refuses to concede this must be prepared also to defend the position that for a builder, who tears down an old building (the dogmatic metaphysics) and erects two new ones in its place ("pure natural science," and the realm of practical rational faith) the demolition of the old structure is nevertheless his chief purpose.

My view has repeatedly been charged with being one-sided, — for example, by Volkelt and Vaihinger. I think, however, with injustice. It never entered my mind to characterize Kant's system simply and solely by its formal rationalism. I see very clearly the other side too, not only the rationalistic and idealistic aspect which is related to Leibniz and Plato, but also the positivistic (although not empirical) side, which approaches the position of Hume. I see, too, that Kant strives to maintain a kind of balance between them, or rather to maintain a judicial position with regard to the two, both of which, under the titles of dogmatism and scepticism, he looks upon as the two heretofore prevailing but false tendencies of philosophical thought. But this does not keep me from seeing that the *Critique of Pure Reason* is primarily planned as an investigation designed to establish, in opposition to Hume's scepticism, the objective validity of the mathematico-physical sciences and the possibility of metaphysics, as a means of rising to the *mundus intelligibilis*. And further, I hold that Kant in his epistemology and philosophical point of view stands nearer to Leibniz than to Locke, — a statement which is not, of course, inconsistent with the fact that his polemic against Leibniz and Wolff comes out more strongly than that against Locke and Hume. He lived in Germany and lectured every year on Baumgarten's metaphysics. Every polemic, from the nature of the case, is aimed more directly against opponents with whom one has more in common than against those who stand further off, in order to emphasize the difference. Had Kant lived among genuine empiricists and materialists, he would have left absolutely no doubt but that he ranked himself with the rationalists and idealists. Besides, he himself remarks that the *Critique of Pure Reason* may well serve as "the proper apology for Leibniz," in the noteworthy concluding section of the article against Eberhard, where he interprets Leibniz's main principles in the spirit of the critical philosophy.[1]

[1] VI., pp. 65 ff.

FIRST SECTION

THE EPISTEMOLOGY

KANT is the founder of epistemology in Germany. Of course not in the sense that investigations of this sort were not in existence before his time. Reflections about the nature and possibility of knowledge have everywhere accompanied philosophical speculation. But Kant was the first among the German philosophers to separate these reflections from metaphysics, and to make of them an independent discipline, — not indeed under the name of 'epistemology' (which first came into use in the second half of our century), but under the title 'transcendental philosophy.' The concept 'transcendental' was coined by him to indicate an investigation devoted, not to objects themselves, but to the form of our knowledge, particularly to the form and possibility of pure rational knowledge.

Unfortunately, Kant did not make the form of empirical knowledge the object of his investigation; otherwise new and more definite problems would have arisen for his transcendental theory.

On the other hand, the transcendental philosophy has retained a very essential relation to metaphysics. Indeed, it may be said that in a certain sense it has absorbed the old metaphysics. Previously, at least in the dogmatic philosophy, the reverse relation existed; metaphysics contained in itself the theory of knowledge, while with Kant all the chief problems of metaphysics appear in the *Critique,* — the ontological as well as the psychological, cosmological, and theological. Unfortunately, again, metaphysical problems demand an independent treatment, not merely an epistemological one. With Kant their rights are not fully recognized; they are not considered from the standpoint of their own nature, but settled from the transcendental point of view. The metaphysical problems, in regard to the soul especially, have suffered from this treatment. Moreover, Kant in this matter follows the procedure of the English philosophers, and this fact has lent support to the view that the critical denial of the old metaphysic is the chief purpose of the *Critique of Pure Reason*, particularly as the promised positive development of the metaphysic was never fulfilled.

I shall attempt now, in the first place, briefly to set forth Kant's position in epistemology. Epistemology has two essential problems,—the question in regard to the nature of knowledge, and the question in regard to its origin. Each affords an opportunity for the rise of great differences in point of view. In answer to the question about the nature of knowledge and of its relation to reality, realism and phenomenalism (epistemological idealism) give contradictory replies. Realism sees in knowledge the adequate representation of a reality which exists independently of it; phenomenalism regards this relation as impossible, and holds that thought and existence are distinct and utterly incomparable. In answer to the question about the origin of knowledge, empiricism and rationalism give contradictory replies. The former maintains that all knowledge arises from experience, ultimately from perception; the latter contends that true knowledge arises from the understanding or from reason, which contain original principles of knowledge, and that out of these science and philosophy are spontaneously created by means of thinking.

The point of departure of all reflection about knowledge, the standpoint of the common understanding, is naïve realism. Phenomenalism arises as critical reflection about the nature of sense-perception; sensations of sight, hearing, smell, and taste cannot possibly represent absolute qualities

of things.   Hence, if our knowledge of things comes from
perception, we have only phenomenal knowledge.   This
view is, however, further opposed by a reflective realism,
which frees true knowledge from sense-perception and
derives it from reason.   Rationalism thus becomes the
basis for reflective, philosophical realism, and it is wont
at the same time to form a union with metaphysical
idealism, or the theory that reality in and for itself is
ideal, and capable of being comprehended in thought; that
it is of the same intrinsic nature as thought, and therefore
penetrable by it.

This development of thought is clearly marked in the
history of Greek philosophy.   The path leads from naïve
realism, through the sensationalism and phenomenalism of
the Sophists, to Plato's epistemological rationalism and realism, which is bound up with metaphysical idealism.   In
modern philosophy, which has Greek thought before it, the
two tendencies have from the beginning run parallel.   Realistic rationalism, which was originally predominant, found
its home in France, the Netherlands, and Germany, with
Descartes, Spinoza, and Leibniz as its chief representatives.
Phenomenalistic empiricism had its home in England, with
Locke and Hume as its leaders.   Rationalism tends towards
a dogmatic and idealistic metaphysic; empiricism tends
towards agnosticism, and indeed (as in the case of the
French philosophy of the eighteenth century) enters also
into relation with materialism, although this union is, properly speaking, impossible.

We are now able to define exactly Kant's position in epistemology.   He unites for the first time phenomenalism and
rationalism.   Previously, rationalism had regularly been used
as a means to support epistemological realism.   Kant, instead of this, uses phenomenalism (transcendental idealism)
as a logical ground for a formal rationalism (knowledge of
objects from pure reason).   Without doubt it is this union,

conflicting with the traditional view, which has greatly obscured the way to a correct understanding of his philosophy. And, in addition, the relation to metaphysics further complicates the difficulty; for rationalism, elsewhere employed as a substructure for a dogmatic metaphysic, is here united with Humian positivism.

A. THE CRITIQUE OF PURE REASON

THE *Critique of Pure Reason*, although originally intended only as a propædeutic for the new system, is of such prime importance that it must always form the centre of every exposition. By its form and content, it dominates all succeeding writings. Since every study of the Kantian philosophy must proceed from it, I have thought it appropriate to follow here, too, the external procedure of the treatise and to pay some attention to the systematic form, chiefly for the purpose of aiding the beginner to free himself from this very form.[1]

---

[1] The *Critique of Pure Reason* is so far the only work in modern philosophy to which a philological commentary, in the strict sense, has been devoted: H. Vaihinger, *Kommentar zur Kr. d. r. V.* Up to this time two volumes have appeared (1881–92); they cover the Introduction and the Æsthetic. Without doubt it is a work of the most self-sacrificing industry, the most conscientious labor, and great acuteness, and it is indispensable for those who intend making investigations in this field. Whether or not the collection and critical examination of every opinion that has ever been passed on Kant was necessary and serviceable for the end in view, I pass over without discussion. One thing at least is thereby accomplished; one receives a downright overpowering impression of the extent to which this work has occupied the minds of later thinkers, as well as of the prodigious burden of problems that have attached themselves to it, for which Kant himself is not without blame. After Garve read the *Critique* for the first time, he is said to have remarked: "If I had written the book, I should have gone crazy over it." What would he have said if he had read this commentary in addition?

E. Adickes's edition (1889) is to be recommended for the beginner who desires a first rapid acquaintance; it facilitates by means of marginal and foot notes the survey of content and connection.

I. Name, Origin, and Composition of the Critique of Pure Reason

The title indicates a judicial investigation and decision regarding the legitimacy of the claims to objective validity made by pure reason and by the concepts to which it gives rise. It is associated with the expression "Critique of Taste," in connection with which the phrase "Critique of Reason" is to be found for the first time in Kant in an announcement of his lectures for 1765,[1] where it is used as a description of the direction which Kant intends to give to his lectures upon Logic.[2]

The name "Critique of Pure Reason" first appears in the letter to M. Herz of February 21st., 1772,[3] as a characterization of the work that he hoped soon to publish. In a letter of the year 1771, the title for a similarly planned work is given as "The Limits of Sense and Reason." And the plan of such a work, of a "propædeutic science," which "teaches the distinction between sense and intellectual knowledge," appears even in the *Dissertation* of 1770.[4] Perhaps there is also in the name a play upon the meaning of "an analytic science," as indeed in the Greek word the two meanings "to analyze" and "to judicially arbitrate" shade off into one another. There is no doubt but that the *Critique* is essentially a conscious attempt to survey and arbitrate boundaries.[5]

[1] II., p. 319.

[2] *Cf.* Baumgarten's *Metaphysik* (p. 607), where the word "critique" is used also in a double meaning: *æsthetica critica* as *ars formandi gustum*, and "critique" in the general sense as *scientia regularum de perfectione vel imperfectione distincte judicandi*. As a general thing the prototypes for many of Kant's *termini* are to be found in Baumgarten; even his propensity for definitions (as it appears, for example, in the Anthropology, together with a fondness for adding Latin terms), is to be referred to the influence of Baumgarten.

[3] VIII., p. 691.

[4] § 8.

[5] [The German text here plays upon the words: *scheidekunst* (which is usually an equivalent for "chemistry," but seems in this context to denote

Fischer, and Vaihinger following him, properly call attention to the fact that Kant always manifests a propensity to appear as an arbitrator in philosophical quarrels. And that is just the rôle he imposes upon himself in the *Critique*, — arbiter in the great suit between rationalism and empiricism, dogmatism and scepticism. And the decree which is to put an end to the old feud is a demarcation of boundaries. Both are right in a certain domain: rationalism, in its determination of scientific method and in its metaphysical standpoint; empiricism, in limiting scientific knowledge to the sphere of possible experience.

Concerning the origin and composition of the work, it is obvious that Kant's remark in a letter to Mendelssohn cannot mean that he composed the book as a whole in the brief time mentioned. In that letter he says that " the result of at least twelve years of reflection was put in shape within about four or five months, as it were on the wing; while the greatest attention was bestowed upon the content, little care was expended on the style, or on making it easy for the reader." [1] Undoubtedly extensive preliminary sketches and detailed elaborations lay before him, which were made use of when the text assumed definite shape, whether they were embodied in their previous form or revised before insertion. This supposition is confirmed not only by the mechanical impossibility of completing a work of such content and size in a few months (especially if the time occupied by his lectures is taken into account), but also by the numerous references to his work in his letters during

any "analytic science "), *scheiden* (to " separate," " analyze," or " take *apart* "), and *entscheiden* (to " arbitrate," " pass sentence on," or " take *a part* ") while the *Critique* is called a *Grenzscheiderin* (" inspector " or " surveyor " of the "frontiers " or " boundaries "), and Kant himself is represented as a *Schiedsrichter* (" arbitrator " or " referee "). The Greek verb κρίνω also means to " separate," " choose," " decide " a contest or dispute, " judge of," " estimate," etc. — TRS.]

[1] VIII., p. 681.

the seventies, [1] and also by the character of the completed work. The manifold incongruities, the great independence, to say nothing of the marked contrariety of the main divisions, and the numerous repetitions, are intelligible only if one assumes that, when Kant came to write his copy for the printer, he had at hand a number of sketches, more or less worked out, the composition of which may have been occasioned by his annual lectures on metaphysics; and he either used these without making any changes, or, as the case may be, adapted them to the context with more or less thorough editorial revision.[2]

The most important point that can be made out about the composition seems to me to be this. The fundamental ideas of all the chief divisions arose independently of the systematic dress with which the *Critique of Pure Reason* is now invested. The main ideas which now form the content of the transcendental Æsthetic, Analytic, and Dialectic were fixed before the schema of a " transcendental logic " was discovered.

---

[1] There is even a sketch of a dedication to Lambert, who had died as early as 1777. See Erdmann, *Reflexionen*, No. 1.

[2] Adickes has attempted in his edition to trace the chronology of the origin of the individual sections. Much will remain doubtful, for revision necessarily makes the seams as invisible as possible. In many cases correct guesses will be made. But clearly the task as a whole cannot be completely carried out. Kant himself could not have done it even with the manuscript for the *Critique of Pure Reason* in his hand. *Cf.* Adickes, *Kants Systematik als systembildender Faktor* (1887); *Kantstudien* (1895); also the works of Arnoldt and Vaihinger. The *Reflexionen zur Kr. d. r. V.* and the *Lose Blätter* furnish much interesting material for the history of the development of the ideas, but the attempt at a reconstruction of the history of the origin of the *Critique* from this material will always leave considerable scope for individual opinion. I am almost inclined to say that the chief worth of such labors consists in the fact that they show in a forcible manner how accidental, arbitrary, and variable the structure of the system really is, although it is apparently so fixed. All of the ideas that appear in the Architectonic of the *Critique of Pure Reason* as fixed supports of the system are exhibited here in endless variations of content and of connection with the whole.

The objects of the investigation were determined by the customary content of the traditional metaphysics, as it used to be treated under the heads, ontology, psychology, cosmology, and theology. The most important concepts and problems were: space, time, matter, motion, unity, plurality, substance, inherence, causality, reciprocity, reality, possibility, necessity, the soul, immortality, the world, infinity, eternity, creation, God.

All of these things, which had been previously treated from the dogmatic standpoint, are dealt with in the *Critique of Pure Reason* from the transcendental point of view, *i. e.*, from the point of view of the question: How far is knowledge *a priori*, which possesses objective validity, possible by means of these concepts? That they all have their roots in the mind itself and are created *a priori*, Kant never doubted; he never shared Locke's doctrine of the "white paper." The new question that he raises is: How far can such *a priori* concepts possess, in spite of their *a priori* character, objective validity? And for this question he discovers the strange and "contradictory" answer that it is due simply to their *a priori* nature. Thus space and time concepts with their derivatives are objectively valid, in as much as space and time outside of us are identical with space and time in us, or in as much as the objects of perception are created by the act of perceiving. The ontological concepts (later called categories) possess objective validity, since the objects themselves are created by the active understanding. On the other hand, the cosmological and theological concepts in general have no objective validity, just because their objects are not posited by thought, but are supposed to exist independently of it.

At first, this new mode of treatment is applied to the space and time concepts. The transcendental basing of mathematics upon the apriority and ideality of the forms of perception already appears in the *Dissertation* of 1770

as a fully developed doctrine. It is transferred without
essential alterations to the Æsthetic of 1781. But also
the subject-matter of the Analytic and Dialectic is here at
least remotely suggested. In particular, there is an anticipation of the discussion contained in the fourth section of
the Analytic, in which the possibility of metaphysics in
general is based upon the concepts of pure reason, and also
of that contained in the fifth section of the Dialectic, in
which the distinction between a sensible and an intelligible
world is presented as the solution for metaphysical problems. In the seventies, then, Kant had come to see clearly
that there is an essential difference between the "ontological" and the "cosmological and theological" concepts; the
former are "objectively" valid, — that is, valid for all possible
objects of thought, — the latter are dialectical.

For this last group of ideas, then, the form of a system
of transcendental Logic with an Analytic and Dialectic is
adopted. Then to this system the doctrine of the space and
time concepts is adapted as a "transcendental Æsthetic."
The motive for using the name "transcendental logic" was
obviously the discovery, which was made late and carried out
with difficulty, that the ontological concepts could be derived from the classification of judgments of formal logic.
And hence the ideas which were in all essential respects
already established were forced into the form of the Analytic
and Dialectic. The long introductory sections in the Analytic and Dialectic have the task of showing that we are here
really and truly concerned with a system of logic, although
a transcendental instead of a formal logic. The traditional
division of logic into a doctrine of concepts, judgments, and
syllogisms, as well as the division into a doctrine of elements
and a doctrine of method, is adopted in its entirety. Categories, ideas, and all, are dressed up according to this schema,
which is added to and subtracted from in order to carry out
this plan. At times it may seem as if Kant is inclined to see

in this arduous labor the chief significance of his work. His feeling of its importance, however, did not prevent his failing to sustain the schema consistently. In particular, the actual working out does not correspond with the Dialectic as the doctrine of the Syllogistic.[1]

---

[1] If the schema were carried out strictly, something like the following headings of the divisions would be reached: —

TRANSCENDENTAL DOCTRINE OF KNOWLEDGE.	CRITIQUE OF PURE REASON.
Introduction.	Introduction.
Transcendental Doctrine of Elements.	Transcendental Doctrine of Elements.
A. Transcendental Theory of Perception.	A. Transcendental Æsthetic.
I. Transcendental Theory of Space-perception.	I. Of Space.
1. Metaphysical Deduction.	1. Metaphysical Exposition.
2. Transcendental Deduction.	2. Transcendental Exposition.
II. Transcendental Theory of Time-perception.	II. Of Time.
1. Metaphysical Deduction.	1. Metaphysical Exposition.
2. Transcendental Deduction.	2. Transcendental Exposition.
General Remarks.	Explications, Remarks.
B. Transcendental Logic, or Theory of Pure Thinking.	B. Transcendental Logic.
[I. Transcendental Analytic, or Theory of the Constitutive or Objectively Valid Forms of Thought.]	I. Transcendental Analytic.
1. Transcendental Doctrine of Concepts.	1. Analytic of Concepts.
a) Metaphysical Deduction of the Pure Concepts of the Understanding.	a) Guides for the Discovery of all Pure Concepts of the Understanding.
b) Transcendental Deduction of the Pure Concepts of the Understanding.	b) Transcendental Deduction of the Pure Concepts of the Understanding.
2. Transcendental Doctrine of Judgments.	2. Analytic of Principles.
a) On the Sensualization of the Pure Concepts of the Understanding.	a) On the Schematization of the Pure Concepts of the Understanding.
b) Systematic Exposition and Transcendental Deduc-	b) System of all Principles of the Pure Concepts

II. The Introduction and its Statement of the Problem

At the beginning of his work, Kant formulates the problem in the form of the question : How are synthetic judgments

<table>
<tr><td>

tion of the Objectively Valid, Pure Judgments of the Understanding.
Remark: Caution against the Transcendent Employment of the Categories.
Appendix: Critique of the Leibnizian Ontology.
[II. Transcendental Dialectic, or Theory of the Dialectical Forms of Thought.]
  3. Transcendental Doctrine of the Syllogism.
    a) On Reason as the Faculty of Drawing Conclusions.
    b) On Ideas as Concepts of Pure Reason.
      α) Metaphysical Deduction of the Ideas from the Forms of the Syllogism.
      β) Systematic Exposition of the Ideas and Conclusions of Pure Reason, and Proofs of their Objective Invalidity.
        1. Categorical Syllogism, Idea of the Soul.
        2. Hypothetical Syllogism, Idea of the World.
        3. Disjunctive Syllogism, Idea of God.
      γ) Transcendental Deduction of the Ideas as Regulative Principles.
Transcendental Doctrine of Methods; or, General Remarks Serviceable for the Doctrine of the Knowledge of Pure Reason.

</td><td>

of the Understanding.
  c) On the Ground of the Differentiation of Objects into Phenomena and Noumena.
Appendix: On the Amphiboly of the Concepts of Reflection.
II. Transcendental Dialectic.

  a) On Reason in General, etc.

  b) On the Concepts of Pure Reason.
  c) On the Dialectical Conclusions of Pure Reason.

    1. On the Paralogisms of Pure Reason.

    2. The Antinomies of Pure Reason.

    3. The Ideal of Pure Reason.
Appendix to the Transcendental Dialectic.

Transcendental Doctrine of Method.

</td></tr>
</table>

a priori possible ? In later expositions,[1] he is fond of emphasizing this formula and its exceptional value. In the *Critique of Pure Reason* it does not play any important rôle. From this fact one may perhaps conclude that it never was of supreme importance, and that the Introduction may well have been added as an afterthought. I agree with Adickes in holding that the investigation was begun and carried on without the formula.[2] In my opinion, it would have been no misfortune if Kant had never discovered it at all. The distinction between synthetic and analytic judgments, which was afterwards so much extolled by him that it deserves to be classic so far as the *Critique of Pure Reason* is concerned, has contributed, by a kind of false clearness, rather to obscure than to elucidate the problem. The formula that would have described the real problem more clearly and adequately is this : By what means and how far is it possible through pure reason (*a priori*) to attain to knowledge of objects ? In reality the Kantian formula reduces itself to this : Synthetic judgments, in distinction from analytic judgments, which have only logical validity, are judgments with objective validity. The proposition in the Dialectic, "all existential propositions are synthetic," can be converted also into "all synthetic propositions are existential propositions." " The relation which arises *per analysin* is logical; that which arises *per synthesin* is real." This formula is taken by Erdmann out of a lecture of Kant's on metaphysics.[3]

[1] *Proleg.*, Controversy against Eberhard.

[2] From Kant's own marginal notes to the first edition (published by B. Erdmann, *Nachträge zur Kr. d. r. V.*), relating to the projected revision that we now have as the second edition, it is evident that Kant once intended at the end of the Analytic to render the whole discussion more pointed by reference to the question : How are synthetic judgments *a priori* possible, either (1) by means of concepts, or (2) by means of construction of concepts (p. 37) ? — a sign that he himself felt that the problem of the Introduction was really isolated from the treatment given in the text.

[3] *Philos. Monatshefte*, 1884, p. 74.

Formally, indeed, Kant defines the distinction otherwise. We shall later see the reason for this. At the beginning of the *Critique* and of the *Prolegomena* he explains it by pointing out that in all judgments a twofold relation is possible between predicate and subject. "Either the predicate B belongs to the subject A, as somewhat which is contained (implicitly) in the concept A, or B lies completely outside of the concept A, although it stands in connection with it. In the former case I call the judgment 'analytic,' in the other, 'synthetic.'" The former may also be termed "explicative," the latter, "augmentative" judgments. For example, the judgment, "all bodies are extended" is analytic, and is *a priori* established; the judgment "a body is heavy" is synthetic.

It is easy to see, and it has been often remarked, that this distinction is an accidental and passing one. Analytic judgments always go back to synthetic judgments — the synthesis, namely, through which the concept is fashioned. The judgment, "Gold is a yellow metal," is oftentimes cited as an example of an analytic judgment. Evidently this judgment presupposes two others that are not analytic: a judgment of experience that there is a body which has all the properties I include under the name "metal," and which in addition is yellow; and secondly, a lexicographic statement that this body is called "gold" in the English language. The judgment is "analytic" only so far as the word together with its meaning is posited as given, and its particular elements are explicated by reflection. In this state of affairs, the individual is originally over against the language, the word is given to him, and he discovers through analysis the elements of its meaning. But, as a matter of fact, the meaning of the word is not originally given, and it is further not something absolutely fixed. "Gold is yellow" is an analytic judgment only so long as no body is discovered which possesses all the properties of gold except that it is white or red. We then should presumably augment the concept "gold" by omitting the mark "yellow," as we should omit the mark "black" from the concept (meaning of the word) "crow" as soon as we came across a "white crow." On the other hand, the mark "black" could by no means be taken away from the concept of a "black-horse" without destroying the concept itself. Its only meaning is "a horse which is black." [1] It is evident how inadequate these distinctions are to afford the basis for an epistemological treatise. Analytic judgments are really judgments about the content of word-meanings. Thus the judgment, "a dragon is a winged, fire-spitting animal with a snake-like body," is an analytic, and therefore an *a priori*, certain, universal, and necessary judgment.

The case is no better with the synthetic judgment. Besides judgments of experience, mathematical judgments are said to be synthetic. Take Kant's favorite example: 7 and 5 are 12; that is a synthetic judgment, for it is in no way possible to discover through analysis the concept of twelve from the combination of 7 and 5. But how is it with the judgment: 3 and 10 are 13? Is it not after all in this case possible to find from the union of 3 and 10 the concept thirteen, and likewise from 3 times 100,000 the concept three-hundred-thousand? Or, on the other hand, from the concept twenty-five to find through analysis that it is the sum of 5 and 20? As a matter of course we could not find in the first instance that the name of the sum of 7 and 5 was twelve; and if thirteen were called 'twelve,' the judgment, otherwise analytic or tautological, that 3 and 10 are thirteen would be also a synthetic judgment. That which really occurs in all arithmetical judgments is merely the rearrangement of the units and their sums according to the schema of the decimal system. The sums of units up to 10 are designated by special names, and so are the 10 × 10, and

---

[1] [As the author observes in the text, the German word *Rappe* (= black-horse) is etymologically identical with *Rabe* (= raven). — Trs.]

10×100 (hundred, thousand) ; the other numbers are expressed derivatively in the form of addition and multiplication. And arithmetical operations are nothing but transpositions, for more convenient comprehension, of groups of units thus formed : 176 and 149 are 325, *i. e.*, one and one hundred are two hundred; seven and four tens are eleven tens, or one hundred (ten-tens) and one ten, or thus, three hundred and one ten ; nine and six are = ten and five; hence, three hundred and twenty (two tens) and five. And the universal axiom that lies at the basis of all arithmetic is that the sum of units is not altered by their transposition in the decimal system.

The real and essential distinction that lies concealed behind this separation of synthetic and analytic judgments is, as has been already said, something else. It is the distinction between two kinds of knowledge which was vaguely before Locke's mind, but was clearly defined by Hume. This is the distinction between pure conceptual (mathematical) knowledge and knowledge of matters of fact. The difference may be stated in this way : In the former case, the understanding is absolutely productive. It itself creates the objects with which it deals. The point, the straight line, parallel lines, the triangle, the circle, the cone, are to be found nowhere in the world except in imaginative representations fashioned in accordance with the constructive principle of the definition. And thus in arithmetic the understanding itself furnishes the concepts of sums, products, powers, roots. And hence it is able to see what kind of relations occur in these constructions that have been called into existence solely by the concept. Hence there is obviously no necessity for the understanding to go beyond the sphere of what it has itself posited. The understanding does not in geometry have to appeal to experience in order to prove its propositions. On the contrary, it demonstrates them from the constructive principle furnished by the definition. And it is just on this account that geometrical propositions are universal and necessary. They hold good for the concept or for the system, which is determined in a purely conceptual fashion. On the other hand, simply for this reason, they are not valid for objects, *i. e.*, for objects which exist independently of the understanding.

The knowledge of matters of fact, on the contrary, as in the natural sciences, astronomy and physics, or in the mental sciences, history, and the science of language, has an essentially different form. The objects in this case are not produced by the understanding, but are found by it. Its task is to reach concepts and formulæ by means of which the object and their relations, as they exist, can be comprehended. Therefore definition and demonstration are not possible here in the same sense as in mathematics. The concepts of objects are formed by comparing the facts given in perception ; and, by observing their behavior, laws are discovered and proved true. Consequently, no strict universality and necessity is here attainable. For necessity exists only where logical deduction occurs, and universality in the proper sense is attributed only to judgments about concepts, or to pure representations conceptually constructed ; whereas judgments about objects given in experience attain only to relative universality, *i. e.*, as far as previous experience shows ; and they always remain subject to modification by further experience. There is no physical law that cannot be changed and transformed by new experience.

That is the essential distinction between forms of knowledge as Hume defined it. There are sciences of the conceptual world produced by the understanding, and sciences that undertake to inform us about given matters of fact.

From the standpoint we have now reached, Kant's problem may be developed as follows : He finds that hitherto men had always attempted to determine the nature and constitution of reality by means of the pure activity of the understanding, independently of experience. This was the attitude of metaphysics, which in distinction from physics pretends to be pure knowledge. Philosophers have always endeavored to determine by mere thinking such propositions as that matter neither comes into nor goes out of existence, that everything in the world has a cause, or that the world must have a beginning in time, a first unconditional cause of its being and its motion, etc. These are, therefore, nothing but mere propositions. Yet doubtless they claim objective validity, and it has been supposed that they are capable of being proved by means of pure reason. Indeed, it is obvious that they can in no way be proved from experience. The question which at this point arises, then, is this: How is it thinkable that that which pure thought establishes as truth which is evident to it, is binding also for objective reality that exists independently of the understanding? Whence the objective (not merely logical) validity of such propositions of the pure understanding?[1]

This is just the Kantian problem. That logical propositions possess logical validity — validity in the conceptual world — is evident, and it is likewise evident that experiential propositions possess objective validity. But the great problem is how propositions that are not based on experience, but on pure thought, can, nevertheless, possess validity for the world of objects. Or is Hume right in saying that all such propositions are impossible?

In this latter case, indeed, metaphysics, and not only metaphysics, but ultimately science in general, would be impossible. Kant insists that there must be a positive solution of the problem. And Kant discovers the solution. He finds the clue to the solution in mathematics, the guiding star of all rationalistic epistemology. Geometrical propositions are,

---

[1] *Cf.* the original conception of the problem contained in the oft-mentioned letter to Herz of the year 1772 with the *Reflexionen zur transsc. Deduktion*, particularly No. 925.

without doubt, pure truths of the understanding, not empirical generalizations. At the same time they possess objective validity. What the mathematician discovers by means of construction and calculation holds good for the corporeal world, and is verified by measurement. How does this anticipation of reality on the part of the understanding come about? How is the objective validity of mathematical judgments to be construed? Kant answers that it is because the space in which geometry projects its *a priori* constructions, that is to say, the space in our representation, is precisely the same space as that in which bodies are. Space is not an empirical datum, but an original construction, a mere form of our perception and therewith of our perceptual world. Bodies in space are nothing but objectified perceptions, and therefore they are subjected to the laws of perception; consequently, everything that geometry establishes for space and spatial representations in general holds good also for filled space or the corporeal world. Now the same principle, Kant discovers, is true of the laws of the understanding in general. The corporeal world is merely the construction of the understanding; therefore the laws of the understanding are *eo ipso* laws of nature. Obviously, the same thing does not hold true for the reality which is not a construction of the understanding. For it, the laws of the understanding have no validity, any more than our geometry has for a world of things that is not in space.

That is the formula under which Kant's critical investigation is really carried on, and the form in which the problem is solved by him. This appears with especial clearness from the Preface to the second edition of the *Critique*. How does it happen that, in place of this definite formula which Kant employs in the treatise ("How can the understanding know objects *a priori*?"), he in the Introduction makes use of the indefinite and transient formula: "How are synthetic judgments *a priori* possible?" When we attempt to explain this we seem to be led to the following considerations: First, Kant starts out from the position that all knowledge *a priori* is to be comprehended under the same formula as mathematics. As mathematics is the most certain and indubitable of sciences, he wants, as it is put in the *Prolegomena*, to bring metaphysics into the good company of mathematics. But unquestionably only pure mathematics is meant, which remains within the conceptual world and the representations of its own construction, — not, however, mathematics applied to reality; it was the necessity and universality of the latter, rather than of the former, that Hume had attacked. Hence mathematics cannot without further modification, be brought under the formula, "*a priori* knowledge of objects." Kant, therefore, sought for some notion that for the time being leaves the question of objectivity *in suspenso*. And at this point he hit upon the conception of the synthetic proposition, in contradistinction to the analytic, which is developed from the pure logical analysis of a given concept. The twofold concept 'analytic-synthetic' had long been familiar to him. As far back as in the essay on *Clearness* (1763), mathematical definitions as synthetic (*gemachte*) were contrasted with metaphysical definitions as analytic (developed from given concepts). After much vacillation in the determination and application of the concepts,[1] he finally comes to define the concepts of metaphysics, too, as synthetic. For this advance the critique of the ontological argument (God's existence cannot be shown from an analysis of the idea of God), and the recognition of the activity of the understanding as a synthesis of perceptions, may have furnished the impetus. And thus he constructs the universal formula: "How can *a priori* propositions acquire objective validity?" Under this formula metaphysics and mathematics are both included. This is a favorable omen. The most contested science is placed to-

1 Erdmann, *Reflexionen*, II., pp. 49 ff., 153 ff.

gether with the one that is most certain and unimpugned for similar treatment before the bar of reason.

The second point to be noticed is that Kant always at bottom adhered to the rationalistic view of the nature of the concept. The very notion of 'analytic' judgments presupposes that concepts are fixed entities which the understanding discovers and clarifies by means of analysis. That is the view that realistic rationalism in all its forms has maintained. True concepts as such have reality; every thinkable essence has at least an implicit claim to reality, a kind of half-reality. This is implied in its inner 'possibility.' When this claim is realized we have reality in the the full sense. Wolff expresses this in the proposition: "Existence is the fulfilment of possibility (*complementum possibilitatis*);" a proposition which is based on the Leibnizian theory of creation, that among the numberless possible things that are in God's intellect, he selects and gives formal reality to those which in their totality set forth the highest degree of possible reality or perfection.[1] With Spinoza, however, the spheres of possibility and of reality coincide; reality for him is nothing but conceivability, necessary logical connection in the world of concepts. Kant began in the sixties to cut loose from this rationalistic position which he had at first occupied, but he never entirely abandoned it. Concepts remained for him ready-made entities that can be taken apart and reduced to their elements. This procedure yields analytic judgments which are necessary *a priori*. One can, however, also add predicates to them that cannot be deduced from their essential marks. The result of this is synthetic judgments.[2]

---

[1] Baumgarten, *Metaphysik*, § 810: *Existentia est realitas cum essentia et reliquis realitatibus compossibilis.*

[2] *Cf.* the long explanation in the polemic directed against Eberhard (VI., pp. 46 ff.). A concept contains two kinds of marks: (1) those that pertain *ad essentiam s. ad internam possibilitatem;* (2) those that are unessential, *extra-essentialia*, which can be separated from the concept without affecting

In this connection the fact that the predicate 'being' or 'real' can never be contained as a mark in the nature of a concept is of prime importance. The judgment in which it is attributed to an essence, is always synthetic. The statement of the problem determines the whole essential structure of the *Critique*. There are fixed concepts, whose objective reality the Æsthetic establishes. The objective reality likewise of the ontological concepts, causality and substantiality, is guaranteed in the Analytic by means of the transcendental deduction. Finally, the objective validity of the ideas of the soul as a simple immaterial substance, and of God as the *ens realissimum*, is investigated in the Dialectic and found to be indemonstrable, because they cannot be represented in perception. But Kant does not discard these ideas. As ideas, though as problematic ones, they remain a necessary condition of our conceptual world.

In all the detailed discussion of Hume's position, the same rationalistic tendency of Kant's thought, his belief in a kind of pre-existence of concepts, comes out very clearly. Hume asks: How must I conceive of the notion of causality for it to be capable of formulating the actual consequence, as it appears in the empirical sciences which employ the idea? Kant starts out from a well-established conception: Cause expresses a necessary relation between one moment of reality, A, and another, B; and he asks how objective

---

its nature. The former are *essentialia constitutiva;* the latter, derivatives (*rationata*). The former determine the real nature, and they are in analytic judgments attributed to the concept; on the other hand, the latter, also called *attributa*, are likewise ascribed to the concept in *a priori* judgments, but either in analytic or in synthetic judgments. "A body is divisible," is an analytic judgment, which follows from the essential mark of extension. "A substance is permanent," is a synthetic judgment, which must be established by something outside of the concept. The lengthy explanation that follows is a sample of the fruitless way in which Kant struggles, first one way and then another, over these concepts of analytic and synthetic. *Cf.* also the chapter on Definition in the *Logick* (VIII., pp. 134 ff.) and the *Reflexionen*, II., Nos. 434 ff., 942, 1351 ff.

validity can be ascribed to this concept. Hume's reconstruction of the concept, making the relation of cause and
effect nothing but the perceptually given relation of regular
sequence of events in time, is for Kant the destruction of
the whole idea of causality. Hume, he declares, destroyed,
proscribed, and banished it. In like manner, the notion of
philosophy, metaphysics, and science in general is for Kant
a *priori* certain, as all genuine science consists in necessary
and universally valid propositions. This is the old rationalistic view. When Hume reconstructs this notion by attributing universality and necessity only to mathematical
knowledge, but not to knowledge of matters of fact, Kant
calls this position scepticism and looks upon it as the
destruction of the possibility of all science.

Moreover, the same rationalism is ultimately involved in
his metaphysical position. Things are in themselves conceptual entities (*intelligibilia, νούμενα*), to which intelligible
reality, but not empirical actuality, is attributed.[1]

---

[1] An exceedingly thorough explanation of the statement of the question,
and particularly of the formula "synthetic judgments a *priori*" is to be found
in Vaihinger's *Kommentar*, I., pp. 253 ff. I agree with the interpretation
of the problem, as it is presented there on p. 317. The question about the
possibility of synthetic judgments a *priori* has in Kant an ambiguous meaning.
It may refer (1) to the psychological possibility, and (2) to the objective
validity of mathematical, ontological, and metaphysical concepts and judgments that reason forms from its own powers. In my opinion, however,
the second question is so much more important for his epistemology, and also
for the significance of his critical investigation, that Kant did not do well to
obscure it under that more general and equivocal formulation. The fact
that the formula is not adapted to a clear and unequivocal comprehension of
the epistemological problem, is indeed most strikingly shown by Vaihinger's
own *Commentary*, which devotes a couple of hundred large octavo pages to
its explanation and to an account of the expositions of others.

I want, however, to devote a word or two to Vaihinger's very searching
discussion, written with polemical reference to my position. Do synthetic
judgments a *priori* as a matter of fact occur in mathematics and pure natural
science? Does that mean their mere existence as psychological processes, or
also their objective validity? And how, accordingly, is the problem to be regarded? Is it concerned with explaining their previously established validity,
or rather with demonstrating their still problematical validity? I may phrase

The point has been raised that along with the inquiry into the possibility of synthetic judgments *a priori*, Kant should have examined also synthetic judgments *a posteriori*. And certainly it would have been a great advantage to his epistemology if he had done so. The fact that he did not do this is to be traced to the rationalistic tendency of his thought. What he is in search of is not a theory of knowledge in general, but a method of metaphysics, *i. e.*, of the pure rational science of reality. Originally (1770) he thought he was in possession of the method for a transcendent metaphysic: but it later turned out to be only the method for a phenomenalistic metaphysic, but nevertheless for a purely ra-

my answer to these questions in the following manner: It is certain that Kant was never really in doubt about the objective validity of mathematics and the physical axioms, as far as their universality and necessity are concerned. It is just as certain, moreover, that Hume had doubted them, and that this very doubt was the point of departure for his examination, the groundless character of which Kant undertakes to set forth. Kant must have regarded this as a doubt to be taken seriously, since he went to such pains to refute it as the transcendental deduction of the pure ideas of the understanding, according to his own utterances, cost him. Hence it follows that the *Critique* had to treat the validity of the contested propositions as problematic until the Deduction had justified their claim. On the whole it does this too; nevertheless, Kant's firm conviction of their validity is apparent everywhere, and in the *Prolegomena* he simply takes them for granted. Inasmuch as he then embodied these propositions in the second edition of the *Critique*, the exposition becomes rather unpleasantly ambiguous, as Vaihinger too finds it. The same vacillation is shown in Kant's replies to the question whether the task consists in explaining or in demonstrating the validity. He says both things, first the one, then the other. But in accordance with the whole character of his treatise, he must ultimately say the second. The validity has been called in question by Hume; I will demonstrate it, will deduce the right of the pure concepts of the understanding, and will render secure the objective validity of mathematical propositions and physical axioms. He says that too; but at the same time he says the other thing still more frequently, — namely, that he is concerned merely with explaining how indubitable validity can exist. Hence it is to be noted that in this sphere demonstration and explanation are very closely allied. If the truth of an *a priori* proposition is demonstrated, it is thereby explained and its *ratio cur* set forth; and conversely, if a proposition cannot be explained. it is a groundless supposition. *Cf.* Adickes's statement of the problem in his admirable essay in Vaihinger's *Kantstudien*, I., pp. 31 ff.

tional science, a 'pure' natural science. He might indeed
have made the 'pure' natural science and its method more
clear by an examination of 'empirical' natural science, but
that lay outside the line of march of his thought. How
synthetic judgments *a posteriori* can have actual validity
seemed to him to be no problem at all. If he had really
raised the question, it would have shattered the whole
structure of the *Critique*. He would have been forced to
reply that there can be no such judgments ; synthetic judgments *a posteriori* are a *contradictio in adjecto*. Or, he might
have asked: If there are synthetic judgments arising from
experience, if there is synthesis arising from sense perception, where, then, is the limit? And are, then, pure *a priori*
judgments possible at all ? It is the unconscious instinct of
self-preservation in the system that causes the Kantian
thought to glide over this as well as over other 'critical'
problems, *e. g.*, the question regarding the form of our
knowledge of the *a priori*.

III. Explanation of some Concepts

Before entering into the details of Kant's solution of the
problem, I desire briefly to explicate a few notions which he
constantly employs. In the first place, I propose to consider
the concepts Perception, Phenomenon, Thing-in-itself.

I shall begin with phenomenon. What is it ? It can be
answered first of all that it is exactly what in ordinary speech
is called a 'thing,' — the perdurable object, with its activities
and relations, which exists independent of the subject. The
moon in the heavens is, in ordinary talk, a thing which is
for itself, but for epistemological reflection it is an appearance, a something that exists for a perceiving subject, but
does not have an absolute existence independent of it.

The matter may be more closely defined in this way:
Phenomenon is a mean between pure subjective individual
sense-perception and the thing-in-itself. Sense-perception

(*sensatio*) is a transitory process in an empirical, individual, consciousness. A phenomenon is more : it is not the *sensatio*, but the *sensibile ;* it is the durable object of possible sensation. The moon is a permanently existing cosmic body of such and such size, mass, and motion.   It really exists, even if no eye sees it, even when it is not visible.   Its real existence is therefore not dependent upon its now being perceived by this or that empirical consciousness.   But, on the other hand, the moon does not exist without relation to a perceiving subject in general ; it is not a thing-in-itself.   All that I mean when I speak of the moon is finally, as far as its content is concerned, given through sense-perception — the appearance of light of a certain intensity, nature, and motion in the heavens, and, I add in thought, of a certain mass, at a certain distance, and of a certain configuration of surfaces, etc. All of this is contained in the sense-perception. We are convinced that, if it were possible for us to steer a definite course in a definite direction through cosmic space, we should come into contact with a body of a determined nature and extension, which would appear to the senses as impenetrable, light-reflecting, etc.   The reality which we predicate of the moon rests altogether upon actual and possible sense-perceptions.   Were it not for these definite perceptions of light and these possible perceptions of resistance, we should not call the moon real.   And if there were no subject whatever to perceive light and experience resistance, we should never talk about the moon as such an object.   The thing-in-itself, or that which manifests itself as the moon to a subject thus organized, might indeed exist, but the moon about which we talk is really only for such a subject ; it is ' phenomenal.'

We may now assert that a phenomenon is an aggregate of possible perceptions for a subject of a certain intellectual constitution, or, in Kant's language, for " consciousness in general."   An actual perception of it is not needed, for a phenomenon can be real and recognized as real without its ever having been given in immediate perception, as, *e. g.*, the farther side of the moon, or the interior of the earth. All that is necessary is that it must, upon the basis of given perceptions, be discovered as possible according to the results of natural laws, as was the case with the planet Neptune before it was actually observed. J. S. Mill developed this idea with the greatest clearness; the empirical reality of a thing (appearance) signifies a permanent possibility of such and such co-existing perceptions of sense. Kant's view is just the same. He developed it most clearly in the sixth section of the doctrine of Antinomies: " There is for us nothing actually given, except the perception and the empirical progression from this to other possible perceptions. For in themselves phenomena, as mere representations, are real only in perception. To call a phenomenon [it ought to read " somewhat "] a real thing prior to perception, means that we must meet with such a perception in the course of experience." [1]

We can now present the Kantian view in the following schematic form. Three things are to be distinguished: (1) The content of subjective consciousness, or the actual sense-perceptions and ideas in a particular individual consciousness (*sensatio*). (2) The objective world of appearance, or the aggregate of all possible sense-perceptions for an all-embracing consciousness, or consciousness in general (*mundus sensibilis*). (3) The reality which exists in itself without any relation to a perceiving subject (*mundus intelligibilis*). The first, the content of subjective consciousness, is immediate only for the individual subject that has these perceptions; the relations between the constituent elements are

[1] In this definition of the concept of phenomenon, which is of essential importance for understanding Kant, I am glad to concur with Falckenberg's exposition in his admirable *Geschichte der neueren Philosophie* (3d edition, 1898, pp. 290 ff. [Eng. trans., pp. 346 ff.] *Cf.* L. Busse, " Zur Kants Lehre vom Ding an sich " (*Zeitschr. für Philos.*, vol. 102, 1893), which shows the difficulty involved in the application of the concept of phenomenon to psychic processes.

accidental sequences in time, conditioned either empirically or through association. The second, the world of appearance, is the same for all subjects of like organization; the relations between the elements are natural laws, universally valid rules for the connection of objects in space and time. The third, the intelligible world, lies outside of the forms of sense-perception; it is only comprehensible in thought as a necessary concept, and therefore unattainable for human knowledge, which is bound down to sense-perception. The content of subjective consciousness is the object of psychological investigation; the world of appearance is the proper object of scientific investigation, particularly of natural science; the intelligible world would be the object of an absolute knowledge. In human knowledge, however, it really appears only as the necessary regulative idea for the critical determination of the nature of our knowledge. If it is made the object of speculative reasoning, there arise the pseudo-sciences of the old metaphysics.

These three stages or forms of reality, the subjective, the objective, and the absolute reality, can be appropriately illustrated by the three stages or forms of intelligence: (1) the animal, (2) the human, and (3) the divine intelligence. The forms of reality are the correlates of the forms of intelligence. This distinction too is important for a comprehension of Kant's thought, as doubtless it was for him also an important point of orientation.

Animal intelligence possesses only subjective sensations and sense-perceptions connected in a merely accidental way by associations. It does not form the idea of an objective world of phenomena, interrelated according to natural laws. The animal does not place himself over against a world of existing things, positing himself as a member of it, and determining for himself his spatial and temporal place in the cosmos. His perceptions (and ideas) remain mere modifications of subjective consciousness.

Human intelligence resembles animal intelligence in that its sensations and perceptions are primarily given as mere subjective modifications. It, however, passes beyond this stage by forming, on the basis of these constituent elements, the idea of objects, and of a great, all-embracing, universally valid, and uniform system of all objects. With this objective world of objective laws, it contrasts the content of subjective consciousness and the sequence of ideas as accidental, as something dependent upon the objective course of events. This distinction between human and animal intelligence depends upon the greater activity of the former. The animal undergoes passive impressions; man actively elaborates, analyzes, and combines impressions, and thereby becomes capable of separating them from himself and positing them for himself. And, on the other hand, he has the power of positing himself as an Ego over against them, and it is this act that constitutes the basis of personality. The faculty of thus spontaneously acting upon phenomena is called understanding.

The divine intelligence for Kant, although an unrealizable ideal, is nevertheless an indispensable concept for the comprehension of the nature of the human understanding. He designates it by the name of an "intuitive understanding." For it, the distinction between being and thinking, which is constitutive for human understanding, no longer holds. God has no existence outside of himself; he is the all-embracing being. His knowledge is absolute knowledge, because he determines reality by his thought. It is mathematical reasoning which enables us to make clear to ourselves this idea of an absolute understanding. In mathematics, the human understanding also by its own self-activity creates the objects of its knowledge; hence, in this case, there is no unknowable element left over, no distinction between appearance and thing-in-itself. Towards reality, however, the human understanding does not bear the relation of a creator; reality must be presented to it in the form of perceptions. Hence, the disparity between thought and being. The divine intellect, on the contrary, bears the same relation to things that the human does to geometrical triangles and circles. It follows, that for God thought and existence are absolutely coincident. That is the ideal of absolute knowledge, and it is an idea of reason necessary for showing the limitation and relativity of our knowledge.

These three stages of intelligence may also be called sense-perception, understanding, reason. In man, the being intermediate between the animal and God, all three are to be found; while the animal possesses sense-perception alone, God reason alone. Sense-perception is the capacity of receiving sensations, the receptivity for affections. Sensation is not a conscious content impressed from outside upon the subject. That is impossible; for the mind has no windows through which something may enter from the outside; a sensation is actively produced, but only in response to an external stimulus. The forms of receptivity are space and time; the product of sense-perception, a plurality of perceptions in space and time. The understanding is the faculty of thinking by means of concepts, of subsuming under rules, and of determining the particular by means of the universal, *i. e.*, of judging. . Its modes of functioning are given in the forms of logical judgment, and the concepts corresponding to these are called 'categories.' The understanding as spontaneity stands in contrast with the receptivity of sense. It introduces law and systematic connection among the individual perceptions. The product of sense-perception and understanding together is the system of nature, arranged in space and time in conformity with law as science presents it to us. Reason is the faculty of passing beyond the empirical world to the supersensuous; its product is the ideal world, the *mundus intelligibilis*. It is, properly speaking, the form of the divine thought that is employed in the intuition of existence in the form of ideas immanent in it.   Human reason is only a feeble reflection of the absolute reason.   In man, reason is primarily employed in the creation of practical ideas, thoughts about something that ought to be real, although it does not exist in the empirical world, and that can and ought to be actualized by reason's own activity, as, *e. g.*, the perfect state.   In the theoretical sphere, reason acts as the principle which limits and regulates the employment of the understanding.   It accomplishes this, in the first place, as a critic of reason, by employing the idea of an absolute knowledge (coincidence of thought and reality) to bring the understanding to the consciousness of its necessary limitation to the world of appearance.   Secondly, it evaluates all theoretical knowledge from its relation to the final purposes of mankind (wisdom).   And thirdly, it directs the immanent employment of the understanding in accordance with speculative ideas, ultimately in accordance with the idea of the unity of reality as a system of realized ideas of purpose.

We may now appreciate the final meaning of the notion of the *mundus sensibilis* and *intelligibilis*.   The world is intelligible for the divine understanding, the *intellectus archetypus*, and it is completely included in God's thought. It is therefore in itself an ideal unity ; the *mundus noumenon* is, as its name implies, an existing system of ideas.   The reality presented to the human intellect is, on the other hand, sensible and phenomenal ; the world of divine ideas manifests itself to it as a sensuous, changing, corporeal world in motion, which it laboriously and imperfectly strives to master, not by means of pure thought, but by experience.

I wish still to make a remark or two about the thing-in-itself, that *crux interpretum*.   It is true that Kant's utterances upon this subject are exceedingly diverse, ambiguous, and indeed even contradictory.   This arises from the fact that the thing-in-itself is not the central principle of his system ; it is a self-evident presupposition.   The object of his investigation, however, is the possibility of rational knowledge. Consequently, the notion of thing-in-itself is really only touched upon as occasion offers. The following points seem to me essential in Kant's conception of the matter.

That he never for a moment doubted the existence of a trans-subjective reality will be regarded as certain by every unbiased reader, even without Kant's own strongly emphasized assurance. It was the primary and self-evident presupposition of his thought at all periods; the *Critique* did not make any change at all in this respect. The notion of the world of appearance, of the *mundus sensibilis*, with which the critical period starts out, implies as a necessary correlate the notion of a real world that appears. Without this, the idea of the phenomenal would be meaningless; the idea, if that were the only reality, would be also the absolute reality. Only upon the presupposition of another sphere to which it is related can it be called phenomenal. An absolute illusionism in no wise differs from an absolute realism.

What can we now, in agreement with Kant, assert regarding the thing-in-itself? If we keep strictly to the standpoint of the *Critique*, we may say: (1) It is not the object of sense-perception; this statement is a mere analytic judgment; (2) it is the object of thought, and, indeed, of a necessary thought. The understanding, inasmuch as it recognizes through critical reflection sense-knowledge as such (*i. e.*, its accidental character and subjectively conditioned nature), frames the correlative concepts of appearance and thing-in-itself. In consideration of this fact, the latter may be called an intelligible entity (*ens intelligibile noumenon*). The concept really does not at first have a positive significance; it is not a thing that is known in its real nature by the understanding, but a somewhat that is opposed by the understanding to the phenomenal as being of a different nature. Since, then, human thought gains a con-

tent solely through sense-perception, the notion of the
thing-in-itself is really without content; it is an empty
form of an *ens*, a mere X, which as a transcendental object
is opposed by the understanding to the empirical object
(the phenomenon).   (3) A noumenon in a positive sense
can exist for an intuitive understanding, *i. e.*, one that
does not have to depend upon sense-perception for its
material.   Hence for the divine intellect things are intuited
concepts (ideas).   For our understanding, this notion, like
that of the divine intellect itself, remains a problematic
concept, — a concept that is thinkable and possible, but
one which, however, we cannot make real by means of
perceptual filling.   (4) To this empty problematic concept
we can, nevertheless, in a certain respect, attribute a content, and that, too, by means of the theoretical reason.   It
is to us, and not to phenomena, that pure thought belongs
(the understanding or reason itself).   This pure thought is
the presupposition of the phenomenal.   In other words, the
phenomenal presupposes the ego in itself, which is certainly
not given in perception as an object, but only in the absolute spontaneous function of thought itself.   If from this
point of view we defined the nature of things-in-themselves
in general, we could say that things-in-themselves are 'intelligible entities,' and that their unity is a *mundus intelligibilis* in the positive sense.   Of course that would be a
mere hypothetical use of the understanding, which we ought
not to employ in a pure rational science like metaphysics
unless, at most, for polemical purposes.   Meantime another
consideration arises.   The practical reason ascribes certainty
and validity to the concept of an absolute and real spiritual
world, although this assurance cannot be employed for theoretical purposes.

So far the matter is clear.   The peculiar difficulty, the
moot question for the Kantian philosophy, arises from the
application of the schema of the Analytic.   Do the cate-

gories apply to things-in-themselves ? Kant gives a definitely
negative reply. They apply only to phenomena; the categories are nothing but functions for constructing the perceptual world; without material data, they have no meaning
whatever. But, on the other hand, he constantly does apply
the categories to things-in-themselves; he imputes reality,
causality, and plurality to them; they affect the subject,
and, conversely, the ego, as a thing-in-itself is affected.
Things-in-themselves accordingly constitute a world of non-
sensuous things which throughout correspond to the things
of sense as they exist in uniform relations, etc. Here, consequently, there seems to be a formal contradiction. Since
the time of Jacobi, Fichte, and Ænesidemus-Schulze, this
charge has been again and again brought against Kant.
Without things-in-themselves, without their reality and
activity, one may not enter into the system; with them, one
cannot stay in it.

A solution of this contradiction is, so far as I see, possible in only one way. A double meaning of the categories
must be distinguished, — a pure logical transcendent, and a
transcendental physical. From this standpoint Kant could
make some such reply as the following to the objection:
I certainly do attribute existence to things-in-themselves,
but this is not the same concept as the category of reality;
the latter, as I say with sufficient clearness, designates
nothing but an existence given in perception, external or
internal, or at least in possible perception. Reality, in this
sense of empirical reality, is, as a matter of course, not attributed to things-in-themselves, but a super-sensuous or transcendent reality is ascribed to them. And the same holds
true for causality. I employ this concept, too, in a double
sense, as indeed the reader of the Dialectic and the *Critique
of Practical Reason* is well aware, — causality according to
natural laws, and causality according to ideas of freedom.
In the former sense, that of the category, cause connotes

nothing at all but the regular temporal precedence of a phenomenon. That can, of course, be ascribed only to things
that are themselves in time; that is to say, to phenomena;
e.g., to bodies with which our senses come into contact. The
external stimulus and the physiological excitation, and, further, these two and the resulting sensation, are related as
cause and effect in the empirical sense. On the other hand,
among things-in-themselves there is, of course, no connection of empirical causality, but a transcendent relation which
is not perceptually represented, but can be comprehended
only by pure thought; it is a relation of inner condition
such as exists between ground and consequence in logical
thought. When I thus explain the matter, I have amply
shown that between things-in-themselves — the members of
the *mundus intelligibilis,* which has its unity in God, the
ens realissimum — there exists a relation of inner correspondence, — a mutual logico-teleological relation to the unity of
the absolute end. All things as existing in God form a
unity, and are related to one another as necessary determinations of parts for the realization of the absolute perfection, just as each part of a work of art or of a poem is bound
up with all the others, not by extrinsic, temporal reciprocity,
but by an intrinsic teleological relation. To be sure, this
remains a problematic idea; reality is presented to us as a
world of appearance, and as a world of ideas it can only be
thought by us, but not perceived. In God's understanding,
we may suppose it is intuitively represented.

If, however, the objection is still urged that all of these
are nevertheless forms of thought, which cannot apply to
the trans-subjective, I bring forward the following consideration. It is true that I, as a matter of course, can think my
thoughts only through my thoughts and forms of thought;
to pass beyond this proscribed circle is impossible. Even
the thought of the thing-in-itself and its reality is an idea,
and as such subjective. I can think the idea of the trans-

subjective, but I cannot think it in a trans-subjective fashion. And hence transcendent reality naturally remains something which I assert and attribute. But I know what I mean when I assert it, and I think you do too. If not, then miracles cannot help you. And a book wherein phenomenon and thing-in-itself are spoken of was not written for you; and your gainsaying, since you do not know what I mean, was not written for me.[1]

IV. The Transcendental Æsthetic

The Æsthetic is the doctrine of sensible knowledge, so far as the latter contains elements that make *a priori* knowledge possible. It is not the doctrine of sense-perception in general, for that belongs to empirical anthropology; nor is it even the doctrine of all the subjective elements in sensation, for that embraces also the sense-qualities, light, color, tone, etc. But it is the doctrine of those elements of perception by means of which knowledge *a priori* is rendered possible. There are two such elements, space and time; and Kant's task is to prove: (1) that space and time originally belong to the subject as forms of its sense-perception, and that they are not introduced from without by means of experience; (2) that by means of them knowledge *a priori* is possible. The first is accomplished in the metaphysical, the second in the transcendental proof. In the exposition the first point stands out so prominently that the other may be overlooked. At least, it was not until the second edition that special paragraphs (Nos. 3 and 4) were devoted to the transcendental deduction, whereas in the first edition they were inserted (as No. 3) in the proof for the ideality of space and time.[2] It is doubtless this that pro-

[1] I shall return to this point about the twofold significance of the categories, the logical and the real, when I come to treat of the doctrine of the "Schematism of the Pure Concepts of the Understanding."

[2] It is noteworthy in this connection that, although in the case of time Kant claims this independence for the transcendental exposition, and arranges for a

motes the usual misunderstanding that the establishment of idealism is the chief purpose of the work. A strong impression that the reader gets from the first pages determines his notion of all that follows. Such is the case with Locke too, for many readers carry away the impression from the first pages of the *Essay* that his sole purpose is contained in the thesis that there are no innate ideas.

The emergence of the "metaphysical exposition" in the Æsthetic is, however, explicable from the history of its genesis. The decision to assume the ideality of space and time was the starting-point of the new philosophy as a whole; it introduced the turning-point of 1770. In the *Dissertation*, however, the chief significance that the ideality of space and time had was found in the fact that it afforded a basis for the possibility of speculative and idealistic metaphysic. Space and time are merely forms of our sense-perception, and as such belong to the *mundus sensibilis.* Hence the real world is free from them. The properties of matter and change, together with space and time, belong merely to phenomena, while thought, which constructs the ideas of God and of immortality, is protected against the "insinuations of sense-perception." The intention of establishing an *a priori* knowledge of the intelligible world by divesting things-in-themselves of space and time, was certainly abandoned in the seventies. There remained only the purpose of discovering the *a priori* knowledge of the sensible world. The 'transcendental' point of view, therefore, should have become more prominent. But, as a matter of fact, this is

paragraph with that heading, he, however, grows weary, as it were, of carrying out the reconstruction, and merely refers to No. 3 of the metaphysical deduction, which was left standing, — a literary curio, to which there is hardly an analogy in all philosophical literature. Did Kant wish to give the reader a hint at the very beginning not to take the matter too seriously and consider himself in duty bound to follow the schematism, which was in other respects so painfully and often pedantically sustained ? At any rate, Kant gave good cause to think so.

not the case. Kant transferred his ideas to the Æsthetic in the same form in which he had first fixed them in 1770, without making any change at all. And it was quite natural that he should do this, since he still regarded the deliverance of things-in-themselves from space and time as an essential advance in speculation. This may be seen from the fact that at the conclusion of the Æsthetic he calls special attention to the advantage natural theology may reap from transcendental idealism. He destroys, as it is later put, insolent materialism and fatalism, together with their pernicious consequences for morals and philosophy, by rendering the conceivability of the objects of theology and pneumatology secure against the demand for their constructibility in space and time.

We turn now to the execution of the work. The metaphysical deduction takes the form of a proof for the thesis that space and time are not concepts derived from experience, but *a priori* perceptions. The demonstration reduces itself in the main to the three following points: (1) Space and time are not got from experience by means of abstraction from given space and time relations, but they are the original presupposition of the apprehension of things as spatial and temporal. To express it otherwise, without the original activity of the subject in arranging the manifold sensations in juxtaposition and succession, there would be no space and time relations. (2) Space and time are irreducible moments of our consciousness; they cannot be thought away, whereas every space and time content given by experience can be thought away. It follows that space and time belong to the subject as a possession that is *a priori* engendered, and not *a posteriori* given. (This argument can perhaps be made more convincing by a slight alteration: Every body can be thought away out of space, and likewise every event from time, but the space itself which the body occupied cannot be thought away, for one cannot think of any gaps in space and time, though, even according to Kant, it is not impossible to think that there is no space or time at all.) (3) Space and time are not general concepts, but perceptions. If they were general concepts formed by abstraction, they would have to have a certain extension. There are not, however, many spaces or times as several examples of the concept, but only one infinite space and time, in which all spaces and times are regarded as limitations. A fourth point in the treatment of space is omitted in the case of time because meaningless, but then, in order to maintain the external parallelism, point three is divided into two points.

After these arguments for apriority, there follow metaphysical reflections upon the nature of space and time, from which their ideality appears. The idea of their absolute reality cannot by any means be maintained. If space is viewed as absolutely existing, then of course empty space, after all bodies are taken away, must, nevertheless, be thought of as existing. But what is this ? Is it an infinite empty receptacle, a receptacle without sides ? And what is time ? Is it the real empty receptacle in which all movements and changes take place? As a receptacle without sides and without extension, then, does its being consist of what is neither present nor future being ? Anything more absurd could not well be thought. Hence space and time cannot be thought of as actual forms of a reality which is contained in them ; for then they would be real nothings. The only alternative is to think them as the forms in which our sense representation of reality is ; they have reality as forms of perception in the subject. Whence it follows that they are not to be thought of as empty, passive forms which like receptacles would be ready to hold things, but as functions for the ordering of the manifold sensations, which have reality only in the function itself. The *Dissertation* of 1770 expressly emphasizes this point : " Neither concept is innate ;

both are undoubtedly acquired. But they are not abstracted from the sensation of objects, but from the activity of the mind co-ordinating all its sense-perceptions according to fixed laws, and thus there undoubtedly arises a kind of immutable and hence perceptually cognizable type. Sensations do indeed call out this act of the mind, but they do not determine the nature of perception. There is nothing here innate except the law of the mind according to which it connects in a fixed way its sensations with the presence of an object." [1]

As we have just remarked, the transcendental deduction in Kant's exposition, even in the second edition, was not made completely independent, or given a prominence corresponding with its importance. It has, however, the task of showing that under the presupposition of the *apriority* and ideality of space and time, knowledge of objects is *a priori* possible. The *Dissertation* also had developed this point of view, and that, too, more definitely and clearly than the *Critique*. Geometrical, mechanical, and arithmetical propositions, that is to say, demonstrated and *a priori* truths, receive objective validity under this presupposition, and only under this. All objects, then, that are presented to our sense-perception necessarily assume the forms of time and space. And everything, therefore, that can be made out about the nature of time and space as such, holds true for them also, as, *e. g.*, the law of the continuity of all changes, or the law that in the material world there can be nothing simple; for the simple can exist in space only as a totality, not, however, as a part.

And the *Dissertation* shows, too, very clearly that this theory alone will do justice to all the requirements.[2] There are besides it two possible points of view. The one looks upon space and time as absolute real *receptacula* of reality. This is the standpoint that Newton assumes, and to which most mathematicians give their adherence. The other re-

---

[1] § 15.   [2] §§ 14, 15.

gards space and time as relations between existing things
and processes, and holds that they would vanish along with
the actual things. This is the view which most German
philosophers after Leibniz represent. The first theory is
adequate for the purposes of the mathematician, but it is
metaphysically inconceivable to think of time as an actual,
continuous stream — it remains a nonsensical fiction. And
thus the notion of space as a system of real infinite relations, without things to be related, belongs to the realm
of fable. Moreover, this view makes natural theology
impossible, for if space actually is the universal receptacle
of reality, then both God and souls must be in space. The
other view, the Leibnizian, might be tenable from a metaphysical standpoint, but it is impossible for the mathematician. " It takes away its exactitude from mathematics, and
places it in the number of those sciences whose principles
are empirical. For if all determinations of space (and of
time) are gained by experience, only from external relations,
geometrical (and mechanical) axioms possess nothing but
arbitrary precision, and only comparative universality, such
as is acquired by induction, *i. e.*, valid for the sphere of
previous observation; then there may be expectation, as is
the case in empirical matters, of sometime discovering a
space possessing other original determinations, and perhaps
even a rectangle with two sides." [1]

[1] The two views here rejected are the very ones through which Kant himself passed. *See* Vaihinger, II., pp. 422 ff. He originally shared the point of
view of German metaphysics, that space is an empirical concept, abstracted
from the relations of external things. He then adopted the second view
(Newton and Clarke), that space is the pre-existent form of the corporeal
world. From this view, which he defended as late as 1768, he freed himself
with sudden reversal, evidently on account of its metaphysical insupport-
ability, and adopted the new standpoint that space and time are *a priori* forms
of the corporeal world (as Newton contends), but consisting together with the
corporeal world merely in sense-perception (which was really Leibniz's view
too, as Kant himself remarks in the *Metaph. Anfangsgründen der Naturwiss.*,
IV., p. 399.)

Hence there remains only our view. It is in itself conceivable, and it satisfies the demands of the metaphysician, who wants a reality free from the conditions of space and time. It satisfies also the demands of the mathematician, and gives him what he needs, namely, an infinite, absolutely homogeneous space (and time), whose determinations are absolutely valid for all objects (of sense). " Since nothing can be given to the senses unless conformable with the primitive axioms of space and the propositions derived therefrom by geometry, everything must necessarily agree with these, although their principle is only subjective, and the laws of sense become at the same time laws of nature. For nature is in minutest detail subjected to the rules of geometry." " Unless the perception of space were originally given by the nature of the mind, the use of geometry in physics would be unsafe. For it could always be doubted whether this notion borrowed from experience would be in precise agreement with reality, since perchance necessary determinations may have been omitted in the process of abstraction,[1] — a suspicion which actually has entered the minds of some people."

I have here quoted these passages from the *Dissertation* because they very definitely set forth the meaning and tendency of the new mode of thought. In the *Critique*, the idea and aim of the transcendental deduction, the demonstration of the objective validity of mathematical propositions, are not clearly brought out. One reason is that the real deduction has been obscured by transferring the schematism of the system from the Æsthetic to the Analytic (under the title " Axioms of Perception "). Another reason is that the exposition is hampered by the insertion of the new formula, " synthetic *a priori.*" Accordingly, the ' objectivity ' of geo-

---

[1] *Negatis forsitan* [*rerum*], *a quibus abstractum erat, determinationibus.* The emendation of the passage by means of the insertion of *rerum* has been very kindly furnished by Professor Falckenberg. It seems to me to be thoroughly successful. In my first edition I regarded the passage as corrupt, but it did not seem to me capable of emendation.

metrical judgments seems to be given in pure perception by the mere construction of the concept, and the application to the corporeal world appears as accidental and accessory so far as the validity is concerned. It is due to this that the controversy arises whether the Æsthetic deals with pure or applied mathematics. If the *Dissertation* were taken as the starting-point, a doubt could never have arisen that the new conception was originally and chiefly concerned with the proof that mathematical principles, without loss of their necessity and universality, hold good also for empirically given magnitudes. The *Critique* too has essentially the same concern, as the deduction of the Axioms of Perception and also the exposition in the *Metaphysical Elements* distinctly show.[1] In the *Prolegomena* for the first time the ideas become more confused: In pure mathematics synthetic judgments *a priori* are possible because we can represent their object in pure perception. Now, however, the relation between the logical premises and conclusion is very nearly reversed, the ideality of space and time is no longer the ground of the possibility of the objectivity of mathematical knowledge, but the certainty and reality of mathematics become the logical ground for the ideality of space and time. At least it is maintained that the former become intelligible only under this presupposition.

If we take the Æsthetic as a whole, we can formulate its argument in the following manner: In our sensible knowledge there emerge two distinct elements, a necessary and constant, and an accidental and variable one; the former as though it were the lasting form, the latter the changing content. The permanent form is space and time; their changing content, bodies with their endless differences, motions, and changes. Space and time appear as altogether constant and intrinsically homogeneous; all spaces and times are entirely one and the same in kind; and they

[1] IV., p. 397.

appear also as unities in the strictest sense. There is only *one* space and *one* time, while the many spaces and times are only accidental divisions of a unitary and self-identical space. The same is true of time. And these facts are necessary thought determinations; we cannot think several spaces or times that do not form a necessary whole. Nor can we think space and time otherwise than as completely homogeneous in their own nature. We are certain that all differences in the relation and the movements of bodies are explicable, not through the special nature of the spaces and times in which they are, but merely through the difference of the things.

How is this fact of the necessary unity and homogeneity of space and time to be explained? Kant says by assuming that space and time are constructed by the mind by means of its own original and uniform functions. If time and space were given by experience and abstracted from it, there is no reason why there should not be several spaces and times intrinsically different, as well as many bodies with different qualities. The particular affections are, as such, accidental and detached, and from them, therefore, the necessary unity and uniformity cannot arise. Moreover, there are three gains from the assumption of this view: (1) We attain herewith the epistemological possibility of viewing all things in space and time as subjected to the universal laws which result from the nature of space and time; or a necessary basis for mathematical physics as a system of universal and necessary propositions with objective validity. (2) We escape the absurd questions into which a system of metaphysics falls that views space and time as absolutely existing reality. Some of these questions ask: Are space and time limited or unlimited? Are there empty spaces and times, and of what does the nature of these consist? What constitutes the difference between nothing and empty time or empty space? (3) We gain also the possibility of an idealistic metaphysic. Reason acquires the liberty of interpreting reality as an ideal world, free from the bounds of space and time; the *mundus sensibilis* sinks to the level of an accidental, though for us human beings necessary, view of reality. Space and time are like Plato's cave, wherein is enclosed the intelligence of sentient man. By the knowledge of the ideality or subjectivity of space and time, reason does not, to be sure, gain the possibility of coming out from the cave, but it does nevertheless reach a clear consciousness of the situation. It surveys the state of affairs, and may sometime discover a means of emerging into the daylight of the intelligible world, guided by practical ideas, if speculative concepts are not to be trusted.

The adoption of a critical attitude towards the doctrines developed in the transcendental æsthetic must in my opinion be circumscribed by the following points: —

1. Kant is right in assuming that space and time are functions of apprehension created by the subject, and not externally derived from experience.

2. He is right also in maintaining that the supposition that space and time have an absolute existence outside of the subject and its sense-perception, is groundless and untenable.

3. On the other hand, we cannot free ourselves from the idea that these functions of apprehension on the part of the subject are fashioned with reference to a trans-subjective reality.

4. And hence the absolute validity of the properties of mathematical space and time for all possible phenomena is not necessary for thought; it is conceivable that the subject in another environment would give rise to other forms of perception.

V. THE TRANSCENDENTAL ANALYTIC

The doctrine of sensibility is followed by the doctrine of the understanding in the second main division of the

Critique. This division contains the theory of scientific knowledge so far as the latter rests upon the functions of the understanding that make knowledge *a priori* possible. In its plan, the Analytic corresponds with the Æsthetic with the exception that in the Analytic the real aim of the investigation, the transcendental deduction, comes out much more clearly. The problem can be thus formulated. In our knowledge of the objective world there appear, in addition to the space and time relations, other formal elements also, which amid all the difference of content remain ever the same ; as, *e. g.* the form of a thing possessing qualities and activities, and likewise the universal uniformity in the relations of things, causality, and reciprocity. The task in this case, as in the Æsthetic, is : (1) to set these elements forth and to establish their *a priori* nature (or " ideality " in the sense in which it is used in the Æsthetic) ; (2) to show that by means of them, objective knowledge *a priori* is possible. Thus in this field also we have a metaphysical and a transcendental deduction.

Before passing to the exposition of these two aspects, I shall make a general preliminary remark. The Analytic is undoubtedly the most difficult and obscure part of the *Critique.* In contrast with it, the Æsthetic and Dialectic are clear and easy. Kant himself is aware of this, and he tries to find the reason in the difficulty of the problem. Undoubtedly we have here to grapple with ultimate and most difficult questions. But the chief cause of the obscurity seems to me to be due to another source, namely, to a certain indecision in Kant's thought.

Schopenhauer, in his " Critique of the Kantian Philosophy," finds the real cause of the difficulty to be a lack of clearness in conceiving the relation of the understanding to perception. And, in fact, the reason can be found in that obscurity. How is the understanding related to the arrangement of phenomena in space and time ? In particular, does it find the order in the time series as a datum, or does it by means of its synthetic functions introduce the order into sensations, which are presented to sense-perception merely as a chaotic throng ? In other words, are the empirical objects of perception given, or do they require to be produced by the activity of the understanding ?

To these questions Kant gives no clear and distinct reply, or rather he both affirms and denies. The Analytic is based upon a demonstration that presupposes the answer that objects are not given, but, in regard to form, are made by the synthetic functions of the understanding, and for that very reason are *a priori* knowable. That would be a purely rationalistic solution of the problem. Inasmuch as the understanding with its immanent laws supervenes on the chaos of sensations, it creates the world of experience or nature. This is a unitary world, consisting in a plurality of permanently existing objects in space, whose activities in time are uniformly related to one another. The Æsthetic does not contradict this, if we conceive space and time, not as passive forms, but as active functions of arrangement (as Kant certainly intends), and then add the thesis of the Analytic that the understanding, in accordance with its own laws, determines the exercise of these functions. Hence all unity in the empirical world proceeds from the highest principle of unity, namely, the transcendental unity of apperception. The understanding is the faculty of reducing all given multiplicity to the unity of the orderly world of appearance, which has its ultimate point of union in the necessary unity of consciousness.

This view, although self-consistent, is, however, inconsistent with another view which it encounters everywhere. The contradictory view may perhaps be termed empiricism. It maintains that objects and forces, temporal sequence and spatial order, are given ; they are not produced by the spontaneous activity of the subject, but must be given through experience. It is the same difficulty that confronted us above in the conception of synthetic judgments *a posteriori*,[1] and one that will come up again in the transcendental deduction. What helps Kant over this difficulty is mainly the dogmatic form of his investigation, which proceeds under the guidance of the schematism. After he had made the great discovery of 1770, which was later embodied in the *Critique* without alteration, that 'pure perceptions' can have objective validity, he raises the question whether 'pure concepts of the understanding' also possess objective validity. And the possibility of an affirmative answer to this question is furnished by the same schema; the latter are conditions under which alone objects can be thought, as the former are the only ones under which they can be perceived. Kant remains content with this schematic solution and makes no genetic examination. In the first edition, he does indeed make an attempt at such an investigation in the 'psychological' deduction, but he discards it in the second. We have here to do only with a transcendental, and not with a psychological investigation. The magic word 'transcendental' excuses one from a concrete examination of facts.

(1) *The Analytic of Concepts and the Transcendental Deduction*

In accordance with the schema of the formal logic described above, the Analytic is divided into two books. The first treats of *concepts*, the second of *principles* (which ought to be called *judgments*), while the Dialectic follows as the doctrine of *syllogisms*. No one will assert that the Analytic has gained in clearness by this division. The real subject with which it deals is the *a priori* and objective validity of judgments, especially of certain of the more universal principles

---

[1] See p. 146.

of natural science. The introduction of the pure concepts of the understanding under the title of 'categories' is calculated to divert attention from the real problem, and to render the deduction more difficult to understand. Obviously, the introduction of this schematization is due to Kant's attachment to the old rationalistic ontology with its fixed and ready-made concepts — substance and inherence, cause and effect, possibility, reality, and necessity. His lectures upon the metaphysics of the "excellent analyst," Baumgarten, lead to the analysis of these concepts, and upon these analyses the Analytic in its new meaning fell back, leaving to a future system of pure reason the completion of the analysis. We turn now to the two parts of the problem, or in other words to the two deductions.

The *metaphysical deduction* of the pure concepts of the understanding is not introduced under this technical name as a heading (this is incidentally used later on in the beginning of § 26), but under the frightful title "Of the Transcendental Clue to the Discovery of all Pure Concepts of the Understanding — First, Second, and Third Sections," almost as if the author had set himself to confuse the reader. The substance of the matter is as follows. When, first, all empirical content is separated from objects, and, secondly, the pure forms of perception, space and time, are left out of consideration, there still remains a residue, the schema, as it were, of their thinkability, — thing and property, force and effect, reality and possibility, etc. The point involved is to make sure of an exhaustive and systematic list of these elements (an inquiry that was of course just as necessary in the case of the forms of perception, but one which, however, was not instituted at all in that instance, for space and time were assumed without more ado as the sole two possible forms). Kant attains this aim by following the track of formal logic. Formal logic seeks to ascertain all formal differences in judgments. Judgment is the peculiar function of the understanding. Hence the fundamental forms of the activity of the understanding can be fully gathered from formal logic. In this way, by somewhat supplementing and adapting the schema of formal differences in judgments which logic establishes, he reaches the celebrated 'table' of twelve categories; and afterwards he never grows tired of following this *a priori* arrangement for every possible and impossible scientific investigation.

There is no interest in following out in detail the minute artifices by means of which the table of the four classes, quantity, quality, relation, and modality, is provided in each case with three categories. Adickes has made the attempt to show the discussions and variations in the text-books on logic that Kant had in mind in this undertaking.[1] Schopenhauer is of the opinion that the twelve categories are all blind windows, with the exception of one, the category of causality. I would make an exception of still another one, the category of substantiality. As a matter of fact, it is these two which Kant regularly cites when he gives instances of the categories. In the systematic representation of principles we shall again meet with the attempt to put some meaning into the others. Moreover, the question also could be raised whether Kant, on the other hand, may not have omitted logical forms that do lay claim to real ontological validity. Laas raises the question with regard to the principle of contradiction, which is also regularly stated as an ontologically valid principle.[2] And where are identity, difference, and similarity? It is also worthy of note that no use whatever is made of the real form of conceptual thought, systematic superordination and subordination. That is employed for the first time in the doctrine of method. In general, it can be said that in Kant's theory of knowledge conceptual thought with its form, classification, does not receive its due; he looks only

---

[1] Kant's *Systematik*, pp. 32 ff.   [2] *Analogien*, pp. 34 ff.

at the arrangement of things in the perceptual connection in space and time, and not at their arrangement in the conceptual system.[1]

We turn now to the *transcendental deduction*, the most difficult thing, according to Kant's own statement, that has ever been undertaken in behalf of metaphysics.

The point to be demonstrated is that the pure concepts of the understanding have objective validity on account of the fact that they are the determinants of all objects of possible experience. Or, in another formula, the laws of the activity of the understanding are at the same time laws of nature. It can be said also that the logical categories are at the same time ontological categories; and this suggests Hegel's identification of logic and metaphysics, which grew out of this thought.[2]

The demonstration rests upon two points : (1) All synthesis of the manifold in sensation proceeds from the spontaneous activity of the subject; the faculty of this spontaneous synthetizing is called understanding. (2) Objective reality, or nature as a unity of objects, first arises when the understanding reduces the manifold to the unity of experience. And the conclusion is that the functions of the understanding are constitutive for objective reality, or that the formulæ which express the activity of the understanding are at the same time objectively valid laws of nature.

Kant repeatedly takes a disjunctive proposition as the starting-point in the demonstration. For objective validity to be confidently attributed to concepts, either the

---

[1] Many attempts to sketch the schema of categories are to be found in Erdmann, *Reflexionen*, II., pp. 149 ff. Here the logical principle of subordination is also employed (No. 483).

[2] The formula does not appear in the *Kr. d. r. V.*, but Kant is not unfamiliar with it; see Erdmann, *Reflexionen*, II., Nos. 159, 1170; *Fortschritte der Met.* VIII., p. 520. In the lectures on metaphysics likewise the doctrine of categories was treated under the title of ontology; see Pölitz, *Kants Vorlesungen über Met.*, pp. 20 ff.

concepts must depend upon the objects, or conversely the objects upon the concepts. A third possibility, the accidental concurrence of a conceptual system that the understanding spontaneously creates, with the inner uniformity of reality itself, in other words, the preformation system, or system of the pre-established harmony of thought and being, is ruled out as an arbitrary supposition. But the first possibility also cannot hold. If all objective validity of concepts proceeded from the fact that concepts depended upon objects, there would be nothing but empirical rules. Such rules, however, could never furnish universality and necessity; and all natural laws, even the most universal, as the law of causality, would then be merely presumptively universal valid rules. Nor would there be any fixed point whatever in the sciences that deal with reality. Empiricism logically carried out is scepticism. Since the latter is impossible, there remains only the second alternative. That is, objects depend upon concepts; or the understanding does not come to know natural laws from experience, but prescribes them to nature.

The matter may be conceived in this way: If there were no understanding, there would be for us no nature either, but only a "throng of sensations," — a multiplicity of unrelated and isolated impressions of sense. The fact that we perceive reality as a unitary plurality of permanent things, as a cosmic whole, subject to uniform laws, is not a consequence of the constitution of reality in itself, which may or may not be unitary and regular (for reality in itself, with its conformity to law, does not pass over into our ideas); neither is it a consequence of our sensibility, which rather conveys to us genuinely separate elements in all sorts of order or disorder. It is rather the act of the understanding, which imposes its unity and regularity upon the given elements of sense-perception, and thereby creates the unitary world of experience.

I shall not enter further into the many variations with which Kant, with wearisome repetitions, presents this idea. I only add the remark that the idea itself, in its universality, is thoroughly justified. Undoubtedly nature, as we perceive and think it, as a system of unitary, permanent things bearing a reciprocal relation to one another, is not conveyed into our consciousness through the senses, but is created by the activity of the understanding. The eyes and ears convey to us separate fragments of perceptions, as they do to animals also. Out of these, the understanding, by reflecting and inquiring, ordering and supplementing, makes the totality of related things that we call nature. We hasten to add that this is, of course, not to be taken as meaning the understanding of the single individual, but the intellectual activity of the generations that are united in the unity of the historical life. It is this which first creates a primitive system of concepts in the words of a language, and later produces in philosophy and science an ever more complete system of reality. If the world, as we now represent it, is in extent and form other than the world of the ancient and mediæval philosophers, this is without doubt the consequence of all the intellectual labor that has in the meantime been expended. The mathematicians and astronomers, the physicists and chemists, have constructed our world; the manner in which it is at present manifested to the senses in no wise differs from that of two thousand years ago.

I return now to say a word further about two points, both of which were touched upon at the beginning. The first is, as it was designated by Kant himself, the psychological or subjective deduction, in distinction from the metaphysical and transcendental. It is the attempt to describe the course by which the understanding determines sense-perception, or to exhibit the "subjective sources" which render the understanding and its activity possible. The first edition furnishes a thorough treatment of this point. It constitutes the main part of the second section on " the doctrine of the threefold synthesis, the synthesis of apprehension in perception, of reproduction in imagination, and of recognition in the concept." The unification of the manifold in perception, which constitutes the essence of empirical knowledge, presupposes: (1) The comprehension of many sensational elements in a unitary perception in space and time. This is possible only by means of spontaneity; that is to say, by means of the *a priori* function of positing the elements in serial form in space and time. (2) This function further presupposes the reproductive synthesis of the imagination; *i. e.*, the capacity of holding fast the elements and their connections, and of recognizing them again as the same; without this capacity no comprehension of the manifold in lasting unities would be possible. (3) The final presupposition is the conception of this union of the manifold as determinations of a unitary object. Only when this has taken place, do we have real or objective knowledge; for this requires us to conceive the many elements as aspects or activities of one and the same object. This unitary object, the bearer of the multiplicity, is not something of definite content; it is a mere X, the counterpart of the formal unity of consciousness in the synthesis of the manifold. And hence this unity of self-consciousness is the prime and absolute condition of all objective knowledge. Where there is no real self-consciousness, no consciousness of an Ego, there is no unitary world, no objective idea of the world possible. Self-consciousness and consciousness of a world, ego and non-ego, are correlates. The animal lacks both the consciousness of self and the consciousness of an objective world. It does not oppose itself as subject to the world as a unity of things; it does not distinguish the self and objects from the sensational and perceptual process, or by hypostatization transform its sensations into phenomena: it remains at the standpoint of the mere sensation.

An example may help to elucidate the matter. The eye receives sensations of light from a luminous point in the evening sky. The animal experiences the sensation of light as well as man, but in its case that is all. Man transcends the given sensation and interprets this shimmer as the light of a cosmic body, say of the planet Venus, for example. He first apprehends repeated sensations as the same light. Then, by the reproductive power of the imagination, he unites the present light in one place with the previous light in another place, and interprets them as the motion of the same luminous body in space and time. He finally relates the light to a permanent object, and defines the latter conceptually as a cosmic body of a certain magnitude, nature, and motion. All that rests upon the spontaneous activity of intelligence; not upon passive receptivity. If it is experience, then experience is essentially the work of the understanding,—not of the senses, as sensualistic empiricism maintains.

In the deduction of the second edition, this exposition, as Kant himself remarks in the Preface, is omitted, because it is not indispensable and the book would otherwise become too voluminous. Since this anxiety does not weigh upon him in other matters (many repetitions and many long schematic observations could be left out without detriment), it is permissible to conjecture that still another cause was at work. I think it was the desire to get rid of the somewhat delicate and equivocal explanation of the nature of the 'transcendental object.' This might appear to him now as an insidious approximation to the "good Berkeley," with whom he had been classified, much to his vexation (in the first review of the *Critique* by Garve-Feder). His own indecision regarding the limits of the activity of the understanding in determining sense-perception may also have been a motive. So he leaves that treatment entirely aside, and comprises the psychological deduction in §§ 24 and

25 in the treatment of the "productive power of the imagination." This undertakes to mediate between understanding and sense, which in the first edition was done by the
threefold synthesis. It asserts that every perception is
produced by constructive activity. I cannot represent any
line without drawing it in pure perception; I cannot represent a circle or cube except by constructing it; I am likewise unable also to represent any course of time, unless I
construct it under the schema of a moving point. Now all
spontaneity comes from the understanding; we may therefore say that the understanding manifests itself as everywhere active in perception itself, and that all perception
contains an intellectual in addition to the sensational factor.
And this constitutes the very moment by which it is qualified to take its place in a uniform system of nature. The
presupposition of the possibility of bringing phenomena
under rules is called by Kant the "affinity of phenomena."
We are able to bring or think phenomena under the laws of
the understanding only because the understanding is an
active formative power in sense-perception itself.[1]

---

[1] Although there is no Ariadne to furnish a thread, still, in order to proffer
consolation to the reader who finds himself entangled in the labyrinth of
Kant's presentations of the relation of spontaneity, or, of the understanding,
to receptivity or sense, I transcribe here a passage from a letter of Kant's to
Beck, of July 1, 1794. (It is among the Kant manuscripts in the Royal
Library at Berlin. Beck's interpretation of his theory was submitted to
Kant, and this letter is the answer to it. See Dilthey, "Die Rostocker Kanthandschriften," *Archiv für Gesch. der Philos.*, II., pp. 638 ff.) "We cannot
perceive the connection as given, but we must ourselves make it; we must
do the relating, if we are to represent to ourselves something as related (even
space and time themselves). It is solely in respect to this connection that we
are able to communicate with each other. The apprehension (*apprehensio*) of
the manifold given, and the act of taking it up into the unity of consciousness
(*apperceptio*) is the same as the idea of a related whole (*i. e.*, possible only
through the act of relating), if the synthesis of my representation in apprehension, and the analysis of it, so far as it is conceptual, give one and the
same idea (that is, mutually produce each other). And since this agreement lies neither in the representation alone nor in consciousness alone,
but is notwithstanding valid (*communicabel*) for every one, it is attributed to

The second point, in regard to which I wish to say a word further, is connected with this. It is the break, already mentioned, in the transcendental deduction, which must be apparent to every attentive reader. It occurs in both expositions. In the second edition, we are told at the close of the deduction [1] that the "pure faculty of the understanding is not competent by means of mere categories to prescribe any *a priori* laws to phenomena, except those which form the foundation of nature in general, as a uniform system of phenomena in space and time. Special laws, inasmuch as they relate to empirically determined phenomena, cannot be fully deduced from pure laws, although they all stand in a body under them." And a similar statement occurs at the conclusion of the deduction in the first edition : "Empirical laws, as such, can indeed in no wise derive their origin from the pure understanding," but they are only particular determinations of the pure laws of the understanding. And the same thing recurs in the deductions of the particular categories or principles. The principle of the permanence of substance is *a priori*, but in order to be able to apply the concept "one must base it upon the permanence of an empirically given object." The law of causality is *a priori*, but the occasion of its application must be given by observing regular empirical succession of time.

But with this the entire demonstration breaks in two. It rests upon the presupposition, with which § 15 began, that "every synthesis, whether it be a synthesis of the manifold content of perception or of conception, and, in the former

some thing binding on every one, but different from the subject, *i. e.*, to an object.

"I may say, as I am writing this, *that I do not at all adequately understand myself*, and I shall wish you joy if you are able to display these simple and slender threads of our faculty of knowledge in a sufficiently clear light. Such superfine splitting of hairs is no longer for me, for I cannot make even Professor Reinhold as clear as I should desire to myself."

[1] § 26, end.

case, whether of sensible or non-sensible perception, is an act of the understanding." "Synthesis does not lie in objects, and cannot be derived from them by means of perception, but it is solely a function of the understanding."— Whence, then, the need all at once of 'empirically determined' phenomena, for a knowledge of the laws of which experience must be superadded? Can laws be drawn from 'experience,' which do not have their source in the understanding? If such is the case, there would be syntheses of phenomena according to principles that originate in the receptivity of sense. If, however, that is the case, if synthesis in general can come from sense-perception, if the law of gravitation can be learned from experience and only from experience, why cannot the law of causality also?

In fact, it is impossible to rest here. One must either go further and adopt pure rationalism, which regards all physics as logically construable and demonstrable, as Spinoza does, or *a priori* deduces nature itself, as Hegel does. Or one must carry out pure empiricism, as Hume does, in intention at least, and say that all natural laws, all truths about matters of fact (in distinction from mathematical truths), even the most universal, are empirical laws. Of course we do not mean by this that nature impresses them upon the senses from without, but that the understanding forms them on the basis of the perceptually given connections in space and time, and tests their truth by reference to these. As the understanding in the case of Galileo and Newton constructed a formula by means of which the endless multiplicity of falling bodies given in space and time could be comprehended, it has likewise given rise to the law of causality. This, however, is not an absolutely pure and rigid law of the understanding, but has been framed with respect to the events that are perceptually given in space and time. And like the law of falling bodies, the law of causality also has been gradually developed by slow and arduous progression on the part of the understanding, until it has finally discovered its adequate formula for the physical world in the law of the conservation of energy. With the surrender of the absolute 'purity,' indeed, the absolute universality and necessity of the law of causality is also given up, and there is then no point whatever at which changes in the construction of phenomena might not be made necessary by continued work on the part of the understanding. Even the law of causality itself would then, as an empirically grounded law, be no more absolutely impervious to improvement through better and wider experience than the law of gravitation. But as the latter does not lose any of its value on account of such a mere possibility, neither does the former. It is the presupposition with which we approach all experience, and the mere conceivability that phenomena are possible which do not correspond with it, we can endure, without suffering any loss of confidence in our knowledge.

If Kant could have been convinced of the untenability of his standpoint, it is hard to say in favor of which side he would have decided. He certainly did not believe in the possibility of a pure logical and demonstrative physics ; and the supposition that he might have formed a higher opinion of the value of the speculative and dialectic method than he expressed about it on the first trials which he made, seems entirely excluded by his view of the nature of scientific knowledge. On the other hand, the overthrow of Hume's doubt of the absolute universality and necessity of the law of causality is a chief factor of his whole critical undertaking. To let that go would mean the surrender of his judicial point of view with regard to empiricism and rationalism. And hence the conclusion that Kant could never have convinced himself of the untenability of his mediating position, that the most universal laws of nature arise purely from the understanding, while special laws of nature come from experience, and with this equivocal conception the gap must be covered up.

(2) *The Analytic of Principles*

The general exposition and establishment of the contention that the forms of thought are constitutive for the phenomenal world, is followed in the second chief division by the exposition and establishment of the principles of the pure understanding in detail.   The clearness of the connection is not aided by the fact that this section is introduced as the transcendental doctrine of judgment, and that judgment, as a faculty of subsuming under rules, is distinguished from the understanding as the faculty which supplies rules.

The chapter on the Schematism of the Pure Concepts of Understanding prefaces the exposition of principles.   Its real purpose is to exhibit the logical modes of thought in the form that they assume as real or ontological categories of the phenomenal world.   In a certain sense they can be designated as the belated definitions of the pure concepts of the understanding, but, in the form that they assume, they are regarded as determining factors of perceptual reality. The matter is clearest in the case of the so-called categories of Relation, — Substantiality, Causality, and Reciprocity. The pure logical content of the category of substantiality is the inherence of the mark in the concept; this relation appears grammatically as the relation of subject and predicate.   The subject is the pure logical substance, to which the predicate is related as something inherent.   Now this same category appears in the real phenomenal world as the relation of the changing quality or activity to the permanent thing.   The logical relation of subsisting and inhering is here reduced to terms of sense in the temporal relation that exists between what changes and what is permanent. The logical content of the category of causality is the relation of ground and consequence; it manifests itself in thought as a relation of logical dependence. If A is, B also is, or if the judgment A is valid, the judgment B also is valid. This same category manifests itself in the real world as the regular succession of phenomena in time. Always, when c (the cause) or a combination of c, c_1, c_2, is present, e (the effect) is also present. Finally, the logical content of the category of reciprocity is the relation of the members of a logical division to one another. The species mutually determine themselves, in that they complete and divide among themselves the extent of the genus. In the real world this category assumes the form of the reciprocity existing between all parts of a totality, ultimately the form of the reciprocity of all space-filling bodies.

The schematization, or reduction to terms of sense, is less successful in the case of the remaining categories. This is due to the nature of these concepts, which were included only by force in the table of categories. I shall not enter into this, but simply add the Latin schema for all these determinations, which Kant inserted towards the close of the section, without, however, entirely carrying it through; I mean the words which in the old editions ran as follows: *Numerus est quantitas phœnomenon, sensatio realitas phœnomenon, constans et perdurabile rerum substantia phœnomenon, — œternatis, necessitas, phœnomena.* By correcting the mistakes and filling in the gaps, we should have the following schema for the definitions of the categories when reduced to sensuous terms or realized: *Numerus est quantitas phœnomenon, sensatio est realitas phœnomenon, constans et perdurabile rerum est substantia phœnomenon, successio regularis est causalitas phœnomenon, commercium physicum universale est influxus idealis universalis s. unio logica essentiarum phœnomenon, existentia aliquo temporeest possibilitas phœnomenon, existentia certo ac determinato tempore est realitas phœnomenon, œternitas s. sempiternitas est necessitas phœnomenon.*

We should have, according to this, really two tables of categories, — a pure conceptual one, and one reduced to sensuous terms; a purely logical, and a table of real categories. The categories of the latter table have objective validity for the phenomenal world. But how is it with the validity of the others? According to the actual argument of the Analytic, they receive real significance only through the fact that they enter into the form of the schemata, and thus determine phenomena. Outside the world of experience they have no significance whatever.

In connection with this, however, another thought presents itself. The pure forms of thought are not limited by sense-perception, but, on the contrary, limit sense-perception. They have in themselves validity for all things that can become objects of thought, and hence also even for things-in-themselves. And that is the older, and at bottom the prevailing mode of thought. It is dominant in the *Dissertation* of 1770. For there we are told that the understanding, through its pure logical concepts, thinks things as they are in themselves. The forms of our sensible perception have no significance for reality itself, since the latter is not in space and time; but our logical forms of thought do have transcendent significance; the real can be only such as it is conceivable for it to be, and what is not possible or conceivable cannot be real. Kant always adhered to this position in principle. The *Critique of Pure Reason*, to be sure, insists that the categories have the significance of real knowledge only in the field of experience, and that they are completely empty without the filling given by perception (and, it is to be remembered, sense-perception alone is possible for us). But, as a matter of fact, even in the Analytic the categories retain the position of transcendent thought entities. Thought extends further than phenomenal reality. And in the Æsthetic and Dialectic the pure logical categories of substance and causality are unhesitatingly applied to things-in-themselves, — in the former instance to explain causally the affection of the ego; in the latter, for the purpose of attributing to the ego causality according to freedom.

Kant's adherence to this is also obviously connected with his metaphysical doctrine of the Ego. The logical nature, understanding and reason, is really the ego-in-itself, while, on the other hand, time and space belong merely to sentiency, to the sense representation of the ego, which as phenomenal can pass away (at death). But there remains the ego as a pure thinking essence, free from space and time, a spaceless and timeless pure thinking spirit. And this is a thought, which, although not realizable in perception, remains nevertheless, a true and necessary idea.

The systematic exposition of synthetic principles follows the schema of the categories, but not without many forced steps. It shows a very varied content of *a priori* elements of knowledge under the four titles : Axioms of Pure Perception, Anticipations of Sense Perception, Analogies of Experience, and Postulates of Empirical Thought in General. If the subject-matter is freed from its connection with the table of categories, one can give to the first section (Axioms of Pure Perception) the heading "Transcendental deduction of mathematics;" to the two following sections (Anticipation and Analogies), the heading "Transcendental deduction of pure natural science;" to which the fourth section (Postulates) is attached as a general remark directed against realistic rationalism and its product, dogmatic spiritualism. That is the schema which Kant himself planned as the basis for the presentation of the *Prolegomena* in the three questions: (1) How is pure mathematics possible? (2) How is pure natural science possible? and (3) How is metaphysics possible? This really justifiable and obvious arrangement is here suppressed for the sake of the table of categories.

The first section (Axioms) contains the deduction of applied mathematics. Its principle is the proposition that all phenomena are extensive magnitudes. All phenomena are in space and time, and have, therefore, like them, extensity attaching to their nature, and along with extensity the derived determinations that they are measurable, divisible, and numerable. Hence they are subjected to the arts of measurement and computation; *i. e.*, geometry and arithmetic are applicable to phenomena. What these sciences find true for that which is in itself measurable and numerable, the pure space and time determinations, holds good also for all things so far as they are in space and time.

The proper place for developing this argument was the transcendental Æsthetic, and it is indeed indicated there under the title of the "transcendental exposition of space and time;" and the "general remarks on the Æsthetic" contribute much to its elaboration. I venture to specify a cause, rather than a logical reason, why its systematic development is deferred to the Analytic. The cause may have been the difficulty about finding a suitable content for the title of 'quantity' in the table of categories. This, to be sure, is also an arbitrary requirement. The quantity, which is equivalent to extension of perceptions, has scarcely anything but the name in common with the logical quantity of judgments (extension of the sphere of the concept).

The second section (Anticipations) contains the first factor of Kant's pure science of nature, namely, the transcendental basis of the dynamic theory of matter. The prevailing science of nature is mechanical. It begins by supposing that matter has no intrinsic differences, but is absolutely homogeneous, like the empty space in which it is contained. Consequently, all differences of bodies are referred to quantitative distinctions; *e. g.*, the different specific weight of bodies is accounted for by the different quantity of ultimate parts that are contained in equal volumes. A cubic centimeter of quicksilver contains thirteen times as much filled space as an equal volume of water. In opposition to this view, Kant contends that the proposition "that the real in space is everywhere the same in kind, and that it can be distinguished only on the basis of extensive magnitude, *i. e.*, of mass," is a pure metaphysical assumption. In opposition to it, one can with fully equal right set up another point of view, namely, that matter fills space without any gaps, but with different intensity. There is no empty space, but "the real has in the case of the same quantity[1] its degree (of resistance or of weight), which, without diminution of the extensive size or mass, can become less and less *ad infinitum*, before it[2] passes into the void and disappears."

To establish this contention, he refers to the fact that the real in space is that which corresponds with the sensation. Now, all sensation has, in addition to its extensity, also a definite *intensity*, or a degree ; it passes through a continuous gradation from zero to the definite intensity. Hence also the real itself, or matter, may have, not only extension (in space), but intensity also, and indeed a different degree in different spaces, though these are all continuously filled. The case is here stated only as a possibility ; the transcendental point of view liberates the understanding from the dogmatism of the mechanical and materialistic physicists, who are metaphysicians in spite of themselves. We shall see later how Kant makes use of this freedom in his natural philosophy.

It is evident enough, moreover, that here too it is only with difficulty that the content receives any relation to the schema of logical categories. The logical function of affirmation and negation has only a loose relation to the concepts of reality and unreality. But the difference between a

---

[1] Read *Quantität*, instead of *Qualität*.
[2] Read *es*, instead of *sie*.

mechanical and dynamical interpretation is connected with that starting-point only by means of the loosest threads of association, — reality — sensation — matter. The idea of the dynamic theory of matter had Kant's adherence, as we shall see further on, long before he had even the remotest notion of a transcendental deduction from the category of quality. And the place of quality in the schema of categories was likewise given before he knew what kind of a content he was to assign to it.

The third section (Analogies) is the most important. It contains the exposition of the fundamental laws of the pure science of nature, namely, the laws of substantiality, causality, and reciprocity.

The primary and basal law of physics is the proposition that "amid all change of phenomena substance is permanent, and the quantity of it is in nature neither increased nor diminished." The physicists, and ordinary common-sense also, have always assumed this proposition as a certain truth. But the question upon what its truth depends has not been raised. Is it based upon experience? Obviously not, for no one has balanced the quantity of all the matter that exists in the world at different times, and established its equality. Does it rest upon logical certainty? Just as little, for the proposition that matter neither comes into nor goes out of existence is not analytic, but synthetic. The judgment that a quantity of matter that existed yesterday exists no longer to-day, contains no logical contradiction. Hence the proposition, if it is to be proved at all, must be proved in a different way. Kant furnishes such a proof, namely, a transcendental one. Except on the assumption of the validity of this proposition, no experience is possible. The proof runs as follows: Experience is an aggregate of phenomena which are regularly conjoined in time. Now, the determination of a phenomenon in time is possible only if there is a permanent upon which all change is recorded, as upon a fixed background. If everything were in a process of absolute change, it would not be possible to determine change itself. Without the permanent there would be no fixed temporal relation of simultaneity and succession. Now, time itself is not such a permanent; neither can it be perceived. The absolute permanent is rather matter, and hence the unchangeableness of the quantity of matter, as the necessary condition of the possibility of experience, is proved in the only way in which it can be proved.

A critical exposition of this proof would direct attention to some such points as the following: Undoubtedly all temporal determination presupposes a permanent. The moving hand does not accomplish anything without a fixed dial-plate over which it moves. What is it that functions as a permanent for our real determinations of time? Is it perhaps the constant mass of matter? It appears not, but rather the uniform motions of the heavenly bodies. They constitute a dial-plate upon which we register all time determinations. Hence it is not necessary for these movements to be absolutely constant. If the movements of the planetary system, measured by those of the fixed stars, are not found to be absolutely constant, they are not on that account unsuited for the time determination of earthly processes. A relative permanence is sufficient for this purpose. The ultimate permanent, according to which we determine changes in time, will, from the nature of the case, never be anything more than an absolute permanent *for us*. A hand of a watch, the point of which took a hundred thousand years to advance the hundred thousandth part of a millimeter would be at a standstill for us. As far as the permanence of matter is concerned, however, at which we should never arrive in this way, the physicists would probably give us the following information about it: What is meant by the assertion is undoubtedly the observation that amid all changes of place, form, and total condition of bodies, the weight remains constant. If water apparently disappears by evaporation, more exact observation reveals the fact that it exists in the form of vapor with undiminished weight. All experiences of this sort are included in the one formula that the mass of matter remains constant. In truth, this is not a principle whose universality and necessity are proved, or really can be proved, either logically or by experience. For, if there were no other reason, in order to prove the constancy of the weight, the constancy of the weight of the weights employed must always be previously proved, and so on *ad infinitum*. The formula is consequently a presumption, a kind of *a priori* presupposition, framed on the basis of all previous experiences, and with which we approach all future experience. If any one wishes to contend that it does not correspond with the truth, — that, on the contrary, matter does come into being and pass away, in some particular instance or even continually, — the impossibility cannot be demonstrated to him. However, that would not seem to be a cogent consideration ; the weight of the presumption is great enough to counterbalance every contention that in a particular case matter has been lost, and to warrant us in asserting with *a priori* confidence that the alleged experience rests upon incomplete observation. And the inadmissibility of this confidence can never be shown. A proof that matter which has once existed can be nowhere found again in the universe, is absolutely impossible.

The second fundamental law of physics is the law of causality. Kant's formula is : " Everything that happens (begins to be) presupposes something upon which it follows according to a rule." The tortuous and wearisome demonstration, which is repeated in several forms, runs of course in the groove of the transcendental schema. The proposition can be proved neither logically (from concepts), nor empirically (by induction). Hence there remains only the transcendental proof that its universal validity is a necessary presupposition for the possibility of experience, *i. e.*, of the conception of nature as a systematic unity of phenomena.

The demonstration contains two moments : (1) The temporal sequence of perceptions in consciousness can be determined only by the objective order of phenomena in time. In other words, the sequence in the apprehension of inner processes is dependent on the regular sequence of natural processes. Hence the law of causality, or the constancy of the course of nature, cannot be deduced from the sequence of perceptions in the subjective stream of ideas (as Hume maintains), but is, on the contrary, the presupposition of its possibility. Or, in the language of the *Prolegomena*, judgments of experience cannot be derived from judgments of sense-perception, but, on the contrary, judgments of perception presuppose judgments of experience. (2) Moments of time stand in a necessary relation of succession. At every point in time the path goes through an *a priori* established time sequence; I can pass from the year 1800 to the year 2000 only by running back and forth through the intervening years of the series. What is true of empty time is true also of filled time, *i. e.*, of phenomena. Phenomena, therefore, also stand in necessary relations of temporal succession.

The important idea, which is here brought out distinctly for the first time, is the differentiation of the subjective train of ideas from the objective course of phenomena. In my subjective consciousness, a given perception may be followed by any other whatever. I perceive how some one shoots a ball on a billiard-table ; I see then the movement of his arms and legs, hear his exclamation, or the remark of a third person, etc. But any other succession of perceptions whatever can arise in my consciousness. In the objective world, on the other hand, in the world of phenomena, a stroke of

a definite force and direction is always followed by a movement of a definite size and direction. We have, then, in this
case strict uniformity ; from what does it come ? Evidently
it cannot be derived, says Kant, from the irregular and contingent sequence of perceptions in consciousness. Neither
can it arise from a transcendent arrangement of things-in-
themselves, which might supposedly be given to us. The
only thing that ever is given to us, however, is a perception. Hence the only alternative is that the regularity is
imposed upon the phenomenal world by the understanding.
The understanding is the principle of all uniformity. As in
the logical necessity of conceptual thought it recognizes
the uniformity of its own functioning, it likewise introduces the same uniformity into the world of phenomena,
and that constitutes the uniformity of nature. The subject
then finds that the uniform connection of nature is the presupposition also of the sequence of perceptions in consciousness. Every sensation is construed as the effect of a
stimulus according to natural laws, and its place in the
temporal course of the contents of consciousness is determined by relating it to corporeal movements in space (of
the hand of a watch, or the motion of the sun).

In all of this, Kant is undoubtedly altogether right in
opposition to sensationalistic empiricism and idealism,
which tend towards pure subjectivism. The distinction
between the subjective content of consciousness and the
objective world of appearance is necessary and important.
And it is undoubtedly true that every one regards the
temporal succession in subjective consciousness as contingent and conditioned, and the temporal succession of phenomena in nature, on the contrary, as uniform and as the
conditioning factor. Natural science is concerned solely
with the objective connection of phenomena.

On the other hand, if a criticism is in place here, the
question is not settled whether ultimately the objective

sequence of phenomena is not, nevertheless, derived from
the sequence of perceptions in consciousness. The laws
of mechanics express an objective succession of phenomena,
but the sequence of perceptions in consciousness is the presupposition of this order. We see, or we are convinced that
we could always see, that when two elastic balls collide,
a definite change in their motion occurs, corresponding with
the mass, velocity, and direction of the balls. Of course, it
is the understanding which formulates the laws, not, however, upon the basis of logical inference, but upon the
basis of the observed sequence. Prior to any sense-perception whatever, even the most perfect understanding
could not foresee the relation of the balls. Adam, even if
he were endowed with the keenest understanding, could
no more have foretold, when he was first created, that a
ball in rest would be set in motion on being struck by
a moving ball, than he could have foretold that it would
fall if he opened his hand. The observation of the sequence of given perceptions first furnishes the understanding with the material for the construction of those formulæ
which we call natural laws. Now, Hume argues, there is no
exception in the case of the law of causality, the first and
most general of all natural laws. The observation that
when we trace the succession of given perceptions, the
same events always occur after the same events, and under
the same conditions, forms the basis upon which the understanding constructs the general formula that the same
phenomena are regularly followed by the same phenomena. The truth of this formula rests upon the same
foundation as the truth of the laws of mechanics or of
gravitation, namely, upon their fitness to formulate the
given connections of phenomena in space and time. If
the law of causality were found to be unfit for this purpose, if upon the most exact observation it were found that
a certain impetus under altogether similar conditions gave

rise to different movements at different times, we should become suspicious of it and finally abandon it. That indeed would be a hard resolution to adopt. For the assumed uniformity of the course of nature is the only basis upon which it can be calculated; but for our thought this calculability is a "happy accident." It is logically conceivable that there may be a connection of phenomena in space and time which do not manifest any uniformity, or whose uniformity is so complex that our understanding is unable to grasp it. It is conceivable that there may be a cosmic system, the regularity of whose movements can never be discovered by us, although it could be understood by a more comprehensive perception and understanding. In like manner, a constitution of the perceptual world is conceivable whose uniformity our understanding never grasped. Then experience in itself would be possible, but impossible for us. Hence the axiom for the "possibility of experience" does not serve the purpose. The causal law must have another foundation, and that is its factual adequacy for the comprehension of given phenomena and their connection in time.

It is thus, indeed, not an absolutely necessary and universal law, but, like all natural laws, a principle whose universality is merely presumptive. Kant would here retort that by this statement we are plunging into the bottomless abyss of scepticism, which destroys all the certainty of knowledge, and in the last analysis leaves only associations, such as those which animals possess. The physicist, however, would not, I think, let himself become disquieted by this, but would reply that the proof of the causal law as an axiomatic presumption, constructed by the understanding upon the basis of all previous experience, is entirely adequate for his purposes. He may pass over the assertion that the causal law has been deviated from in a particular case, with precisely the same confidence with which Kant passes over the pos-

sibility that more exact observation may contradict the
universal uniformity.   Indeed, he will not let himself be
diverted by fruitless anxieties from that well-established and
indispensable axiom, and be induced to assume a "miracle."
The impossibility of an explanation in accordance with natural laws can never be demonstrated.   Moreover, another
thing must be added.   The pure *a priori* establishment of
the causal law in its merely universal form is no advantage
whatever for the purposes of the physicist.   Since Kant,
nevertheless, appeals to experience for the particular laws,
to the observation of the given time sequence ("temporal
succession is the sole empirical criterion of causal relation;"
"knowledge of actual forces can be only empirically given,"
etc.), all physical laws, with the sole exception of this
"fundamental principle," remain mere empirical propositions.   Hence they lack strict universality and necessity.
One can say only that if this law is a causal law, it is
universal and necessary; but one can never absolutely establish that proposition, since perception of temporal succession
is the only criterion.   Every observation can, indeed, be
corrected by succeeding observation.

In conclusion, I regard as fruitless Kant's effort to iso-
late certain most universal principles from their connection
with natural laws, and to base them solely upon the nature
of thought.   The law of the conservation of energy has been,
in the same sense as all the other laws of physics, constructed by the understanding with reference to the given
connections of phenomena in space and time.   And its
validity, from an epistemological point of view, is not different in kind from that of all other propositions about
matters of fact.   It is not associated with the principles of
pure mathematics, but belongs to the sphere of natural laws,
whose validity rests upon their adequacy to explain given
phenomena.

I shall merely mention the third Analogy.   It is the prin-

ciple that all substances, in so far as they are coexistent,
exist in a state of reciprocity; or, in other words, that the
universe is a unitary system. This is a presupposition with
which physics does, as a matter of fact, approach the investigation of reality. It assumes that there is no absolutely
isolated or inert reality. That which is not active does not
exist. The form of the proof is analogous to the two previous demonstrations. As permanence of matter is necessary
for the perception of the duration of time, and the validity
of the causal law for that of succession in time, the validity
of this principle, likewise, is necessary for coexistence to be
an object of possible perception. It seems to me that the
proof could have been more obviously drawn from the nature of space, as the proof in the case of the second analogy
was drawn from the nature of time. All spaces are recipro-
cally determined, hence also filled spaces or phenomenal
substances.

I may add here a remark about Kant's view of the content of the causal relation. He has not developed this in a
connected way. His view does not diverge far from Hume
on the one hand, and from Leibniz on the other. Causality
in the phenomenal world signifies for Kant, as for Hume,
nothing but regularity in the sequence of phenomena. Real
causal efficiency cannot of course occur here, for phenomena
are ideational products. As such they can no more produce
an effect than concepts can. But, as concepts logically determine one another, phenomena likewise can mutually determine their place in space and time. Or, more precisely, the
place of each one in space and time is determined with relation to that of all the others. On the other side, Kant conceives of the intelligible causality of things-in-themselves,
which indeed can produce a real effect, after the pattern of
the Leibnizian pre-established harmony. The *noumena* stand
in the divine understanding in a relation which one can
designate as an *influxus idealis*. They determine one an-

other, like the parts of a work of art, with logical and teleological necessity.

The fourth section, the Postulates of Empirical Thought in General, furnishes a content for the fourth class of the table of categories, but this, like the former cases, is effected only at the cost of great trouble. It does not contain new natural laws, but a criticism of realistic rationalism concerning the use of the expressions, "possible," "real," and "necessary." The old rationalism gave to what was merely conceivable the predicates "possible" and even "real." Thus Descartes based the "reality" of his spiritualistic concept of the soul as an *ens mere cogitans* solely on the conceivability of such a being. I can form a clear and distinct idea of it. And likewise the reality of the concept of body as *res extensa*, and of God as the *ens realissimum*, is founded on their conceivability. The case is the same with Spinoza. An idea is true, not on account of its agreement with an object, but because it possesses *denominationes intrinsecas* of a true idea; that is, inner possibility or conceivability. And likewise Leibniz assigns to what is conceivable, if not complete reality, nevertheless a kind of semi-reality, namely, that of possibility. And he holds that the possible may become real; that is, if its reality does not conflict with another *possibile*. In the language of his metaphysics, everything possible or conceivable becomes actual, in so far as it possesses, in addition to its inner possibility, compossibility also with all other realities.

Kant by his 'Postulates' puts an end to these attempts at a magical production of reality out of a pre-existing conceptual world. That which may claim the predicate "real" must be given in perception, or be inferred from previous perception under the guidance of natural laws. That which may claim the predicate "possible" must be capable of being given in possible experience. Without reference to perception, therefore, pure thought as such is in no condition whatever to treat of the real and the possible.

The point of the discussion is directed against spiritualism, which subscribes to the doctrine of soul-substances that occupy no space. Such a thing can never be an object of experience. And therefore it is neither a real nor even a merely possible being, but a pure creation of thought. It remains to be noted that we are here, of course, concerned with empirical reality, not with a transcendental or intelligible reality, which may, nevertheless, belong to such creations of thought.

In the second edition, Kant included in this discussion the Refutation of Idealism, which may also be positively described as the proof of a 'formal materialism.' For our experience, there are no substances except space-filling matter. The corporeal world is the real world, and the only way in which I can interpret psychical processes or connect them with reality is by relating them to the corporeal world. For our scientific knowledge, therefore, they are a *posterius*, not the *prius*, as Berkeley held. But this, of course, does not exclude the view that the entire corporeal world exists only for the subject, which interprets it by means of its functions of perception and thought. 'Material' materialism, which fails to remember this, is just as false as the 'material' idealism of Berkeley. This observation would have been quite natural at any rate, but Kant was very sensitive on this point, ever since he had been included with Berkeleian idealists. He did not want to have anything at all in common with Berkeley.

(3) *Phenomena and Noumena*

With the systematic presentation of the synthetic principles, the exposition of the new positive epistemology is brought to an end. It has been shown how the form of the objective world is created by the synthetic functions of intelligence, and how an *a priori* knowledge of it is thereby rendered possible. The introduction to the following section clearly marks this termination: " We have now not only traversed the domain of the pure understanding and carefully examined every part of it, but we have also measured its extent, and assigned to everything therein its proper place." But, Kant continues, the geographer or describer of this land cannot yet regard his task as finished; for it is an island, "surrounded by a wide and stormy ocean, where many a fog-bank and many an iceberg that soon melts away seems to the mariner, on his voyage of discovery, a new country, and, while constantly deluding him with vain hopes, engages him in dangerous adventures, from which he can never desist, but which he can never bring to a termination." Hence the geographer of this land of truth is obliged, for the sake of the future voyager in these regions of ideas, to make a chart also of the oceanic surroundings with their illusive countries. This is the task of the Dialectic.

Two small sections are inserted between the Analytic and the Dialectic. They settle accounts between critical or phenomenalistic idealism and realistic idealism. They may be described as the introduction to the Dialectic.

The first section, on the "Division of all Objects into Phenomena and Noumena," contains Kant's critical discussion of Plato, the first founder of idealism. Beyond the corporeal world, which the common understanding takes as the truly real world, Plato posits another world as the really real, namely, the world of ideas. Corporeal things, he found, these particular trees and men, cannot be the truly real. They are constantly involved in a process of becoming and passing away. Therefore they *are* not. On the other hand, amid the change of individuals, the universal form, the type, remains. Therefore it really *is*. Individuals are apprehended by sense; the universal form is conceived by the understanding. Therefore one can say also that the real world is the world as it is for the understanding. The world as it is represented by the senses is mere appearance, a fleeting shadow-image of the pure essence. Thus we have the division of things into αἰσθητά and νοητά, into a *mundus sensibilis* and a *mundus intelligibilis*.

In this distinction, Kant says, Plato is quite right. It is the beginning of all sound philosophy to recognize that bodies are not the absolutely real, but only mere appearances. But he is wrong in holding that the *mundus intelligibilis* is the real object of the knowledge of the understanding. On the contrary, it is the *mundus sensibilis* to which the human understanding is adapted. Its concepts have value for knowledge only as functions for the construction of phenomena. If there were no phenomena, concepts would be just as meaningless as eyes would be if there were nothing to see, or ears if there were nothing to hear. Accordingly, the concept of a noumenon cannot be used in the positive sense, as Plato employs it, of the real as it is known by means of the understanding. It has merely a negative significance: non-phenomenon. Nevertheless it is a necessary concept, necessary, that is, "in order to limit the pretensions of sense-perception." Sense-perception has the tendency to posit its knowledge as absolute. The common understanding also does so, since it regards its perceptions as absolutely real things. And the materialistic philosopher with systematic dogmatism likewise does so when he maintains that corporeal substances are in themselves real, and more, the only thing that is in itself real. As opposed to this point of view, it is necessary to remember that reality which is given in perception is only phenomenal. And of this we are reminded by the concept of the *mundus intelligibilis*.

(4) *The Amphiboly of the Concepts of Reflection*

This section contains Kant's critical account of Leibniz. Three times does Kant here repeat his criticism of the chief points of the ontological system of the old monadology. These repetitions show clearly that the section was compounded of loose fragments written at different times. The common source of the errors of Leibniz's ontology, Kant finds in the fact that he intellectualized phenomena, *i. e.*, that he traced bodies back to intelligible things (monads), and created his ontology for these. Such a system may be suitable for intelligible things, but not for sensible things, to which he nevertheless applied it. Take the principle of the *identitas indiscernibilium*. Of course, in the conceptual world two completely similar things are identical. There cannot be two concepts with the same content. But that does not prevent two things in the perceptual world from being completely similar without coinciding. Likewise, in the conceptual world real determinations are not annulled. In that sphere only logical contradiction nullifies. But in the perceptual world there are real determinations that are cancelled which do not involve a logical contradiction, *e. g.*, two moving forces which act upon a certain point in opposite directions. Lastly, the monadological treatment of the concept of substance and of space and time is criticised. The fact that Kant evidently intended to utilize the table of categories for this criticism, though he did not carry out his design, prevented a coherent and detailed critique of Leibniz. It would not have been at all superfluous for Kant to have discussed, above all, the concept of a substance with inner determinations. However, Kant returns to this point under the title of 'Paralogisms.'

(5) *The Method of the Critical Philosophy*

I propose at this point to insert a remark on the question of the form of the knowledge of the *a priori*. It has been for a long time the object of lengthy discussions. The controversy is as much over the *quæstio facti* as over the *quæstio juris*. On the one side it is maintained that Kant gets the knowledge of the *a priori* from experience, although he does not acknowledge its experiential origin, or carry it out from this standpoint. In this respect, therefore, he stands in need of correction and completion. This view is represented especially by J. Fr. Fries. On the other side it is contended that the knowledge of the *a priori* must be itself knowledge *a priori*, and that it cannot be discovered in experience; that Kant's investigation is not an empirical and psychological or anthropological one, but transcendental in character. Kuno Fischer and Cohen maintain this view.[1]

There is no doubt that Kant wishes utterly to disregard the empirical and psychological basis of his investigation. If the knowledge of the *a priori* rested upon experience, all that the *Critique* has gained would be lost, and there would be no pure knowledge at all, but only empirical knowledge. The necessity and universal validity of the principles of mathematics and of pure natural science could not then be saved, and the possibility of real science in general would be denied. At any rate, the possibility of philosophy would be disallowed; for it, as far as its notion is concerned, is nothing else than pure rational knowledge derived from concepts.[2] Corresponding with this, Kant everywhere claims for his system apodictic certainty and systematic completeness. With these the system stands or falls. Hence it is self-evident that it can no more be based upon experience, upon

---

[1] J. B. Meyer, *Kants Psychologie* (1870), pp. 5 ff., gives a survey of the history of this controversy.

[2] See above, p. 109.

inner, anthropological experience, than upon sense observation. The ultimate bases must be rational truths. Since the bases of the system of metaphysics are the *a priori* forms of sense-perception and of thought (upon which the possibility of a system of rational knowledge depends), the principles which express the *a priori*, metempiric, and transcendental character of space, time, and the categories, must themselves possess certainty of some other kind than empirical certainty. They must be rational truths.

It is obvious that this is what Kant intends. The point is raised, however, that as a matter of fact he has reached these *a priori* elements by empirical means; namely, by means of reflection over actual perception and thought. The process of the long search and the final discovery of the categories is carried out before our eyes (in the *Reflections*). And there can be just as little doubt that the proposition that human perception has the form of spatiality and temporality is an anthropological generalization.

What attitude would Kant adopt towards this problem ? I think one might from his standpoint make the following statement: It is true that we become conscious of the functions of thought and perception on the occasion of their exercise. We can also say that they themselves do not exist as innate and fixed forms, but are constructed along with the sensation itself. And, further, the human mind attains distinct notions of them only at a high stage of development. Complete clearness in regard to them is reached, however, only by means of critical reflection, the result of which is given in the Æsthetic and Analytic. The fact that this insight is gained by reflection does not at all deprive them of their rational character. Even the principle of contradiction has been discovered by reflection upon the nature of thought, but it does not on that account become an empirical truth. As soon as the understanding thinks it, it thinks also its necessity, and sees in the principle the nature of conceptual thought, or its own nature. Now, the case is similar with the categories or with the synthetic principles. In them too the understanding comprehends its own nature. By reflection upon its activity, which exists for it in its product, the sciences, it recognizes in the principles the form of its activity, which is the constructive principle of objective knowledge. In the axioms of geometry, it formulates its constructive principles of space, and, since it formulates them, it becomes sure of their universality and necessity. In the principles of the pure science of nature, we have just such axiomatic principles, which the understanding, since it formulates them, immediately recognizes as the principles of its constructive activity in the sciences, and thereby perceives their universality and necessity. Hence they as well as the mathematical principles are rational truths. Mathematical propositions are also discovered in time on accidental occasions. But their mathematical existence does not rest upon that fact, but on the fact that they are conceived and demonstrated. Hence they are rational truths. Likewise the rationality of the *a priori* is also entirely consistent with its discovery by reflection.

One may admit the validity of this observation. Rational truths do not lose their character because they arise some way or other in empirical consciousness. Otherwise there would be no such truths at all. But the question remains whether Kant is right in maintaining that the principles of " pure natural science " have a rational character in the same sense as the propositions of pure mathematics, or those of formal logic. It is this point that in my opinion is rightly contested. If with Kant we start from reflection upon the form of the sciences, there arises an essential difference between the form of pure mathematics or logic on the one side, and of physics on the other. In the former case, it is by pure thought that the truth of the propositions is established; they are deduced as logical consequences. In the latter case, on the contrary, we have to reckon with an irrational factor, which renders it impossible to decide upon the truth of propositions by means of mere immanent reflection; we must consult sense-observation. And this irrational factor does not disappear even in the ultimate principles. It is attached to the laws of biology and chemistry, and likewise to the laws of mechanics, and even to the principle of the conservation of matter and of energy. It is a presupposition, of the highest degree of probability and trustworthiness, which we make about the course of nature, but it is not of a purely rational character, like the principle of contradiction. We cannot think that concepts and judgments have a relation other than the one we formulate in the law of contradiction, or that the conclusion is not valid if the premises are valid. In this case, the understanding is entirely in its own sphere. But we can think, *in abstracto*, that a change may occur without following upon another according to a rule. Kant would say that it certainly may be thought from the standpoint of pure logic, since there is no formal contradiction, and since the law of causality is a synthetic principle. But, he would urge, the understanding cannot think it without destroying itself, and without allowing the sciences to become a prey to scepticism. But it may be replied to this, that that is just the question. Hume maintains, and many physicists will believe him, that the sciences extend just as far with the presumptively valid principle as with the *a priori* and absolutely valid principle. What they need is a working maxim for their investigation, and they have that in the law of causality or the principle of the uniformity of nature, even if it is not a law of the pure understanding, but merely a principle constructed by the understanding on the basis of the datum, and found to be useful.

Kant shows in regard to this point a fatal tendency to think in a circle. What Hume doubted was the strict (not the presumptive) universality or necessity of all judgments of fact, and hence also that of the propositions of physics or of applied mathematics. Kant undertakes to demonstrate this universality and necessity in opposition to Hume, but really he keeps continually presupposing them. In the concept of science as such, according to him, the apodictic character, the universality and necessity, is contained as an essential mark. Whoever denies that scientific principles possess this character is maintaining that there can be no real science : he is a sceptic. But scepticism is contradicted by the existence of the sciences, *i. e.*, the mathematical sciences of nature. Therefore the necessary presuppositions of the possibility of science are proved to be valid, *i. e.*, the *a priori* and transcendental nature of the categories, or the pure rational character of the most universal and fundamental principles is established. And then, conversely, the *a priori* principles guarantee the universality and necessity of the sciences.

If one places himself at the standpoint of evolutionary biology, the question about the general character of the *a priori* assumes a different aspect. One will then probably reach the following view : The perception of space and time, which can now be regarded as an *a priori* endowment of the individual, has been developed, along with the brain and the sense organs, in the life of the species. And the same holds true of the functions of thought, which in their fundamental features are now perhaps inherited with the brain organization, and developed by the categories of language. And association would then be regarded as the primitive form of the connection of phenomena, out of which active thought had gradually arisen, as it still arises from it in the development of the individual. And it would further follow that a future metamorphosis of the forms of perception and thought would not be beyond the range of what is conceivable and possible.

VI. THE TRANSCENDENTAL DIALECTIC

Analytic and Dialectic are respectively opposed to each other as the proof of scientific and the critique of pseudo-scientific metaphysics. The former is the "pure natural science," the latter the traditional school metaphysics with its speculations about God, the world, and pure spirits. The task of the Dialectic is to show the impossibility of this metaphysics as a dogmatic science.

- In this we have the announcement of a significant turning-point in the history of philosophy. The old school philosophy took its character from theology. The philosophical faculty and its instruction served as a general preparatory school of theology. The old phrase *philosophia ancilla theologiæ* still had its meaning for the Wolffian philosophy, although the handmaid liked to appear rather independent, sometimes even domineering, and thereby caused much trouble for her old mistress. Nevertheless, the final aim of the Leibnizio-Wolffian metaphysics was to lay the basis for religion and theology. The metaphysics developed by Kant in the Analytic could be better described as *ancilla physicæ*. It is based on Newton's mathematical science of nature. Kant utterly rejects on principle a speculative metaphysic as a substructure for theology. His philosophy really undertakes to secure the foundation of religious belief solely by means of ultimate reflections upon the nature of knowledge.

In the Dialectic, then, he undertakes to show the impossibility of theologizing metaphysics. And at the same time he seeks to establish the conviction that the destruction of the old metaphysical substructure for theological dogmatics is not a loss, but a gain, for religious belief. An unstable foundation does not support, but endangers the structure erected upon it. Theologizing dogmatism always produced scepticism as its counterpart, which made it a business to undermine the fundaments of faith that were laid by the

philosophy of right intentions. And as this effort, from
the nature of the case, must necessarily be successful, the real
effect was that religion too was drawn into the ruin of the
dogmatic philosophy. Or, without metaphor, the proofs of
religion by well-meaning philosophy called forth the criticism
of the understanding, whose freedom had been threatened.
And the ever victorious criticism of the proofs shattered also
belief in the conclusion. Fallacious proofs are always a
danger even for a good subject.

In place of the old unreliable fundaments, Kant even here
refers to another, and in his conviction an absolutely trustworthy support for religious faith. It is the incontrover-
tible facts of the moral self-consciousness. The consciousness
of duty, of vocation, of the worth of spiritual and moral
goods, does not arise from the understanding, neither does it
depend upon proofs of metaphysics and natural philosophy.
But it is the expression of the inner nature of man himself.
Therefore it is not assailable by sceptical reflection. If the
continuance of religious belief is hereby secured, it rests
upon a foundation which cannot be shaken.

As a preliminary to the treatment of the particular parts
of the transcendent metaphysics, there is also here, in the
Introduction and the first book, a general discussion of the
origin, position, and meaning of the notions it employs.
Under the name of 'Ideas,' they, as the products of reason,
are contrasted with the categories as the products of the
understanding. For the sake of the *parallelismus membro-
rum*, one might assign to these sections the heading : Metaphysical Deduction of the Ideas. And this would then be
followed in the second book by the transcendental deduction
and the systematic presentation of the Ideas, the conclusion
of which is that a transcendental deduction is in this sphere
impossible.

When the deduction of the Ideas as necessary products of
the intellect is taken out of the logical schematism, which

contrasts them as the elements of the syllogism with the categories as the elements of judgment, it may be expounded in the following manner.

Knowledge conformable with the understanding, as it is systematized in the sciences, everywhere refers beyond itself. It always deals only with elements that are dependent upon others. Every space-image is limited and determined by other space-images, and these are in their turn limited and determined by others, and so on without end. The same is true of every period and every determination of time. But it is no less true of everything that fills time and space. Every motion, every action is caused by other motions and actions, and these in their turn by others, and so on *ad infinitum.* Consequently, every element of reality in the given phenomenal world is dependent upon others outside of it, which again are dependent upon others. The understanding can never get a firm footing: it sees itself ever driven from the conditioned to the conditioning elements, which are themselves in turn again conditioned.

To escape this unrest, the mind creates the concepts of the Infinite, Eternal, Unconditioned, and Absolute. Kant gives the intelligence in the exercise of this function the name of 'reason,' in distinction from the understanding, which always goes back to the antecedent conditioning factor. And the concepts which thus arise, he calls " Ideas." Reason, therefore, transcending the particular and relative, is by the necessity of its own nature forced to form the concept of the absolute. The relative cannot ultimately be without an absolute, the limited and finite without the encompassing infinite, the conditioned without an unconditioned. And hence reason puts itself at the standpoint of the absolute, and undertakes from that point of view to deduce the conditioned.[1]

[1] Erdmann, *Reflexionen*, II., 352 : " An Idea is the representation of the whole, in so far as it necessarily precedes the determination of the parts. It

Only with the attainment of this view-point, does knowledge reach its final goal. It can attain rest only in the absolute system, which proceeds from the absolute and develops from it all that is relative and conditioned. Perfect knowledge would be a philosophy which deduced the whole of reality from a unitary principle, a first being, which fashioned the world in accordance with Ideas. To deduce and comprehend the whole of reality from these creative Ideas would be knowledge in the absolute sense. As we do not know a book, a poem, or a work of art until we can develop all the particulars from the idea of the whole, we should likewise have complete knowledge of the world if we could develop the nature and order of all the parts from the idea of the whole. The philosophy of Plato, or Hegel, or Leibniz, is in truth the idea of perfect knowledge.

In this respect Kant is in thorough accord with realistic idealism. The idea of absolute knowledge is quite correctly defined by those philosophers. Their mistake is to think that they can produce, or indeed, like Hegel, that they have produced, a system corresponding with this idea. The human intellect can grasp the idea of perfect and absolute knowledge, but cannot carry it out. It is an idea, a concept, with which no corresponding object can be given in experience. The understanding assigns to itself the task of furnishing a system of world-science. But it is a task that never can be completed; for the infinite is and can never be given to the human understanding. It can, progressing further *in indefinitum,* conjoin phenomena in time and space, but it will never attain to the whole. Beyond every cosmic system, there remains a wider and more comprehensive sys-

can never be represented empirically, because in experience one passes from the parts through successive syntheses to the whole. It is the archetype of things, since certain objects are possible only through an idea. Transcendental ideas are those in which the absolute whole as such determines the parts in the aggregate or series."

tem. Beyond every period of evolution there remains an infinity of more comprehensive periods. And the case is exactly similar with regard to the task that speculative reason undertakes : to furnish a system of world philosophy, to explain reality from an idea of the whole, or the chief end of the creator. We are not as successful with our system of world-philosophy as with our system of world-science. The only indication for such an interpretation of the world is the moral world within us, which manifests itself for us as an absolute end. But we go wrong at every step, if from that standpoint we venture upon a teleological interpretation of history or nature.

The Ideas, however, retain their significance and necessity. They are problems, or demands, which serve as regulative principles to determine the employment of the understanding. The concept of the world-science, or the idea of reality as a unitary whole, determined in accordance with all-prevailing laws, instigates investigation, and leads to an ever-increasing extension and unification of experience. The concept of world-philosophy impels us to estimate rightly the value of our knowledge, and forces us to recognize the limitation of our knowledge, not only from the standpoint of its extension, but also from the standpoint of its significance. By comparing such knowledge as is possible for us with the idea of an absolute knowledge, we recognize the fact that science is not the final goal of human existence. Were it possible by means of science to realize that end, and to think the thoughts of the Creator, science would then appear as the most distinctive task of life. If it suffices merely to give us a slight acquaintance with the phenomena of our spatial and temporal environment, its importance declines in comparison with the practical and moral interests. The understanding and science become merely an instrument for higher purposes of life.

In the second book we have the systematic presentation

of the Ideas, together with a criticism, instead of the deduction. The subject matter is furnished by the schema of the disciplines of the old metaphysics, rational psychology, cosmology, and theology. The fourth discipline, the ontology, the true as well as the false ontology, was treated in the Analytic. (The latter was discussed in the two concluding sections.) Subsequently, the attempt was made to subordinate this given matter to the schema of the transcendental logic. As the Dialectic is construed as the doctrine of the syllogism, these disciplines, likewise, must submit to being brought by all kinds of artifices under the view-point of the categorical, hypothetical, and disjunctive syllogism. That this is all the idle play of a capricious scholastic subtlety, needs no elaboration. And it is just as little necessary to dwell upon the fact that the introductory remarks upon the nature and origin of the ideas, have meaning only for the theological and cosmological ideas. I shall proceed now to make a brief survey of the dialectical Ideas.

(1) *The Rational Psychology*

The critique of this discipline depends essentially upon the following points. People argue from the unity of the self-conscious subject to the simplicity of the soul substance. The soul cannot be a compound; hence it cannot be an extended thing; therefore it cannot be a material thing; consequently, it is a spiritual substance. As such it cannot be destroyed. A substance cannot be destroyed by division as far as its substantiality is concerned, but only in its form and connection. The soul substance cannot be divided into parts, hence it is imperishable, and, in the case of the identity of self-consciousness, immortal. — Kant, on the other hand, maintains that the soul is not given to us in perception, like the body, as a permanent object. The unity of self-consciousness is given solely in the act of relating the manifold of inner experience. Without perception of a permanent, the application of the category of substance has no meaning.

This view is in its entirety completely established. The concept of substance is constructed for the perception of the material world. In this field, the principle of the permanence of substance has its definite meaning. The mass of matter remains the same amid all changes of place, motion, and form. The sphere of inner psychic processes in no way affords an occasion for the establishment of a similar principle. The proposition that the substance of soul-entities is unchangeable in quantity, is a proposition without any meaning. The unity of self-consciousness is solely functional. — This destroys at the same time the metaphysical proof for immortality. Kant is right also when he contends that religious belief sustains no loss on that account; for it never rested upon cunning arguments, but upon the need of the heart.

(2) *The Rational Cosmology*

The critique of rational cosmology occupies the second main division, entitled "The Antinomy of Pure Reason." The discussion in this chapter is somewhat prolix, but it contains an important and early established element of the critical philosophy. The appearance of an intrinsic self-contradiction within reason itself, as Erdmann shows,[1] attracted Kant's attention as early as the sixties, and essentially influenced the development of the system of transcendental idealism. Only on the supposition that the world in space and time is merely phenomenal does the contradiction disappear. Thus, in the exposition of the Dialectic, the doctrine of the antinomies appears also as a supplementary confirmation of transcendental idealism. On the presupposition of realism, the contradictions are absolutely insoluble. Moreover, the critical philosophy ex-

[1] *Reflexionen*, II., p. xxxv.

hibits itself here most advantageously in the rôle of referee and arbitrator, which it assumes towards all preceding philosophy.

Unfortunately, in this case too the ideas are distorted by an irrelevant schematization, and sometimes are disfigured beyond the point of recognition.

The problems of infinity are the real point of departure for the discussion. Progressive synthesis of phenomena in space and time leads to the problem of the infinite, just as progressive analysis also does. Does analysis ever reach a point beyond which it cannot go ? Finally, tracing out causal connections, whether the procedure is progressive or regressive, leads to the problem of an infinite series. Rational cosmology had attempted to solve the problems by pure thought. But the result of these attempts was that reason became entangled in insoluble contradictions. It discovered, instead of one solution, two contradictory ones, and each seemed capable of being demonstrated with equal force. (1) The world is necessarily finite in space and time. — Its finitude is unthinkable. (2) The world is composed of ultimate simple parts. — The simple is unthinkable, and it is impossible to construct from the simple (unextended) the extended world. (3) The chain of the causal series must have a final link, upon which it depends. — There can be no link in the causal series that the understanding can regard as final, that it must not necessarily view as due to an antecedent cause. Thus reason itself is cleft in two, and necessarily affirms and denies the same thing. If it seeks to rest in the finite, thought contradicts it by reaching out beyond every arbitrary limit. If it strives to place itself at the standpoint of the infinite, thought proves ineffectual and perception contradicts it.

Instead of taking up these real and genuine problems as such, and for their own sake, and following them out to their logical conclusions, the exposition, in its present form,

goes off on a side line after another " System of Cosmological Ideas." There are four cosmological ideas that are
dialectic: (1) The idea of the creation of the world; (2)
the idea of the simple (the simplicity, spirituality, and
immortality of the soul) ; (3) the idea of freedom ; (4) the
idea of a necessary being. They are the same ideas, as
one may see, that Kant elsewhere brings forward as the
real object of all metaphysics : God (here treated separately
in (1) and (4)), Immortality, and Freedom. The doctrine
of the Antinomies, accordingly, contains all the dialectic
concepts of pure reason. It might have included the whole
Dialectic, even the critique of rational psychology (under
(2)), and theology. Nevertheless, these four ideas are here
patterned after the cosmological idea, and yoked to the
schema of categories. And thus Kant gets the following
four pairs of antithetical propositions, which are to progress
according to the categories of quantity, quality, relation, and
modality: (1) The world has a beginning in time, and is
limited in regard to space. — It has no beginning and no
limits. (2) It consists of simple parts. — There is no
simple substance in the world. (3) There is freedom, *i. e.*,
there are phenomena which cannot be accounted for by the
law of causality. — There is no freedom, but everything
happens in accordance with natural laws. (4) There is a
necessary being. — There is no necessary being.

And now it appears that in these four contrary theses, two
great tendencies of thought are opposed to each other, which
throughout the entire history of human thought have carried on a never ceasing struggle. They are the rationalistic
and dogmatic on the one hand, and the empiristic and
sceptical tendency on the other. One can also name them
the idealistic and the materialistic tendency. They are
pitted against each other in Greek philosophy, in Plato
and Epicurus. In modern times we have the same opposition in the theological philosophy of the Church, on the one

side, and, on the other, in the tendency that proceeds **from** the natural sciences, and is employed in this service; or, in the language of traditional censure, the philosophy of good intent and the philosophy of evil intent. The well-meaning philosophy, working in the interests of theology, demonstrated the necessity of the beginning of the world in time (creation), of simple essences (monadology, immortality), of the freedom of the will, and of a necessary being (God). The empiristic and materialistic mode of thought, which was based on the natural sciences, contested all of these things. It found that a beginning of the world in time, the spirituality and immortality of the soul, causeless events (of free will), and a necessary being, are simply things that are not given in experience. Hence they are unreal and chimerical. Hume, or the *Système de la nature*, here comes into conflict with Leibniz.[1]

---

[1] The composition of the doctrine of antinomies is a difficult problem that scarcely admits of a complete solution. It seems that the exposition is based upon a sketch which was early drawn up and originally worked out as an independent treatise. This, according to the original conception, was designed to include the whole dialectic, that is, Kant's entire critical discussion of the old metaphysics, in both its forms of dogmatic affirmation and dogmatic negation. The discussion was to embrace the following four heads: (1) The creation or infinity of the world; (2) Immortality; (3) Freedom; (4) God. The third and fourth sections of the doctrine of antinomies especially refer back to this earlier sketch. They clearly presuppose that the doctrine of the antinomies was intended to set forth the whole dialectic controversy of previous metaphysical speculation, and to bring it to a judicial decision. Then, however, the schema of the transcendental logic was discovered, and the Dialectic was assigned the position of the doctrine of the syllogism. Consequently, the doctrine of the antinomies had to be forced into the schema. It received its place under the title of the hypothetical syllogism, and had to surrender a part of its content for the equipment of the categorical and disjunctive syllogisms. The critique of rational psychology, schematized as the doctrine of the categorical syllogism, deprived it of an essential part of its content, namely, the critical discussion of the theory of monads as a support for psychology and metaphysics, particularly for the proofs of immortality. The only thing left for it was the discussion of the atomistic theory, which is replaced by the dynamic theory of matter. On the other hand, the rational theology, framed as the doctrine of the disjunctive syllogism, deprived the fourth cosmological idea of its real content (the cosmological proof for the

The solution of the antinomies may be described as substituting for the *aut — aut*, a *nec — nec*, or an *et — et*. The former is used to solve the first two antitheses. Sound human understanding has the feeling that it must be possible to give a simple affirmative or negative answer to the question whether or not the world is finite in time and space; and likewise to the question whether the ultimate parts of which the world consists are simple (unextended) or extended. Indeed, as soon as the metaphysician attempts an answer, the contradiction appears. If he says that the

existence of a necessary being). Thus the first and third ideas were the only ones really left for the rational cosmology. The third idea, the idea of freedom (which does not really belong at all among the cosmological ideas), was made into a long-drawn-out chapter. *Cf.* Adickes, *Kants Systematik*, §§ 60 ff., and the numerous passages in Erdmann's *Reflexionen*, in which Kant turns these notions around, first one way and then another. Kant's dexterity in schematizing, as well as the kaleidoscopic character of all of these schematizations, is brought out with extraordinary clearness. *Cf.* also an interesting sketch of the doctrine of antinomies in Reicke, *Lose Blätter*, I., pp. 105 ff. The propositions of the antinomies are here contrasted as principles of empirical employment in the world of appearances and of rational employment in the world of things-in-themselves.

Relating to Phenomena.

The principles of the exposition of phenomena posit them collectively as conditioned, hence not as absolutely posited : —

1. No absolute totality (totality *secundum quid*) of composition, hence the infinite progressus ;

2. No absolute totality of decomposition, hence no unconditioned simple.

3. No absolute totality of the series of procreation, hence no unconditioned spontaneity ;

4. No unconditioned necessity (all things can be taken out of time and space).

All these propositions are objectively certain as principles for empirical employment, but contrary to reason.

Relating to Things-in-Themselves.

Principles of the rationality or comprehension of the same. From the universal to the particular absolute synthesis : —

1. Unconditional All of the dependent whole. Origin of the world (*in mundo noumeno datur universitas*).

2. Unconditioned simple (*monas*).

3. Unconditioned spontaneity of action (*libertas transsc.*).

4. Unconditionally necessary existence (*necessitas absoluta, originaria*).

These propositions are subjectively necessary as principles for rational employment in the whole of knowledge. Unity of the manifold of the knowledge of the understanding. They are *practically* necessary in respect to the . . .   (Breaks off.)

world is finite, the question is raised about what exists
beyond the limit. Is it empty space and empty time?
What are they, and of what do they consist? And why
should not a filling be possible? In fact, are they conceivable at all without a filling? Or are space and time
themselves limited? As soon as one attempts to grasp
these thoughts, one is conscious of their impossibility. If
one adopts the opposite view, and says that the world has
no beginning in time and no limits in space, this conception
will not bear analysis. If it has no beginning, an infinity
must have elapsed before the present point could be reached.
Can an infinite time have elapsed before a definite terminus?
The case is similiar with space. Does the world exist as an
infinite in space? If I stood upon the farthest visible fixed
star, would a new world of fixed stars lie before me? And
if I repeated this a thousand times, and a thousand times a
thousand times, would I then be no nearer the boundary?
If I could multiply this by itself as often as I pleased,
would all that be infinitely small in comparison with the
infinity of actual extension? The understanding becomes
dizzy and it clings again to the finite, saying that "infinite" and "real" are mutually exclusive predicates.

The process of division leads to a similar result. The
understanding in this instance is at first inclined to assume
ultimate parts. Are these extended? If so, then they are
not ultimate. Why could not that which is extended be
further divided, at least in thought? On this supposition,
we never reach a termination. We do not come to an end
until we posit the ultimate parts as simple (unextended).
But what is the result of that? Is it not just as impossible
to compound extended bodies out of unextended parts as to
make a line out of points? How many points make an inch
and how many monads a body? Hence this position also
is untenable, and the understanding once more seizes upon
extended atoms.

Lastly, is the causal series finite or infinite ? Obviously it cannot be infinite. There must be a final member in the series that does not depend upon any other,— a something that exists through itself, a necessary being. If there be no necessary being, there could be no contingent being either, that is, nothing that exists merely through something else. Dependence on something else cannot proceed *ad infinitum*, neither can a suspended chain be infinite. It must have a final link, by which it may hang upon a peg. But, in fact, as soon as one attempts to designate such an ultimate, unconditioned, and necessary thing, the contradiction emerges. There can never be any such ultimate. The understanding cannot refrain from inquiring after the cause. And hence the understanding is driven ceaselessly hither and thither between the two contrary principles, impelled and again repelled, and can never find rest.

The solution which Kant offers runs as follows : Space and time, as well as bodies and motions of bodies, and therefore the causal series also, are not something absolutely existent. They are only phenomena, which the subject fashions by means of productive synthesis. They are only in and through the function of synthesis. This function is by nature neither a finite, nor an actual infinite, but a potential infinite. It can always be carried out further. Take the numerical series, for illustration. It is not finite, for I can by addition always pass beyond any particular number whatever. But neither is it infinite. It does not exist anywhere as a ready existent, infinite series. It has only potential infinity in the notion of the possibility of further synthesis. Now precisely the same thing holds true in the case of space and time. They have potential infinity in the synthetical function. I can prolong every line *in indefinitum*, and likewise every lapse of time. But in the corporeal world that fills space, and in the stream of events that fills time, I can never arrive at a point, on the other

side of which empty space or empty time begins. And the
same is true of division. As every number is divisible *in
indefinitum*, so are every space and every space-content.
And likewise in the causal series *regressus* and *progressus
in indefinitum* are proposed as a solution ; there can be no
final member in the series.

In fact, that is the only possible solution of these problems. If one regards space and time as things existing in
themselves, the dilemma as to whether they are either finite
or infinite cannot be avoided. If they are real only in the
functions of synthesis, the question loses its meaning for
the understanding, although not for perceptive thought.
But Kant does not maintain the latter. The appearance
remains, but it no longer deceives one who knows what it
signifies.

The solution of the third antinomy, to which the idea of
freedom gives rise, is different. In this case, the *aut — aut*
(there is freedom of the will — there is no freedom) is replaced by an *et — et*. The same act, on the one hand, must
be regarded as causally conditioned, and, on the other, can be
viewed as free. The former view applies to it as a member
of the phenomenal series, the latter as a manifestation of the
intelligible ego. We shall later return to this point. Moreover, as was previously noted, the idea of freedom does not
really belong among the cosmological ideas. It has a place
in the original conception, which, under the title of " Antinomies," was to furnish a solution for all the old dogmatic and
sceptical systems of metaphysics. In the exposition of the
antinomy, Kant has enveloped it in a cosmological cloak.
It is introduced under the title of the first uncaused cause.
The solution of the antinomy discards this cloak altogether.

The fourth idea is the idea of the necessary being. This,
it is clear, cannot be separated from the idea of the first,
unconditioned cause, and really belongs to the cosmological ideas. It cannot, however, be freely developed in this

connection, because it really belongs to the critique of rational theology, which was cut off from the antinomies. In the doctrine of the antinomies, it is disposed of in the same way as the previous problem. The *aut — aut* gives way to an *et — et*. The proposition that everything has accidental and conditioned existence, and that there is no necessary being, is valid for the world of appearance. But this does not interfere with the proposition that "there is also a non-empirical condition of the whole series, *i. e.*, an unconditioned, necessary being," or that "the whole series is grounded in an intelligible being, which is therefore free from all empirical conditions, and rather contains the ground of the possibility of all these phenomena."

(3) *The Rational Theology*

The critique of rational theology has seven sections. The first two contain what may be called the metaphysical deduction of the concept of God, which is derived from the disjunctive syllogism. The succeeding sections contain the transcendental critique (in place of the deduction) in the form of a negative answer to the question whether the objective validity of this concept can be theoretically demonstrated.

The concept of God is the same as that already developed by Kant in *The only Possible Ground of Demonstration of the Existence of God* (1763). God is the sum total of reality, *i. e.*, the unity of all thinkable reality (*omnitudo realitatis*). God is the *ens realissimum*, who unites in his nature all possible positive determinations, so that every positive predicate without limitation is attributed to him. God, therefore, is the primeval cause of the possibility of all being, out of which that of every entity must be regarded as derived by limitation; so that there is no entity which would not be posited in God's being.

The critique has then to decide whether objective validity can be procured for this concept in the same way as for the pure concepts of the understanding. A critique that confined itself exclusively to the limits of the Analytic would content itself with a mere reminder that reality, in the sense of the category, signified an object of possible experience, or one that can be given in perception, and that such reality could be attributed of course only to particular things, and not to the sum-total of all that is conceivable. God, as the absolutely transcendent being, could naturally have only intelligible reality, the reality of a thought entity or an idea, and hence absolute reality in the sense of the Platonic, or Spinozistic, or Hegelian system, according to which conceivability is just the criterion of absolute reality. Nevertheless, since discussions about the reality of the idea of God have played such an important rôle in the history of philosophy, Kant thinks it advisable "to draw up in detail the records of this process and deposit them in the archives of the human reason, for the prevention of future errors of a similar kind." And so he presented at length the possible forms of argument for the purpose of showing their fallacious nature.

There are three modes of proving the existence of God by means of speculative reason : the ontological, the cosmological, and the physico-theological.

The ontological proof infers the existence from the idea of God itself. The unreality of the *ens realissimum* cannot be thought, or, with Spinoza, *Dei essentia involvit existentiam*. — Kant's criticism amounts to the following : Existence is no mark of a concept. " Being is no real predicate," *i. e.*, no ideal content, that could constitute an element of a concept. A hundred real dollars contain no more ideal content than a hundred possible (thought) dollars. Hence the existence of a thing can never be inferred by means of a logically necessary (analytic) judgment from the concept of it. It can be demonstrated only by means of its direct presentation in perception, or by proving that it is connected with given perceptions in accordance with empirical laws. All existential propositions are synthetic, or everything real is contingent. Necessity, that is, conditioned necessity, is attributable, not to things, but only to judgments, assuming that they are inferred from valid premises. Or Kant holds, with Hume, that "the contrary of every matter of fact is possible."

It is easy to see that this criticism is valid only from the empirical standpoint. A representative of rationalism, Spinoza for example, would reply that the criticism does not touch his conceptions. My ontological argument, he would assert, does not refer to the existence of God in the world of sense-perception. I remain in the intelligible world, and am not concerned with the empirical, but solely with the transcendent, reality of God. A critique of the ontological proof would consequently have to be planned along entirely different lines. It would have to show that the concept of a unity of all ideal reality is intrinsically impossible, that it does not have in itself the *denominationes intrinsecas* of a true concept. If one puts God in a line with dollars, it is indeed easy to show the absurdity of the ontological proof. Kant in the criticism substitutes for the true and genuine idea of God, which he rightly develops in the exposition, the spurious and vulgar representation of God as a particular being, — a method of representation that can scarcely with justice be attributed even to Descartes, against whom the conclusion of the criticism is directed. What, however, prevented Kant from criticising the ontological proof in the only form in which it was intended or had meaning, seems to be the circumstance that his own thoughts move in precisely the same direction and make God the unity of the intelligible world. Whoever ascribes absolute intelligible reality and unity to the intelligible world, naturally cannot deny the ontological proof of God, except in the meaningless form to which I have referred.

The cosmological proof according to Kant runs as follows: If the contingent and conditioned is, the necessary and unconditioned also must be. Now, the contingent is real. Hence the necessary also is. The proof of the major premise is that the contingent and conditioned has its existence through something other. Now there cannot be only dependent existence; the *regressus* cannot proceed *in infinitum*. There must be an existence which is through itself, *i. e.*, a necessary being; and this necessary being is the most real being, God.

The criticism of the proof rests upon many points, but I call special attention to the following: (1) The necessary being is not necessarily the most real being. Any limited being whatever can just as well be unconditionally necessary. Therefore, from the concept of a necessary being, even if it were a valid concept, the existence of God as the most real being could not be proved (section 3). (2) The proposition that the necessary being is the most real being is really nothing but the converse of the proposition advanced by the ontological proof, that the most real being necessarily exists, and therefore these propositions are disproved together. (3) The concept of a necessary being is not a valid concept. The existence of a thing can never be represented as absolutely necessary: its non-being can always be thought. Or, in other words, necessity and contingency are not applicable to things, but merely to thought. We are given the task of finding a conditioning factor for every conditioned element. In reality, in the world of possible experience, we can never discover a conditioning factor that is unconditioned. — Again we must remark that the criticism affects only those who posit God in the series of empirical conditions, and hence as a particular being with empirical reality and causality.

The physico-theological proof, since it starts out from empirical data, does not properly belong in a critique of the attempts of pure reason to construe reality *a priori*. And it is really only touched upon by Kant in this place. The proof is that we meet with such order, purpose, and beauty in the world " that language in the presence of wonders so numerous and inconceivable has missed (? lost) its force, and number its power to reckon, and even our thought all bounds, and our conception of the whole dissolves into a speechless astonishment — the more eloquent that it is dumb." This purposive order is not a necessary result of the nature of the elements. The latter behave, as far as we see, with indifference towards every arrangement. Therefore the order must be referred back to an ordering intelligence, and, further, to a cosmic intelligence, for the world manifests itself, so far as our experience reaches, as a unitary system.

Kant lets the presuppositions of the proof pass, but attacks the conclusion that God, the *ens realissimum*, exists. The proof, at most, points to a world architect for the domain of experience, but not to a creator with the predicates of an *ens realissimum*, infinite, eternal, almighty, omniscient, etc. Consequently, it does not at all serve the purposes of speculative theology, which is thrown back upon the *a priori* proofs, ultimately upon the ontological argument.

Kant does not enter into the question how far the argument from empirical analogy goes towards establishing belief in the existence of a world-constructing intelligence. He remarks only that the proof, as the oldest, clearest, and best suited for the common human reason, deserves to be mentioned always with respect. He observes too that reason cannot be oppressed by any subtile speculation to such a degree that a glance at the wonder of nature and the majesty of the structure of the world would not arouse it immediately from brooding indecision as from a dream. Still, he intimates, on the other hand, that the conclusion cannot bear the strictest transcendental criticism. Perhaps freely acting nature, "which is the source of all power and perhaps also of human reason itself," is the ultimate principle of the construction of the world, and not to be derived from any other, — an observation which recalls Hume's *Dialogue on Natural Religion*. What right have we to take this petty brain excitation, called reason, for a model of the constructive principle of the world ? That would be no less audacious anthropomorphism than it would be groundless arachnomorphism if spiders, dwelling upon a planet inhabited by them alone, were to derive the order of the world from a cosmic spinning power. Kant could on this point have referred to Hume's treatment as a complement to his critique of the proofs of God. Hume gives, what Kant does not give, the criticism of natural theology from the standpoint of empirical reflection. In accordance with the purely rationalistic design of the *Critique of Pure Reason*, Kant really has space only for the purely *a priori* metaphysics and a critical discussion of it. His critical inquiry, in regard to how far reason can *a priori* know reality, excludes on principle from the outset every discussion that enters upon the concrete nature of reality. It must, indeed, be admitted that it is thoroughly rational to inquire whether metaphysics *a posteriori* is not possible, whether the question regarding the nature and constitution of reality does not permit of an answer based upon the whole of empirical knowledge, although not in the form of apodictic propositions, nevertheless in the form of well-grounded opinions. That is the course which the metaphysics of Schopenhauer and Fechner follows.

The concluding section of the Dialectic, entitled " Appendix," is not unimportant. From another standpoint, it might even be regarded as a main division. It contains the positive treatment, or, if one chooses, the "transcendental deduction" of the Ideas of reason, — a limited and conditioned, but nevertheless a real deduction. The ideas of reason are not, indeed, like the fundamental principles of the understanding, real constructive principles of nature, but they are, nevertheless, necessary principles for the employment of the understanding. They are *regulative*, but not *constitutive* principles, Kant says with his everlasting art of drawing distinctions. Reason from its nature aims at an absolutely unitary and complete system of knowledge. It takes as its ideal the logical system and aims at a complete and thorough-going organization of reality in accordance with the schema of a conceptual hierarchy of forms and rules. And it necessarily carries this ideal over to its conception of reality; with the result that reality manifests itself as a conceptual system. The law of logical classification, namely, generalization and conceptual division carried out to their uttermost, is accordingly a synthetic proposition *a priori*, which as an heuristic principle possesses objective validity. The highest ideal of rational knowledge is, however, unity in accordance with ideas of purpose. Absolute knowledge would be a synthesis of all things in accordance with teleological laws. And it would follow from this, that reason, in order to attain the highest degree of speculative contentment, cannot forbear applying this assumption to reality. Hence it must make the presupposition of this assumption, namely, that the first ground of the world is to be conceived after the analogy of an intelligence that creates in accordance with ideas. And this will put us on our guard against thinking that we can determine the original cause of the world and of the unity of the world in itself, and according to its essence. "We have merely presupposed a something, of which we have no conception at all, which we do not know as it is in itself. But, in relation to the systematic and purposive order of the universe, which we must presuppose in all our study of nature, we have thought this unknown being by analogy with an intelligent existence, *i. e.*, in respect to aims and perfection to which it gives rise; we have endowed it with those attributes that, judging from the nature of our own reason, may contain the ground of such a systematic unity." Or, if we separate the thought from these somewhat painfully qualified sentences, human reason cannot refrain from imposing upon things its teleological conception, as well as its logical nature. Reason may claim that it is derived from the same original source from which things also arise; that consequently a conception conformable with its nature cannot be altogether unsuited to the nature of things and their source, even if it should not be in a position adequately and exhaustively to reflect the nature of things and their ultimate ground. In the second half of the *Critique of Judgment*, these ideas are further spun out.

VII. The Doctrine of Method

Under the title of the Doctrine of Method, there follow a series of reflections about the theme of the *Critique*, chiefly about the subject matter of the Dialectic. These are placed under some titles (Discipline, Canon) taken from the schema of a logical doctrine of method. The second and third sections of the Discipline of Pure Reason form, together with the Canon of Pure Reason, a kind of epilogue similar to the last two sections of Hume's *Enquiry Concerning the Human Understanding*. They show that these investigations are not only not dangerous or injurious for morals and religion, but are, on the contrary, necessary and useful. They emancipate reason from negative as well as from positive forms of dogmatism. And reason, when thus liberated, cannot refrain from taking sides with the positive view regarding God and a future life. The practical interest is altogether upon this side. Hence, let us calmly permit the light of day to be shed upon all doubts. "External peace is a mere illusion. The seeds of distrust which are in the nature of the human heart must be exterminated. But how can we exterminate them if we do not give them freedom, aye, even nourishment to bring forth leaves, in order that they may make themselves known and be thereafter utterly extirpated ? "

If one brings together the expositions of the Dialectic (including the Doctrine of Method), and follows out the spirit of the third and fourth sections of the Doctrine of Antinomies, which perhaps are the clearest reflection of the original conception, one can state the problem in the following manner: The question involved takes the form of a critical discussion between the new metaphysics and the previous metaphysics. All previous metaphysics was dialectical, *i. e.,* it had not, like the other sciences, a fixed stock of recognized truths. It contained only contested propositions and allegations, which were always opposed by a contradictory contention possessing an equal claim to logical necessity. All previous philosophy exhibits nothing but a perpetual war between two opposing tendencies. The one tendency, the rationalistic and idealistic, aims at furnishing an absolutely fixed theoretical basis for practical and religious truths. It teaches us to view the world as the creation of a rational being. It conceives the logical and ontological ideas in such a manner that the spirituality and immortality of the soul, and the freedom of the will can be grounded upon them. In opposition to this, stands the empirical, or the dogmatic and materialistic tendency. By means of sceptical reflection it destroys these conceptual constructions and demonstrations. The view of reality that cosmology and physics, biology and history evidently present to us, does not at all compel the understanding to regard nature as the work of an extramundane intelligence. Its inferences lead neither to a first cause (an act of creation), nor to the possibility of a teleological explanation of the world. And the same is true of immortality and freedom. Unbiased theoretical consideration shows that the psychical life runs parallel with the physical, and hence that they both come into and go out of existence together; that likewise all the processes of the inner life, volitional processes not excepted, manifest regularity and causal connection in the same sense as the physiological. The exemption of certain phenomena from the domain of natural explanation is altogether inadmissible.

Thus the two stand in direct opposition. The one emphasizes the practical interest of reason. It is ready to sacrifice the theoretical to it. Philosophical speculation must necessarily lead to a result that can be consistent with morals, religion, and the maintenance of the laws of society. The other lays stress upon the scientific interest, and is ready to sacrifice the practical to it. Its motto is: The truth above all! The understanding must see things as they are. It must without scruple form the ultimate hypotheses and draw the final conclusions, untroubled as to whether the world or the philosophy which it constructs may contradict the demands of the heart. And these consequences are either that science knows nothing of God, freedom, and immortality (Hume), or, it denies them altogether and regards God, freedom, and immortality as creations of the imagination (*Système de la nature*).

That is the state of the controversy. Kant's adjudication results in declaring that both are right, and both are wrong. They are right in what they assert, but wrong in what they deny. The sceptical and materialistic philosophy is right in its demand that nothing must be withheld from free scientific investigation. The understanding has the right of investigating everything and calling everything in question. It is also right in its contention that all theoretical proofs for the objective reality of the ideas of God, freedom, and immortality are fruitless. But that philosophy is wrong if it then discards these ideas altogether as meaningless products of fancy. The rationalistic and idealistic philosophy is entirely right when it insists upon the validity of these ideas. But it puts itself in the wrong if it undertakes to establish this validity by objective proofs. The certainty of these propositions depends, on the contrary, upon the subjective need of reason, in which, of course, a speculative as well as a practical necessity expresses itself. — Hence, faith must not encroach upon the domain of science, any more than science must do violence to faith. Both are equally indispensable for the spiritual life of man. Both have their place side by side; for the understanding is the seat of knowledge, and the heart the seat of faith.

Such is Kant's position. As far as the heart and the speculative impulse (of reason) are concerned, he takes sides with idealistic philosophy. But in the position that things must be made intelligible according to the laws of the understanding, he adopts the point of view of materialistic philosophy. Transcendental idealism, however, is the bridge over the apparent contradiction. The understanding pertains to the *mundus sensibilis*, and reason, particularly practical reason, pertains to the *mundus intelligibilis*. Moreover, the understanding cannot refrain from granting the reality of the latter, although only as a "limiting idea," towards which it strives, without being able to give it positive content.

B. The Prolegomena and the Second Edition of the Critique

I shall conclude the exposition of the contents of the *Critique of Pure Reason* with a remark upon the two succeeding revisions of the subject.

The *Prolegomena to Every Future Metaphysic which can Appear as Science*, published two years after the *Critique*, is, as far as its subject-matter is essentially concerned, an epitome of the main work, to which it frequently refers. It lays stress upon the chief points, and puts them in a different setting without any essential change in meaning.

As Kant himself describes the difference, the *Prolegomena* follows the analytic, instead of the synthetic method. While Kant was composing it, the first reviews of the *Critique of Pure Reason* came to his notice, notably the criticism in the *Göttingische Gelehrten Anzeigen* (Jan. 19, 1782), which was written by Garve and revised by Feder. This led Kant to incorporate in the *Prolegomena* a number of exasperated replies.[1] There was one point that particularly irritated him, and that was, being classified with Berkeley. The *Critique* was described by Feder as a work that contained a "system of higher idealism." Kant saw in this an application to his system of the favorite method of attack of those " whose philosophy, is the history of philosophy," namely, of giving old party names to new ideas,— a procedure which in Catholic polemics has been elaborated into a system. In that literature, the history of philosophy is nothing but a *catalogus errorum*. The various -isms stand ready like so many coffins for the reception of all new, non-approved ideas. Kant protests against the method in the most spirited way. With the tone of strong self-consciousness, he declares that there are really new and very serious ideas in his book, which concern the very existence of all previous systems of metaphysics. He solemnly suspends

---

[1] Erdmann has separated — even typographically — these later insertions from the original composition. But such a strict separation cannot be carried out. In the introduction to his edition of the *Prolegomena*, and in his essay, entitled *Kants Kritizismus in der 1. und 2. Aufl. der. Kr. d. r. V.*, which appeared as an introduction to his edition of *Kr. d. r. V.*, Erdmann deals with the progress of Kant's thought in connection with the reception it met with from his contemporaries, and traces the development up to the appearance of the second edition. The main idea is directed towards the establishment of the interpretation that the chief purpose of the *Critique* is the proof of the impossibility of transcendent knowledge, and that this negative aim again reasserted itself, although it is obscured here and there by the emergence of the positive aspect (the proof of the possibility of rational knowledge within the domain of experience). The determination of the deviations of the later writings from the first edition, like the interpretation of the chief purpose, seems to me untenable.

all metaphysicians from their labors until they have satis-
factorily answered his question about the possibility of
synthetic knowledge *a priori.* In particular, he protests
against the assertion that he follows the same road as the
" good Berkeley." His idealism has nothing to do with the
idealism of that man, who opens the door for the extravagance of the imagination. On the contrary, he concludes
that " imaginative extravagance cannot arise in an age of
enlightenment, unless it conceals itself behind a system of
scholastic metaphysics, under the protection of which it may
venture to rage against reason. But it is driven from this
its last retreat by the critical philosophy." In a series of
remarks upon his historical relation to his predecessors,
Kant connects his investigation, not with Berkeley, but
with Hume, who, he says, was the first really to state the
problem of the critical philosophy, although he did not solve
it. He emphasizes the empirical and agnostic moments
which are common to both him and Hume. With Hume he
teaches that all our knowledge is confined to possible experience, and he points out that the *Critique* first proved
by principles the impossibility of transcendent speculation.
In opposition to Berkeley, he lays stress upon the realistic
elements, and shows that he not only assumed as self-evident
the reality of things-in-themselves, but also distinctly held
to the empirical reality of bodies.[1]

---

[1] I shall only remark further that the Göttingen review, although it is not
always relevant, is not so foolish as it has been represented, either in the
form given it by Feder or in the original composition of Garve. Indeed, I
should say that it is not bad for the first notice of such a difficult and strange
work. And it really gives, for a German review, little cause for complaint on
the score of immoderateness. This is especially true of Garve's work, as it
was afterwards printed in the *Allg. Deutschen Bibl.* (Appendix to Vol. 37–52,
Part 2). Moreover, the charge against Feder of arrogance or malicious misrepresentation is also entirely unfounded. For the whole subject and the
correspondence between Kant and Garve, which arose regarding the matter,
cf. A. Stern, *Ueber die Beziehungen Garves zu Kant* (1884). Furthermore,
Feder has shown that he was capable of understanding Kant, in his "Versuch

In the parts which are intended as an abstract of the *Critique*, another moment is prominent, namely, the rationalistic. He there lays stress upon the claim that the critical philosophy alone can account for the form and validity of the rational sciences of mathematics and pure natural science. Since these disciplines exist as recognized sciences, the correctness of the critical epistemology is thereby based, as it were, upon a fact. If it is the only possible explanation of the possibility of those rational sciences of objects, its truth is thereby demonstrated. On the other hand, this system of philosophy supplies the mathematical knowledge of nature with a trustworthy epistemological basis, that secures it "against all chicaneries of shallow metaphysics, because of the indubitable objective reality of its propositions." Lastly, the critical philosophy assists metaphysics to obtain the sure method of a science, by closing up the false way of transcendent speculation, and by pointing out to metaphysics its necessary and possible task. That task consists in forming a system of philosophy according to rational principles. In this undertaking, both the theoretical principles of the systematic unity of the employment of the understanding, and of the practical principles of a reason that is guided by the idea of a final purpose must find place.

einer möglichst kurzen Darstellung des Kantischen Systems" (*Philos. Bibl.* von Feder und Meiners, III., pp. 1-13, 1790). In twelve pages, he has here written for his pupils a summary of the *Critique of Pure Reason*, formulated both concisely and intelligibly in twenty-five propositions. For Feder's further experiences with the Kantian philosophy, and the "amputation of his celebrity as instructor and author," see his *Autobiography* (pp. 115 ff.), which is worth reading in other respects. He was a candid man, who is not, indeed, to be ranked as an independent thinker, but neither is he by any means to be regarded as a conceited numskull. It is a pity that Kant had such a mean opinion of him — but of what one of his opponents did he not have a low opinion? If he had permitted himself to come to terms with the empirical tendency, as Feder and more particularly Ænesidemus represented it, his philosophy would necessarily have had a light cast upon it that would have prevented many a misunderstanding. Furthermore, it is worthy of note that he repeatedly suggested to Beck to make a comparison of the Humian and Kantian philosophy (*Archiv für Gesch. der Phil.* II., pp. 617, 619).

"Idealism," however, appears here, as in the earlier work, a mere means, "the only means of solving the problem upon whose solution the fate of metaphysics entirely depends," and towards which the whole *Critique* is exclusively aimed, — the problem, namely, of establishing the possibility of synthetic knowledge *a priori*. Transcendental and epistemological idealism, which teaches the conception of space and time as forms of perception, and of things in space and time as phenomena, renders knowledge of the phenomenal world *a priori* possible, by means of the *a priori* construction of phenomena in space and time. And it also renders the existence of a supersensuous world certain, as the necessary correlate of the world of phenomena, and thereby guarantees our philosophical view of the world against the "impudent contentions of materialism, naturalism, and fatalism, that seek to restrict the field of reason."

These points are characteristic also of the changes made in the second edition, which appeared six years after the first. The realistic and agnostic aspects are here and there somewhat more strongly emphasized by means of omissions and additions. A few observations on the "Object of our Ideas," which seemed to be capable of misinterpretation in the sense of an absolute idealism, are left out. A "Refutation of Idealism" is inserted. The transcendental deduction is confined more strictly to its epistemological purpose by separating it from the psychological exposition. Further, the limitation of the pure employment of the understanding solely to the domain of possible experience is emphasized thus early in the deduction. On the other hand, the view of the *Prolegomena*, that mathematics and pure natural science are recognized sciences of a purely rational character, is brought into the introduction of the *Critique*, not to the advantage of its clearness. The significance of the transcendental deduction of the pure concepts of the understand-

ing is in this way made less important, — Kant remarks
incidentally that it was not all necessary for those sciences,
— and at the same time and for the same reason the positive construction is given less prominence in comparison
with the critical limitation. — Nevertheless, Kant is right
when he says in the Preface that the changes do not affect
the propositions and the grounds by which they are demonstrated, but only the form of exposition. It is certain that
Kant himself entertained the conviction that his thought
had not undergone any changes since he definitely adopted
the critical standpoint.

This is particularly true of two points, his attitude
towards rationalism and towards idealism. In regard to
rationalism, the character of the epistemological system
is the same in the second as in the first edition. This
is brought out with particular clearness in the new Preface. If in the course of the elaboration it is occasionally
somewhat obscured by the element of realism and the
critical limitation, there is, nevertheless, not a moment's
doubt but that the chief interest is to establish the possibility of rational knowledge, although only of objects as
phenomena. It must be admitted that there are occasional
utterances, which emphasize the refutation of transcendent
metaphysics to such an extent that, if we had only a few
fragments of this character from Kant's writings, we should
have to classify him with Hume. The most radical remark
of the sort is the one he introduced in the Preface of the
Metaphysical Elements of Natural Science (1786). There
the basis of the system of the *Critique* is said to be the
proposition "that the entire speculative reason can never
transcend objects of possible experience." "If it can be
shown that the categories can have no other use except
merely in relation to objects of experience, the answer to the
question how they make experience possible is indeed
sufficiently important to lead to the completion of this

deduction, wherever possible.   But in regard to the chief aim of the system, namely, the limitation of pure reason, it is nowise necessary, but merely serviceable."

Such passages are worthy of note, inasmuch as they show how the consciousness of the design of his own work became temporarily obscured in the ardor of polemical or conciliatory efforts.   But, notwithstanding, there can be no reasonable doubt that the Æsthetic and Analytic, in their entire plan, are conceived as proofs for the positive assertion that there is rational knowledge of objects (as phenomena), and not for the negative contention that there is no knowledge beyond the limits of possible experience.   And, in the last analysis, the same holds true of the Dialectic also.   It does undertake to overthrow the old dogmatic metaphysics, but only for the purpose of demolishing at the same time sceptical and materialistic metaphysics, and of laying the foundation for a new system, namely, the metaphysic that employs the Ideas as regulative and practical principles.

How strictly Kant adheres to his formal rationalism is apparent from the very context in which the above cited passage occurs.   In the Preface itself to the *Metaphysical Elements*, he develops his rationalistic conception of philosophy in the most definite way: " The name of real science can be given only to that whose certainty is apodictic. Knowledge, which can attain only empirical certainty is only science improperly so-called."   " A rational doctrine of nature, therefore, deserves the name of a science of nature only when the natural laws which lie at its basis are known *a priori*, and are not merely empirical laws."   " Since in every doctrine of nature only so much real science is contained as there is knowledge *a priori*, every doctrine of nature will constitute a real science only in so far as mathematics can be applied to it."   It is on this account that Kant refuses to regard chemistry and psychology as real sciences.   Furthermore, he himself later took an opportunity

to expressly correct the passage first quoted,[1] in which connection there occurs also a noteworthy remark upon the
"discovery of alleged contradictions" in his work. "They
disappear of themselves entirely, if one views them in connection with the whole." He might have said, in the language of Protestant dogmatics, if one views them *ex analogia
fidei*, or from the standpoint of the general rationalistic
character of the system.

Kant's attitude towards idealism also is equally unchanged
in its main features, although the heat with which he protests against a kinship with Berkeleian idealism has produced
here and there a magical transformation in the exposition.
One can bring the problem of idealism under three heads:
(1) Do bodies exist as real things outside (*extra*) of us in
space? (2) Have bodies absolute reality independent of all
ideas? (3) Is there something absolutely existent beyond
(*præter*) our ideas (things-in-themselves)? Kant since 1770
never really vacillated for a moment in his answers to these
questions. We can formulate them as follows: (1) Undoubtedly, bodies exist outside of us as real things. To be
a real thing is nothing else than being given in external
perception in space as an object. (2) These things, bodies,
are not things-in-themselves. They are real as phenomena
only for a perceiving subject. Without any subject at all,
without the content of its sensations and the forms of its
perception, we should never talk at all about bodies and their
reality. These two points are developed with particular
clearness in the critique of the fourth Paralogism in the
first edition. Its place was taken in the second edition by
the equivocal Refutation of Idealism (in the Postulates of
Empirical Thought), but that section says nothing to the
contrary. (3) There are things-in-themselves, which exist
in complete independence of our representation and thought.
They are not, indeed, given in perception, and consequently

---

[1] *Teleol. Prinzipien*, **IV.**, p. 496.

empirical reality is not attributable to them, like bodies. — To these three propositions Kant always adhered. Bodies have empirical reality, along with their transcendental ideality; while things-in-themselves, on the contrary, do not have empirical, but transcendental reality. This is of course not capable of realization in perception, but is a necessary idea for thought.

Kant's strong opposition to Berkeley, at times carried out at the risk of being misunderstood, and pushed so far that he can find nothing whatever in common between Berkeley and himself, is due to his decided aversion to dogmatic idealism, which denies reality to the corporeal world, and does so for the purpose of claiming it solely for the facts of inner sense. In opposition to this, Kant maintains that the facts of external perception possess reality in precisely the same sense as those of inner perception. Or, in other words, the really objective world is the world of things in space. It alone is an object of real objective perception and real objective or scientific knowledge. The facts which are only in inner sense possess a subjective and contingent character, while the perceptual world constructed in space is the world that is common to all, and that is determined by recognized natural laws. The psychic life becomes an object of objective knowledge for others only through its manifestations in bodily phenomena and movements. Indeed, the subject itself connects its inner experiences with bodily processes, and constructs them in time by relating them to movements. It localizes them in the objective world by means of their relation to the bodily life.

SECOND SECTION

THE METAPHYSICS

LITERATURE: Kant did not carry out his intention of elaborating the metaphysics (if one leaves out of consideration the *Metaphysical Elements of Natural Science*). [Eng. trans. by Bax, Bohn's Library, London, 1883. A volume entitled, *Kant's Cosmogony*, by W. Hastie (Glasgow 1900), contains translations of Kant's *Examination of the question whether the earth has undergone an alteration of its Axial Rotation*, and of his *Universal Natural History and Theory of the Heavens*.] Jäsche's contemplated edition of the lectures, which was even announced by the publishers (1802), never made its appearance. Thus we have chiefly to rely upon the treatment of the subject in the critical writings. Besides this source, there are the later publications from the remains: The *Reflexionen*, edited by Erdmann, containing Kant's memoranda in Baumgarten's text-book on metaphysics; also the copies of *Lectures on Metaphysics* (1821) and on the *Philosophy of Religion* (1817), both edited by Pölitz. The lectures on religion probably date from the winter semester 1785–86. On Pölitz's metaphysics, as well as on a few existent manuscript remains, there are two very minute investigations: E. Arnoldt, *Krit. Exkurse* (pp. 370 ff.), and M. Heinze, *Abh. der sächs. Ges. d. Wiss., philos. hist. Kl.*, 1894. The latter contains supplements from the manuscripts. In addition, there are two essays by Erdmann in the *Philos. Monatsheften*, 1883–84. The significance of these sources consists in the fact that they furnish a positive presentation of Kant's thoughts, which in the Dialectic are put in a negative form. The lack of fixed dates, however, renders it difficult to utilize them. Still, they all belong to the period when the critical philosophy was established in its fundamental outlines. (The notes for the psychology, cosmology, and theology in Pölitz, which are the earliest, Heinze places in the years 1775–80; Arnoldt, 1778–84. No objection seems to me to stand in the way of the latter date.) In addition, there are imperfect ideas and notes of Kant's hearers. Still, one gets the impression that especially the later sections of the metaphysics and the philosophy of religion reproduce, rather faithfully on the whole, the content of the lectures, although deficient in particular respects. To be sure, if our knowledge of Kant were gathered solely from these fragments, we should never obtain a clear idea of his type of thought, and we probably should not regard it as worth the trouble. Dogmatic metaphysics and critical reflection are here interwoven in a strange way. One can hardly understand how pupils who were not already conversant with the *Critique* could follow these lectures. One thing, however, comes out very clearly, namely, that the old metaphysics had much more influence upon the lectures, and hence also upon Kant's thought, than any one would suppose whose knowledge of Kant was derived solely from the *Critique of Pure Reason*. This may have been simply adaptation to tradition, that existed in the form of Baumgarten's compendium, which, by the way, on account of its wide range, compactness, and precision, was very suitable for a text-book. Or it may have been due to the concurrence of the old with his own metaphysics, the content of which was determined long before the critical reflection upon its method was definitely conceived. It may also have been done for pedagogical purposes, which for Kant had ultimately a moral, and, in a certain sense, a culture significance. In any case, one sees that these notions had for him permanent importance and truth, although truth in a different sense from the truths of physics. It can perhaps be said that Kant did not entirely abandon a single one of his fundamental views on theology, psychology, and physics, as they were formulated in the precritical writings. Most of them recur, only with altered significance, in the critical writings.

Hegel, in the Preface to his *Logic* (1812), writes that in consequence of the Kantian movement the rare spectacle of a cultivated people without a metaphysics is now witnessed in Germany; science is, in other respects, a richly adorned temple, but without a holy of holies.

It surprises us to hear that Germany at that time was without metaphysics. We are rather accustomed to speak of a superabundance of metaphysics at the time of the speculative philosophy. And it would have surprised Kant also to hear that he had destroyed metaphysics. Certainly nothing was further from his intention than that. On the contrary, he everywhere emphasizes that he is interested in the definite establishment of metaphysics, and that he intends to raise it from its previous condition of insecurity to the rank of a science. The *Critique* was originally intended to be nothing but the epistemological substructure for the metaphysics, as is especially apparent from the series of letters to M. Herz, written in the seventies. For the first time, in the long letter of February 21, 1772,[1] the *Critique of Pure Reason* is described as a work which "contains the sources of metaphysics, its methods and limits." In 1773 it is called "Transcendental philosophy," which must precede the metaphysic of nature and of morals. And that is its permanent position in the *Critique* itself, as is shown in the Introduction and the concluding section (Architectonic of Pure Reason).

The same standpoint is maintained also in the writings that follow the *Critique of Pure Reason,* viz., the *Prolegomena,* the *Metaphysical Elements of Natural Science,* and the *Fundamental Principles of the Metaphysic of Morals.* It is, however, brought out with very especial distinctness in the retrospective survey which Kant makes in connection with the prize-subject of the Academy, *Upon the Progress of Metaphysics since Leibniz and Wolff.* Here his philosophy is set forth as the first and only great advance in metaphysics since those days. "The transcendental philosophy," Kant says, "has for its object the founding of a metaphysic whose purpose, as the chief end of pure reason, is intended to lead reason beyond the limits of the sensible world to the field of the supersensible."[2] And he repeatedly defines metaphysics as a science "of advancing from knowledge of the sensible to that of the supersensible," as is suggested also by the old name, μετὰ τὰ φυσικά, *trans physicam.*[3] The critical philosophy is the first to show how this advance may be accomplished with safety.

One sees that Kant took his official title of Professor of Metaphysics with entire seriousness. His task is not to

[1] VIII., p. 693.   [2] *Ibid.,* p. 533.   [3] *Ibid.,* p. 576.

destroy metaphysics, but to upbuild it. He regards all his undertakings in the sphere of philosophy as preparatory for that purpose. When sending to Mendelssohn his *Dreams of a Ghost-Seer*, he wrote to him, on the 8th of April, 1766, as follows: "I am so far from regarding metaphysics itself, objectively considered, as trivial and dispensable, that I am convinced that even the true and lasting well-being of the human race depends upon it." This remained his permanent and fundamental point of view. In an age that is on the point of losing faith in metaphysics, "when people seem to regard it an honor to speak contemptuously of metaphysical speculations as mere subtleties," he undertakes to intervene in its behalf. "Metaphysics is the real and true philosophy." [1] Metaphysics, "the favorite child of reason," "is, perhaps more than any other science whatever, by its very nature rooted in us, as far as its fundamental features are concerned. And it can by no means be regarded as the product of an arbitrary choice, or as an accidental expansion in the progress of experience, from which it altogether separates itself." [2]

Indeed, the *trans physicam* gives the direction to Kant's whole thought; the *mundus intelligibilis* is its goal. The first step towards it is the transcendental idealism. By means of the principle of the ideality of space and time, it establishes the ideality of matter. The corporeal world is nothing but phenomenal, and sense-perceptions are the material out of which it is upbuilt. The Æsthetic and Analytic show how the intellect makes the corporeal world from that material. Thereby the great obstacle is forever removed that stands in the way of an idealistic metaphysic. That obstacle is materialism, which takes corporeal objects for things-in-themselves, aye, for the only things, and thus exalts physics to the rank of the absolute science, which leaves room for no other science. The second step is the removal of pre-

---

[1] *Logik*, Introduction, IV.   [2] *Prolegomena*, § 57.

vious mistaken attempts to erect an idealistic metaphysics — the refutation of the pseudo-sciences of rational psychology, cosmology, and theology. These false sciences were also hindrances towards the attainment of the supersensible, inasmuch as they led reason along a false path, and brought it into conflict with itself (in the antinomies), and thus robbed it of its self-confidence and delivered it bound into the hands of scepticism (like Hume's). The Dialectic, that makes known this result, is in so far accounted as a "negative advance." Its procedure is like that of a wanderer, "who has turned off the right road and goes back to the place from which he started, in order to discover his bearings." [1] The third and final step is the knowledge of the true relationship of the human reason to the *mundus intelligibilis*. This is based upon two factors. The first is that, by means of the practical reason, which is *a priori* legislative for the will, we transcend the sensible world, and belong immediately to the intelligible world, the kingdom of ends. There is, therefore, nothing more certain than that reality in itself is an order in conformity with ends, a realization of ideas. The second factor is that the speculative reason cannot help interpreting the world as a unitary system. The ultimate and supreme systematic unity, however, is unity in accordance with ideas of purpose. Consequently, this is the necessary and final presupposition of the theoretical reason in regard to the nature of reality. It cannot, indeed, realize this idea; it cannot demonstrate that nature is a system of realized ideas of purpose, in the way a machinist can do with a machine, or an art critic with a drama. In this instance, human reason itself has imposed the idea of purpose upon reality, — a thing which it did not do in the case of the world. The teleological interpretation of the world is applied only to the *intellectus archetypus*. Meanwhile, human reason can gain an insight

[1] VIII., p. 522.

into one other thing, and that is the purposive necessity of its own limitation. The morality of freedom for man depends precisely on the fact that, although his knowledge is confined to the sensible world, he can freely determine himself by means of his will in the supersensuous world — which would not be the case if he possessed a theoretical knowledge of the supersensuous.[1]

These are the three steps in the transition from the sensible to the supersensible world. In the outline of the Prize Essay, they are designated as follows : " The doctrine of science as a safe advance ; the doctrine of doubt as a halting place ; the doctrine of practical wisdom as a transition to the final goal of metaphysics. The result is that the first contains a theoretical and dogmatic doctrine, the second a sceptical discipline, and the third a practical and dogmatic discipline."

Metaphysics arises everywhere from the insufficiencies of physics. The inadequacy of common knowledge to attain the idea of knowledge, and the inadequacy of common reality to reach the idea of perfection, engender the impulse towards transcendence. This was the case with Plato, the first in whom the impulse towards transcendence led to the creation of a system of metaphysics. It is the same with Kant, in whom the two motives, the insufficiency of empirical science, and the worthlessness of empirical reality, were no less active. The desire for transcendence is the soul of his philosophy. What he calls reason, the faculty of Ideas, is really nothing else than the desire for transcendence, which has its roots in the feeling of the unsatisfactory nature of the given. The understanding belongs to the sphere of phenomena ; it limits itself to construction in this field. But the mind is more than mere understanding. As reason, which transcends and limits the understanding, it soars above nature to a higher order of things.

[1] *Kr. d. pr. V.*, Dialectic, ix.

I shall now attempt to sketch briefly Kant's metaphysical views, by indicating their relation to the main problems and tendencies of his thought. But I shall first make two preliminary remarks.

The epistemology and the metaphysics, the critical phenomenalism in the former case, and the objective idealism in the latter, are not completely in harmony. The epistemology requires that we should on principle remain within the world of appearance, while the metaphysics leads us to the *mundus intelligibilis*. Kant the epistemologist says that the thing-in-itself is for us an undetermined x, merely a limiting concept. "The transcendental object, which may be the ground of this appearance that we call matter, is a mere somewhat, and we would not understand what it is, even if somebody could tell us."[1] Kant the metaphysician is quite conversant with the thing-in-itself. "In the world of the understanding, the substrate is intelligence; the act and cause, freedom; the common interest, blessedness arising from freedom; the first principle, an intelligence in accordance with an idea; the form, morality; the nexus, a nexus of ends. This world of the understanding even now lies at the basis of the world of sense, and is the true self-dependant." Or, "*mundus intelligibilis est monadum, non secundum formam intuitus externi, sed interni repræsentabilis.*" Or, "the *mundus intelligibilis*, as an object of perception, is a mere undetermined idea, but as an object of the practical relations of our intelligence to intelligences of the world in general, and to God as the practical first principle, it is a true concept and definite idea: *civitas Dei.*"[2]

These notes are not dated, but they probably belong to the seventies. However, the view expressed in them, Kant the metaphysician never abandoned. And Kant the epistemologist contents himself with saying that everything

---

[1] Amphiboly, III., p. 235.
[2] Erdmann, *Reflexionen*, II., 1159, 1151, 1162.

which is not for the understanding but for reason, although not perceptually knowable, is nevertheless thinkable and really true. The moral certainty is the final guarantee for this. Some one may say that the critical epistemology, when it was given its final form after the year 1772, was no longer strong enough completely to fill in all the parts; the idealistic metaphysics maintains its position alongside of the official system, but it has the value only of a private opinion of Kant's, with which he did not care to dispense. But one must then add that this private opinion was older than the epistemological system, and it was so deeply rooted in his thought that he would sooner have given up the Analytic than the *mundus intelligibilis.* The epistemology was originally conceived simply as a foundation for the idealistic metaphysics. The Kantian metaphysics has, certainly, a somewhat peculiar variability, a kind of shifting between knowing and not knowing. Every statement that a thing is so, is followed by the qualification that properly speaking it is not so, upon which there ensues a final assertion that it is so nevertheless.

The second remark to be made is that Kant's metaphysics has restricted itself to the sphere of pure knowledge *a priori.* It rejects on principle every consideration of experience. It undertakes to give philosophy the dignity of a science derived from concepts. By clinging to this notion of philosophy, Kant was prevented from following the path which Schopenhauer later adopted — that is, from making phenomena the starting-point for philosophy. In truth, metaphysics is possible only by means of observation and interpretation of perceptually given reality. The actual form of all metaphysics is an interpretation of the sense-given corporeal world from the personal inner life. From Plato to Hegel, and Schopenhauer, and Fechner, all metaphysicians have thus regarded it. They all interpret the world either from thought or from the will, that is to say, from inner experience. Even Kant, as a matter of fact, follows the same course, but he does not want it called by that name. His metaphysics spurns borrowing from experience, and thus it always retains something, as if it existed only *per nefas*.

The metaphysics has two main problems, — the ontological and psychological, and the cosmological and theological. I shall proceed now to indicate Kant's solution of both problems.

I. THE ONTOLOGICAL AND PSYCHOLOGICAL PROBLEM

This is the question in regard to the nature of reality in general. It has evoked three types of solution: Materialism, Spiritualistic Dualism, and Idealism (in the metaphysical sense).

Kant, as has been often said already, ranges himself on the side of idealism. The real itself is an ideal nature. The intelligible world is a system of concrete ideas. It is thus thought with intuitive knowledge by the absolute understanding. It is thus thought in abstract knowledge by the human understanding, to which the perception of the ideal world is permanently denied, since it possesses only sense-perception. The ideal world, accordingly, for the human understanding has not empirical reality, that is, it is not a datum of sense-perception, but it possesses intelligible reality, that is, existence for thought.

Such is the solution of theoretical philosophy. Materialism is utterly impossible, *i. e.*, for metaphysics. But for physics, on the contrary, it is an adequate, and indeed indispensable presupposition that everything that is real manifests itself in space as a body or a function of a body. But epistemological reflection adds that bodies are mere appearances; that they are real only for a perceiving and thinking subject. Precisely for that reason, the subject and its activity cannot be interpreted as a function of a body.

The thinking ego is, on the contrary, a presupposition of
the possibility of the corporeal world, which is a product
of its activity.   One must of course guard against falling
into the error of spiritualism, which supposes that the ego
is known as an object or a permanent substance.   The ego
is given only in its function, as subject, not, however, as
object.   We have no perceptual knowledge of it, as we
have of bodies, but only a concept (in Berkeley's language,
a "notion," not an "idea," or perceptual representation).
It is the concept of a perceiving and thinking subject, whose
functional forms are space and time, categories and ideas.

That is the one aspect.   The same subject has, however,
still another side, namely, the one which it applies to practical philosophy.   It is a rational faculty of desire, practical
reason ; and the moral law is the form of its functioning.
The intelligible character takes rank with the transcendental
unity of apperception as a description of the nature of the
ego.   And here we have reality itself as it is in itself, that is,
as purposive reason, positing itself as its own end.   What
human nature is in miniature, the divine nature is in its
fulness : Reason, positing and realizing ideas.

I shall now touch on a few problems that suggest themselves in this connection.   First, how is the pure ego related
to the empirical ego ?   The subject of the pure volition, the
intelligible character, and the subject of pure perception
and thought, do not belong to phenomena.   On the other
hand, every act of the will and of intelligence, so far as it
manifests itself in the empirical consciousness in time, does
belong to phenomena.   What remains, then, to determine
the subject ?   And conversely how far can one say that a
thought, a volition, or a feeling is a mere appearance of a
self-existent being ?   To the former question, Kant, it seems,
must answer that only the form of the ego in general
remains as a principle of determination.   In this case, the
ego as *individual* would belong to the phenomenal sphere.

And for this very reason the categories, and consequently unity and plurality also, cannot be employed to define things-in-themselves. Obviously, however, this is contrary to Kant's real view. In particular, he maintains that the ego as an intelligible character is an individual.

The answer to the second question is also difficult. Evidently the opposition of phenomenon and thing-in-itself was originally thought of as the opposition between the corporeal world and the ideal world in God (*mundus sensibilis —— intelligibilis*). And the phenomenal world, or the objective world of perception, *a potiori* always remains for Kant the corporeal world. On the other hand, the epistemological system reduces the facts of the world of consciousness also to phenomena, if for no other reason, on account of treating time on a parallel with space. And then Kant constructs also an " inner sense," which is to bear the same relation to the processes of consciousness as the external senses bear to the corporeal world. It will, however, it seems to me, always remain inexplicable what use there is for this inner sense, if we disregard the formal necessity in the system. It likewise remains inexplicable how a thought or a feeling as a phenomenon can be brought into opposition to a thing-in-itself. A motion, a facial expression, a word written or spoken can be interpreted as an appearance of an inner process. But in the case of a thought or a feeling, to be thought and felt are absolutely identical with their existence. They are precisely that which appears, *i. e.*, that which manifest themselves in the sensible world as perceptual physical processes. Finally, it also remains inexplicable what use there is for the ego as a thing-in-itself, or a transcendental object. It is solely a function and nothing else. In the ego as a thing-in-itself, Kant is still adhering to something like the old soul-substance.

I may here touch upon a related question. How are body and soul, the physical and psychical phenomena,

related to each other ?   It is the old moot-question concerning the *commercium animœ et corporis*.   Kant does not
enter into it in detail; in the second edition it is only
mentioned.   He maintains that the *Critique* has obviated
the whole difficulty.   One may designate the solution it
gives as phenomenalistic parallelism.   The very same thing
which manifests itself to the inner sense as a thinking and
willing being, appears to the external sense as a body ; or,
in other words, there is a parallelism between psychical and
physical phenomena in the sense that the same thing which
arises in my consciousness as sensation, idea, or feeling,
would manifest itself in the perception of the external
senses as a physical process in my body.   The question
regarding the possibility of interaction between body and
soul reduces itself to the question, how both external and
internal sense-perception can take place in a being at the
same time.   Or, if we turn our eyes from the world of
appearance to the world of things-in-themselves, the question would arise how there could be interaction between
the intelligible substrate which lies at the basis of the
phenomena of the inner sense, and the intelligible substrate
of the corporeal world.   These are questions neither of
which we can answer, but which contain nothing at all
contradictory.   Why could not two things the nature of
which is unknown, stand in a reciprocal relation to each
other ?   They may be thoroughly homogeneous.   In this
connection the view that appears distinctly in the critique of
the second paralogism in the first edition, keeps suggesting
itself, that the psychical side is the genuine reality, and the
physical is mere appearance.   This is precisely the view
of Schopenhauer and Fechner, who clearly develop this
conception.

    Kant does not enter upon a more detailed exposition of
the parallelistic theory.   The *Critique* is too much occupied
with the refutation of the old spiritualistic psychology and

its doctrine of immortality for Kant to undertake the construction of his own doctrine in a coherent system of psychology. Nevertheless, he reserved a place for it in his system alongside of the rational physics. Thus we receive no answer to problems like the following, that meet us from any epistemological point of view: Do psychical processes correspond with the functioning of all parts of the body, or only with the functioning of certain parts, e. g., the brain, or even only with a definite point in the brain? It is the old question in regard to the seat of the soul that keeps thus recurring. It is the question which Lotze and Fechner answer in opposite ways. Kant thinks to do away with it by the reminder that the soul is not in space, but space is in our perception.[1] — Neither did he discuss in any greater detail the question concerning the extension of mental life. This is disposed of by a reference to the universal parallelism between phenomena and things-in-themselves. A more detailed discussion would have led to the problem of the gradations of mental life (as with Leibniz), and of the nature of psychical life itself, e. g., whether it is at bottom will or idea. These are questions, moreover, which were not altogether strange to Kant, as is shown in Pölitz's *Metaphysics* and the *Reflections*.[2]

II. Immortality

The problem of immortality, which constitutes the ultimate goal in Kant's critical philosophy, as it does in the old metaphysics, is treated almost exclusively in a negative

[1] In a short essay, *Zu Sömmering, über das Organ der Seele* (1796, VI., pp. 457 ff.), he agrees with Sömmering in holding that the soul has virtual, although not local, presence in the fluid contained in the cavity of the brain, — a view which is related to that developed by Lotze in his *Medizinische Psychologie*.

[2] A unique gradation may be mentioned from Pölitz (pp. 214 ff.): The animal soul has only an external sense; the human soul has both external and internal sense; pure spirits (merely a problematic concept) have only an internal sense.

manner in the *Critique of Pure Reason.* Speculative reason
can give neither an affirmative nor a negative answer to the
question of a future life. It belongs to the tribunal of the
practical reason, and this decides in favor of the affirmative.
In regard to the form of the future life, as we have to think
it in Kant's sense, we receive but scant information. He
treated the subject in much greater detail in the lectures, as
is shown by Pölitz's *Metaphysics* and Erdmann's *Reflections.*
We have in those works Kant's original presentation and
the later development side by side. According to the original conception, which may be gathered also from the *Dreams
of a Ghost-Seer,* although it is there presented with an air
of scepticism, the soul is a simple, unextended, spiritual
substance. At birth this substance enters into *commercium*
with a body, with which it stands throughout life in a relation of reciprocity. Furthermore, this relation is a restriction upon its spiritual activity. The soul is in the body,
as in a prison or a cave. At death it withdraws from this
commercium, and it lives on as pure spirit. Such is at least
the philosopher's favorite presentation. However, he adds
proofs for its continued existence. He gives a Platonic
ontological proof from the nature of the soul as vital force;
then the moral proof from the demand for recompense; and,
lastly, a cosmological proof from the "analogy of nature."
The soul develops capacities, such as the speculative impulse and the moral will, for the full employment of which
the earthly life does not afford opportunity. Accordingly,
from the principle that nature produces nothing without a
purpose, it follows that there are organs fashioned for a
future condition, as is the case with the organs of fœtal life.
The condition that ensues is a life of pure spirit. "The
sciences are the luxuries of the understanding, which give us
a foretaste of that which we shall be in the future life." [1] —
This treatment, which rests upon the basis of spiritualistic

[1] Pölitz, *Met.,* p. 249.

dualism, is, without any explanation, placed alongside of a view that presupposes phenomenalism. "The separation of the soul from the body consists in the metamorphosis of sense perception into spiritual perception, and that is the other world." Then the *commercium* with the *mundus intelligibilis*— in which the spirit, "according to Swedenborg's lofty thoughts," exists even at present, without, however, being conscious of it, on account of its sense-perception— takes the form of the intuition of the spirit. The communion with all good spirits, in which the spirit then sees itself, is heaven, and the communion with the evil, hell.[1]

We have here the notion of the future life, to which Kant adhered also in the critical period. It is indicated in the "Discipline of Pure Reason in Relation to Hypotheses."[2] Against dogmatic denials of immortality, one may bring up the "Hypotheses of Pure Reason": "The body is nothing but the fundamental phenomenon, to which, as a necessary condition, all sensibility, and consequently all thought, relates in the present state of our existence. The separation of soul and body forms the termination of the sensible exercise of our faculty of knowledge, and the beginning of the intellectual. The body would thus be regarded, not as the cause of thought, but merely as its restrictive condition, and at the same time as promotive of the sensuous and animal, but therefore the greater hindrance to the pure and spiritual life." Or, "this life is nothing more than a mere appearance, *i. e.*, a sensible representation of the pure spiritual life. The whole world of sense is but an image, hovering before our present mode of knowledge, like a dream." These are, he concludes, merely problematical judgments, but nevertheless they cannot be confuted; they "cannot properly be dispensed with (even for our own satisfaction) as answers to misgivings that may arise." It is noteworthy, too, that

---

[1] Pölitz, pp. 255 ff.

[2] III., p. 516; *cf.* critique of the 4th Paral. in the 1st edition, III., p. 612.

the *Critique* also further permits the use of the old proofs for immortality, with the exception of the ontological proof that is based upon the notion of the soul-substance. "The proofs that may be serviceable for the world preserve their value undiminished; nay, they rather gain in clearness and unsophisticated conviction by the rejection of dogmatical assumptions. For reason is thus confined within her own proper province, namely, the arrangement of ends, which nevertheless is at the same time an arrangement of nature." After this follows the proof from the analogy of nature, referred to above.[1]

III. The Freedom of The Will [2]

The third concept, which Kant regularly names together with God and Immortality as the great concern of metaphysics, is Freedom. In the practical philosophy, it becomes the real support in the ascent to the intelligible world. Following the order of Kant in the Dialectic, I shall here briefly indicate the nature of the concept.

Kant distinguishes two meanings of the word: practical and transcendental freedom. The former belongs to the phenomenal, the latter to the intelligible world.

Practical freedom signifies the power of a being to determine its act by means of the rational will independent of sense impulses. Such a capacity is possessed by man, whose volition is indeed affected by sensibility, but not necessitated as in the case of animals.[3] It is more closely defined as a power which, "by means of representing what is remotely

---

[1] Critique of the Paralogisms, 2d edition, III., p. 288.

[2] The main references are: *Kr. d. r. V.*, third cosmological Idea and Canon (III., pp. 371 ff., 530); *Proleg.*, § 53; *Grundlegung zur Met. d. Sitten*, 3d section; *Kr. d. pr. V.*, Critical Exposition of the Analytic, V., pp. 98 ff. In addition, see *Reflexionen*, II., pp. 426 ff. and *Vorlesungen über Metaph*, pp. 180 ff., 204 ff.

[3] III., p. 371.

useful or hurtful, overcomes the impressions of our sensible faculty of desire. But these considerations of what is desirable in relation to our whole state are based upon reason." [1]

Perhaps it would have been possible "for reason in its practical employment" to have stopped with this notion of freedom, and Kant in the passage last quoted shows a tendency to this procedure. It is adequate, and the only view that is of use in the explanation of the processes of the moral life, especially of responsibility. But, notwithstanding, that is not Kant's meaning. On the contrary, he maintains that practical freedom necessarily presupposes transcendental freedom.[2] Without it, the former would be no better than the freedom of a turnspit. An *automaton spirituale* is just as much an automaton as an *automaton materiale*.[3]

Transcendental freedom, which is valid as it were beyond the domain of possible experience, has first of all the negative significance that the law of empirical causality is not valid for things-in-themselves. Obviously, the causal law, which determines the temporal sequence of phenomena in accordance with a rule, has no application to things that are not in time. But beyond this it has a positive meaning. It is a second form of causality, in addition to the empirical. It is explained as "the power of inaugurating a state of things by itself," as "a spontaneity, which can of itself begin to act, without the necessity of premising another cause."[4] The concept becomes more closely defined through its sphere of application. It is the *intelligibilia*, the pure entities of the understanding, to which this power pertains. And there are two orders of beings to whom it applies: God, the primordial Being, and man as practical reason, man-in-himself (*homo noumenon*).

Freedom belongs primarily to God. This is an implica-

---

[1] III., p. 530.
[2] III., p. 372.
[3] V., p. 102.
[4] III., p. 371.

tion of the concept of God. The first and most real being (*ens originarium realissimum*) cannot be determined by something outside of itself. Its action is absolute spontaneity. The notion of creation expresses this as an absolute positing of the being of things.

In a narrower but real sense, freedom belongs to man, *i. e.*, to the *homo noumenon*. In the first place, it is attributable to him in the negative sense of the analytical judgment that man, as an intelligible being, is not subject to the causal law of the empirical world. It has, however, also a positive significance, since man as a pure intelligible being (*homo noumenon*) has the power " of initiating, independently of natural causes and entirely of himself, a series of events." The effects of human causality according to freedom are thus phenomena in time. "The idea of freedom occurs solely in the relation of the intellectual as cause to the phenomenal as effect." Wherefore Kant refuses to ascribe real freedom to God, since the effects of his causality are things-in-themselves, not phenomena.[1] And in the case of man, the same act is, on the one hand, "in respect to its intelligible cause, to be regarded as free, and still at the same time, in respect to phenomena, and as a consequence of them, to be regarded in accordance with the necessity of nature."[2]

The exposition of this strange view of the twofold causation of certain phenomena, first, by means of things-in-themselves, and, secondly, by means of phenomena, is followed by the doctrine of the intelligible and the empirical character. This harmonizes somewhat better with the system of transcendental idealism. Actions are conditioned by means of the empirical character and the solicitating circumstances. The result is that actions, precisely like other natural phenomena, can in the case of perfect knowledge be foreseen with utter certainty. The empirical character,

---

[1] *Prolegomena*, § 53.　　　　[2] III., p. 373.

however, is the manifestation of the intelligible character in time. The intelligible character, finally, is to be viewed as free intelligible activity. And thus one can rightly say of every action contrary to law, " that, although as a phenomenon in the past, it is completely determined, and in so far inevitably necessary, yet the agent need not have done it, since it, together with all his previous actions that determine it, belongs to one single manifestation of his character, which he himself fashions." " The sentient life possesses, in virtue of the intelligible consciousness of its existence (in the eyes of conscience), the absolute unity of a phenomenon." [1]

Kant regards freedom in this sense as the absolute presupposition of moral responsibility. The processes of the moral self-consciousness, the consciousness of guilt and of repentance, cannot be explained, except on the presupposition " that everything which arises from human volition has for its source a free causality. This, from youth on, expresses its character in its actions, which on account of the uniformity of their procedure render a natural connection knowable. The natural connection, however, does not make the disposition of the will necessary, but, on the contrary, it is the consequence of the immutable principle voluntarily adopted." [2] The justification of this presupposition cannot be demonstrated to the understanding. We cannot exhibit the reality of causality according to freedom, and neither can the *how* of its possibility be theoretically explained. The sole ground for its assumption is that it is the necessary presupposition of the possibility of the moral life. The denial of it leads to an *absurdum morale*, which it is impossible to admit. The speculative reason can accomplish only one thing, that is, it can by differentiating the sensible and the intelligible world disclose the possibility of conceiving freedom. If we fail to draw this distinction,

[1] IV., pp. 102 f.   [2] V., p. 104.

and if we take phenomena for things-in-themselves, there remains absolutely no place for freedom.

In Kant's actual use of the concept of freedom, the two meanings, the practical and the transcendental, often merge into each other. This is especially obvious in the *Reflections*. The relation between the two meanings is mediated by means of the concept of rational causality. The latter can pass as the concrete definition of practical, and also of transcendental freedom. The understanding or reason is just *homo noumenon*. It is defined in the epistemology as pure spontaneity, in contradistinction to sensibility, or receptivity. Its causality is causality in accordance with concepts or ideas. Precisely the same is characteristic also of causality according to freedom, — pure spontaneity and determination of the will by means of a concept or a law. "*Ought* expresses a possible act the ground of which is nothing else than a mere concept." Thus the indefinite notion of the intelligible and its effect receives perceptual filling and at the same time practical signification.

It is obvious, furthermore, that this whole conceptual structure is attended by numerous and serious difficulties. Kant suggests a theoretical one, which arises from the relation of man as *ens derivativum* to God. If one assumes that "God, as the universal and original being, is the cause also of the existence of substance (of the intelligible subject), it seems that one must also concede that the actions of man have their ground in the causality of the highest being." [1] His solution is that God is creator only of *noumena*, but not of phenomena, whereas actions are phenomenal. Kant himself finds this solution "brief and illuminating." I am afraid, however, it will satisfy no one except himself. The intelligible character ought really to be intelligible activity. — Besides, there are practical difficulties. If reason is the intelligible essence of man, what is the source of evil? Is

[1] IV., p. 104.

it sensibility ? That is not and cannot be Kant's meaning.
What, then, becomes of the imputation contained in the
question, for what purpose was the causality of reason in
accordance with freedom devised ? If the source of evil is
not sensibility, it must be reason. But can reason be untrue
to itself ? And if it were, if all evil actions were " the
result of immutable principles of evil voluntarily adopted,"
whence the disapproval with which conscience, which after
all is nothing but the practical reason, pronounces judgment
upon its own act ? And how does this affect the possibility
of a change of life, if the intelligible character has posited
itself through an intelligible act ? Is not the necessary
consequence the intolerable doctrine of the immutability of
the will, which is absolutely irreconcilable with the facts of
the moral life ?

But enough of criticism. So far as I see, the doctrine of
transcendental freedom has been no gain in any way. As
Kant holds it, the concept of the *homo noumenon* as a cause
of phenomena, and thus too of the same phenomena that are
also caused by natural conditions, is neither thinkable nor
even consistent with his own fundamental notions. He
would have to say that the intelligible nature produces by
means of intelligible causality intelligible effects, which
manifest themselves in the phenomenal world as a system
of diverse processes in time. And it is further impossible
to define the facts of the moral life in accordance with that
principle. My conviction is that the notion of practical
freedom alone is both adequate and sufficient for these
purposes.

IV. The Cosmological and Theological Problem [1]

The second great problem of metaphysics is the question
concerning the existence of God and his relation to the

[1] For Kant's " natural theology," in addition to the Lectures, which show
very definitely the real tendency of the Kantian thought on this subject, the

world.   There are in this field also three opposing views :
Atheistic Atomism, Theism, and Pantheism.   Kant takes
sides with theism, or at least with a form of theism that
diverges decidedly from anthropomorphism, and approximates to pantheism.   A very suitable designation of his
view would be the later expression of pantheism that " God
is a supramundane being, in whom reality is immanent."

If we start from the point of view of the cosmological
problem, the question is : Has the world original unity,
or is it a merely accidental aggregate of many independent
essences (atoms) ?   Kant holds to the unity in a double
sense.   All things in space are in a relation of reciprocity,
and all things-in-themselves constitute an original unity
of the *mundus intelligibilis* in God.   The phenomenal reciprocity in space is the manifestation of the ideal *nexus*
of things in the intelligible world.

This view is one of the most permanent factors in Kant's
thought.   It meets us as early as in the *New Explication*
(Prop. XIII.) and the *Natural History of the Heavens* (Preface).   It forms the basis of the *Only Possible Demonstration*,
and lies at the foundation of the *Dreams* and the *Dissertation*
of 1770.   It recurs in the treatment of the concept of God
in the *Critique of Pure Reason*, as well as in numerous
metaphysical *Reflections* of the remains, and the *Lectures*.
All reality is embraced in unity in the *ens realissimum*.
In other words, God is the *omnitudo realitatis*, in whom
the reality of all beings is posited, and from whom it is
derived by processes of limitation, in a way similar to that
in which all spaces arise through limitations in the one
space and are enclosed in it.[1]   In every respect, this

following are to be especially noted : *Kr. d. r. V.*, The Dialectic, chiefly the
Appendix; the *Prolegomena*, especially §§ 57, 58 ; the essay on *Was heisst
sich im Denken orientiren?* (IV., pp. 342 ff.) ; *Kr. d. pr. V.*, the last sections of
the Dialectic; *Kr. d. Urt.*, especially the concluding section (§§ 85 ff.); *cf.*
the *Reflexionen*, II., pp. 452 ff.

[1] " Every world presupposes a primary source, since no *commercium* (reci-

view has a twofold purpose. On one side it is directed against atomistic pluralism. The world, as it is, cannot be conceived of as arising from an original plurality of absolutely independent substances, but only from a fundamental unity. Thus it is a proof of God. The other aim is directed against anthropomorphic theism. The unity is an essential, not an artificial and accidental one, like that which a builder gives to his material. Things are in God, not outside of him. Hence his efficacy is not incidental or miraculous, but is everywhere active. *Mundi non est architectus, qui non sit simul creator.*[1]

These ideas seem to lead to a pantheistic view. But that is not Kant's meaning. He would say it is true that things are in God and God is in things, but God is not the sumtotal of things. God is the unitary principle that fashions things, but is not merged in things. The relation of God to things is perhaps intelligible through the relation of the understanding to concepts. Concepts are in the understanding and the understanding is in the concepts, but it is not identified with them. It is not the sum-total of them, but their presupposition, the principle by means of which they are posited. Thus God is the supramundane principle, by means of which the "natures of things," existing ideas or things-in-themselves, are posited. Obviously, this does not include bodies, which are nothing but the representation of things in our sense-perception. That which God creates is the intelligible world, the world of *noumena*.

This differentiation of God from the world — not from

procity) is possible except in so far as they all exist through one being. This is the sole way of gaining an insight into the connection of substances by means of the understanding, so far as we perceive them, as they exist as universals in the Godhead. When we form a sensible representation of this connection, it is brought about by means of space. Thus we can say that space is the phenomenon of the divine omnipresence." Pölitz, *Metaphysik*, p. 113 ; *Dissertation*, § 22. *Reflexionen*, pp. 219 ff.

[1] *Diss.*, § 20.

the corporeal world of phenomena, which does not exist at all for him, but from the intelligible world — is merely touched upon in the *Critique of Pure Reason*, but is often discussed in the *Lectures*. God, as the primordial being, stands above the world, not in the world. That which is in the world is the totality of things in reciprocity. Between God and things, however, there is no reciprocity. The relation is only one-sided. God has an effect upon things, or rather he effects things, but things do not act upon him. All reciprocity of things is possible through him alone, but he himself is not within this *commercium*. This follows immediately from the concept of him as *ens originarium*. If he were *in commercio* with others, he would be determined by them, and would depend upon them. Hence, he would not be *ens originarium*, for such a being can be thought only as independent.[1]

The foregoing sketch gives in outline the permanent form of Kant's philosophical view of God and the world: God is the original being, which as *intellectus archetypus* posits ideal reality. And our intellect sees this ideal reality shining through the phenomenal world, as the real world that is the ground of the latter.

The critical period brought with it no change in the content of this view. It affected only the method of metaphysics. In reply to the question whether we can demonstrate the truth or objective validity of this view from pure reason, the critical philosophy, after the vacillation of the earlier writings, answers with a completely decisive "no!" But it gives a no less decided affirmative answer to the question whether we have ground to as-

---

[1] Pölitz, *Vorlesungen*, pp. 109, 302, 332. *Cf.* the exposition of the rational theology from a later lecture as given in Heinze's work. There Kant argues against pantheism as follows: Pantheism is either the doctrine of inherence — that is, Spinozism — or that of the aggregate. Both are impossible. God is an essential unity(*monas*), not an aggregate, and God is the *ground* of the world, not its substance.

sume its truth. The existence of God is the most certain
element of our metaphysic; an irresistible need of our
reason forces it upon us. The establishment of this need
is, on the basis of the *Critique*, the proof of the existence
of God. From a consideration of the introduction to the
rational theology in the *Lectures*,[1] we may distinguish three
modes, or even stages, of this demonstration: the transcendental, the physico-theological, and the moral proof.

The transcendental demonstration is the same as appears
in a negative light in the criticism of the ontological and
cosmological proof. In its positive form, it has the following character: Speculative reason cannot relinquish
the concept of an original being in whom the unity of reality is posited, and in whom things are bound so together
as to give rise to the possibility of reciprocity. The task
that is imposed upon it by its own nature is to exhibit reality as a unitary system in a system of logically connected
concepts. The presupposition of the possibility of such a
completion of knowledge is that the nature of things con-
forms with this; *i. e.*, that reality in itself is a logical system,
an *omnitudo realitatis noumenon*. This is the content, too,
often overlooked, of the Appendix to the Dialectic, with its
"transcendental deduction of all ideas of speculative reason."[2] The psychological and theological ideas, especially
the latter, are really necessary factors of our thought. They
cannot, indeed, be realized in perception, simply because our
perception is sensuous. But that does not in the least prevent their "being assumed as objective and hypostatic." If
the idea of a logical *omnitudo realitatis* lies at the basis of
the greatest possible empirical employment of my reason,
" I am not only justified, but also forced, to realize this idea,
i. e., to posit a real object for it. Therefore, after the analogy
of the realities in the world, of substances, causality, and
necessity, I may think a being that possesses all these in the

---

[1] Pölitz, pp. 268 ff.　　　　[2] III., p. 452.

highest degree of perfection, and may conceive this being as an independent reason, which by means of ideas of the greatest harmony and unity is the cause of the universe." That is to say, God or the intelligible *ens realissimum* is a necessary presupposition for the perfect employment of my reason, and therefore a necessary conception for me.

That is the first element of the Kantian, or transcendental theology. It leads to deism, or the notion of God that is determined merely by means of pure concepts of reason, as a necessary, supreme, and original being, in whom all reality has its unity. The physico-theology advances a step further. It establishes theism, which defines the supreme being as intelligence and free will. Its starting-point is the order and purposiveness that we meet with in nature, especially in living nature, and which we can in no way conceive except by presupposing a being that fashions things in accordance with ideas. We do not, indeed, reach in this way any extension of our scientific knowledge; for we cannot perceptually realize such a creative intelligence and its activity. But, nevertheless, reason does not find ultimate contentment until it attains to this idea. For " the highest formal unity is for it the purposive unity of things, and the speculative interest of reason is thereby rendered necessary, namely, its interest in regarding all the harmony of the world as if it sprang from the intention of a supreme reason." And as an heuristic principle the inquiry after the final end renders an indispensable service also to the empirical investigation of the structure of life.[1] This is more fully elaborated in the *Critique of Judgment,* and we shall return to it later.

The crowning-stone is furnished by the moral theology. It is not until we arrive at this point that we gain a concept of God that is serviceable for religion. The physico-theology as such leads no further than to a technical intelligence of

[1] III., p. 461.

great perfection.[1]   The moral theology is the first to define
the primordial being by means of the moral predicates,
"justice," "goodness," "wisdom," and "holiness."   Thus for
the first time it becomes the object of religious belief.   God
is the supremely good and all-powerful will that guarantees
the realization of the highest good.   The *ens realissimum*
now becomes the *summum bonum*, its nature and will are
determined by the moral law, which for that very reason is
referred to it as law-giver and judge.   The demonstration
of this, which is elaborated in the *Critique of Practical
Reason*, is suggested also in the *Critique of Pure Reason* (in
the section on the Ideal of the Highest Good) :[2]   " It is only
in the ideal of the supreme original good that reason can
find the ground of the practically necessary connection of
the two elements of the highest derivative good (morality
and its corresponding blessedness)."   Without God and the
future life, " the glorious ideas of morality, although objects
of approbation and of admiration, cannot be springs of purpose and action.   For they do not fulfil the whole aim which
is natural to every rational being, and which is *a priori*
defined and necessitated by pure reason itself."   Or, as it is
stated in the *Lectures*, without God and a future life one
arrives at an *absurdum morale* that is just as weighty as an
absurdum logicum.   Consequently, a being that is both the
supreme ruler in the moral world and the creator of nature,
is a necessary assumption for our reason. — The moral theology, however, at the same time renders the service of freeing us from superstition and necromancy, which are easily
connected with demonology.   If God's will is determined
solely by the moral law, every attempt to seek his good-will
and favor by any other service than that of a moral life is
vain and useless.

[1] This is brought out excellently in the concluding section of the *Kr. d.
Urt.*, §§ 84 ff.
[2] III., pp. 534 ff.

Such is Kant's natural theology. I desire to further elucidate it by comparing it with two opposite doctrines,
namely, with anthropomorphism on the one hand, and with
Spinozism on the other.

We have defined God's nature by ascribing to him reason
and freedom. Do we not thus fall into anthropomorphism?
Certainly, Kant says, if we suppose that we can dogmatically
define God's nature by means of the forms of the human
reason and the human will. But that obviously cannot be
our intention. No such discursive understanding as the
human understanding is attributable to God, since he has no
sense-perception to which objects are given, but only an
"intuitive understanding," which posits things by means of
its thinking, in some such way as the mathematician does
his objects. We cannot, indeed, form any sensible representation of the nature and possibility of such an understanding. And the same holds true of God's will. Obviously
a pathologically incited will, like the human, which presupposes sensible wants, cannot be ascribed to the all-sufficient
being. Hence a dogmatic anthropomorphism is far from our
view. But that which we regard as possible and indispensable is a symbolic anthropomorphism. As art represents
God in human form, not in the sense that he really actually
exists in this form, but for the purpose of rendering him
pictorially conceivable, theology likewise ascribes to him
the spiritual attributes of man in their highest perfection, for
the purpose of representing to ourselves in this symbol his
absolute perfection and holiness, and of holding it as an ideal
before our eyes. And thus speculative philosophy also may
employ the concept, not as an objective determination of his
nature, but as "analogical knowledge." "If I say we are
forced to view the world as if it were the work of a supreme
understanding and will, I am really saying nothing more
than that the world is related to the unknown as a watch,
a ship, and a regiment are related to the artist, builder, and

commander. Hence in this experience I know this unknown, not indeed as it is in itself, but still as it is for me, namely, in respect to the world of which I am a part." Or "as the furtherance of the happiness of children (a) is related to the love of parents (b), so the welfare of the human race (c) is related to the unknown in God (x), which we call love."[1]

It follows from this that the concept of God is one that appertains not to physics, but to morals. In physics, we are interested in an objective determination of things and their causal connection. For that purpose, the concept of God is thoroughly inadequate; "if a physicist takes refuge in God as the author of things, it is a confession that he has come to an end with his philosophy."[2] On the other hand, a proper concept of God is, from a practical point of view, of very great significance. It furnishes the moral law with a dynamic, which it does not have in sentiency considered by itself. It lends to the heart peace and security against fate; it wards off the ruinous influences of irreligion and pseudo-religion.

As Kant refuses to accept dogmatic anthropomorphism, he also rejects Spinozism. A remark of Jacobi's, that the *Critique of Pure Reason* is an "aid for Spinozism," he disclaims as "a scarcely intelligible insinuation."[3] In fact, Kant had no adequate first-hand knowledge of Spinoza's system, and looked at him entirely too much through the spectacles of the prevailing expositions. Atheism and fatalism are for Kant the fundamental features of his system: atheism, which makes God a sum-total of things in space and time, and even asserts that he has space and time as essential determinations in himself;[4] and fatalism, which regards mechanism as the universal form of all that exists and

---

[1] *Proleg.*, §§ 57 f.   [2] *Kr. d. pr. V.*, Dial., VII.
[3] *Was heisst sich im Denken orientiren?*   IV., p. 349.
[4] V., p. 106.

happens, with a denial of freedom and purposes. Nevertheless, he could have agreed with a good deal in the actual system of Spinoza. This agreement is not confined to the polemic against the anthropomorphic representation of God, and the assertion that God is not an individual that evinces himself in miracles. But Kant might even have sympathized with much in the positive construction of Spinoza's system. His explanation that God = *omnitudo realitatis* = the totality of everything possible or thinkable, is not far from Spinoza's *substantia constans infinitis attributis*. And likewise his definition that reality is in God and God in reality, is not far from Spinoza's *Deus rerum omnium causa immanens*. But there are essential differences also. Kant makes the moral predicates of prime importance in the concept of God, whereas Spinoza confines himself to the transcendental determinations. Accordingly, Kant, as was shown above, seeks to establish the supra-mundane nature of God. God is not merged in the world, and his relation to the world has not the form of logical necessity of thought (*efficere* in Spinoza), but the form of a free creative act. Theology designates God's efficacy by the word 'creation.' Kant accepts the word and the concept. God's efficacy is an absolute positing of the being of things, *creatio est actuatio substantiæ*, in distinction from human production, which applies only to the manifestation or combination of things, not to the existence of substance. If we represent this notion of creation with permissible symbolic anthropomorphism, artistic production perhaps affords the most suitable image, more suitable than the mathematical method that Spinoza employs, in order to dogmatically determine the efficacy of the substance. God as creative understanding thinks in intuitive ideas, in some such way as the creative genius thinks in images.

V. MECHANISM AND TELEOLOGY

In connection with the cosmological and theological views arises the question regarding a mechanical or teleological explanation of nature. Kant discusses the problem in the *Critique of Judgment.* It did not correspond with his purposes to include this in the *Critique of Pure Reason,* the criticism of pure *a priori* metaphysics. Even the brief treatment of the physico-theological proof is out of place. Accordingly he combined it with the criticism of taste, to form a third *Critique.*

The problem is treated according to the fixed schema. The reader is guided through the Analytic, Dialectic, and the Doctrine of Method, and is led to and fro to the point of exhaustion between understanding and reason, reason and judgment, and determining and reflective judgment. It would be difficult to convince one's self that all this ceremoniousness was necessary to exhibit these fundamentally simple ideas. The following is the outcome. The question, formulated as an antinomy, whether all natural phenomena are to be explained mechanically, or whether certain natural products render a teleological explanation necessary, is not to be solved by a simple yes, or no. The natural products that give rise to the problem are organic beings. The understanding does not succeed if it undertakes to explain them, like all other natural phenomena, as mere effects of natural mechanism. Their peculiarity consists in the fact that in them the whole cannot exist without the parts, while also, conversely, the parts are only possible through the whole, in that it produces and preserves them. The eye serves the body as an instrument, but it itself arises only in and through the whole. And the idea is absolutely incomprehensible that somewhere and at some time an eye could arise for itself through an accidental combination of parts, like a mechanical product, a stone, or a clod of earth.

Every attempt to carry out such an idea is frustrated. The same is true of the whole. The understanding cannot be satisfied by attempts to explain mechanically plants and animals by means of a mere collision of atoms in motion, as the old atomic view undertook to do. The more the attempt is carried out in detail, as in Lucretius, the more apparent does its absurdity become. The understanding accordingly sees itself forced to assume for this sphere a different form of origination, namely, a form that explains the existence of the part from the existence of the whole, that is, to adopt the teleological view. It regards the whole as pre-existent in the idea or the concept (as purpose), and then explains how the thing becomes real by means of causality in accordance with concepts (purposive activity). We have empirical knowledge of this kind of causality in the experience of our own activity in the production of works of art. On the other hand, the concept of a natural force which acts purposively but yet without purpose and aim, as a concept of a species of force of which experience affords no example, is utterly fanciful and empty.[1]

One cannot escape from this assumption by assuming a gradual development of the higher forms of life from lower and more simple ones. Even the first and simplest organisms already possess the character of the organic; that is, the whole renders the part possible. If one wants to explain the first forms of life as springing directly from the womb of mother earth, one must therefore "ascribe to this universal mother an organization purposively adapted to all these creatures. But then one has only pushed the ground of explanation further back, and cannot lay claim to have made the generation of plants and animals independent of the conditioning final cause."[2]

[1] *Ueber den Gebrauch teleol. Prinzipien*, **VI.**, p. 493.

[2] *Critique of Judgment*, § 80. Kant evidently shows an inclination towards the evolutionary view in biology, which is closely connected with his evolution-

But now for the other side of the case. If we assume that an intelligent being originates plants and animals by means of purposive causality, the conception is absolutely useless for an explanation of things. In the first place, we have no kind of knowledge at all of the nature and mode of acting of such a being. We can offer a teleological explanation of human products of art, for we have a knowledge of man, his ends, and his mode of activity; but the cosmic intelligence, of which organic beings are to be viewed as artistic productions, and its mode of activity, are never given in any perceptual form. It is, therefore, merely a problematic concept, whose objective reality cannot be established. Hence this concept is of no service in any way to the physicist. It accomplishes nothing in its attempts to explain natural phenomena. We could offer such an explanation only if the cosmic intelligence were a known force of a known and regular form of activity.

But there is still another consideration. We can frame no sensible representation of the final purpose of nature.

ary cosmology. The emergence of new forms through a gradual transformation of existent conditions of life, under the influence of different conditions, is a familiar notion to him. Only the original emergence of organic beings by *generatio æquivoca* — that is, " the generation of an organic being by means of the mechanism of raw, unorganized matter " — is to him a preposterous idea; an idea which, nevertheless, he attempted to think, as is seen, among other places, from a fragment in Reicke (*Lose Blätter*, I., p. 137): " I also have at times steered into the gulf, assuming here blind natural mechanics as the ground of explanation, and believed I could discover a passage to the simple and natural conception. But I constantly made a shipwreck of reason, and I have therefore preferred to venture upon the boundless ocean of Ideas." " The principle of teleology in the structure of organic, especially of living, creatures is as closely connected with reason as the principle of active causes in the perception of all changes in the world. To suppose that any part of a creature which bears a constant relation to a genus is purposeless, is just as bad as to suppose that an event in the world occurs without a cause." But evolutionary biology is to him a rash venture of human reason, which finds no encouragement in experience, according to which all production is *generatio homonyma*. Still it is " not precisely absurd, and there may be but few even of the most acute natural scientists to whom it has not sometimes occurred."

We cannot regard the particular species of animals and plants as absolute ends in themselves. The truth is that the existence of many, regarded in themselves, seem to us completely worthless, however artful and formally purposive their structure may be. Neither can we form a representative idea of the final purpose of the whole cosmos, for which the existence of all these beings would be a necessary means. One reason for this is that we do not look upon nature as a unitary system. The only being that we recognize as an end in itself is man, as a rational being. But if we posit him as the ultimate goal of the universe, not only is the objection valid that the employment of means for this purpose is utterly inconsistent with our ideas, but also in the narrower sphere the facts cannot be made to tally with this supposition. Nature seems to deal with man in precisely the same way as it does with its other products, and human generation and decay is part of the general course of nature.

Hence the understanding remains in this field, as it were, in a state of suspense. It cannot carry out the mechanical explanation at this point, although, on the other hand, it cannot be demonstrated that such an explanation is impossible. It cannot divest itself of a teleological conception, but, on the other hand, it cannot really carry it out. Accordingly, it will employ the two principles alongside of each other. On the one side, it will cling to the general maxim to look upon all natural phenomena in accordance with a mechanical explanation. Scientific explanation is explanation from physical causes. On the other side, it will look upon organic things as if they were products of an intelligence that works in accordance with purposes,—a procedure which, as an heuristic principle, is indispensable in the biological sciences, and which in part has shown itself to be fruitful. No one could understand the construction of the eye, for example, who knew nothing of the purpose of the organ, namely, vision. One will remain conscious, however, that this is only a subjective principle of reflection, not an objective principle of explanation, like mechanical causality.

The final reach, however, to which the understanding may attain is to recognize herein its own subjective condition. It is due to the very nature of our discursive understanding that the mechanical and teleological conceptions cannot be reduced to a unity. For an understanding to which things that it thinks by means of concepts must be given in sense-perception, the contingency of the matter is in permanent contrast with the necessity of the form. For an intuitive understanding, which posits things by means of its concepts, the teleological and causal points of view may be coincident. Or, objectively expressed, in the intelligible substrate of nature, there may occur a union of the manifold, in which mechanical and teleological conjunction are one and the same. We may represent this unity to ourselves after the analogy of the unity that exists between the parts of a work of art or a poem. And thus we may symbolically represent the efficacy of the creative principle by means of the creative activity of the artist, which also transcends the opposition of mechanism and teleology. A poem is not produced, like a boulder, by means of external addition of parts, nor like a product of handicraft, by means of methodical contrivance, with reference to the subsequent realization. But the genius produces together both the form and material of his work of art, as in organic development form and material grow together.[1]

Kant did not further pursue this discussion. Its evident presupposition is the objective idealism in his metaphysics, which views reality in itself as a system of existent Ideas. The subsequent speculative philosophy, which was fond of emphasizing its connection with the *Critique of Judgment*, carries out the idea that reality is an ideal composition,

[1] §§. 77, 78.

which we, by means of the dialectic method, interpret or imitate. This philosophy overcomes the opposition between teleology and mechanism, like that between thought and being.

The critical philosophy does not trust the human understanding to take this step, for it is not an intuitive understanding. Kant stops exactly where scientific investigation stops. One can say that he gives really nothing but an exact description of the procedure of our biological investigation. This seeks the physical causes of the process of life, and presupposes that such are everywhere existent. It discards hyperphysical causes as explanations, since they furnish the natural investigator with no explanation. On the other hand, biology presupposes that all parts and functions of the organism have a purpose (or at least originally had). The explanation of the structure is not completed until we recognize the relation to the purpose, namely, the preservation of life. Where this is the case, as for example with the eye, the natural scientist says, "Now I understand." Where it is not the case, as with the brain or the process of generation, he says, "The matter is a riddle to me." And even if we could describe in minutest detail the physical process involved in generation, the union of germ-cells and their nucleus or what-not, we should not understand the matter until we gained a clear insight into the significance that parental generation has for the preservation and development of life.

Above all, it is to be noted that Kant has really a transcendent metaphysic. He gives his complete adherence to it as the rational view of the world. But it is not possible as *a priori* demonstrable knowledge of the understanding, as scholastic philosophy tried to be. From such a standpoint, only mathematical physics is possible, which is concerned solely with phenomena and their necessary relations in space and time. Reason, on the other hand, necessarily passes beyond the phenomenal world to the intellectual world, which is a world of existing ideas that are conjoined by logical and teleological relations, and are intuitively present in the divine intellect. In the world of appearance, especially in organic life, there are gleams now and again of the ideal world. In the moral world, however, we comprehend it in its absolute reality; the entities of practical reason are as such members of the intelligible world.

It is clear that this is the Platonic-Leibnizian philosophy. Kant had it constantly before his eyes in Baumgarten's textbook. Reality, as the understanding thinks it in contradistinction to sensibility, is a system of monads, which are joined in a unity by means of pre-established harmony, or an *influxus idealis*, like that which exists between the parts of a construction of thought or a poem. The ultimate ground of the unity of things is their radical unity in God's being, while bodies, on the contrary, are merely *phænomena substantiata*. Kant never discarded any of these ideas. He only gave them another interpretation. They are not truths demonstrable to the understanding, like mathematics and physics, but necessary ideas with which reason can never dispense. The only point at which reason went astray was in attempting to include these ideas among those that are capable of manifestation in sense-perception. The *Critique* has shown the impossibility of such a procedure. The illusion which led to it has been discovered and exposed, if not destroyed, and thus it can no longer deceive. He who has understood the *Critique of Pure Reason* will no longer expect to find God and the soul as objects in nature among other objects. In other respects, however, the critical philosophy does not at all impugn the truth of these ideas. They constitute absolutely essential elements of our knowledge. In the new philosophy, in the ideas of speculative and practical reason, they find a new and better support than they possessed in the old proofs of the under-

standing. As the Reformation discarded "good works" only
in order immediately to require them again in a new form
as fruits of faith, Kant likewise discarded the notions of
the old idealistic metaphysics, on the ground that they were
barren as pure knowledge of the understanding, only for
the purpose of immediately reinstating them again as necessary ideas of reason. The distinction is suggested also in
the Analytic when it says that "to think an object and to
know an object are not the same." For us sense-perception
is essential to knowledge, and it is merely the phenomenal
that is given in perception. The truly real, accordingly,
can only be thought by us, but never perceived. It can
never, therefore, possess empirical reality for us, but intelligible, transcendental reality alone.

VI. The Metaphysical Elements of Natural Science [1]

This little work is described by Kant (in a letter to
Schütz, September 13, 1785) as a chapter containing the
concrete application of the *Metaphysics of Nature* that
he intended to write. This preliminary work is given out
in advance because the metaphysic must retain its character
as entirely pure, whereas here an empirical concept is presupposed. He does this also for the purpose of having
ready at hand something that he may later employ as concrete illustrations, and thus make the presentation comprehensible. But the pure metaphysic of nature did not
appear, any more than the metaphysical elements of psychology, which in this same letter he promises as an appendix to the Doctrine of Bodies.

---

[1] See **A.** Stadler, *Kants Theorie der Materie* (1883) ; and **A.** Drews, *Kants
Naturphilosophie als Grundlage seines Systems* (1894). The former gives a
systematic and complete exposition of Kant's treatment, the latter deals with
his whole natural philosophy, and criticises it from the standpoint of Hart-
mannian realism.

The present work does not of course organize its material in accordance with the demands of the subject-matter, but in accordance with the schema of categories. It is closely connected with the system of fundamental principles in the *Critique of Pure Reason.* The second part, the Dynamics, is the most important. It is the further elaboration of the "Anticipations of Sense-perception." Its object is to establish a dynamic theory of matter, and by means of it a dynamic explanation of natural phenomena in place of the mechanical. The essential ideas, however, are much older than the *Critique.* They are in their main features already contained in two small treatises that date from the fifties : in the *Physical Monadology* (1756), and in the *New Doctrine of Motion and Rest* (1758). In the later writing they are easily remodelled according to the principles of the *Critique,* although it seems to be very questionable whether it is always an advantage to the clearness and logical result.

The form of natural philosophy with which Kant took issue from the beginning of his scientific career was the atomistic-mechanical view. There were two elements in this conception, that most extensively dominated the opinions of physicists, which were chiefly objectionable to him. The first was its opposition to Newton's natural philosophy, and to the attractive force that matter possesses, which is presupposed by the Newtonian theory. The second was that the atomic view tends to approach the doctrine of empty space in its explanation of natural phenomena.[1] In regard to the former, as we have already seen, the application of the power of attraction to the explanation of cosmic structures belongs to Kant's oldest scientific undertakings. Its derivation is for him, therefore, a chief requisite of every theory

---

[1] Upon the development of the atomic theory of matter and the opposition that Newton displays towards this conception, see the thorough and instructive work by Kurd Lasswitz, *Geschichte der Atomistik vom Mittelalter bis auf Newton.* 2 vols., 1890.

of matter. But the atomistic and mechanical theory does not and cannot do justice to this requirement, inasmuch as it admits to matter only one form of action, namely, the transference of motion through impact and impulsion in a state of rest. This fact at once shows the inadequacy of the view. If it takes refuge in the position that this form of activity alone is immediately given and evident, Kant retorts that attraction and its effect at a distance "is not in the slightest any more unintelligible than the original power of repulsion."[1] The sole advantage that action caused by impact has over that caused by attraction, is that in a certain sense it is given in sense-perception. But that is no advantage for the understanding, to which, by means of his dynamic theory, Kant wishes to give once more its natural freedom against the restrictions of sense representation.

The same thing holds true in regard to the second element, namely, empty space and the corollary of an absolute space-filling by means of mere extension, with which the atomistic and mechanical physics operates. Kant finds that the absolute void as well as the absolute plenum, or absolute impenetrability, are wholly arbitrary suppositions, which commend themselves because they may be in a certain way perceptually represented. But the understanding is by no means forced to suppose them. Indeed, in the last analysis, they are nothing but occult qualities, "bolsters for lazy reason." Neither the concept of absolutely empty space nor that of absolute impenetrability is given in experience. Experience shows only a greater or less degree of resistance. The plenum and void are, therefore, *entia rationis*, in which reason, in its desire for the absolute, delights, but from which the understanding, with its attention fixed upon phenomena, must turn aside. "The absolute void and the absolute plenum are in the science of nature pretty much the same thing as blind chance and blind fate are in metaphysi-

[1] IV., p. 405.

cal cosmology, namely, a bar to inquiring reason." And
therefore "everything that relieves us of the need of taking refuge in empty spaces is a real gain for natural
science." [1]

Now the dynamic concept of matter that Kant opposes
to the mathematico-mechanical view is as follows. Matter is
defined as the movable which fills space and possesses motive
power. Two primary powers constitute its nature: the
powers of repulsion and of attraction. The repulsive power
is the first, without which space-filling cannot be made intelligible at all. Atomism, indeed, bases this upon mere
existence in space; the mere fact that a body is in one place
prevents it from penetrating another body. Kant maintains that the exclusion of a body that is seeking to enter
the space that another body occupies presupposes a repulsive power; otherwise it is nothing but a consequence of
an occult quality. This power is the original power of
expansion; thereby matter fills space and repels other
bodies from it. But a second fundamental power is necessary. If matter had merely a power of expansion, it would
completely dissipate and thus destroy itself. Consequently,
the activity of this power must be limited by a power that
acts in the opposite direction, that is, the power of attraction. If this alone were operative, it would likewise annihi-
late matter, inasmuch as it would contract the matter
into a point and thus destroy the space-filling. Space-
filling is possible only through the opposition of the two
forces. And from this point of view one can at the same
time deduce an original difference in the character of the
space-filling, dependent upon the difference of the proportion of the powers. In this way the "chief of all problems
of natural science," namely, the explanation "of an *ad
infinitum* possible specific difference of matter," would be
solved, without the supposition of an absolute impenetra-

[1] IV., p. 427.

bility and absolute empty space, — a supposition that restricts the understanding.[1]

In the *Physical Monadology* these concepts are formed on the presupposition of monadic centres of force that merely, together with their activity, fill space. On the other hand, in the *Metaphysical Elements* the view of scholastic metaphysics is abandoned, that makes matter consist of ultimate and simple parts whose aggregate appears to the senses as an extended body. That view may satisfy metaphysical needs, but it cannot be reconciled with the requirements of the mathematical science of nature, which cannot do without the demand for infinite divisibility both of space and of matter also. The critical philosophy, which interprets matter as mere phenomenon in space, finds no difficulty in regarding matter itself as that which is extended through space, and which for that very reason fully shares in the spatial quality of absolute divisibility.

Thus the new theory, inasmuch as it attributes both extensity and intensity to matter, seems to be the refutation of the atomistic and mechanical philosophy of nature, which regards matter solely as an *extensivum*, and of the monadology, which undertakes to reduce it to pure *intensiva*.

I shall not enter into the use that Kant makes of this notion for the interpretation of the other qualities of matter and also of the laws of motion. Neither shall I take up the question whether the new notion of matter as continuously extended, but endowed with different degrees of power, and therefore filling space with different intensity, is altogether consistent with the presuppositions of the critical epistemology. It may be seen at this point how strenuously Kant's old stock of metaphysical notions resisted reconstruction at the hands of the critical epistemology.[2]

---

[1] IV., p. 428.

[2] There is no reason for taking up Kant's last work on natural philosophy, the *Uebergang von den metaphysischen Anfangsgründen zur Physik*. Neither

VII. Concluding Remarks

The goal of all Kant's efforts is the establishment of a scientifically tenable metaphysic according to a new method. And in this he is concerned with a metaphysics that will lead beyond the physical world to the world of true being, the *mundus intelligibilis.* From his first work to the last line that he wrote this is everywhere present as the fundamental tendency of his thought. The means vary, but the end remains the same.

Kant early became convinced that the means employed by the traditional metaphysics were useless for its purpose. It attempted to rise to the world of ideas by means of the teleological explanation of natural phenomena (physico-theology). Kant saw clearly, as is shown as early as the writings of the year 1756, that natural science is necessarily immanent; it never leads beyond physical causes to hyperphysical or ideal causes. He accordingly sought for a new procedure for metaphysics, and at first he thought that he had found it in a new form of pure conceptual speculation. According to this, God is not the cause of things, in the sense of being the mechanician or efficient cause in time, of the physical world and its various forms. But God is the logically necessary presupposition of their conceptual existence in the form of their true nature or essence. This was his view as early as the fifties, and it was elaborated in the *Ground of Demonstration* of 1763,

has physics, the *a priori* concept of which ought here be given, suffered any loss because Kant could not more fully complete the work, nor has the knowledge of his philosophy been enriched by the parts so far published (*Altpreuss. Monatsschr.*, XIX–XXI, edited by Reicke with his customary care).   One can here see all the blemishes of the Kantian thought exaggerated as in a concave mirror.   The constant manipulation of given thought-elements to make them fit in with a fixed schema seems to be carried out to such an extent in his last manuscript that it cannot be viewed without pain.

though there a sceptical hesitation was already exhibited towards his own thoughts.

A new attempt to discover the true method of metaphysics appears in the *Dissertation* of 1770. One may already describe it as the transcendental method. By means of pure concepts of the understanding, it is possible to reach a pure intelligible reality that is free from the conditions of sensibility. As *a priori* knowledge of the sensible world is possible by means of the forms of sensibility, so through the pure forms of thinking, *a priori* knowledge of the intelligible world is possible. Of course, this is nothing more than symbolical knowledge, since we have not an intuitive understanding.

With some modifications of this standpoint we reach the final and definitive form of the method of metaphysics in the critical philosophy. First of all, the view is retained that the understanding creates metaphysics *a priori* through pure activity, but it is metaphysics in a new signification, *viz.*, as pure science of nature. The *Critique of Pure Reason* shows the possibility of a phenomenalistic metaphysics as science. But, on the other hand, the understanding, according to the new view, does not lead *trans physicam*, into the land of the truly real. Its concepts have the significance only of concepts of the constructional forms of phenomena. But now another faculty comes into play. What understanding cannot do is accomplished by reason, which leads to the ideal world that exists in and for itself. And it does this in two ways. First, as *theoretical* reason, in virtue of the striving towards the unconditioned that is implicit in its nature, it leads beyond the world of the conditioned and relative. Nature, the reality in space and time, cannot by any means be thought of as existing in the absolute sense. The contradiction involved in the fact that it can neither be thought as finite nor as infinite, shows its inner impossibility, or its unreality in the absolute understanding. The human spirit can find satisfaction only in the thought of reality as an existing world of ideas, as a complete system of eternal essences whose unity is constituted by inner teleological relations. And this conclusion is suggested in an especial degree by the presence of those peculiar forms, organic beings, whose possibility cannot be explained from merely mechanical causes. Secondly, the *practical* reason, by virtue of its unconditional command to realize ideas in the world of sense, leads necessarily to the assumption that an ideal world forms the basis of nature. How on any other supposition could ideas enter as formative principles into nature? The rational being that posits itself as absolute end for itself, posits itself necessarily as a member of a kingdom of ends, and further posits this kingdom as the absolute reality itself.

Thus the reason, which thinks and realizes ideas, leads beyond the spatial and temporal world of phenomena to an ideal eternal reality. This reality, it is true, cannot be given in our (sense) perception. For man as a rational being, its reality is not less certain, though this is of course not reality in the sense of reality as a pure concept of the understanding (which only signifies 'given in sense-perception'), but transcendent intelligible reality. The concepts of the understanding are realized by means of perception; while the objective validity of ideas cannot, from the nature of the case, be attained in this way. But that is not required for a proof of their validity. Kant continued to hold fast to the position of the *Dissertation* of 1770. Reason possesses a transcendent significance, and limits sensibility, while sensibility does not limit reason. Sensibility restricts understanding, which is valid only in so far as its concepts are realized. But in respect to reason it has no authority, and it transcends its sphere when in the form of dogmatic materialism it rises against the theoretical reason and its ideas of God, freedom, and immortality, and will admit nothing as real except that which is an object of sense-perception in space and time. This is a restriction that has validity only for the investigations of natural science. Still less has sensibility any authority against reason in its practical application. In this field, subservience to the arrogance of sensibility becomes an offence against human dignity. Indeed, from an ultimate religious point of view, sensibility in general is what is accidental, false, and to be shunned. When the rational being puts off his corporeal existence, he will be finally free from sensibility and its limits. Metaphysics will attain its complete truth after the great metamorphosis, in the eternal life.

APPENDIX

Empirical Psychology and Anthropology [1]

Between the exposition of the theoretical and the practical philosophy I introduce a sketch of the psychology and anthropology, including also the philosophy of history that is connected with the latter. These disciplines stand in numerous relations to both the fundamental parts of the system. The psychology is closely connected with the epistemology and metaphysics, the philosophy of history with the moral philosophy and politics. Unfortunately, these subjects were not completely developed. Since they are not sciences that can be derived from rational concepts, they remain outside the boundaries of a proper system of philosophy as Kant defined it.

[1] LITERATURE : It is a permanent source of regret that the Anthropology, which was a favorite subject of lectures with Kant, was not prepared for the press by him while he was still mentally vigorous. We should then have had a work rich in facts and in important ideas ; and perhaps the revision of the empirical science might have exerted a favorable influence even upon the elaboration of the pure philosophy. The *Anthropologie in pragmatischer Hinsicht*, which was first prepared for the press in 1798, shows many traces of old age. This was supplemented by the publication of manuscript lectures of Kant, belonging perhaps to the first half of the eighties : *I. Kants Menschenkunde oder philosophische Anthropologie*, edited from manuscript lectures by F. Ch. Starke, 1831. Menzer assigns these lectures to the year 1784, or at any rate between 1778 and 1788 (*Kantstudien*, III., p. 68). In addition to these, there is the psychology in Pölitz's *Metaphysik* (pp. 124 ff.), and the *Reflexionen Kant's zur Anthropologie*, edited with an introduction by B. Erdmann. Finally, in this field belongs a whole series of short essays, among the earlier of which we may mention especially the *Beobachtungen über das Schöne und Erhabene*, and among the later those concerned with the philosophy of history. Also the *Critique of Judgment* and the works on moral philosophy contain some material pertaining to these subjects. — *Cf.* also J. B. Meyer, *Kants Psychologie* (1870); A. Hegler, *Die Psychologie in Kants Ethik* (1891). [E. F. Buchner, *A Study in Kant's Psychology with Reference to the Critical Philosophy*. (Psych. Rev. Monograph Supplement No. 4) 1897.]

In the first place, psychology according to Kant is an experiential science, and as such, therefore, does not belong to philosophy in the proper sense of the word. Indeed, it cannot even be called a science in the proper sense, like physics, which is based on mathematical principles. Psychology is only a collection of purely empirical facts, something like chemistry, only it is in a still worse position than the latter in that it is restricted to observation, and cannot employ experiment. "It can therefore never become more than an historical, and so far as possible a systematic account of the internal sense, *i. e.*, a natural description, but not a science of the mind, not even an experimental doctrine of psychology."[1] Why, since the phenomena of the inner sense are in time, it is not possible to employ arithmetic, Kant does not tell us. Nor does he explain to us how he conceives empirical and rational psychology to be related, — all of which is in keeping with the failure of his "Theory of Experience" to give any real explanation of concrete problems.

Nevertheless, this discipline, which is rated so poorly in regard to its scientific form, is not without importance for the construction of the critical philosophy. Indeed, one may say that the latter has borrowed its entire outline from psychology. The doctrine of the mental faculties must have afforded the form and the division for the critical procedure. The schema that lies at the basis of all of Kant's thought is the old division of the mental faculties, first into those of knowledge and desire, and further into a higher and a lower, or an ideal and a sensuous faculty of knowing and desiring. This obvious principle of division, that had come down to modern times through the scholastic philosophy, and had been retained by Leibniz and Wolff, Kant found in his text-book of psychology, Baumgarten's *Metaphysic* (*vis cognoscitiva et appetitiva, inferior et superior*). He adopted

[1] *Metaphysische Anfangsgründe der Naturwissensschaft*, IV., p. 361.

this schema and made it the basis of his investigation. The *Critique of Pure Reason* examines the faculty of knowledge, and the *Critique of Practical Reason* the faculty of desire. In both these we find the intention of separating sharply the higher faculty from the lower, and securing for it independence as against the latter. With this purpose the *Dissertation* of 1770 begins, and the critical philosophy has always held fast to it. In the philosophy of Leibniz and Wolff, sensible knowledge is defined merely as knowledge of the lower rank, as confused rational knowledge. But the difference is rather one of kind, or of the source from which it is derived. Sense knowledge is founded on receptivity, knowledge of understanding upon spontaneity. And the same is true in the practical sphere. According to Wolff's doctrine, the sensuous impulses are "confused" strivings towards happiness that are clarified, purified, and systematized by means of reason. In this field, also, Kant sets up an absolute difference in kind: the sensuous impulses aim at pleasure, while reason has for its goal the moral law.

Kant's anatomical impulse then carried him on to further divisions. Within the faculty of sense it is necessary to distinguish external and internal sense, sense-perception and imagination. In the intellectual faculty, reason and judgment are to be separated from understanding. Moreover, he brought into connection with judgment a third fundamental faculty of the mind lately called into prominence by Mendelssohn and Tetens. This was the faculty of feeling pleasure and pain. By distinguishing in this field also a lower and a higher side — pleasure and pain connected with sensations (pleasantness and unpleasantness), and with the imagination (beauty and ugliness) — he obtained a schema for the third Critique, the *Critique of Judgment*.

We cannot here undertake an exposition of the details of the empirical psychology. But I shall still say a few words regarding the Anthropology and Philosophy of History. The Anthropology considers man as a species in relation to other living beings. It passes over into Philosophy of History, since the nature of man can come to complete development only in the course of ages, and in connection with a political state.

The nature of man can be defined in the general formula, ' Man is a living being endowed with the capacity of reason ' (*animal rationabile*). His vocation, like that of all living beings, is to develop all his natural powers to the highest stage of perfection. This general formula, however, embraces two special characteristics. In the first place, in the case of man it is only in the life of the species, not in that of the individual, as with animals, that all the natural powers attain complete development. Secondly, among animals these powers develop spontaneously, by means of instincts ; man, on the contrary, must develop and form his natural powers by the help of reason. The goal of this process of culture, which constitutes the real content of the historical life, is man as a completely rational being (*animal rationale*), a being that determines his life and actions entirely by reason. It was the Stoic type of human perfection that Kant had before his mind. The complete sovereignty of reason, and complete freedom from the passions, constitute the *status perfectionis*. Emotions like scorn, sympathy, repentance, shame, have no power over the perfect man ; he acts in accordance with principles, not according to feelings. Emotions are only provisional springs of action with which the wisdom of nature endowed man, as it endowed animals, until reason is sufficiently developed to assume the guidance of life. When regarded from the standpoint of perfection, emotions and passions are to be viewed as disturbances, the latter comparable with drunkenness, and the former with chronic illness.[1]

[1] *Anthropologie*, §§ 72 f.

The way to complete culture is shown by history. The Philosophy of History is the attempt to interpret the facts of history from this point of view. In the *Idea of a Universal History*, Kant furnished an outline for such an interpretation.[1] He distinguishes three sides in the development of human nature : the cultivation of the powers in the various accomplishments, arts, and sciences; civilization through the limitation of the individual's own will by social control; finally, moralizing by means of religion, custom, and education. In this way the moral nature will become gradually free from the natural sway of impulse, and morality, as the free determination of the will through the moral law, will become possible.[2]

The means that nature employs to urge men to set out in this course of development are the three great passions, desire for gain, desire for power, and desire for glory. They belong to man as *animal sociale*. He desires not merely to exist, but to live with others in order to become conscious of his own superiority in comparison with them. The will to live becomes in man the will for power, and this is the fundamental impulse of man as *animal sociale*. It constantly urges him on to develop his own powers of body and mind, in order to maintain and further his position in society. And, on the other hand, it becomes a motive which leads the individual to establish a judicial and political order, in order, by the limitation of this impulse, to ward off the

---

[1] It is noteworthy that in the Philosophy of History also Kant is the forerunner of the speculative systems. He himself describes his *Idea* as an "*a priori* clue." We find that he even made an attempt at an *a priori* history of philosophy. In Reicke's *Lose Blätter* (II, pp. 285 ff.) there is the following passage : "Can a history of philosophy be written mathematically (this must mean dogmatically, or from concepts)? Can we show how dogmatism must have arisen, and from it scepticism, and that this necessarily leads to criticism ? — Yes, if the idea of a metaphysic inevitably presses on human reason, and the latter feels a necessity to develop it; but this science lies entirely in the mind although only outlined there in embryonic form."

[2] *Anthropologie*, Conclusion.

destruction that threatens him from the attacks of others. Thus antagonism in society is the contrivance by means of which nature brings man unwittingly nearer his goal. Kant here follows entirely in the track of Hobbes. Desire of gain and desire of power are the great basal impulses, that, in the case of man alone of all animals, render "the war of all against all" the natural condition of society. But just because of the evils that war brings in its train, the creation of a state becomes necessary. And in this way an artificial condition of peace and of security is attained, in which, however, antagonism and competition are not entirely destroyed, but only limited, and prevented from passing into violence and deception.[1]

In this way, however, the happiness of the individual is not secured. Indeed, one may say that the increase in culture is purchased at the cost of happiness, if by happiness one understands the natural feelings of comfort. Those powerful impulses of human nature, desire for gain, desire for glory, and desire for power, never permit man to attain satisfaction. The animal is at peace as soon as his physical wants are satisfied. In the case of man, there is added to the physical wants the necessity that springs from the idea of acquiring more, and of attaining superiority. If one judges the matter from the standpoint of the individual's happiness, one could with Epicurus call these things imagined necessities and insane impulses. One might even say that from them arise all the evils and all the vices of culture. On this point Rousseau was right. Culture as such does not render men either happier or more virtuous. Folly, hypocrisy, maliciousness, are specific qualities of man which are entirely wanting in the irrational animal. Moreover, they increase with culture. Nevertheless, nature or Providence is justified by the course of human history. .It

---

[1] *Anthropologie* §§ 82, 83. *Idee zu einer allg. Gesch. in Weltbürgerlicher Absicht*, IV., pp. 146 ff.

brings man constantly nearer to the goal to which his view was originally directed, though of course not by the smoothest and shortest road. This goal is the complete development of all his natural powers, especially of his powers of reason. The final goal, which of course lies at an indefinite distance, is a community of peoples, living entirely in accordance with the moral law, and employing in friendly rivalry all the powers of reason. The everlasting peace is represented as the final result.

Thus we reach the idea of history as the education of the human race. Kant, in giving a natural history of the human species, developed the ideas that Lessing at the same time was treating from the point of view of religious development. In this account he entirely divests himself of anthropomorphic ideas. Nature has so mingled egoistic and social impulses in man that the struggle for existence in its highest form, as struggle for social superiority, must necessarily result. But, on the other hand, there arise the motives that lead to the establishment of political and judicial government, through the agency of which the injurious effects of the egoistic impulses are obviated without affecting their force as influences in behalf of higher culture.

This point of view overcomes the opposition between the optimistic and pessimistic estimate of human nature and history. Kant does not share the optimism of Shaftesbury and Rousseau regarding the essential goodness and amiability of our race. His judgment of the character of man as shown by experience approaches the harsh estimates of Hobbes and Schopenhauer. But while he cherishes no illusions regarding actual conditions, he has a lofty faith regarding the destiny of man and his future. He believes in the continuous progress of the race, and in the final and definitive victory of the good. The kingdom of reason and of right, the kingdom of complete culture and morality, it will come, no matter how hard the struggles may be by which it is attained.   " The education of the human race," thus we read at the end of the *Anthropology*, " is wholesome, but harsh and severe.   It requires many efforts and transformations of nature, which extend almost to the destruction of the whole race, to produce from the disunited and self-contradictory evil a good that man did not intend, but which, once being present, preserves and maintains itself." [1]

Thus Kant opposes Rousseau's sentimental demand for a return to nature with the manly and courageous motto, " On to humanity."

[1] E. v. Hartmann, in a treatise entitled *Zur Geschichte und Begründung des Pessimismus*, has tried to represent Kant as the father of pessimism. With what justification appears from what has been said.   Nietzsche perhaps could have quoted Kant the anthropologist with more reason.   It is likewise Kant's view that the development of the species, the progress of the human type in the course of history, is effected by means of great and powerful egoistic impulses, by the will to live, only that Nietzsche's distortions and exaggerations are lacking.   And one must remember that this is not Kant's only idea.

SECOND BOOK

THE PRACTICAL PHILOSOPHY

THE central principle of Kant's practical philosophy is the *idea of freedom*, not in the technical sense of the system, but in the general acceptation of *spontaneous self-activity*. In epistemology, Kant opposes sensationalism by making knowledge the product of the mind's activity. And in the same way, he combats hedonism by basing ethics entirely on spontaneous activity. The value of man's life depends solely on what he does, not on what happens to him. And the same notion forms the leading principle of the subordinate disciplines. In the philosophy of the State and of Law, the constitution and laws of a state have value only when they are based upon the freedom and spontaneous activity of citizens who are regarded as the end. An autocratic form of government may, under certain circumstances, be very conducive to the peace and well-being of its subjects; but it is as much inferior to a republican, or representative form of government as a machine is to an organism. The same principle runs through the philosophy of Religion. Religion is believing in God and fulfilling his commands — the moral law — freely. Thus the church is nothing but the voluntary association, formed to fight against evil, of all the righteous and true believers. With the true church there is contrasted the priestly church, which degrades the people into passive laity, for whom the priest makes the creed and performs divine service. Finally, in the pedagogical works true education is distinguished from mere training by the fact that it has in view the self-activity and the freely acting good-will of the pupil.

FIRST SECTION

THE MORAL PHILOSOPHY

LITERATURE: Among the precritical writings, the *Beobachtungen über das Gefühl des Schönen und Erhabenen* (1764) is of special importance for Kant's ethical views, and contains contributions for a moral characterology. After hints of a change in his theory of morals in the *Dissertation* and the *Kritik der reinen Vernunft*, Kant published the *Grundlegung zur Metaphysik der Sitten* (1785), the first systematic exposition of his ethical views. It contains preliminary sketches that were subsequently omitted, and, above all, the important notion of a kingdom of ends. *The Kritik der practischen Vernunft* adds, in particular, the moral theology, and the *Kritik der Urteilskraft* [Eng. trans. by J. H. Bernard, 1892] contributes to the same subject. The systematic exposition of the ethics, according to the principles laid down in these writings, is contained in a work that belongs to his old age, *Anfangsgründe der Tugendlehre*. In the Anthropology there is much that concerns moral dietetics. Interesting fragments of earlier attempts at construction are contained in Reicke's *Lose Blätter*. [J. G. Schurman, *Kantian Ethics and the Ethics of Evolution*, 1881; Noah Porter, *Kant's Ethics* (Griggs Philos. Classics), 1886.] For the development of Kant's ethical views, *cf.* F. W. Förster, *Der Entwickelungsgang der Kantischen Ethik bis 1781* (1893), and P. Menzer, in Vaihinger's *Kantstudien*, II., pp. 290 ff., III., pp. 41 ff. Also, A. Hegler, *Die Psychologie in Kants Ethik* (1891); A. Cresson, *La morale de Kant* (1897). [T. K. Abbott's volume, entitled *Kant's Theory of Ethics* (1883), contains English translations of the *Grundlegung zur Metaphysik der Sitten* (*Fundamental Principles of the Metaphysic of Morals*), the *Kritik der pract. Vernunft* (*Critique of Practical Reason*), the general Introduction to the *Metaphysiche Anfangsgründe der Sittenlehre* (*Metaphysical Principles of the Science of Morals*), and the preface and Introduction to the *Metaphysische Anfangsgründe der Tugendlehre* (*Metaphysical Principles of the Doctrine of Virtue*).]

I. The General Character of Kant's Moral Philosophy

The character and position of moral philosophy in Kant's system is described by the name which he gives it, "metaphysic of morals." By means of this title, it is paralleled with the "metaphysic of nature." Like the latter, it is a system of pure rational laws, valid *a priori*, applying, not to the realm of nature, but to that of freedom. But, on the other hand, the name implies a contrast with the "physics of morals." It is not to be a theoretical science of the origin, importance, and effect of subjective and objective morality in the life of human experience, but a system of pure *a priori* valid formulæ, without any relation to the guidance of life according to the teachings of experience. The pure concepts of the understanding are absolutely indifferent to any particular content of experience, but are valid *a priori* for every possible experience. And, in the same way, the moral law is completely unconcerned with life and particular circumstances. It is valid *a priori* for every rational being, quite irrespective of what the conditions of life may be. The concepts of the understanding do indeed require for their objective validity confirmation through experience; for otherwise they are only empty thought-forms. But, for the moral law, it is not essential that it shall be obeyed anywhere in the real world. It does not determine what is, but what ought to be, what abides, even if what is actual everywhere follows a different course. In truth, there is no way of demonstrating that the moral law anywhere determines the nature of the real. Morality, as an act of freedom, can never be found as a fact in the empirical world. The metaphysic of morals has nothing at all to do with actual occurrences, with life and history as empirical facts. These things belong to the "physics of morals."

As this point is of great importance in understanding and estimating the value of Kant's moral philosophy, it will be well to consider it at somewhat greater length.

One may give the title of "physics of morals" to the theoretical consideration of morality as empirical facts of ordinary life. As an empirical living being, man belongs to nature, and all theoretical knowledge of his character and development forms a part of natural science in its broader sense. That is as true of psychical anthropology, including the philosophy of history, as of physical. All these disciplines consider man purely as a natural product, just in the same way as the zoölogist considers any other species of animal. Investigation into the history of his development may show how the species man has differentiated itself into various races in adapting itself to different conditions of life in different quarters of the globe. In the brief essays *On the Various Races of Mankind* (1775), and *Determination of the Concept of a Race of Men* (1785), Kant pointed out the way to this mode of treatment. If this procedure were ever able to show how mankind originally had evolved from an earlier form of life, Kant would have nothing to object. Then, too, sociology and philosophy of history consider man as a social being. The former may show how in a common life certain uniform relations necessarily grow up, and how these become, through the specific character of man, who differs from other gregarious animals in possessing higher intelligence and more strongly marked individuality, rational usages, consciously adopted and maintained, in distinction from the social instincts of animals. Again, it may go on to show how these usages assume different forms among different peoples, corresponding to the various conditions and ends of life, but how they everywhere have the tendency to promote life in the sense of preserving and raising the historical type. Finally, the philosophy of history may attempt to gain an insight into the unity of all the data presented by empirical history, and to discover in them progress towards a final purpose, perhaps the complete development of all the natural powers of humanity. In doing this it may represent the moral and legal usages as essential conditions of progress toward this goal. — All these would be purely theoretical sciences, investigating the uniform connection of given facts according to the law of causality.

And to the same sphere belong also disciplines like politics or pedagogy that deal with the problems of some special department of life, and even those that profess to furnish guidance for life in general, like morality in the popular sense of the word. These are all technical disciplines that really belong, as far as content is concerned, to the theoretical sciences. They convert into a rule that which theory expresses as a law. Medicine is nothing but the sum of the applications of the knowledge that physical anthropology possesses. It may be connected with the latter as a mere corollary. In like manner, the ordinary laws of morality, as a set of practical or technical precepts, might be added or annexed to general anthropology, as "pragmatic" anthropology. Kant has himself furnished an example of this in his *Anthropology with a Pragmatic Purpose*. All this belongs to the "physics of morals."

Now, a "metaphysic of morals" is entirely different from all this. It is not at all concerned with what happens, but only with that which should happen, whether it now is taking place anywhere or not. It sets up a law for the realm of Freedom. This is something that lies entirely outside the realm of nature, that is, outside of the real world in so far as the latter is known as an object. It lies in the intelligible world. Since obedience to the moral law is an intelligible act of free will, it does not belong at all to the observable facts of empirical reality. Real occurrences, which are objects of knowledge, belong entirely to the phenomenal world, and are to be explained according to the law of causality. The only thing that is evident as a fact is the consciousness of the unconditional obligation of a law that commands categorically. The effects and purposes of the action do not enter at all into this consciousness. In like manner, it is altogether free from inclinations and conditions of the possibility of the action. It contains only the form of a universal law by means of which all action is to be determined. Now, this law is the sole object of practical philosophy in the true sense, as opposed to pragmatic and technical disciplines that have wrongly assumed the name of practical, when really they are only offshoots of the theoretical sciences.[1]

Thus Kant's practical philosophy, or the "metaphysic of morals," is in principle completely divorced from empirical reality, from the life of the individual, and from the historical life of humanity. It is not at home on the earth among men, but in the transcendental world of purely rational beings. It is the natural law of the *mundus intelligibilis.* The moral law is suspended over life merely as a norm for passing judgments upon the will. It does not have its origin in life, and from the very nature of the case no knowledge of its effectiveness in life is possible. — It is another question whether Kant always remained true to this fundamental conception in elaborating it in detail. Probably such a purely transcendent morality cannot always be carried through. So soon as we attempt to deal with concrete norms, over and above the mere demands of formal accordance with the law, the special empirically given content of life will necessarily claim recognition. "Thou shalt not lie," is not a rule for purely rational beings as such, but for those who communicate their thoughts by speech and other symbols. "Thou shalt not mutilate, destroy, or defile thy body," is a rule only for those rational beings who have a

---

[1] *Cf.* especially the first preface to the *Critique of Judgment* (VII., pp. 377 ff.).

body with the organs in question. In a pure "metaphysic of morals" there should really be no mention of any of these things. Of course the content of such a 'science' would be very scant.

II. The Elaboration of the System

The system of the "metaphysics of morals" was long delayed, although Kant had intended, as early as 1785, to undertake at once its complete elaboration.[1] First there appeared as a prolegomenon the *Fundamental Principles* (*Grundlegung*), which, according to the preface,[2] was intended to represent the *Critique*. Then followed still another "*Critique*" of *Practical Reason*, — in reality quite an unsuitable title, as Kant himself recognized: the practical reason requires no critique. The theoretical reason, or the understanding, requires criticism because it has a tendency to over-step its limits. But the practical reason is not subject to any criticism, to a judicial sentence before any other court as to its claims. It is itself the final court of appeal regarding all human affairs. Instead of a "Critique" we might have expected an "apology," or rather an "apotheosis" of the practical reason. But after the *Critique of Pure Reason*, it seemed to Kant that this doctrine, too, must have a critique as a prolegomenon. And when the critique was written, in this case also the doctrine was long in following. Not until 1797 did it appear, and then not as a "system," but under the apparently stereotyped titles, *Metaphysical Principles of Doctrine of Virtue*, and *Metaphysical Principles of Right*. It was not until the second edition (1798) that the two works received the common title, *Metaphysic of Morals*. These works exhibit Kant's tendency to undertake all sorts of preliminary discussions, which developed into a kind of dis-

---

[1] *Cf.* the letter to Schütz, of Sept. 13, 1785.   [2] IV., p. 239.

like to give a final exposition of the real question itself. They also show his ever-increasing tendency towards schematic uniformity in the construction of his system, the pernicious effects of which Adickes has traced throughout Kant's entire period of authorship in his acute investigation, entitled *Kant's Schematic Tendency as a Factor in the Construction of his System*. To this latter tendency in particular is to be ascribed the fact that the working out of the system (the doctrinal part, as Kant says) is lacking, or remains in the form of " Critiques." The elaboration of the *Critique of Pure Reason* had left such deep traces on Kant's mind that his thought always fell again into this groove. This is the limitation of the human understanding that we so often meet with. If one has once happily solved a problem by means of a certain method, one tries to solve all the problems of the world in the same way.

The *Critique of Practical Reason*, which therefore remained the chief work on moral philosophy, follows the *Critique of Pure Reason* step by step, not only in its intrinsic method, as the *Fundamental Principles* does, but also in its external divisions. We have the same statement of the problem regarding the possibility of synthetic judgments *a priori;* the same divisions into a Doctrine of Elements and a Doctrine of Method, into Analytic and Dialectic, with a table of categories and antinomies. If the schema was not adapted to the epistemological investigation, it is here still more ill-fitting. Kant's thought had become enslaved by the schema : it looks more at the fixed form of the system than at the facts. He is not troubled by the fact that his ideas suffer from this fixed arrangement, that necessary investigations are lacking, and empty, formal notions find place. He rejoices in the thorough-going analogy, and finds in this an important confirmation of the truth of his system. In what follows, I propose to

treat merely the fundamental conceptions, without following in detail the schematic execution.

(1) *The Form of Morality*

The form of morality is determined by the essential
character of the critical philosophy, formal rationalism.
This element comes out so clearly just at this point that
no one can mistake it and find the main purpose in something else, *e. g.*, in phenomenalism or the determination
of limits. The undertaking is to show that the practical
reason, like the theoretical, is *a priori* legislative. Moral
philosophy, as metaphysics in the *Critique of Pure Reason*,
is traced back to a transcendental logic : the moral law
is a purely logical law of action.

The point of departure for the investigation is here, as in
his theoretical work, the division of human nature into two
sides, sensibility and reason, which are related to each other
as matter and form. In the *Critique of Pure Reason*, we
have the understanding as spontaneity opposed to sensibility as the receptivity for impressions. It is the function
of the understanding to bring the manifold of sensation
to a unity subject to laws. In the *Critique of Practical
Reason*, sensibility has the form of a plurality of impulses
that by means of objects are stimulated into a variety of
desires. Impulses aim at satisfaction. The satisfaction
of all the impulses, posited as the common goal of sensibility, is called *happiness*. Also here we have reason as
the formal principle opposed to sensibility. As in the
theoretical sphere reason is the origin of the laws of nature,
so here it assigns a law to the realm of voluntary action.
This is the moral law. The moral laws correspond in the
sphere of the will to the pure concepts of the understanding
in the realm of intellect. Like the latter they possess universality and necessity, and in a twofold sense. That is,
they are valid for all rational beings, and they admit of abso-

lutely no exceptions.   Here as in the theoretical field their *a priori* character is established by means of these marks.

Of course the difference that we already described, that in the theoretical field the universality refers to what is, and in the practical to what ought to be, shows itself here.   Natural phenomena correspond without exception to natural laws ; but, on the contrary, action is not invariably controlled by the moral law.   It should be so controlled, but it is not.   But that the universality of obligation is not merely an empty and arbitrary demand, perhaps on the part of the moral philosophers, but rests upon a real law of reason, is shown by the fact that all men know and recognize it, if not in act, at least in passing moral judgments.   In estimating the worth of our own actions and those of others, there is always presupposed an underlying standard.   This is the moral law, and just in this way is its universal validity recognized.

It is noteworthy, as a further parallel, that the characteristic position of man, both in a theoretical and practical regard, rests upon this union of sensibility and reason.   The nature of human knowledge is determined by the fact that there must enter into it both perception and understanding.   Understanding without sensibility is a description of the divine intelligence, while sensibility without understanding is the condition of the brutes.   In like manner, the human will is characterized by the fact that reason and sensibility are always united in action, the former determining the form of the will, and the latter furnishing the object of desire.   Reason without sensibility characterizes the divine will, whose nature is expressed in the moral law, which alone determines its activity.   Sensible impulses without reason result in the animal will, made up of lawless and accidental desires, subject to the natural course of events.

Now, just on this point rests the characteristic nature of morality, which is *action out of respect for a law*.   Among

beings above and below the human race there is no obligation
and no morality, but only the act of will. The divine will
corresponds completely with the divine reason: it is holy,
not moral. The will of the lower animal is made up of
passive excitations of impulse: it does not act, but is passive
as a part of nature, and consequently is entirely without
moral quality. In the case of man, morality rests upon the
control of the sense impulses by the reason. Through the
fact that man as a rational being prescribes a law to himself
as a sensible being, obligation first arises. Here we have
a volition that contains a moment of negation, — even of
contradiction.

The point of departure and the basis for moral philosophy
are found in the analysis of the moral consciousness. This
reveals just that consciousness of the opposition of duty and
inclination, the consciousness of obligation, as the original
phenomenon in the field of morality in general. The interpretation of these facts is the first problem of moral philosophy. Kant solves it, as we have indicated, by tracing it
back to the opposition of reason and sensibility. The inclinations are all derived ultimately from sense impulses,
while the consciousness of duty proceeds from reason, as is
evident from the fact that obligation presupposes a universal
law as norm. Every system of moral philosophy that does
not recognize the absolute nature of this opposition, that
attempts, like eudæmonism, to explain obligation by some indirect derivation from the inclinations, destroys, according to
Kant, the very essence of morality. For this reason he
constantly treats eudæmonism not only as a false theory,
but as a moral perversity. He sympathizes, however, with
the morality of the common man, who finds as unconditionally given in his conscience the opposition of duty and
inclination. One can at once say that Kant's system of
morality is the restoration of the common morality of conscience with its absolute imperative, as opposed to philo-

sophical theories of morality, which all undertake some explanation of that imperative.

The second point that results from an analysis of the moral consciousness is the fundamental form of moral judgments of value. A will is morally good when it is determined solely by duty, or the moral law. In so far as the will is determined by inclinations, whether these are bodily or mental, coarse or refined, its actions can have no moral value. They may in such cases correspond with the moral law. But legality is not morality. The latter rests solely upon the form of the determination of the will. It is only when duty is done out of respect for the law, without any reference to the results of the act for the inclinations, that we have the habit of will that alone possesses moral value. The ordinary reason always makes these distinctions with complete certainty. It distinguishes what is morally good from what is useful and agreeable, and also from what is merely in accordance with law and duty.

The content of the general moral consciousness may consequently be expressed as follows, in the form of a demand: Let the moral law be the sole determining ground of thy will. It has the form of a categorical imperative: Thou shalt do what the law prescribes, unconditionally, whatever consequences may result. Impulses that seek happiness, and the dictates of prudence speak in hypothetical imperatives: If you would obtain this or that, if you wish to consult your advantage, you must do this or that, or leave them undone. You must not be intemperate if you would not injure your health or your good name, and so act contrary to your happiness. The pure practical reason may command the same line of action. But by means of its form as unconditional imperative it can unmistakably be distinguished from all such prudential rules. Even if no injury could ever result to one from lying, or from a dishonorable act, the imperative retains its force. This is the mandate of the reason, the expression of its nature. Universality and necessity, not comparative and conditional, but absolute and unconditional, constitute the essence of all rationality.

For this very reason, universality is the touchstone through which the rational origin of the will's motives may be infallibly recognized. If the maxim of the will cannot be represented as a universal law, it is not derived from reason, but from sensibility, and the resulting act is without moral value, or non-moral. One may accordingly express the categorical imperative also in the formula: Act so that thy maxim may be capable of becoming the universal natural law of all rational beings. If it is from its very nature incapable of this extension, then it proceeds from the arbitrariness of sensibility, and not from reason. For example, the question may arise whether it is right for me to tell a lie to rescue myself or some one else from a difficulty. The maxim of the decision of the will might be: If by a lie or by a promise that I do not intend to keep I can obtain an advantage that is greater than any disadvantage for myself or others that may result, then I regard it as allowable, and will act accordingly. Now attempt to represent this maxim as a universal natural law of willing and acting. One sees at once that it is impossible: it would destroy itself. If every one constantly acted in accordance with this maxim, no one would ever believe the statements or promises of another, and accordingly there would be an end to statements and promises themselves. Lies and dishonesty are self-contradictory: they are possible only on the condition that they do not become universal natural laws of speech and conduct. The liar and deceiver wills at the same time that there shall not be lying and deceit; for he does not wish others to deceive him. The reason in him, therefore, is opposed to the sensible nature, which regards merely its momentary advantage.

And just in this fact lies the real ground for rejecting such a condition. Reason and sensibility are related as higher and lower. If one lies, he follows the lower faculty of desire; he permits the animal in him to rule, following his desires and fears. He divorces himself from his character as a rational being and renounces his humanity. The worth of man rests on the fact that reason rules in his life and is not subordinated to the impulses of sense. In virtue of his reason, man belongs to a higher order of things, an intelligible and divine world. As a sensible being he is a product of nature. How shameful and degrading it would be to subject his divine part to the animal nature, to renounce his citizenship in the kingdom of rational beings, and content himself with merely an animal existence. It is an absolute inversion of things to subject the reason, which from its very nature is its own absolute purpose, to the sensibility that it is naturally intended to serve. Justice ($\delta\iota\kappa\alpha\iota o\sigma\acute{v}\nu\eta$), to use Plato's phraseology to express Kant's thought, consists for man in every part of his soul performing its proper function. It is necessary that reason, the part that is divine in nature and in origin, shall rule, and that the will shall obey its commands and make them the law of its action, and that the system of sensory and animal impulses shall provide for the preservation of the bodily life in strict subjection to reason, and without causing the mind disquiet and disturbance.

We here touch upon the deepest side of the Kantian theory of morals, where it passes over at once into religious feeling. To this we shall return immediately. But first I wish to consider another of the fundamental notions of the system, that of freedom.

Freedom is the postulate of morality as something internally consistent. A being without freedom, a being whose activities are determined by causes either outside him or in him, is never the subject of a moral judgment. And it makes no difference whether this causality is mechanical or mediated through ideas. An *automaton spirituale* is not less an automaton than a bodily one. Freedom therefore signifies absolute spontaneity, the ability to act unconditionally, and not as determined by causes. The possibility of this notion was shown in the *Critique of Pure Reason*. There it was proved that empirical causality is valid in the world of phenomena, not in the intelligible world. It is therefore thinkable that the same being stands under the law of causality as a member of the phenomenal world, but as a *noumenon*, possesses causality according to the concept of freedom. This notion, which remains problematical from the speculative standpoint, is rendered certain by means of the practical reason. The moral law commands unconditionally. Its fulfilment must therefore be possible. In other words, there must be a will that is not determined by sense solicitation, but that determines itself merely through the idea of the law. That is a free will. Freedom, or the capacity to make the moral law the absolute ground of determination of the will, without regard to all the solicitations of inclination or to the influence of fixed habits, education, natural disposition and temperament, is directly posited in the recognition of the moral law itself. Although the understanding may not be able to explain it, the absolute validity of the notion is not less certain. Thou canst, for thou oughtst — common-sense recognizes at once the necessity of the connection.

With the concept of freedom that of autonomy is closely connected. The moral is not a law imposed by some external authority, but the essential expression of reason itself. The theological theory of morality, that derives the law from the arbitrary will of God, and finds its sanction in the power of the Almighty to punish and reward, is refuted by the notion of autonomy. There is no being except I myself that can say "thou shalt," to me. Another will can say "thou must," but that is a hypothetical imperative that always has some external sanction — if you would avoid or obtain this or that. That is heteronomy, and a will that is determined in this way never has any moral value. It is true the moral law is God's will; but God's will and the will of the rational being harmonize spontaneously, as being both expressions of the nature of reason itself. It is not binding as an arbitrarily imposed command that might even have been different.

And now I return to the point already mentioned: the moral law is the law or natural order of the intelligible world. The intelligible world is the kingdom of rational beings, of which God is the sovereign. In this world every rational being has full citizen rights and is a constituent member, furnishing from his own will the law that here obtains. In Rousseau's republic every citizen is subject and yields obedience only to laws that he assents to as a part of the legislative body. In the republic of spirits a similar autonomy prevails. There, no one is determined by means of causes external to himself, as takes place in nature where external conditioning is the rule, but there is nothing except free self-determination, which is at the same time in harmonious agreement with the reason of others.

In this way the moral law receives at Kant's hands a metaphysical and cosmical character. It is the natural order of what is actually real, of the intelligible world, while the law of causality is merely the natural order of the phenomenal world. It is for this reason that he so earnestly tries to show that the moral law is not merely the law for all men, but for all rational beings in general. It is a law of transcendent import, the most intimate law of the universe itself. In so far as man realizes this law in his life, he belongs directly to a different order of things from that of nature. During the earthly life this relation is concealed. Our faculty of ideas is limited by sensibility, and can conceive only what takes place in space and time. It cannot conceive freedom and eternity. Nevertheless, as moral beings, we are immediately certain that we are not merely natural beings belonging to the phenomenal world, but that as rational beings we belong to a truly real, a spiritual and divine universe. Is the earthly and temporal life merely one phase of our existence? If so we may suppose that when we put off the body we shall be free from the obscuring of consciousness by sensibility, and that the mind will then completely and with full consciousness recognize itself as a member of that real world, which it already knows through action and faith, though not through sight. Eternal life would be life as a purely rational being, without the trouble and limitation of the life of sense.

It is Kant's Platonism that is here evident as the fundamental form of his ontology. The *Critique of Pure Reason* and the *Critique of Practical Reason* unite for the purpose of establishing an ethical and religious view of the world on the basis of objective idealism, — a mode of thought that in its essential features is older than the critical philosophy. We found it already in the *Dreams of a Ghost-Seer* as the serious background to the humorous representation of Swedenborgianism. Criticism, looked at as a whole, appears even from the beginning as the new method of establishing a Platonic system of metaphysics.

These are the fundamental concepts of Kant's moral philosophy. They form, as we have already said, the most complete contrast to the empirical and eudæmonistic point of view. This latter appeared to Kant not merely false and superficial, but also perverse and profane. It reduces morality to self-love. Enlightened self-interest demands virtuous conduct, though in moderation, and as a means which best conduces to happiness. It makes reason subservient to the sensuous desires, and denies the possibility of a disinterested action, and thereby of any genuine morality whatever. In so far as it has any influence on action, it poisons morality at the root. Moreover, it is nothing but weak sophistry that "can exist only in the confusing speculations of schools which are bold enough to close their ears against the heavenly voice (of reason) in order to maintain a theory which does not cost much racking of the brain." The ordinary man of unsophisticated understanding, with the "wise simplicity" of Rousseau, dismisses at once these shallow arguments. He holds fast to the clear distinction between actions performed from a sense of duty and from inclination, and maintains its absolute significance for moral judgments of value.

Not only eudæmonism, the morality of enlightened self-interest, but the morality of feeling is abhorrent to Kant. He especially condemns the sentimental and rhetorical form that seeks to furnish moral stimulus by dressing up moral heroes, and by representations of actions that lie beyond the limits of duty. The morality of reason alone, with its fixed principles, affords a permanent basis for the moral will. The sentimental procedure produces merely momentary emotions that soon evaporate, and in doing so render the heart dry and dead.

It is worthy of note that also in these points the critical philosophy represents a reaction against Kant's past. The writings of the sixties show everywhere traces of the mode of thought that he now so decidedly rejects — the eudæmonistic morality of perfection,[1] and the English ethics of feeling. And also in this field the change dates from the revolution of 1769. In 1785 (in the announcement of his lectures),[2] he spoke of Shaftesbury, Hutcheson, and Hume as his predecessors whom he followed in investigations in the field of moral philosophy. But, in a remark in the *Dissertation* of 1770 [3], he dismisses Shaftesbury and his followers with contempt. Pure reason alone is to be considered. As contrasted with it all empirical principles are "impure."

---

[1] *Cf.* II., p. 307.　　　[2] II., p. 319.　　　[3] § 9.

(2) *The Material of The Will*

Up to this point Kant's thought is on the whole simple and clear. The difficulties and vacillations begin with the problem of finding an object and end of action for the will that is only formally determined. Two ends are possible, happiness and perfection. The adoption of the one or the other of these constitutes the difference between the systems of moral philosophy to which one can apply the names Hedonism and Energism.

The former finds the ultimate end in pleasure, the latter in complete development of character and activity. Even Kant takes account of these two ends. He hesitated long, however, in deciding regarding their relation to morality proper, even after the critical point of view had been discovered. I shall deal first with happiness and its relation to morality.

The analogy of the practical with the theoretical seems to demand that the matter of the will should be furnished by sensibility. The impulses of sense all aim at satisfaction ; in the last resort they may together be said to seek happiness. This accordingly would be the goal of natural volition and action. The moral law, according to the same analogy, would have to be represented as a condition of the possibility of this end, perhaps because it would harmonize the various desires and bring unity into the actions of the many persons whose actions have influence on one another's happiness. From this standpoint, happiness would be the effect, but not the motive of the will. This is determined *a priori* by reason, not *a posteriori* by the results to be expected, just as the pure concepts find their application and illustration in experience, although they do not originate in experience, but are necessary to its possibility.[1]

---

[1] Pölitz, *Kants Vorlesungen über Metaphysik*, p. 321 : " Worthiness for happiness consists in the practical agreement of our actions with the idea of

Another mode of establishing a necessary relation between virtue and happiness is by making the consciousness of virtue the source of happiness. This was the position of the Stoics, for whom the wise man as such is happy, whatever his external conditions of life. Internal happiness (εὐδαιμονία) is not dependent upon external fortune (εὐτυχία), but is derived entirely from the individual's own will and the consciousness of his personal power and worth. Spinoza is a representative of the same standpoint.

This combination, too, is not unknown to Kant. A long and interesting sketch, published by Reicke in the *Loose Leaves*,[1] contains, among other things, the following thoughts:[2] "The material of happiness is sensible, but the form is intellectual. Now, this is not possible except as freedom under *a priori* laws of its agreement with itself, and this not to make happiness actual, but to render its idea possible. For happiness consists just in well-being in so far as this is not externally accidental, or even empirically dependent, but as based upon our volition. This must be active, and not dependent upon the determination of nature. . . . It is true that virtue has the advantage that it carries with it the greatest happiness in the use of natural endowments. But its higher value does not consist in the fact that it serves as it were as a means. Its real value consists in the fact that it is we who creatively produce it, irrespective of its empirical conditions, which can furnish only particular rules of life, and that it brings with it self-sufficiency. . . . There is a cer-

universal happiness. When we act in such a way that there would result, if every one acted in the same way, the greatest amount of happiness, then our conduct has rendered us worthy of happiness. — Good conduct is the condition of universal happiness."

[1] I., pp. 9 ff.

[2] Förster and Höffding (*Archiv f. Gesch. der Philos.*, VII., p. 461, Vaihinger's *Kantstudien*, II., pp. 11 ff.) place this sketch, perhaps rightly, in the seventies. Reicke, from external evidence, is inclined to fix the date in the eighties. Even this does not appear to me impossible. It is only certain that it is to be placed before the *Grundlegung*.

tain stock of contentment necessary and indispensable, and
without which no happiness is possible; what is over and
above this is non-essential. This is self-sufficiency, — as it
were, *apperceptio jucunda primitiva*." [1]

This in essence was the Stoic solution of the relation between virtue and happiness. Kant found it nearer home in
Shaftesbury and Pope. It is at bottom the view of Aristotle
and Plato. Not pleasure, but virtue, is the highest good and
final purpose. Or the exercise of the specifically human
powers and capacities is what gives an absolute meaning and
value to life. Since, however, the possession of this good is
directly connected with the consciousness of one's own worth,
one can say: Virtue insures at the same time happiness.
But this name does not, of course, imply the satisfaction of
all the desires of sense, but just the consciousness of possessing that which alone has absolute worth.

In the later expositions these positions are abandoned.
In the *Fundamental Principles* the notion of happiness plays
no part whatever. The concept of a kingdom of ends is

---

[1] I add a few more sentences: "Happiness is not really the greatest sum
of enjoyment, but pleasure arising from the consciousness of one's own ability
to be contented, — at least this is the essential and formal condition of happiness, though still other material conditions are necessary." — "Morality (as
freedom under universal laws) renders happiness as such possible. Though it
does not depend upon it as its purpose, it is the original form of happiness,
which, when one possesses, one can dispense entirely with pleasures, and bear
many evils of life without any loss of contentment, — indeed even with a
heightening of it." — "Morality is the idea of freedom as a principle of happiness (a regulative principle of happiness *a priori*). Accordingly, the laws
of freedom must contain *a priori* the formal conditions of our own happiness
without any direct reference to it." — "Freedom is in itself a power independent of empirical grounds for acting or refraining to act. — I am free, but
only from the compelling forces of sense, not also from the limiting laws of
reason. — That 'freedom of indifference' by means of which I can will what
is contrary to my will, and which allows me no certain ground for counting on
myself, would necessarily be in the highest degree unsatisfactory to me. It
is essential, then, to recognize as *a priori* necessary a law according to which
freedom may be limited to conditions that render the will self-consistent. To
this law I can bring no objection, for it alone can establish, according to
principles, the practical unity of the will."

introduced, but even this finds no further extension and application. The formal determination of the will by the law is here the only dominating conception. On this depends the worth of man. As a rational being, he belongs to the higher order of things. In the second half (Dialectic) of the *Critique of Practical Reason,* on the other hand, after the first part has repeated the formal determinations of the *Fundamental Principles,* pleasure appears prominently as a necessary element of practical philosophy. It is here combined with virtue (as the worthiness of happiness) into the concept of the highest good, and in this form serves as basis or moving principle of moral theology. The "postulates" — God and immortality, together with the complete adjustment of happiness and worthiness — are founded on this notion. In the end, all natural connection between virtue and happiness is rejected. Kant now emphatically denies the view of the ancient philosophers that there is any natural connection between the two. For him the connection is now "synthetic," not "analytic." Entirely reprehensible is the position of the Epicureans that makes virtue an external means to happiness. But the Stoic view is also untenable, that the consciousness of virtue is itself at once happiness. Obedience to the law, he explains here, is motived by "reverence," — a feeling that has absolutely no kinship with the pathological feeling of pleasure. The truth is rather that man, as a sensible being, feels oppressed by the moral law which restrains his self-love and lowers his self-conceit by the demand for obedience that it makes. Obedience to the law also brings with it, indeed, a feeling of exaltation and self-respect, but neither have these the character of pleasure. "Contentment" (*Selbszufriedenheit*) really signifies only a negative pleasure in its existence.[1]

Nevertheless, happiness is an essential object of the rational will. Virtue is indeed the highest good (*bonum*

[1] V., p. 123.

supremum) ; but it is not therefore the complete and per-
fected good (*bonum consummatum*), as an object of desire for
finite, rational beings. For that purpose happiness is an
essential condition. And this is true not only from the partial standpoint of the man who makes himself his own end,
but even in the judgment of impartial reason, which regards
happiness in general as itself an end in the universe. For
to desire happiness, and also to be worthy of it, and yet not
to share in it, is a condition of things that cannot at all
accord with the perfect volition of a rational being.[1] Since,
now, the connection of the two elements is not analytic,
" in accordance with the rule of identity," but synthetic, the
question how the highest good is practically possible requires
a transcendental solution.

The key to this transcendental solution is again naturally
found in the distinction between the sensible and the intelligible world. In the sense-world, happiness is not propor-
tionate to worthiness, and so the adjustment is postponed to
the future life. The practical reason ensures the possibility
of the highest good by means of the two postulates, immortality of the soul and the existence of God. Immortality, or
rather life beyond the grave, makes possible an indefinitely
prolonged advance towards moral perfection, consequently
towards worthiness for happiness. The existence of God, as
an all-powerful and holy will, and at the same time the
author of nature, guarantees the second element of the highest good, happiness in proportion to worthiness. Further,
since to bring the highest good into existence through free
volition is a requirement that is *a priori* necessary, the possibility of doing this must be a necessary postulate of practical reason. Or, in other words, the truth of the existence
of God and of the life beyond the grave is apprehended by a
necessary act of rational faith. It is not the object of theoretical knowledge. For this, perception would be necessary,

[1] V., p. 116.

and this is impossible for us who are limited to sense perception in space and time. Moreover, it is not the object of a command, imposed either internally or externally; for that is impossible. But it is guaranteed by an inextinguishable conviction that is posited along with my rational nature itself. The rightly constituted person can say: "I will God's existence, and that my existence in this world shall include, over and above the life of nature, membership in an intelligible world. Finally, I will my own immortality. I hold fast to these beliefs, and do not allow them to be taken from me. This is the single case where it is inevitable that my interest should determine my judgment, since I am not permitted to renounce any of its demands."

Moral theology is thus based on the lack of natural connection between virtue and happiness. The desire of the human will, which is unable to unite in this world the two indispensable elements, morality and happiness, by means of necessary concepts, becomes an imperative demand to pass to the region of the intelligible for what is necessary to complete our theory. Without God and immortality, without a transcendental world-order, the realization of the highest good, which is enjoined by the moral law, would not be possible.

In the form in which these thoughts are presented in the *Critique of Practical Reason,* there are many sides open to criticism. It reminds one somewhat too much of the police argument for God's existence: if one does not receive reward or punishment here, he will find it laid up for him in the next world. And Schopenhauer's gibe is not entirely unjustified, that Kant's virtue, which at first bore itself so bravely towards happiness, afterwards holds out its hand to receive a tip. Even formally the combination of the two factors is open to criticism. Happiness for Kant is the satisfaction of the inclinations of sense. Now, are there still inclinations of this kind in the other world? We are supposed to be in an intelligible world where sensibility is entirely lacking. And how does the matter stand with regard to the infinite progress towards moral perfection? In the other world is there still time in which change and progress can take place? And how is moral progress itself possible for a being without sensibility? The *noumenon* is "a purely rational being," "an intelligible character." In what, then, can its progress consist? It appears as if Kant would have to postulate indefinite continuance in time in the form of sensible existence in order to render progress and compensation possible. It would be necessary for him to adopt something like the East Indian notion of rebirth and transmigration of souls.

Nevertheless, if one disregards the somewhat wooden form of exposition, and holds fast what is essential in Kant's thought, one will estimate the doctrine differently. We may say that Kant here really touches upon a strong, if not the strongest, motive of religious faith. The unsatisfactory nature of the present world, the conflict of the natural order of events with the irrelinquishable demands of the spirit, is the strongest motive to transcend the visible order and to seek an invisible one. The fact that in the natural course of events, as observation shows, the good and great are often oppressed and perish, while the vulgar and the wicked triumph, is the goad that drives us to deny the absolute reality of nature. It is and remains the final and indestructible axiom of the will that reality cannot be absolutely indifferent to good and evil. If, then, nature is indifferent, it cannot be the true reality. Then only behind or above nature, as mere phenomenon, can the true world be discovered, and in it the good is absolutely real; *i. e.*, in God who is the absolutely real and the absolutely good. It was Plato who first united the notions of the absolutely real and the absolutely good in the concept of God. And since that time philosophy has never abandoned this thought, and it is this that constitutes the essential element in Kant's thought. This point of view would have been attainable without using happiness as the vehicle of the postulate. Kant really does happiness too much honor in making it, or the lack of correspondence between it and virtue in the empirical world, the coping-stone of his entire system. If he had set out from the notion of a kingdom of ends, his road would have been shorter and smoother. He who wills the kingdom of ends believes in the possibility of its realization. He who lives for the kingdom of God, and is ready to die for it, believes in God.

At this point we return to the second definition of the object of volition — perfection as the end of the will. If Kant had given, as he intended, an exposition of his system about the middle of the eighties, this notion might perhaps have played an important rôle. As it is, it occupies an unimportant place in the *Metaphysical Principles of the Doctrine of Virtue*, as an end of the will that is necessary in addition to happiness. As the two ends which duty prescribes, although they must not be motives of will, Kant here names our own perfection, and the happiness of others. Under the head of our own perfection, the cultivation of all our powers and talents, bodily, mental, and moral, is enjoined. To promote these with all our strength is a duty. On the other hand, it is never one's duty to promote one's own happiness, " since every one inevitably does that spontaneously." Nevertheless, it may even become a duty to promote one's own happiness as a means, although not as an end, since disappointment, pains, and want furnish great temptations to transgression of duty. On the other hand, it is not a duty to promote the perfection of others — that is their own business — but to work for their happiness. In doing this, one performs a grateful service if one simply makes concessions to their inclinations, but undertakes a thankless task if one regards their real advantage, although they themselves do not recognize it as such.

Here, just as little as in the *Critique of Practical Reason,* is any attempt made to unite in an organic way the "necessary purposes" and the formal law. In the former work, happiness, both for ourselves and others, is without any mediation declared to be a necessary object of desire for the practical reason. Here Kant takes the same position with regard to perfection. If Kant had not been so hardened in formal rationalism, if he had not so blindly maintained in the sphere of the will the absolute separation of form and matter that in the *Critique of Pure Reason* determined the form of his critical philosophy, if he had been able for a moment to lay aside the axiom that the good will is that which is determined solely by the form of the law, and that all determination of the will by the matter of volition proceeds from sensibility and renders it "impure," he would necessarily have arrived at a different system of ideas from the concept of perfection as the end of the will. He would have seen that man as a rational being aims at the establishment and enlargement of a kingdom of reason, of a kingdom of humanity, of a kingdom of God upon the earth. The moral law is the natural law of this kingdom in the sense that its enlargement depends upon obedience to the law. Transgression against the law, on the other hand, has, as a natural effect, disorder and destruction.

This line of thought is not entirely foreign to Kant. He employed it in the concept of "end in itself," which he ascribed to rational beings as a distinguishing characteristic, in the related notion of a "kingdom of ends" or a "kingdom of God" in contrast with the kingdom of nature, as he speaks of it in the *Critique of Pure Reason* in Leibniz's phrase. The notion is also the foundation of his philosophy of history (in the *Idea of a Universal History*). It recurs in the *Fundamental Principles* in the following passage: "The kingdom of ends would actually come into existence by means of maxims whose rule the categorical imperative prescribes to all rational beings if these maxims were universally followed." [1] But it is not employed seriously. The horror of rendering the determination of the will "impure" by any matter of volition prevented Kant from following up this thought. In the *Critique of Practical Reason* it no longer played any part. Here nothing but formalism prevails. This work begins at once with the propositions: [2] "All practical principles which presuppose an object (matter) of the faculty of desire as the ground of determination of the will are empirical and can furnish no practical laws." "All material practical principles are as such of one and the same kind, and come under the general principle of self-love or personal happiness." With these "propositions" the notion of purpose is *a priori* debarred from entrance into the practical philosophy, at least from any influence on its main problem. At a later point, in the Dialectic, we have not the concept of "perfection" or of a "kingdom of rational beings," but that of happiness suddenly reappearing from some unknown quarter, and presenting itself, after having been previously rejected as derived from sensibility, as an *a priori* necessary element of the complete good, and one that reason has to recognize in addition to virtue.

One must say that anything so internally inconsistent as the *Critique of Practical Reason*, with its two parts, the Analytic and the Dialectic, with the form and the matter of the will, the law and happiness, is perhaps not to be met with again in the history of philosophical thought. Kant, however, is so certain of his *a priori* procedure that he unhesitatingly rejects, as forming a single *massa perditionis*, all previous forms of moral philosophy, Epicurus and the Stoics, Shaftesbury, Wolff, and Crusius, since they all have started with material grounds of determination. The crit-

---

[1] IV., p. 286.   [2] §§ 2, 3.

ical metaphysic of morals is the first and only true system of moral philosophy.

If Kant had taken the concept of a kingdom of ends as his starting-point, and if, instead of forming his ethics after the pattern of his epistemology, he had elaborated it as a practical discipline, establishing or maintaining its natural connection with anthropology and philosophy of history, his thought might have attained something like the following form, which seems to me more felicitous.

The vocation of man, the purpose that God or nature has prescribed to him, and whose accomplishment is the business of the historical life, is the development from animality to humanity through the employment of his own reason. Education, civilization, and moralization, are the three parts of the process of humanizing. The final goal of the process of development is to form a united and harmonious kingdom of rational beings in which the moral law, as a natural law, shall determine volition and action, or in religious language to build up the kingdom of God upon the earth.

Man stands in a twofold relation in regard to this vocation. The sensuous impulses that he shares with the animals (the lower desiderative faculty) resist it, because in the process they suffer loss. The sense impulses are restrained by the advance of culture. On this point Kant shares Rousseau's conviction. But man has also a "higher desiderative faculty," practical reason, and this has as its end nothing else than the enforcement of its own demands. From this view-point the explanation of the essential concepts of moral philosophy would be as follows:

Morality is the constant resolution of the will of a being who is at once sensuous and rational to follow reason as opposed to the impulses of sense. It gives to action the form of universal conformity to law, instead of the accidental and arbitrary character that belongs to sensible impulses. Moral laws are universal laws of conduct, that, in so far as they determine the will, direct its activity towards the ultimate end. Duty in the objective sense is the obligation to determine action by reference to the moral law. Freedom is the corresponding capacity to determine conduct in independence of the incitations of sense, and in accordance with the moral law. The moral worth of the individual depends upon his disposition. Conscientious performance of duty carries with it moral worth and dignity, irrespective of the amount and extent of what is accomplished. For the latter is not dependent on the will alone, but also upon fortune.

Happiness is used in a double sense, and corresponding to this its relation to sensibility is different. In so far as the word denotes the satisfaction of the sense impulses, virtue is not a means of promoting one's own happiness. But in so far as the realization of the higher desiderative faculty (the practical reason) is accompanied by the feeling of satisfaction, one may even say, if one likes to name this feeling happiness, that virtue is the only means of attaining the true happiness, which, in the case of a rational being, depends before everything else upon self-respect, and is inseparable from morality and the maintenance of the dignity proper to man. — Complete humanizing and moralizing, together with the happiness that is their result, constitute the highest good. This is a mere idea to which there can be no corresponding object in the sense-world. The significance of the idea consists in the fact that it sets a goal for empirical reality as manifested in the historical life, to which the human race is required to approximate through constant stages of progress.

Belief in God is the moral certainty that the highest good is the ground and goal of all things. Perfect divine service is a life spent for the honor of God, and in the service of the highest good.

In this way we might have all of Kant's essential thoughts without the formalism.

III. Criticism of the Moral Philosophy

In what has been said we have already indicated the standpoint from which Kant's moral philosophy is to be criticised. According to my opinion, it is just that which Kant regarded as his special service that constitutes his fundamental error. This is the expulsion of teleological considerations from ethics. I shall attempt to show this in describing the place of teleology in the historical development of philosophy. In undertaking this, I emphasize the fact that the criticism has reference only to Kant's moral *theory*, not to his moral *views*. These are better than his theory, and I shall return to them in the next section.

All philosophical reflection upon the nature of morality sets out from two points: (1) from the fact of moral judgment, (2) from the fact that the will is directed towards some end. From the first point of view, one reaches the problem regarding the final standard in passing judgments of value upon human actions. From the second standpoint, the question regarding the ultimate end or the highest good presents itself. In this way, arise the two types of moral philosophy, — the ethics of duty, and the ethics of the good. The original form of the ethics of duty is to be found in religious theories of morals: the law of God is the final standard of judgment and of value. Theological ethics, Christian and Jewish alike, declare that an action is morally good when it agrees with the command of God, and that a man is morally good when he makes the Divine command the law of his own will.

Philosophical ethics is inclined to the form of the ethics of the good. Greek ethics is entirely dominated by the question regarding the final end of all volition and action. Two tendencies manifest themselves at this point: that toward hedonism, and that toward energism. The former places the highest good in a state of feeling, pleasure; the latter, in an objective condition of character and realization of purposes: the complete development of all the human powers and capacities, and their complete realization is the highest good. Aristippus and Epicurus belong to the first side, Plato, Aristotle, and the Stoics to the second. The two tendencies approach each other in so far as the first asserts that a happy life can be attained only by virtue and ability, and the other concedes that virtue and ability has happiness as its necessary though not intentional result.

Modern ethics begins in the seventeenth century with the abandonment of the theological form of the ethics of duty prevailing in the school philosophy. An immanent basis for ethics was sought, instead of the transcendent foundation in the will of God as expressed in the ten commandments. This is gained in the same way as in Greek ethics. For the distinctions of value in what is good and what is evil are based on the recognition of a highest good, and on the relation of will and conduct to it. This highest good was defined as self-preservation, realization of the complete character, human perfection, complete development of humanity (in the systems of Hobbes, Spinoza, Leibniz and Wolff, and Shaftesbury). Then a volition or action whose natural result is in harmony with this end is declared to be good. At the same time, egoistic hedonism, which makes the individual's own advantage the absolute ground for the determination of the will, made its appearance. The distinction between good and evil is then reduced to the difference between greater or less certainty and cleverness in attaining this end. On the other hand, the theological form of moral philosophy also perpetuated itself. Kant takes Crusius as its representative.

The fundamental distinction between the chief types is that the theological ethics of duty is formal, the philosophical ethics of the good, teleological. The latter derives the distinctions of value in human conduct and relations in a last resort from the effects in relation to an ultimate end. The former has regard merely to the formal agreement of the will with the law, or to the formal character of the will's determination by means of the law : the moral good is absolutely good, not good for something.

Now, Kant's position was determined in this way. Originally he occupied the standpoint of the Wolffian morality of perfection. To this was added in the sixties, by way of a basis and complement, the English morality of feeling with its anthropological tendencies. The critical philosophy brought a complete reversal : Kant went over to the side of formal moral philosophy ; only, the pure reason takes the place of God as the autonomous source of the law. Henceforth he rejects the teleological conception, not merely as false, but as dangerous for morality itself. A will is good solely on account of its formal determination by the law, not on account of what it wills or what is effected through it.

I am unable to convince myself either of the dangerous character of teleological ethics, or of the tenability of this purely formalistic theory of morals. The latter sees only what stands nearest, and leaves entirely unsolved the problem of a general theory of life and of conduct.[1]

If one attempts, as is reasonable, to find a reconciliation, one may take as a basis the distinction between two kinds of judgments regarding the value of human volition and conduct, the subjective-formal and the objective-material. The first refers entirely to the disposition, to the relation of the will to the moral judgment of the person acting. And since we name an action good in so far as it results from a consciousness of its moral necessity, the content may be what it will. The Arab, as an avenger of blood, the fanatic who persecutes the enemies of his God, acting, not from

---

[1] A detailed account of the controversy between teleological and formalistic moral philosophy is given in my *System der Ethik* (4th ed. 1896), I., pp. 201 ff., 314 ff. [English translation by F. Thilly, pp. 222 ff., 340 ff.].

personal hatred, but perhaps overcoming personal inclination
or universal sympathy for his kind, and following the " categorical imperative " in his breast, acts morally. And his
moral maxim would perhaps stand the test that Kant demands — act in such a way that thou canst will that thy
maxim should become a universal law of conduct. " Certainly I will this," he might say, and even Kant could not
prove the logical impossibility of this maxim prevailing as a
law of nature.

But, we should now add, this is not the end of the matter.
A second and quite independent question is whether aveng-
ing blood, and persecuting those of a different faith, are good
when considered objectively. Our moral sense condemns
both. Why ? Evidently because they are in contradiction
with our idea of a peaceful and equitable common life, with
our conception of the value of freedom in our intellectual
life, and of the worthlessness of forced convictions, and with
our experience regarding the injurious influence of repression
and protection in the spiritual life. Or, in a word, because
the objective results of such ways of acting do not tend to
promote, but to disturb and destroy the highest good, quite
irrespective of what are the subjective motives of the person
acting, whether he kills or persecutes from inclination or
from a sense of duty.

And now we would go on to assert that the real problem
of moral philosophy does not consist in discovering the
subjective moral value of the actions of the individual.
It has done all that it can do in this connection when
it has established the principle that one acts morally, from
a subjective point of view, when one acts from a feeling
of duty, out of reverence for the absolute command. But
the problem is rather to determine the objective value
of actions and relations, or to explain the different moral
evaluation placed upon them (varying among different peoples and at different times). Ethics will seek to determine

why lying, stealing, killing, adultery, etc., are condemned, and truth, honesty, friendliness, and faithfulness in the marriage relation are good.   In this investigation, it will find that actions of the sort first mentioned tend to disturb and to destroy man's social life, and thereby to undermine the foundations upon which all healthy human life must rest.   Lying is not evil because it cannot be posited as universal without destroying itself, but because, so far as in it lies, it destroys an essential good, namely, the confidence that is the fundamental condition of all social life among men.   And in like manner, thieving, and adultery, and impurity, are reprehensible because they destroy goods, like property, the material basis of all human culture, and the family life, the medium in which the spiritual life of man is maintained and handed down.   In general, vices are objectively bad because they are destructive forces; virtues are objectively valuable because they act as forces to preserve and promote the kingdom of reason and of humanity.   The capacity for logical universalization, however, is a useful means of discovering the result of any kind of action.   It is difficult to say how a single action may result in any particular case.   But it becomes clear what its nature is, what general tendency it possesses, as soon as one asks what the result would be if every man always acted in this way.

Finally, teleological ethics is able to derive from its own principle what is valuable in the purely subjective morality.   It shows that the habit of determining one's actions from a sense of duty, which we call conscientiousness, has the tendency to preserve the content of human life.   What actually determines the will in this case is uniformly the objective morality of the community and the time.   Custom and law, however, usually tend to preserve this community life: a people whose custom and law tended towards disintegration would be incapable of living, and would perish. In so far, then, as conscience has objective morality as its content, it has the tendency to determine the conduct of the individual in the direction of the preservation of the community, and also to influence his actions as a member of the community.

Thus the teleological moral philosophy attains a unitary view of the moral world. It is able to derive both the form and the matter of the will, to speak in Kant's phrase, from a single principle. The will that is directed towards the highest good, wills at the same time its own determination by the moral law, as the norm upon whose maintenance the possibility of its realization depends. In this it may, of course, happen that this or that particular impulse sometimes determines the volition in a direction opposite to the norm. We have in this all the valuable elements of the Kantian ethics. We have the autonomy of the will in a twofold sense. As independent of external authority, the moral rational will wills the highest good, and in doing so gives itself the law. And, as independent of sensibility, the rational will, not the lawless impulses of sense, furnishes the motives of life. In like manner, we have freedom from hedonism and egoism. The rational will does not will pleasure as the absolute good, but an objective state of things. And the object of its will is not merely itself, or its own existence and advantage, but the preservation and development of the spiritual and moral life of the community, and of itself as a member of the community. And so we say with Kant that the worth and significance of a life depends entirely upon the good that man does, not upon the good or evil that he suffers.

On all these points, the Kantian morality is significant of an exceedingly healthy reaction against sensualistic and egoistic eudæmonism, which was then to some extent in vogue, especially in the polite world. Think, for example,

of La Mettrie and Helvétius. It is the reaction of the
sound morality of the people against the sophistical view
of the court and the gentry. On the other hand, as a
philosophical theory of morality, it is just as untenable as
the old theological view. Above all, it is unable to discover the unity of form and matter of the formal and real
motives of the will. As in the old theological moral philosophy, so also in Kant, the content of what is morally
good is in the last resort given by command of God, and
the end of the will, eternal blessedness, is only accidentally
connected with morality by means of the will of God. Moreover, he brings in, as matter of the will, happiness or even
perfection in addition; but he cannot find the natural connection of these with the moral law and so takes refuge in a
supernatural connection. He had really before him all the
elements for a teleological interpretation, — the concept of
a kingdom of ends, the unity of rational beings, perfection
and happiness as necessary objects of volition, the moral
law as the natural law in the domain of freedom, — but
as if by some fatality they were held apart. More than
once, it seems as if he must reach a proper synthesis, especially in the second section of the *Fundamental Principles*,
as, *e. g.*, in the remark :[1] "Teleology considers nature as
a kingdom of ends, morality views a possible kingdom
of ends as a kingdom of nature." But he does not draw
the conclusion that the moral law is the natural law of
the kingdom of ends, in the sense that on its realization depends the maintenance and actualization of that kingdom.
He had the analogy that the laws of the state are the
natural laws of civic society, in the sense that the preservation of the state as a social unit depends on the
maintenance of the legal order. Nevertheless, he does not
discover the formula of solution. He is so intent on the
pure law of reason and its logical universality, so much

[1] IV., p. 284. Footnote.

in love with the purity of the pure will that is determined solely by means of the law, that he turned away in horror from the derivation of its validity from the matter of volition as from a sacrilegious defilement of morality.

Instead of this, he toiled over the absolutely vain attempt to squeeze a "matter" of volition out of the "pure" law of the logical universality of the motive of the will — *ex aqua pumicem*, one might say, inverting his quotation. Lying and suicide are morally impossible actions, for when made universal, they destroy their own possibility. Suicide would destroy life, and in this negate itself, and so with lying. These things, therefore, can occur only as irregular exceptions, and are thus contrary to reason and its logic. If in the case of these negative commands there is still a certain significance in this rule of universality — the same which belongs to the universal validity of legal commands — the positive duties resist most decidedly every attempt at an investigation of this kind. Consider the attempts to derive the duty of cultivating our own talents, and the duty of charity: " As a rational being man necessarily wills that all his powers should be developed because they are useful and given to him for all kinds of possible purposes." And: Even if absolute egoism could exist as a natural law, yet no one could will it, " since many cases might occur when he would require the love and sympathy of others." It is evident that Kant here drops his formula and falls back on the matter of volition, even appealing to egoistic motives. Thus the facts of the case emphatically reject his theory. Nevertheless he does not abandon it, but clings to it on principle: all derivation of duties from ends is empirical, false, and ruinous.

The cause of all this difficulty lies in the mysterious prominence that epistemology had won in his thought. It hindered the free, spontaneous development of Kant's ethics, as it did also of his metaphysics. It determined both the problems and the form of their solution. Above all, it is responsible for the unfortunate theory that makes the human will a union of practical reason which merely sets up a law, and sensible impulses that merely clamor for egoistic satisfaction. Thus arises the empty concept of a pure will as the complement to "pure" perception and thought. And the mysterious over-estimation of "pure" thinking then led to the clearly untenable assumption that the "pure" will is the good will. And from this there resulted, as a further consequence, the denial of any moral difference whatsoever between the material grounds that determine the will. In principle, it is quite indifferent for the moral value of the action whether the satisfaction of sense desires, the love of fame, the good of a people, the salvation of a people from the bonds of injustice and false-hood, is the end that determines the will, in so far as they are all material principles of determination. At least, between the moral theories that adopt material principles, between egoistic hedonism and the Aristotelian and Stoic ethics of perfection, there is said to be no difference. According to Kant, they all reduce in· the last resort to Epicureanism. Epicurus alone had the courage of his convictions. One may well say that the consequences of a false principle cannot be carried further.

And with this unfortunate theory of the will is connected the tendency of Kant's moral philosophy that from the first does violence to feeling. It is commonly called rigorism, but I should rather name it negativism. To act morally is to do what one does not want to do. Of course, according to Kant the natural and sensuous will always aims at the satisfaction of its desires. Duty, however, commands unconditionally that we shall allow nothing but the law to determine our will. Even the virtuous man might really always prefer to follow his sensuous inclinations to luxury, ease, etc. But the "idea of the law," with its "thou shalt not," or "thou shalt" interposes. And so, practising the hard virtue of repression, he does what he does not want to do. Greek moral philosophy, on the other hand, with its sound theory of the will, regards virtue as a joyous, positive mode of action, as the attraction of the will by a noble and beautiful purpose. In "perfection of character" and "completion of will," the human being attains that which his deepest nature seeks. To be sure, Kant at bottom holds to this also; he defends himself against Schiller's reproach, he struggles with his own negativism, but vainly. For he held fast to the principle that a will is only good when it is determined solely by the "idea of the law," and that all material determinations are reducible to happiness. And, as a consequence, duty remains that which one does not want to do, and virtue abstinence from that which one really desires.

I refrain from showing how this fanaticism for "purity," or fixed formalism, is connected with the inability of Kant's moral philosophy to account for important facts of the moral life as they exist, as, e. g., the conflict of duties, a doubtful or erring conscience, the moral necessity of a white lie, etc. Kant made shift as one usually does in such cases: he denied the possibility of that which could not be derived from his theory, or did not agree with it, and in this way he was led to deny the reality of the most evident facts.

However, let this suffice for criticism. We propose now to consider Kant's philosophy from another and a more pleasing side.

IV. KANT'S MORAL PERCEPTIONS AS BASED IN HIS PERSONALITY

The moral perceptions of a man are not the result of his moral theory, but arise from his personal character. The theory is an attempt at their explanation, and is also partially determined by other influence of all sorts. Thus, in Kant's case, his moral perceptions have their root in his personality, while their exposition in his moral philosophy is very greatly influenced and perverted by his epistemology. I shall attempt to give an account of these perceptions themselves. It is to them that the Kantian morality owes the influence which it has exercised, and still continues to exert.

Into Kant's moral personality, or personal character, two moments, as we have already intimated, entered as determining factors.[1] He had a strong will, but not a vigorous or even an amiable nature. He had formed his character through his will, and was a self-made man in the moral sense. And it was his pride that his moral quality was not a natural endowment, but the work of his own will. From the Essay, *On the Power of the Spirit to Control its Morbid Feelings by mere Resolution*, which he added as the third essay to that collection of essays called *The Controversy of the Faculties*, we learn how he brought his weak body into subjection by means of discipline that was continued even until his old age. The universal principle of his Dietetics reads: "Dietetics must not tend towards luxurious ease, for indulgence of one's powers and feelings is coddling, and results in weakness." His inner life was regulated according to similar principles. In the same passage he reports how by discipline of his ideas and feelings he had gained the mastery over the tendency to hypochondria, and had attained peace and cheerfulness, though in earlier life it had rendered his life almost unbearable. This self-control " also enabled him to express himself deliberately and naturally in society, and not according to the mood of the moment." Thus from a character naturally weak and retiring he developed the bold self-sufficiency that lies in the blood of bolder and more self-assertive natures. In like manner, the

[1] p. 54.

active sympathy that he showed for those about him appears to have been grounded in the moral consciousness of duty rather than to spring from a warm heart. It seems not improbable that he was thinking of himself when speaking of a man "in whose heart nature has placed little sympathy, who is naturally cold and indifferent to the sufferings of others; perhaps, being endowed with great patience and endurance, he makes little of his own pains, and presupposes or even demands that every other person should do the same." When such a person does good to others merely from a sense of duty, and without any promptings of inclination, his act has a much higher value than if it were the result of a "kind-hearted disposition."[1] At least, one gets the impression from his biography that he did not possess a heart that was naturally very sensitive to what happened to others. Thus his interest in his sisters and their families, for whom he did much, had not the directness and heartiness of a lovable nature. One might almost say that there was an excess of rationality about it. He puts a low estimate on enjoyment — it is only activity that is valuable and gives worth to man — and likewise condemns the soft, tender, "moving" feelings. Only the "vigorous" emotions (*animus strenuus*) find favor in his eyes. Stoic apathy, independence of things and mastery over them is his personal ideal. It is obvious how strong an influence this exercised upon his moral theory.

A second point where his ethics was in close touch with his personality is found in his democratic feeling for the people, which always made him sympathize with the common man against the social pretensions of the aristocracy. This feeling is not unconnected with his own descent. Rousseau, his favorite author, even at that time a famous writer, and much affected in the polite world, knew how to understand and sympathize with the artisans, peasants, and

[1] IV., p. 246; V., p. 284.

shepherds, with whom he had shared bed and board in his youth. And in the same way Kant always remained faithful in his moral feelings to the circle of humble people from whom he had sprung. He is not at all inclined to grant that the advantage which the rich and polite claim to have in culture and manners is a real advantage. Their advantage consists more in what they enjoy than in what they do. He does not even recognize any merit in their charities. "The ability to give to charity," he says, not without a certain harshness, " is usually the result of the advantage given to various men by the injustice of the government. This brings about an inequality of fortune that renders charity to others necessary. Under these circumstances does the help that the rich may vouchsafe to those suffering from want deserve the name of charity, which one is so ready to apply to it in priding one's self on it as a virtue ? "[1]

Not to the rich and the noble do we owe thanks, but to the laboring and productive masses. He called them once " the people most worthy of respect,"[2] who have borne the pains and cost of our culture, without enjoying the fruit that usually belong to endurance and self-denial, in order that the few might have freedom and abundance.

These sentiments show that Kant belongs to the great movement which took place about the middle of the century, in which sympathy for the life of the people burst through the aristocratic ideas of rank that had hitherto prevailed in society. He thus belongs to the group of great writers who not merely created a new literary epoch, but founded a new epoch in the life of the German people. It is the period when the people, the long unnoticed masses, and their spiritual life were again discovered. Möser, Hamann, Herder, Goethe, and Pestalozzi had a share in bringing it about. Goethe, for example, in a letter to Frau von Stein (Dec. 4,

---

[1] *Tugendlehre*, § 31 ; *cf. Kr. d. r. V.*, Doctine of Method, p. 161.
[2] Preface to the 2d edition of the *Kritik der pract. Vernunft*.

1777) says: "How much that dark journey (to the Harz in winter) taught me in the way of love for those who are called the lower classes, but who certainly are the highest in God's estimation. There we find all the virtues united: limitation, contentment, straightforwardness, fidelity, joy in the most moderate fortune, innocence, patience, patience — endurance in the face of privation."

One can say at once that Kant's morality is that of humble folk, the morality that he had learned in his parents' home. Conscientious and faithful performance of moral demands without thought of reward, with hard work and often severe self-denial, was the mode of life and of thought in which he grew up. With this corresponded a mood, not gloomy but somewhat austere, that was only slightly modified by the consciousness that they were living as God had willed it, and by the hope of a better life beyond the grave, in which the powers and natural talents that here lie under the pressure of necessity, will have opened up to them a freer field for their activity. That is essentially the mode of life and the attitude towards it that Kant has before him as a moral philosopher. His morality is not that of the ruling classes, or not that of the artist or poet, but the plain morality of the common man. The morality of the ruling classes (*Herrenmoral*), of which one hears so much talk nowadays in Germany, is individualistic and egoistic. Its philosophy is to live the life of the impulses, giving them free vent without any thought of a law, and without reference to others, or even at the cost of others, of the herd of humanity who are produced wholesale by nature for the service and enjoyment of the ruling class. The "artistic" morality is equally individualistic and egoistic. It also claims for itself a special standard, a morality of its own, which leaves room for the free development of the natural talents, and the elevation of the imagination above the common things of every-day reality. As opposed to a morality

of this kind that claims to be for distinguished persons, the
morality that flourished at the court at Versailles and perhaps also at Potsdam, and again at every seat of a petty
grand-seigneur in Prussia, where sophists and court philosophers retailed "enlightenment" in the form of egoistic eudæmonism, — in opposition to morality with exemptions for the
privileged classes, Kant sets up his account of morality, the
simple morality of the common people. It has no exemptions for the gods or demigods of this earth, but its laws
possess strict universality.   It did not address itself to
"volunteers" of morality, but preached simple obedience ; it
knew nothing of meritorious conduct, but only of obligation.
In opposition to the tendency of the upper classes to estimate the worth of life from its accidental filling, to make
the social judgment of a man's importance the final standard of evaluation, he took as the foundation of his morality
the principle: "It is not possible to think of anything anywhere in the world, or even outside it, that can be regarded
as good without any limitation except only a good will."
The will, however, is not good through what it achieves, but
good in and for itself, because it is determined only through
the feeling of duty, and not through inclination.   Whether
you rule states and win battles, whether you render humanity richer by miracles of art or science, whether with
weary feet you tread the furrows as a ploughboy, or on the
remotest outskirts of the city you make harness or patch
shoes, — none of these things have any significance at all for
your moral worth.   For this standard it matters not what
external fortune or natural gifts you may possess, but all
depends upon the disposition and faithfulness with which
you perform your duty.   If you do not follow your own inclinations and moods, but obey the moral law within, you will
rise to a plane of grandeur and dignity that will always remain far from those who follow after happiness, or guide
their actions merely according to maxims of prudence.   You

belong then, whatever your place in this earthly existence, to the kingdom of freedom; you are a citizen of the intelligible world, citizen of the kingdom of God.

Kant here stands in close connection with the Christian view of life and attitude toward it. I do not mean with the worldly, courtier Christianity of fashionable people, of the cavalier type, who rejoice in duels, but with the original spirit of true Christianity. Its depreciation of the world and its pomps and glories, its indifference to all external distinctions of culture and education, the absolute value that it places upon the good will, the fidelity with which one serves God and his neighbor, its insistence on the equality of all men before God, — these are all characteristic of Kant's view of life. He stood quite outside Christianity in its ecclesiastical form, where under the protection of the state it forces on people its doctrines and creeds; but to the Christianity of the heart and the will, as it was and still is practised among the common people, his relation was close and intimate. Indeed, one may say that his morality is nothing but the translation of this Christianity from the religious language to the language of reflection: in place of God we have pure reason, instead of the ten commandments the moral law, and in place of heaven the intelligible world.

It is only when we take this standpoint, then, that we gain a real understanding of Kant's moral philosophy. But it seems to me that here lies also the secret of the influence that it has exerted. This has not been due to the form of conceptual construction that it employs, but to the perceptions upon which this construction is based. These moral views corresponded to the temper of the period, which in Germany enthusiastically honored Rousseau as the true pioneer and guide. The thoughts through which Kant expresses the strongest sentiments of his time are contained in propositions like these: "Every man is to be respected as an

absolute end in himself, and it is a crime against the dignity
that belongs to him as a human being to use him as a mere
means for some external purpose" (think, e. g., of bond-
service and traffic in soldiers), and : " In the moral world the
worth and dignity of each man has nothing at all to do with
his position in society." The truth of these ideas is limited
to no particular period, and they possess a very real significance for our time that has perhaps grown somewhat insen-
sible to their force.

Even the first point, the emphasis on the power of the
will as opposed to natural disposition, has its permanent
value. It is the fashion to say that Kant aroused the generation of the illumination who were sunken in weak and
selfish sentimentalism. His doctrine of the categorical imperative is supposed to have tempered the race of freedom's
warriors. I do not know whether or not the voice of a
philosopher is able to accomplish so much. In that great
conflict there were perhaps stronger influences at work than
the feeling of duty. I do not know either whether the age
of the illumination deserves all the hard names that have
been provided for it by a later time. We can at any rate
say that on the whole it was a time of unusually hearty
and vigorous effort in the cause of truth and right, for freedom and education and all that makes for the progress of
humanity, and also especially for the elevation of the back-
ward and oppressed classes. The present age has scarcely
cause to pride itself as contrasted with that generation. But
there is no doubt that the appeal to the will to assert itself
in the face of natural impulses has its justification and its
necessity in every age. The fundamental form of all moral
teaching is as follows : You do not really will when you are
moved by the impulses of sense ; your real self, your true
will, is directed toward a higher goal. And your proper
moral dignity rests upon the fact that you are ruler of
nature, not merely of what is external to yourself, but of

what is in you, and that you fashion your life according to
your own volition.   An animal is a natural product, and
just for this reason it has no real moral value, however
beautiful and admirable it may be.   This highest and absolute value you can bestow on yourself, even if you have
received little from nature or from society.   You cannot
attain happiness by the unaided efforts of your will; that
depends also on the natural course of events.   But something that is higher than happiness, you and you alone can
gain for yourself, *i. e.*, personal dignity, which includes worthiness to be happy.   It is indeed possible that you may be
unfortunate, but you can never be miserable : the consciousness of personal worth will provide you with strength to
bear the hardships of fate.

In conclusion, I may add a word regarding the coping-
stone of the Kantian philosophy, the doctrine of the primacy
of the practical reason.   This also is closely connected with
Kant's personal feelings.   It is a protest against attaching
too much importance to science, and estimating too highly its
importance for life, as had been the fashion since the days
of the revival of learning.   For three hundred years the
maxim of the Renaissance that education is the presupposition of morality, had been accepted.   Then Rousseau entered
his emphatic protest.   This came closely home to Kant; he
felt the truth to which the prevailing opinion had hitherto
rendered him blind.   And his entire system of philosophy
became for him a means for the confirmation of this truth.
The critical philosophy degrades scientific knowledge to a
technical means of orientation in the world of phenomena.
It follows, of course, that the possession of such a technique,
however valuable it may be as a means for all purposes of
culture, cannot decide regarding the personal worth of a
man.   So long as one believed that through science and
philosophy it was possible to obtain absolute insight into
the nature of things, and the being of God, these things

appeared to have some part in constituting the dignity of man. Now Kant declares that knowledge of this kind is absolutely impossible, and in its place he set *practical faith*, which rests solely on the good will, not on knowledge and demonstration. And this faith is the only way of approach to the super-sensible world, which through it stands open to all alike, to all, that is, of good will. Learning of the schools, theology, and metaphysics are of no advantage here.

This point also was doubtless of essential importance in helping the Kantian philosophy to find an entrance. Belief in metaphysics and dogmas was in process of vanishing, and natural theology was losing its credit. To many it seemed that science had perhaps spoken its last word in the *Système de la nature*. Then Kant brought faith back to a place of honor. Science can afford us no final philosophy. Its certainty always rests upon the faith that has its deepest roots in the will.

It is my deepest conviction that in this doctrine Kant teaches us definitive truth.

SECOND SECTION

THE THEORY OF LAW AND OF THE STATE

LITERATURE: The works that are here of main importance are the short essays: (1) *Idee zu einer allgemeinen Geschichte in weltbürgerlicher Absicht* (1784); [Eng. trans. by W. Hastie in *Kant's Principles of Politics* 1891]; (2) *Ueber den Gemeinspruch: Das mag in der Theorie richtig sein, taugt aber nicht für die Praxis* (1793); (3) *Zum ewigen Frieden* (1795); [Eng. trans. by W. Hastie in *Kant's Principles of Politics* 1891]. The systematic presentation in the *Metaphysische Anfangsgründe der Rechtslehre* (1797); [Eng. trans. by W. Hastie in *Kant's Philosophy of Law*, 1888]; this belongs to the period of extreme old age, and contains scarcely anything regarding the theory of law and the state that is not better expressed in the treatises mentioned above. We shall therefore follow these entirely in our exposition. The same is true of the second essay (*Streit mit der juristischen Fakultät*) of the collection called *Der Streit der Fakultäten* (1798). There are long reflections of an unsystematic sort on philosophy of law in the second volume of the *Lose Blätter* edited by Reicke. *Cf.* also an essay by Schubert, "I. Kant und seine Stellung zur Politik," in Reimer's *Histor. Taschenbuch* (1838); and Friedländer in the *Deutsche Rundschau* (1877)

I. ITS RELATION TO HIS PHILOSOPHY OF HISTORY, AND ITS HISTORICAL STARTING-POINT

In giving an exposition of Kant's theory of the state and of law, we may best set out from his views on the philosophy of history which we have already touched on in connection with his anthropology (p. 290). History is to be regarded as the natural movement of the human race towards complete culture as its goal, *i. e.*, of a complete development of all the capacities with which nature has endowed mankind. In the *Idea of a Universal History*, the ideal was formulated as " the complete culture of the human race by means of its own reason." The animals have the perfections of their species by endowment of nature, but man must himself attain his perfection in the long warfare called history. The means to this end, it is further explained, is antagonism within society. Man is a social being in that he can develop his capacities and find recognition for them only in society. And for this reason he seeks for society. But he is not a social being like a good-natured, peaceful, gregarious animal. He is rather the most unsocial of all creatures. Three strong natural impulses, the three great passions, love of glory, love of power, and love of gain, render each one the enemy of his fellows. It is just these impulses, however, that overcome natural indolence, the tendency to ease and animal comfort, and goad him on to a constant struggle for superiority.

From this arises the most important and most difficult problem that the human race has to face: to find a form which will permit a common social life on the one hand, and which will afford at the same time the greatest possible play to the antagonism that is essential to progress. The solution of this problem is found in the state. In the state, or in civic society, the absolute freedom of the state of nature is limited by laws that the individual is compelled by force to obey. Thus a peaceful common life and harmonious cooperation become possible. Nevertheless, in this organization there is no cessation of the struggle for property, glory, and power: privileges and property even here are prizes that call out men's powers. Thus is gained the most favorable condition imaginable for the development of all man's natural capacities. The motive, however, to pass from the *status naturalis* to the *status civilis* is found in the evils attendant on a state of nature, which is a condition of war and violence where no man is free from constant danger.

As soon as this undertaking has been completed, a final and most important problem meets us. This is to regulate the relations of the states to each other according to principles of right, or, in other words, to bring into existence a cosmopolitan unity of states founded on laws of justice that shall bring war among the states to an end. An everlasting peace, accompanied by unceasing rivalry between peoples and individuals, is the condition that will make possible the completion of the process of human education and moralization, or, in other words, the realization of the highest good. With the achievement of this end, the historical development will have reached its goal. The motive that urges men towards an international community of law and right proceeds again from the suffering of the people which accompanies the *status naturalis* among the states. This condition of unlimited freedom is a condition of open or latent war of all against all. The more oppressive this condition becomes, the stronger the motive to establish the universal rule of justice.

So much regarding the connection of Kant's theory of law and of the state with his philosophy of history. Before entering into details in the exposition of his ideas, it seems to me useful to describe the political and social conditions under which Kant grew up, and which he saw around him when a man. These conditions form the background with which his ideas stand in strong contrast.

The actual state in which Kant lived was an absolute monarchy, a form of government that might lead to the highest development of the power of the state, or to the most insane and worthless despotic government, according to the personality of the ruler. As examples of the latter we may mention the *Maitressenwirtschaft* and the exports of soldiers practised by many German princes of last century. The traffic in soldiers, active or passive, was a common practice; Kant often refers to it. In the eyes of the princes men formed one product of their country among others. "Many rulers regard their people as if they were only a part of the kingdom of nature."[1]   A war for dynastic ends, or merely to satisfy their irrational personal temper, seemed to them to afford the chief use for this natural product.

Society, as Kant saw it in his time, had strict distinctions of rank.   An hereditary nobility was sharply separated from the common people.   The latter were divided again into two classes.   There were first the humble citizens, a somewhat destitute and oppressed people.   Of these the only persons who gained any prominence were a few of the larger merchants distinguished for their wealth, and the scholars and academically trained officials who were held in somewhat greater respect.   And, secondly, there was the peasant class who were held in servitude.   These, as bond-servants, cultivated the lands of their lord, and oftentimes they were not considered as much more than useful household cattle. Indeed, at that time the law was that servants were inherited or transferred along with the soil.

Public discussion of political and social questions was practically debarred.   There was no press that had any real importance.   The newspapers were under regular police control, and printed only things that were perfectly harmless.   The magazine treated affairs of private life and literature.   Books were written only by scholars for scholars. That was true at least of the first half of the century, in which Kant's views were formed.   During the second half the intellectual life began to have freer scope, and literature gradually became a power.   Nevertheless its legal position remained the same : freedom, where this was enjoyed, rested upon favor and not on legal right.   Any moment an offensive expression might lead to the suppression of an author's work, or even to the most brutal ill-treatment of the offending author himself, as the fate of Möser and Schubart and other outspoken men showed.

[1] *Pädag.* VIII., p. 464.

Kant's political views were formed in opposition to the actual condition of things just described. Over against the prevailing state of affairs in which men were debased and humanity dishonored, he set his ideas of the dignity of man, freedom, equality, and justice. The central point of his thought is the notion of freedom. This has its origin in ethics. As a rational being, man is an autonomous law-giver, and an absolute end in himself. On this fact rests the dignity that belongs to him. Both these points recur in the politics; every citizen is ideally an autonomous co-worker with the law, and an independent centre of ends and claimant of rights. A system of law (*Eine Rechtsordung*) that would make it possible for one to be used as a mere means for the purposes of another, would be contrary to the idea of right (*des Rechts*). Right essentially presupposes the equality of all persons as having rights due to them; that there are no prerogatives or privileges. To employ the power of the state to maintain privileges, or to oppress the poor, would be a reversal to the opposite of the very idea of the state. The task that pertains to the state as such is to maintain a universal system of law that shall be the same for all. It is required merely to adjust matters so that the freedom of each one can exist along with the equally limited freedom of every other. It is obvious that Kant's idea of the state conflicts strongly both with the aristocratic arrange-ment of society and the absolute state of the eighteenth cen-tury, where everything is ruled through the police and for the public interest.

Let us turn our attention now to details, and first cast a glance at Kant's views of the origin of the state.

II. ORIGIN OF THE STATE

Kant follows here in the main outlines the thought of Hobbes, although the treatise on politics that is inserted in the collection, *On the Common Saying*,[1] has the title, "Against Hobbes." The origin of the state is really derived from the egoistic and anti-social impulses of human nature. If the phrase *bellum omnium contra omnes* does not occur here, the mode of thought is the same; for another time he expressly says that Hobbes's proposition, *status hominum est bellum omnium in omnes*, is wrong only in that it should read, *est status belli*.[2] Egoistic beings whose treatment of others is determined by love of glory, love of power, and love of gain, as the strongest motives, are constantly in a condition of at least potential war with each other. The impossibility of enduring this state of things forces them to form a state, and not sympathy and a brotherly disposition; for from these would never arise a state whose very essence is law and compelling power. On the other hand, a "population of devils" would adopt a system of law with compelling force if they only had intelligence to recognize what was necessary for their own good.[3] The essence of the state is made up of nothing but a supreme authority having the right and the power of legitimate compelling force against illegal violence. In the state all give up their unlimited freedom, which just because it is unlimited is insecure (the *jus in omnia*), in return for a freedom that is limited by universal laws and protected by the power of the state. The peace and security afforded in a sphere that is limited and guaranteed by law is better for every one than the unlimited freedom and insecurity of the state of nature. And thus we can even say that the establishment and maintenance of the state is for every one's interest. And from this standpoint one may regard the state as resting upon contract, *i. e.*, upon the free will of all. Only one must not understand by the contract an historical fact, but a rational idea. This was also at bottom Hobbes's opinion. What he really wished to

[1] VI., pp. 321 ff.   [2] VI., p. 194.
[3] VI., p. 433.

denote by that term was not the history of the state's origin, but the explanation of its continuance.

III. The Constitution of the State

In the general principles laid down, the influence of the dominant ideas of the eighteenth century, the theories of Locke, Montesquieu, and Rousseau, is unmistakable. The outlines of a constitutional state, as opposed to a state founded merely on arbitrary power, are marked out by three notions, — freedom, equality, and political independence. Freedom denotes that it is not allowable to employ force against a member of the political body except in defence of the law, but not in behalf of his own best interest. The latter corresponds to the paternal government exercised over those under tutelage, and not to the form of constitution demanded by free citizens. Equality means that all are subject to the law alone, and that all are subject to this in the same sense. There are to be no private rights founded on social distinctions, no class privileges, no prerogatives of birth, but all positions are to be open to every one according to the measure of his capacity. Hereditary lordship and servitude are inconsistent with the principles of a constitutional state; they cannot be regarded as proceeding from the general will of the people in the original contract. We can only suppose that a privileged class of nobles arose by the use of violence, and not by the consent of all, as did the general authority of the state. The limitation of freedom, which was originally universal and the same for all, through the compulsion of law, on the assumption of the rational notion of contract, is something that must apply equally to all.[1] And as for servitude, "no one can by a legal act cease to be master of himself and come to the same level as cattle."[2] The third point was the independence of the

[1] VI., p. 329.   [2] VI., p. 325.

citizens as sharing in the legislative power. The political counterpart of moral autonomy is to obey only those laws that one has decreed as a member of the legislative power. Nevertheless this right does not belong to all who live under the laws. Besides women and children, who are naturally dependents, those persons also are to be excepted who have no political independence, but are in the service of others. This is an exception that it might be difficult to justify for an individualistic and rationalistic theory of the state, which recognizes men only as abstract rational beings. Kant discusses only the difficulty of distinguishing between the dependent and the independent and active citizens.

Kant's ideal of the form of a political constitution was one in which the legislative power should be in the hands of a popular assembly, while the administration of the laws should be left to a relatively independent executive power. The value of a political state depends essentially for him upon the guarantee that it provides for lawful government, and the protection it affords against the lawless misuse of power, which is the internal disruption of the state. To construct the constitution of such a state is the most difficult of all problems; for from the notion of the government as the highest authority, it follows that as such it cannot be subjected to any controlling power, or that no legal judgment can be passed upon it. The highest authority cannot be controlled or brought under compulsion; that is an analytic proposition. The problem therefore is to find a form in which an absolute power of this kind can be embodied that will exclude the possibility of its arbitrary misuse. A democratic form of government, in which all the authority, legislative, executive, and judicial, is in the hands of the people or their chosen representatives, affords no security on this point. On the contrary, it tends towards despotism and arbitrary rule, and is especially unfavorable to intellectual freedom.[1] A strong monarchy is much more easily able to allow this free play, as the government of Frederick the Great showed. If the irresponsible ruler regards himself as the highest servant of the state, and acts on this theory, that is, as the protector of the independence of the country from without, and the preserver of justice and freedom from within, an absolute monarchy may be a good and legitimate government. Of course, there is no guarantee in this form of government against misuse of its powers.

From the very nature of the case there is no completely trustworthy security. "From such a crooked stick as man, nothing exactly straight can be formed."[2] A relative security against the abuse of the highest authority is, however, attained by dividing its powers or functions. In this Kant followed the doctrine of Locke and Rousseau. It is of chief importance that the legislative and administrative powers should not be united in one person. That results at once in the form of a despotic government. In a constitutional state the legislative power must necessarily be in the hands of the people. Kant deduces this in the following way in the *Theory of Law*.[3] Since the law can do no wrong (an analytic proposition), the making of the law must be in the hands of all, so that every one shares in its decree, and therefore in the law really obeys his own will. *Volenti non fit injuria.* In subjection to the legislative power stands the government, as the vehicle of a relatively independent executive authority. This may be either a physical person (a prince), or be intrusted to a body of men. The executive " stands under the laws and owes obedience to them as to another person or sovereign." Consequently, it may be called to account by this sovereign and deposed, but cannot be punished, for that would be an act of the executive power to which alone it pertains to compel one by force to act accord-

[1] IV., p. 167; VI., p. 418.   [2] IV., p. 149.   [3] § 46.

ing to law.[1] Finally, the judicial power is separated from both the other two. It lies in the hands of judges and juries. This would be the form of constitution through which a legitimate use of the highest authority is to the greatest degree secured. Kant names it the republican constitution.[2]

We may here refer briefly to the question of the right of revolution, which was then a burning one. Kant shows clearly the logical impossibility of this notion. A right to oppose with violence the legally constituted government, which is in actual existence and in possession of the legislative, executive, and judicial powers, perhaps on account of the abuse of its powers, is a clear contradiction. If this 'right' were incorporated in a paragraph of a constitution (there was such a paragraph in the French constitution of 1793), it would mean " the demand for a publicly constituted opposing authority that should protect the right of the people against the government, and so on *ad infinitum*." [3]

Instead of any such impossible arrangement, Kant advocates the free and public criticism of the government. This is the only instrument of control that is possible or necessary for the protection of the rights of the people : " the freedom of the press is the only palladium of popular rights." Then

---

[1] § 49.

[2] Among the political constitutions of his time, Kant may have regarded that of the United States of North America, the foundation of which he followed with warm sympathy, as approximating most closely to his ideal. Not that of England; for he regarded this as only a slightly concealed form of despotism — not, however, a parliamentary despotism, as has been thought, but a monarchical despotism. By bribing the parliament and press, the king has really absolute power, as is shown above all by the fact that he has waged many wars without and contrary to the will of the people. Kant had in general a very unfavorable opinion of the English state. In one of the fragments published by Reicke (*Lose Blätter*, I., p. 129) we read : " The English nation (*gens*) regarded as a people (*populus*) is the best totality of men considered in their relation to one another. But as a state among other states it is the most pernicious, violent, dominating, and quarrelsome of them all."

[3] VI., p. 335; *Rechtslehre*, § 49, *Remark A*.

it is contemptible to rouse prejudice against this. "To inspire
the ruler with anxiety that disturbance might be excited in
the state by means of private and public discussion, is equivalent to arousing mistrust in him against his own power, or
even hatred against his people." [1]

The question remains whether or not, when even this last
means of protecting themselves against abuses has been
taken from the people, a breach of formal right, although
legally impossible, may not nevertheless be necessary when
regarded from a moral and historical point of view. Kant
would deny this by asking if it is allowable to do evil that
good may come. His philosophy of law excludes on principle
teleological considerations, just as his moral philosophy does.
Along with all his love of freedom, Kant has in general still
a strong inclination to posit absolutely the duty of obedience
to the legally constituted government. Doubtless this is
connected on the one hand with the formalistic positing of
all duties as absolute, and also with his pessimistic view of
human nature. Only by absolute subjection to an absolute
power is it possible to unite such egoistic and unruly animals,
and to keep peace between them. All pessimists are abso-
lutists, as witness Hobbes and Schopenhauer; while a
breach of the existing law (*Recht*) in behalf of the higher
right of the idea affords but slight hesitation to the optimistic idealists. An account has already been given of Kant's
practical decision when the question met him whether he
would obey the inner call to criticism (in the field of religion), or the declared will of the government (the express
command of the king to refrain from criticism and subject
himself to the religious dogma). In this case he regarded
silence as the duty of a subject. Even if old age and natural
timidity of temperament urged him in the same direction,
his conduct was yet in accordance with his principles.

[1] VI., p. 336.

IV. The Function and Limitations of Government

The real function of the state Kant finds in the establishment and preservation of a system of laws. The essence of law consists in the legitimate limitation of the freedom of each individual, to correspond with the equally limited freedom of all others. The perfection of a system of laws is shown by its capacity to make possible the greatest attainable amount of freedom on the part of individuals, together with a full guarantee of justice. One might say, that as in Leibniz's metaphysics, the best possible world is defined by the fact that in it the maximum of compossible reality is realized, so the best system of laws is that which allows the realization of the largest amount of compossible freedom.

In this statement the limits of the functions of the state are also implied. The state is not justified in limiting the freedom of the individual further than regard for the maintenance of right demands; to protect against injustice and violence from within and from without is the whole duty of the state. Positive provision for the well-being of the individual lies outside its province. Least of all is it called upon to provide for spiritual well-being, or to exercise an influence upon thoughts and beliefs. If the executive power should attempt at all to fix limits to what shall be investigated and promulgated in the scientific, philosophical, or religious sphere, by absolutely forbidding criticism of certain dogmas, and thus absolutely fixing them, the result would be injurious to intellectual progress, and that would be "a crime against human nature whose real vocation consists in making progress." [1] These are the thoughts that W. v. Humboldt elaborated in his *Attempt to Determine the Limits of the State's Influence*. J. S. Mill, in his essay *On Liberty*, represents a similar standpoint.

[1] IV., p. 165.

Into the details of the theory of law I will not enter. They would be on the whole of little importance, and in many points astonishing and unpleasant, — the treatment of marriage is notorious.[1] Its fundamental character is the strict formalism that completely excludes teleological considerations. The formalistic treatment of punishment adopted by Hegel has long dominated the development of the theory of punishment. The constant neglect of the causes of crime on the one hand, and of the effects of punishment on the other, as is demanded by pure formalism, has perhaps even extended its evil effects to practical penal legislation and administration. Only in most recent times has the causal and teleological point of view begun to gain ground in criminology. It is to be hoped that in the coming century this view will lead to a crusade against crime that shall be richer in results than the efforts of the nineteenth century that were founded on the Kantian and Hegelian theory of punishment.

V. THE IDEA OF EVERLASTING PEACE

Everlasting peace was the favorite idea of Kant when he was growing old. The condition of its possibility lies in a universal union of states under just laws. To promote this is a duty, just as it was declared to be a duty to promote the formation of the national constitution. Kant hated war, although he did not fail to recognize its "culture mission," its influence upon the development of political life and power, and even upon that of personality.[2] Nevertheless war is contrary to reason and right, it subjects all the affairs of men to chance and violence, it develops the

---

[1] For Kant's true views on marriage one must go back to the exposition in his *Beobachtungen über das Gefühl des Schönen und Erhabenen* (II., p. 251). In the *Rechtsphilosophie* we have only the really "deplorable" (Schopenhauer applied this name to the whole work) fancies of an old man, for which one cannot hold the real Kant responsible.

[2] *Kr. d. Urb.* p. 270.

worst impulses of human nature, since it breaks through the bounds of law and morality.   Thus war is "the destroyer of all that is good," "the origin of all evil and all wickedness."   Kant has many bitter things to say about the "gods of the earth" who wage war as sport, who sacrifice nothing and "do not in the least suffer the loss of their hunts, country-houses, gala-days, etc., who decide upon war from trivial reasons as if it were a pleasure party, and to preserve respectability calmly leave its justification to the diplomatic corps, who are always on hand for this purpose."[1]   But he also condemns emphatically even wars prosecuted from serious reasons, e. g. wars undertaken to gain for a country a boundary or addition necessary to its safety.[2]   The patriotic oratory that one hears at the present time, with its glorification of war, and of the warlike and victorious king, Kant would have felt to be a sign of lamentable moral regression. In the "illuminated" eighteenth century, reason may not have been able to suppress war, but at all events it did not so far forget itself as to praise it.

Nor would the aged Kant lend a willing ear to the laudation of clever and unscrupulous politicians.   His impressions of the politicians have great similarity with the views expressed by Plato.   He describes them as persons who make possible everything impossible, except the dominance of right upon the earth, which they rather regard as something absolutely impossible.   He regards them as empiricists lacking in ideas, who see no further than the advantage of the day, but are not able to estimate things in their large relations.   In distinction from this, it will remain the permanent task of philosophy to view things from the standpoint of ideas, or as Spinoza would say, *sub quadam æternitatis specie*.   And philosophy will be right in refusing to listen at all to the wretched and disgraceful objection of unpracticality.   This reproach is often raised

[1] VI., p. 418; VII., pp. 163, 403.   [2] VI., p. 451.

against Plato's *Republic:* but ideas are not refuted by vulgar appeal to alleged contradictory experience. Rather experience has to be measured by ideas and formed after their pattern. The philosopher should set up an archetype, and the task of the politician should be "to bring, in accordance with this, the existing constitutions ever nearer to the highest possible degree of perfection. For no one is able or has the right to determine what is the highest plane that humanity is able to reach, and how great the gulf must remain between the idea and its fulfilment, just because freedom is able to transcend every limit that may be assigned." [1]

Like the idea of a perfect system of laws in a state, the idea of an international union of states, united by law, and the consequent substitution of a legal process for violence and war, is a necessary idea of reason, and as such perfectly legitimate. It is the duty of the politician to work for its realization ; the "thou canst for thou oughtst" holds not merely in private morality, but also in public matters concerning the laws.

However, Kant discusses also the influences that, even without the good will of the politician, on whom one cannot finally count, are at work for the realization of that idea. He refers especially to two points. (1) The evils that war entails are constantly becoming greater and more oppressive to the people. To the evils of present war are added the intolerable burdens of preparing for the future war, and of paying the debts of the last one. Further, along with increasing intercourse between peoples, the circle of those who suffer indirectly from the effects of a war will constantly be enlarged. The increase of these evils will continue to strengthen the impulse to get rid of them. As they have been strong enough to induce savages to submit to the rule of a political constitution, they will

[1] *Kr. d. r. V.*, § 1 of Dialectic.

also be effective in compelling the states to give up their savage freedom. (2) The growth of republicanism, or the increasing influence of the people in the government. Kant was convinced that the people, who had to bear the burdens, would not decide on war so lightly as the princes did, who regarded it as a kind of glorious sport. He had in mind the dynastic wars of his century, the wars of Louis XIV., Charles XII., and Frederick II. He saw in the events of his time symptoms full of promise for the increasing influence of republican ideas, — the establishment of the great republic beyond the ocean, and the transformation of France from a dynastic to a republican form of government.[1] Even nearer home he saw traces of the same tendency. In Prussia and Austria powerful and enlightened princes were beginning to promote the enlightenment of their subjects. It is true that there might even have been at work here a kind of craft of idea ; the increase that the princes sought in the sinews of war necessitated the development of all the intellectual and economic resources of their people. It seemed even here that the outcome must be a change from a dynastic state with its subjects to a popular state with its independent citizens. Thus even philosophy has its millennium.[2]

When we look at the matter from the end of the nineteenth century, it seems that the course of development since Kant's time can scarcely be regarded as the fulfilment of his prophecy. In this sphere also " a strange and unexpected movement of human affairs has taken place, just as in other respects too, if one looks at it in the large, nearly everything in it is paradoxical." [3] The growth of republicanism has not only failed to abolish war, but it has changed very greatly the sentiments of the people with regard to it. Since the duty of defence has become uni-

---

[1] *Streit der Fakultäten,* 2 *Section,* §§ 6 ff., **VII.,** pp. 399 ff.
[2] IV., p. 143.   [3] IV., p. 167.

versal, a condition of affairs produced by the revolution, war has become something in which the people really share, and consequently become popular in a certain way that was never possible in a dynastic war carried on by professional soldiers. The assumption that the people would not desire war on account of the burdens that it entails is a mistake in one respect. It is true that the people love peace, but there is something that they love more, and that is victory and the glory of war.

In order to become conscious of the interval that separates the views of the nineteenth century from that of the eighteenth, one may read a discussion of war in H. v. Treitschkes's treatise on constitutional monarchy.[1] Here we find war called " a necessity of political logic," that is implicit in the very concept of a state. " A state that renounces war, that subjects itself at the outset to a tribunal of nations, yields up its own sovereign power, *i. e.* its own existence. He who dreams of everlasting peace demands not only something that is unattainable, but also something nonsensical, and commits a schoolboy fallacy." And not only with logic, but also with ethics is the demand for an everlasting peace in irreconcilable conflict. " The hope of banishing war from the world is not only senseless, but deeply immoral. If it were realized it would transform the earth into a great temple of egoism."

Would Kant have given up his idea of everlasting peace as a mistake in the face of such objections, or before such fiery rhetoric ? Perhaps he would not. Perhaps he might have said that he had not, at any rate, anticipated the indirect course that history had taken ; but nevertheless, that he could not see in this anything more than a slight and perhaps necessary deviation, which did not lead away from the real goal. It is certainly obvious that purely dynastic wars are no longer possible. And, he might continue, there can

---

[1] *Historische und politische Aufsätze*, III., pp. 533 ff.

scarcely be any doubt that the dread of going to war has increased among European peoples with the universal duty of defence. Look, for example, at France. How prudent this people, formerly most warlike and most devoted to military glory, have become since military service was made universal. Perhaps it requires only a great and general European war, long prolonged and inconclusive in result, with the dreadful sacrifices of property and blood that it would entail, to cause the love of peace among the nations, which is now obscured by thoughts of glory and revenge, to manifest itself with lively force.

With regard to the "schoolboy fallacy," or even the moral questionableness of the idea of everlasting peace, he might propose the following considerations. The subordination of a state to a foreign power would certainly destroy its sovereignty and its essence. But in this connection we are dealing with the free recognition of a universal court of the nations with power of arbitrating all disputed questions. It is undoubtedly true that a nation would prefer to appeal to arms rather than submit to an unfavorable decision where their vital interests were at stake, or might even anticipate such a decision in this way. Nevertheless, arbitration may gradually and without any compulsion gain such a degree of favor that the use of force would constantly become more rare, and arbitration more highly prized by those states that had adopted it. Perhaps also the opposition to foreign powers in the east and west may make it necessary for the European states to form a closer union in one political alliance and to suppress all internal quarrels. As for "the temple of egoism" into which it is said peace would transform the world, it is at least going somewhat too far to say that war alone gives rise to sacrifice and heroic courage, and also that it produces nothing but these virtues. The lower brutal impulses perhaps find in war as favorable conditions for their development as the higher ones, and the stock exchange, if that is what is meant by the temple of egoism, has always known how to make profit in time of war.   Further, the author wishes to defend only the ' just ' war.   Does he not see that he is hereby assuming that the same war as carried on by the other party will be unjust ?   Indeed, is it not true that merely by introducing the idea of what is just and unjust into the relations between peoples, he admits that there is right and wrong in this field, and that therefore a judicial decision is not in principle impossible, and is perhaps even demanded by reason, or even, as he has said, " a necessary idea of reason," whose realization, it is true, may be long delayed ?   Moreover, Kant might add, he had an example in the man who regarded the peacemakers as blessed, not from any selfish or cowardly desire of peace for himself — he could have had peace, but chose rather conflict and the cross — but from desire for God's kingdom of love and of peace upon the earth ; and that therefore even in a panegyric on war a little more care and attention in the choice of expressions would appear to him to be in place.

THIRD SECTION

THE THEORY OF RELIGION AND THE CHURCH

LITERATURE: The chief work is *Religion innerhalb der Grenzen der blossen Vernunft* (1793). With this are connected a few short treatises: *Ueber das Misslingen aller philos. Versuche in der Theodicee* (1791); *Das Ende aller Dinge* (1794); and finally the first section of *Der Streit der Fakultäten* (1798). — *Cf.* E. Arnoldt, *Krit. Exkurse*, pp. 193 ff. ("Kant's Verhältnis zu Lessing"), and "Beiträge zur Geschichte von Kants Leben und Schriftstellerthätigkeit in Bezug auf seine Religionslehre und seine Konflikt mit der Regierung" (*Altpreuss. Monatsschrift*, XXXV., Heft 1 and 2).

Kant's philosophical theory of religion attempts, on the one hand, to furnish a philosophical exposition of the doctrines of the Christian church. On the other side it undertakes to limit these doctrines in harmony with the demands of a purely rational faith, or to sift out what is no longer tolerable to the enlightened philosophical and moral consciousness.

In general, the discussion follows the lines of theological rationalism, which since the middle of the century had been increasingly victorious over the old orthodoxy. The theologians of the illumination, following the example of the great philosophical rationalists, differed in important respects from the traditional doctrines, and found it necessary to omit and to transform certain things to bring the Scriptures and the dogma into harmony with their own beliefs. In doing this, they were only illustrating what inevitably takes place whenever absolute authority is claimed for a written document. Intelligence can preserve the freedom that is its essence only by interpreting and construing. It is the form in which progress and the continuity of historical faith are brought into harmony. The fact that the illumination period had but slight reverence for the historical induced a freer use of the right of interpretation and transformation than would otherwise have been the case. Kant shared with his time the contempt for the historical and the factual, as opposed to the doctrinal and rational.

The peculiar characteristic of Kant's rationalism is the decided emphasis on morality. This corresponds to the tendency on the part of the critical philosophy to turn from the speculative to the practical. The practical reason, the moral standard, is for Kant the touchstone of what is true and of value in all religions. Religion rests on revelation: the Bible as God's revelation is authoritative. Kant maintains unconditionally that the truth of every external revelation is to be tested and measured by the divine in us, by its harmony with the moral law. The Bible must be interpreted according to the standard of morality, not morality according to the standard of the Bible. We cannot even know the son of God to be such, except through the fact that he corresponds to an idea of the divine that we have in us. External verifications, *e. g.* miracles or prophecy, cannot in the last resort be recognized as affording proof; for one reason because we know of them only through fallible tradition. But another reason is that the power to work miracles in itself confers no moral authority. Can not, according to the church doctrine, the devils also work miracles ?

The value as well as the truth of religion is to be estimated according to a moral standard. Churches and church doctrines have value only because, and in so far as, they are serviceable for the moral education of the human race. If their influence is in the opposite direction, they are injurious and objectionable. And herein lies the great danger of all ecclesiastical institutions: they tend to attribute an importance that does not belong to them to all kinds of external things,— acts of worship, good works, or even mere faith in church dogmas or historical facts,— to the exclusion of

morality. And, on the other hand, men have an inclination
to excuse themselves from the only true divine service,
leading a good life, by the performance of such external
statutory divine services. In opposition to this, Kant says
that whatever has no significance for the moral life is superfluous or dangerous. That is true both of religious actions
and doctrines. All doctrines in which it is not possible to
find a moral meaning, like the dogma of the trinity, the
resurrection of the body, and others of the same kind, lie
beyond rational faith.

I cannot enter upon a detailed exposition, but will indicate in a general way the contents of the four parts of the
chief work. The first discusses the doctrine of sin, or of human depravity. The radical evil in human nature (original
sin in theological language) is not sensibility, but a tendency
toward impurity of disposition, as showing itself in a failure
to make the law the only determining ground of the will, and
therefore in allowing one's self occasional lapses from its
demands. This tendency is thus to be regarded as a free
intelligible act, and not as a natural endowment. The subject
of the second treatise is the doctrine of justification. The belief in Jesus as the son of God is explained philosophically to
mean that the son of God is the ideal of humanity which God
approves, and which corresponds completely with the will of
God. In the practical faith in this ideal, and in actively
striving to realize it, the individual gains the approval of God,
an approval that likewise partakes of the nature of grace, in
that human effort is never able to attain to perfection. In
historical religion, the sonship of the God-man is figured by
means of the virgin birth, to indicate the exemption of the
ideal man from the debasing effects of sensibility.

The third and fourth essays treat of the church, in its
true nature or " idea," in its historical form, and in its degen-
eration from the true " idea." The church in its " idea " is
an ethical community of men under merely moral laws, as

opposed to the political community which is ruled by legal enactments. Such an ethical community would represent a kingdom of God upon the earth, whose members, living together in fraternal agreement, had entirely adopted the will of God as their will. In the historical form, this ethical community appears as the visible church, with holy books and laws fixing the nature of the creed and mode of worship. This is a necessary form; for the people are still incapable of apprehending and maintaining rational faith in its pure form; and therefore the beneficent doctrine is given to them in the form of a divine revelation handed down in canonical books, and expounded by professional teachers who enjoy public esteem and respect, and is impressed upon the senses through symbolical acts. The purpose to be attained in all this is "that pure religion shall by degrees be finally freed from all empirical motives, and from all ordinances which have merely a historical basis, and which provisionally unite men for the promotion of the good by means of an ecclesiastical form of belief, so that at last the pure religion of reason may prevail universally." "The veil under which the embryo first develops into man must be laid aside, if he is to come to the light of day. The leading-strings of the holy tradition, together with its annexed provisos, the statutes and observances, which did good service in their time, become gradually unnecessary, or even hindrances, when he attains to manhood's estate."[1]

Finally, in its degenerate form, the church appears as an institution for compelling the maintenance of the statutory requirements in creed, worship, and church government. Here the statutory demands take precedence over the moral. The essential part of divine service is not an upright life, but the fulfilment of certain ecclesiastical duties. The first commandment, and the first condition of divine approval and of happiness, is subjection to the rules of the church.

[1] VI., p. 219.

For fulfilling this requirement the "believers" are promised divine favor in this world and the next, although living immorally and obeying the demands of their sensual desires. To the "unbelievers," on the other hand, punishments hereafter are held out in prospect. Thus we have a complete perversion of true religion; all kinds of "pious nonsense" are commanded as a sort of heavenly court service by means of which one may win by flattery the favor of the ruler of heaven. On the other hand, the true and the upright, those who are conscientious and truly pious, who do not think this emulation to win the favor of the heavenly court is worthy either of themselves or of God, are threatened with divine wrath, and sometimes, at least, are made sensible of the wrath of the church. Thus the degenerate church enters directly into the service of the devil.

The history of the church shows itself to be a continual struggle of the true church and religion with the priestly church. It begins with the great conflict of the founder of Christianity against Judaism, which had become perverted through superstitions and trivial compulsory requirements. What Jesus really accomplished was to found the invisible church as an ethical community of all God's true children upon the earth. The spirit of original Christianity is found in a purely moral and rational faith, instead of in belief in creeds and in popular superstitions, in a pure life devoted to God and one's neighbor as the only divine service, instead of in the performance of lifeless and exacting ceremonies. It is true that when Christianity became organized into a church, as an institution with worldly interests and worldly power, it degenerated in the direction of a priestly church having compulsory services and creeds; nevertheless, the motives that gave it birth still remained effective in it. The Reformation was an earnest attempt to free the church from perversions. But this great struggle for freedom of conscience was soon followed, even inside the reformed

church, by the re-establishment of a new ecclesiastical serf-
dom in a compulsory creed. The demand that one should
believe certain dogmatic formulas and historical facts, took
the place of the good works required previously, and oppressed
the consciences of sincere men more heavily than the old
burden of external performances. It was not until our
period of illumination, that there appeared to be a hopeful
prospect of a final deliverance of reason from ecclesiastical
authority, and of the restoration of the pure faith of practical
reason and the purely moral divine service.

Religion within the Bounds of Pure Reason is the last of
Kant's great works written in the full vigor of his intellect.
It is a most energetic attack, carried out with extraordinary
power of feeling and thought, on all churches and religions
based on statutory requirements, which establish a tyranny
over the soul by means of fear and superstition. It is also a
strong protest against all external piety that attempts by court
service and homage to gain divine favor through flattery.

Lessing would have been delighted with this work. The
Lutheran orthodoxy, which makes correct belief the only
act that is well-pleasing to God, is rebuked in especially
keen and cutting fashion. The *fides mercenaria* is worse
than any other ecclesiastical servitude. An upright man
would sooner agree to do anything else, "because in the case
of all other forced service he would at all events only be
doing something superfluous, but in this case something
opposed to his conscience."[1] Kant often returns to this
point, evidently referring, though not in express words, to
the new condition of affairs created in Protestant Prussia by
Wöllner's religious edict. In general, the entire work is an
emphatic protest against the new priestly government. He
emphatically demands freedom to investigate and to teach
for the teachers of rational religion and for the scholars who
expound the Scriptures (the philosophers and theologians).

[1] VI., p. 270.

They ought "to be left absolutely free by the secular power in employing their results and discoveries; for otherwise the laity, who derive their religious instruction entirely from the clergy, would be compelling the latter to adopt their views."[1] To him the fixing of the creed forever, with the apology that the people are not yet ready for freedom, appeared as insupportable arrogance, as an interference with the government of God, who has given reason the duty of guiding us into an increasingly perfect knowledge of the truth. The bigotry that was then in favor in high places was dealt with most unsparingly. Prayer, churchgoing, sacraments, if these things are practised to gain the Divine approval, or to make one's self a favorite with God, are disgraceful fetiches. The Shaman priests of Tungus and European prelates, the prayer mills of Thibet and ceremonial devotional exercises, are placed side by side, with the sarcastic remark added that there is no distinction between them in principle, though there is in external form.[2]

The end and aim of all priestly government, according to Kant, is political power. To obtain this, the priests attempt to gain an influence over the minds of the ruling powers, and in particular to represent to them the advantage that "the state might derive from the unconditional submission to which spiritual discipline has accustomed even the thought of the people. But in this way the people become accustomed to hypocrisy, their honesty and fidelity are destroyed, and they grow cunning in avoiding the true performance even of their political duties."[3]

The government in which Wöllner was a minister took offence at these views, as was to be expected. The order in council, of which we have already spoken,[4] was its answer to them. It is not too much to say that the hate that expresses itself in this order was not without cause. If the

---

[1] VI., p. 214.   [2] VI., p. 275.
[3] VI., p. 280.   [4] Page 49.

illumination was to be overcome, if a compulsory form of religious faith was to be re-established and supported by every means in the power of the secular government, Kant's philosophy of religion could not be tolerated, — indeed, Kant's whole philosophy should not have been permitted to continue in existence. If the ecclesiastical and political reaction in Prussia had had time to establish itself, it doubtless would have been forced to suppress the critical philosophy as a whole. The death of Frederick William II. preserved the Prussian state from this disgrace. However, we have a subsequent proscription of the spirit of Kant's philosophy. This belongs to the time of the Holy Alliance. In an order regarding religious instruction in the gymnasium, of the year 1826, we read: Above all things, the teacher must remember "that the state is concerned to make true Christians of the members of its schools, and that therefore they must not be instructed in mere so-called morality, which hangs in the air and has been deprived of all real support, but there must be inspired in them a God-fearing disposition, which has its roots in a well-grounded knowledge of the Christian truths of salvation." This is directly contrary to Kant. It is the inversion of his demand that religious faith should have its basis in morality.[1]

Besides the political tendency, there was in addition another sentiment that helped to bring about this change; for the romantic generation, with its enthusiasm for the historical, the Kantian religion was too thin, abstract, and rational. This age had lost its faith in reason, and demanded a stronger support for life and faith than rational propositions could afford. In particular, it sought to base religion again upon tradition, on historical facts and supernatural revelations. However greatly Kant may have aided in overthrowing the old rationalism, through his personal feelings

[1] *Cf.* my *Geschichte des gelehrten Unterrichts*, II., p. 323.

and sentiments, he belonged entirely to the Illumination. For him religion is nothing more than the general metaphysical background for his rational thought and action. He did not feel the need of a really positive religion, still less the necessity for direct intercourse with the supernatural. Every such attempt to gain this kind of intercourse (prayer, means of grace) he personally rejected. He sees in these things only sentimentalism, and a presumption that, along with all its boasted humility, leads easily to the assumption of special intimacy with the heavenly powers, and a contempt for any one less highly favored. Kant's religion, which is based merely on the general relation of the finite to the infinite, and on the natural revelation of God in reason and conscience, is a cool and matter-of-fact form of the religious life. This generally happens where a strong and independent intellectual life, united with strict conscientiousness in thinking and acting, is the fundamental form of mentality. It is also the religion of Lessing and Spinoza. If this form of religious experience is inferior to more concrete and robust forms in the strength of its immediate effects upon the mind, it is not exposed to the numerous perversions to which the latter incline, — magic and sorcery, superstition and fanaticism, priestly intolerance, and contempt for healthy reason and common morality.

It is true that it has little advantage for political purposes. Kant would not regard that as a defect. The emphatic passage with which he closes his little essay, *On the End of all Things*, shows clearly his opinion regarding the employment of religion, and of Christianity in particular, in support of the various purposes of the secular government: "If there ever should come a time when Christianity ceased to be lovely and of good report (which could easily happen if it should put on, instead of the humble spirit, the weapons of arbitrary authority), then, since there can be no neutrality on moral questions, the dominant tone of men's thought must be unfavorable and antagonistic to Christianity. And the antichrist, who is held to be the forerunner of the last days, would begin his government, — although it would be of short duration, — founded perhaps upon fear and selfish advantage. Then, however, since Christianity was intended to be a universal world-religion, but was not afforded by fate conditions favorable to becoming so, the (perverted) end of all things in a moral sense will appear." Arnoldt assumes that this essay increased to the utmost the anger of the Berlin authorities against the source of these courageous warnings and admonitions, and furnished the last motive for the Cabinet order of Oct. 1, 1794. Although, as we have seen (p. 50), the movement against Kant had been already recommended and decided upon, this passage may nevertheless have rendered its execution more easy for the government. The history of the nineteenth century reveals with striking clearness to him who has eyes to see that Kant's gift of prophecy did not deceive him here. The hatred of ecclesiastical and political Christianity, first on the part of educated people, then on the part of the masses, was the direct result of the attempts to employ religion to gain worldly power. The fact that Christianity has always been able in these circumstances to restore itself, is striking proof of the inner vitality of the religion of the cross and of worldly renunciation.

As embraced in formal propositions, the following points sum up Kant's doctrine of religion :

1. *The essence of religion* is not belief in supernatural beings (demons, demiurges) that occasionally influence the course of nature and man's destiny, but a belief in God, in a will that directs everything for good, and that realizes itself in nature and in history.

2. *The proof of religion* is not afforded by historical facts (miracles, revelation), but by the moral law, the will in ourselves that is directed towards the highest good.

3. *The function of religion* is not to subject the will or the understanding to any powers of this world or the other, but only to strengthen it as the power to will the good.

I believe that these formulæ might still to-day be taken as a basis for a philosophy of religion.

APPENDIX

THE THEORY OF EDUCATION [1]

Of Kant's thoughts on education I shall discuss only two points, both of which are closely connected with his ethical and political views.

His belief in the effectiveness of a moral instruction that shall take as its function the mere representation of the moral law in its purity, is associated with his concept of freedom and the autonomy of the moral law. He returns repeatedly to this point, as, *e. g.*, in the "Doctrine of Method" in the *Critique of Practical Reason,* in the fragment of a moral catechism in the *Metaphysic of Morals,* and also in the *Religion within the Bounds of Pure Reason.* By leading children to reflect upon concrete cases laid before them, and directing them in applying the moral law to these cases, they become themselves conscious of the law, and cannot help acknowledging its authority and making it a principle of the will. On the other hand, Kant emphatically rejects the process of making morality attractive by holding up the advantages and rewards that will result, either in this world or the next, from its performance. In like manner, he is desirous that the disgraceful nature of vice, rather than its harmful conse-

---

[1] Kant's pedagogy is found only in the notes that he made for the public lectures that the members of the philosophical faculty were required by the government to give in turn. These notes were prepared for publication by Rink. They are loose sheets written at various times and without any systematic form : — as printed the same thoughts are repeated two or three times. The lectures treat of bodily habits and training, and especially of the education of the will. The subject of school instruction is only touched upon, and no discussion at all is given of the particular disciplines. There is a good edition by O. Willmann. In addition to this work, the writings on moral philosophy contain remarks on the form of moral education.

quences, should be emphasized. He condemns with equal vigor the excitement of the feelings and emotions by the representation of unusually noble characters and actions, such *e. g.* as takes place in novels. The character must be based upon principles. He emphasizes very strongly the necessity of early training the will by means of discipline. The purpose is to restrain natural wildness by accustoming the child to law and actions based on uniform principles. This negative influence is the prerequisite of the positive training of the will, which uses, as its essential means, the mere representation of the moral law in its purity.

The second point is his decided disapproval of a state system of education. This was the logical consequence of Kant's cosmopolitan and humanistic mode of thought. The end of education has to do with men, not with citizens. Or, in a last resort, we may say that it is concerned with humanity: the complete development of the powers of man is its absolute end. For this reason " the basis of a plan of education must be made cosmopolitan." [1] This must not proceed from the state or from the prince. For these have in mind only the immediate purposes of the state or the dynasty. They would at best direct education to develop skill, " merely in order to be able the better to employ the subjects as tools for realizing their own purposes." Therefore the establishment and direction of the schools should be left entirely to the judgment of the most enlightened scholars. " All culture begins with a private individual, and radiates out from this centre. Only through the exertions of people of broad sympathies, who appreciate what is best in the world, and are capable of forming an idea of a better condition in the future, is it possible for nature gradually to approximate to the realization of its ends."

With this in view, we can understand the lively interest that Kant took in Basedow and in his philanthropic under-

[1] VIII., p. 463.

takings in Dessau. With the latter's aims he was in essential agreement, and he welcomed the undertaking chiefly as an attempt at an experimental school, which would be followed by future "normal" schools. To a still greater extent would Kant have sympathized with Pestalozzi's efforts; for these were based entirely upon the idea of freedom and self-activity. The object on which Pestalozzi set his heart, and which aroused Fichte's enthusiasm, was to deliver men from the indolent, stupid passivity in which the lower classes especially were forced to live by the influence of the secular and ecclesiastical government, and of the schools that were open to them. It is exactly the same end that Kant has in view. Freedom, independence, personal responsibility, are the conditions of human dignity, and therefore the necessary ends to be attained in education.

Would Kant approve of the course that education has taken in the nineteenth century? He would certainly recognize gladly the improvements in the external equipment of the schools, the large expenditures for all educational institutions from the common school to the university. Also in methods of instruction he would find great and salutary changes, among other things, the exercise of the understanding and the judgment instead of the mere mechanical learning by rote. On the other hand, he would perhaps see many things that would cause him serious doubt. Thus he would scarcely approve the fact that the schools have passed almost entirely into the hands of the state government, that instruction and education are regulated, down to the minutest details, by ordinances (instruction and examination regulations), and burdened by constant control. Certainly he would have wished to see a highly developed private school system alongside of the system of public schools. And probably he would not abandon as unfounded his fear that the state might aim too exclusively at practical capacity for its particular purposes, and not at the absolute ends of humanity. In particular, he would perhaps find in the "patriotism" that is now dominant in many places something directly opposed to the final end of humanity. The glorification of nationality and the state would appear to be almost a second religion, and in some places in Europe, *e. g.* in the French state school, it has become the first and only religion, since the old religion has been banished from the schools. And would Kant withdraw his opinion regarding instruction in religion after a visit to our schools ? In a remark added to the fourth part of *Religion within the Bounds of Reason*,[1] he complains of the lack of sincerity, and demands that education should especially concern itself to cultivate this virtue from the earliest years. He then proceeds : " Now, if one compares our mode of education, especially in religious matters, or better in the doctrines of belief, where it is regarded as sufficient to make a pupil a believer, to have him remember accurately the answers to the questions involved, without paying any attention to the truth of the creed, or understanding at all what he asserts, one will no longer wonder at the lack of sincerity which makes pure hypocrites at heart."

The Theory of Beauty and Art

The æsthetics of the critical philosophy is found in the *Critique of Judgment*, where it is connected by a slender association of concepts with the critique of natural teleology.[2] Kant's reason for taking the judgments of taste from the field of empirical psychology, and placing them in

---

[1] VI., p. 289.

[2] B. Erdmann's edition has an introduction that gives an account of the origin of the work and the history of the text, together with information regarding Kant's relation to the printed text of his works in general. *Cf.* K. Th. Michaelis, *Zur Entstehung von Kants Kr. d. Urt.*, Berlin, 1892 ; Goldfriedrich, *Kants Aesthetik* (1893) ; Victor Basch, *Essai critique sur l'éstétique de Kant* (1896), a thorough and penetrating work.

the series of the *Critiques*, is that he discovered in them a certain universality and necessity that refer to transcendental principles, and therefore require criticism.   Their insertion in the schema is the result of the following construction.   In the *Critique of Pure Reason* we have understanding, judgment, and reason.   This series was combined with the classification of the new psychology, — faculty of knowledge, faculty of feeling, and faculty of desire.   The third *Critique*, for which a place had been found in this way, assumed the precise form of its predecessors, and thus in the investigation regarding beauty and art the entire machinery of the *Critique of Pure Reason* is reproduced.   We have the Analytic and the Dialectic, the table of categories and the Deduction, and even the Doctrine of Method makes its appearance at the end, though only as an empty title, as indeed the others are too.   Think, for example, of the motley content that is united under the title of "Deduction."   First, there is a deduction that deduces nothing, dragged out for some pages, then the doctrine of natural and artificial beauty, the theory of art, the conditions of its production, and the classification of the fine arts.   Or notice how the schema of the categories is employed to divide up the exposition of the characteristics of the beautiful and the sublime.   Never has a ready-made schema, that was designed for a wholly different purpose, been more wrongly imposed upon a content.   It is an evident consequence that the subject matter suffers severely in clearness of arrangement as well as in essential quality.   I shall explain very briefly the fundamental concepts employed in Kant's treatment.

The predicate " beauty " is ascribed to anything when it is the object of disinterested pleasure, *i. e.* pleasure that does not proceed from either the lower or the higher faculty of desire, but arises out of pure contemplation.   Æsthetic pleasure is based on the fact that the object sets the faculty of knowledge in free play.   It is not, however, logical thought that is here aroused, or even reflection on the suitableness of the perception for a concept, but sense-perception and imagination. The purely formal adaptation of the object for the faculty of knowledge is recognized with a kind of thankful joy, and to the thing is ascribed the predicate "beautiful" in distinction from the predicates "pleasant," "useful," "perfect," or "good." The complete separation of pure beauty from judgments of this kind is the essential business of the critical æsthetic.

The sublime is another variety of æsthetic pleasure. Although it conflicts with the interests of sensibility, and to this extent gives rise to unpleasantness, it nevertheless at the same time arouses in man the consciousness that in virtue of his reason he is raised above the finite world of sense, and thus affords pleasure. Sublimity is therefore, just as little as beauty, a quality that belongs to the object. It exists only in the feeling that it arouses in the subject. Kant distinguishes two forms, the mathematically and the dynamically sublime. The former is aroused by magnitude in space and time, which, defeating the efforts of the imagination to comprehend it, calls out at the same time the rational idea of the infinite as completed totality. The latter has its source in what is powerful, overwhelming, fearful. As merely sensible beings, the idea of these things depresses us; but, as moral beings, they at the same time inspire us by bringing before our minds our independence of all natural powers.

The critical æsthetic is distinguished from dogmatic theories in this way. The latter suppose that beauty is an objective property of the thing that is confusedly represented through sense. Kant, holding fast here also to his idealistic standpoint, makes it depend solely upon the subject and its modes of functioning.

The connection of the æsthetical with the moral is something that Kant stoutly maintains. In the case of the sublime, this connection is directly given. The idea of a moral law, and of a will that remains steadfastly true to the law of its own nature in the face of all the attractions and menaces that come to us through sense, is in itself sublime. Thus poetry that represents the sublime in a perceptive form, as tragedy does, exerts directly a moral influence upon the mind. But even the sublime in nature has the same effect, since it leads beyond the finite to the infinite, and to the faculty of ideas. In like manner, the love of beauty " has as result as well as presupposition a certain liberality in the mental attitude, *i. e.* the independence of pleasantness from mere sense enjoyment. An interest in the beauty of nature for its own sake is always a mark of goodness." [1] " Beauty is the symbol of what is morally good ; " and thus sensibility for beauty is akin to interest in the good.[2] It is the *artes ingenuæ* and *liberales* that lead us from the desire for enjoyment to the desire for perception, and that free men from the slavery of the senses.[3]

The relation of æsthetics to the philosophy of nature is another point of importance. This is based on Kant's view of the nature of artistic talent and artistic production. The former is a kind of natural force, and to the latter belongs the form of a product of natural laws, not that of something made according to design. Artistic genius as an inborn productive faculty creates, as does nature, purposively, and yet without design, and without employing concepts. The artisan works according to rules that he has learned, and produces something in accordance with his notion or purpose. Artistic genius is " the native power of mind by means of which nature gives rules to art." " How it produces its results it cannot itself describe or define by scientific rules ; and, accordingly, it is not in its power to create such things at will or

---

[1] *Kr. d. Urt.,* § 29, Remark § 32.

[2] *Ibid.,* § 59.

[3] *Metaphysik* (Pölitz), p. 188.

according to a plan, or to give another person such directions as would enable him to produce similar results." [1] We see that Kant rebelled against the theory current in his time. He rejected the old classical theory of imitation, of which Gottsched was the representative. Works of art are creations of genius, not the products of technical skill that mechanically puts together given materials according to fixed rules.

It is this very fact that forms a basis for uniting in one whole the two parts of the *Critique of Judgment*, the critical æsthetics and the critical teleology of nature. Genius, as has been said, is a natural force, and this natural force acts in accordance with æsthetic ideas in man, the microcosm. In this fact, then, we have a suggestion that nature may also act in a similar way in the macrocosm. And, in like manner, natural beauty, which is so closely related to the beauty of art, suggests also that there is manifested in nature a force that works purposively according to ideas, though without intention. If we now add the fact that beauty is also a symbol of morality,[2] the circle is complete. Natural beauty and the beauty of art, the product of artistic genius, are both intimations of the nature of the original ground of all reality, which is expressed from another side in the moral nature of man. Kant might have united with his ethico-theology, these reflections as æsthetico-theology.

It is a permanent source of regret that such fruitful thoughts were prevented from developing themselves freely by the hindrances imposed by a useless schematism. If these had been swept away, it is certainly true that the notion of " pure " beauty and also of the " purely formal" æsthetic, with which Kant set out, could not have maintained themselves. But this would have been no loss except to the framework of the pure *a priori* philosophy. On the other hand, the essential nature of Kant's system, its

---

[1] *Kr. d. Urt.*, § 46.   [2] *Ibid.*, § 59.

connection with objective idealism, would have been made more evident. It is well known that it was the *Critique of Judgment* that afforded a starting point for the subsequent speculative philosophy. This was also regarded by Goethe and Schiller as the work in which Kant approached most nearly to their own way of thinking. That nature and art are one in their deepest nature, nature creating according to æsthetical laws, and the imagination of the artist working in accordance with natural laws, is precisely Goethe's view of the world.

CONCLUSION

The Effects of Kant's Philosophy and its Relation to the Present Time

The immediate effects of the *Critique* were like those of an earthquake. Everything that had hitherto stood fast tottered or fell in ruins. For the first moment the dwellers in the old structures stood helpless and gazed at the ruin brought about by him who had so ruthlessly undermined their foundations. Then followed a period of feverish activity. Some endeavored to repair the ruins, to close up the gaps in the walls and cover them with a temporary roof. Eberhard and Feder belonged to this class. Others, like Jacobi and Aenesidemus-Schulze, busied themselves in investigating the foundations of the provisional new structure that Kant had himself erected. Then came younger men, Reinhold and Fichte, who began to construct new systems in the Kantian style. And soon the impulse toward construction was stronger than ever before. One magic castle after another arose on the ruins of the old metaphysics. Ever bolder, richer, and more fantastic became the systems. Kant's new system, incomplete both internally and externally, seemed poor and bare at that time. At the time of Kant's death, the critical philosophy was regarded by the majority as a standpoint that had been superseded. A decade or two later Hegel's influence was universal, and the *Critique* noteworthy only as the starting-point of the entire revolution.

I cannot here enter into details regarding the remarkably great and sudden influence of the *Critique*, and the quick victory, equally astonishing, that the speculative philosophy gained over it. How fiercely the force of this philosophical revolution swept against existing opinions is shown more clearly perhaps than anywhere else in the autobiography, which we have already mentioned, of the Göttingen professor, Feder.[1] While still a reputable author and an esteemed teacher, he found himself forsaken by his students as one who had opposed Kant, or, what was the same to the enthusiastic youth, one who had not understood him. His colleagues treated him contemptuously, so that he voluntarily resigned his professorship, though still vigorous, and left Göttingen. Even the universities that had hitherto been most prominent, Göttingen and Halle, the new secular and political seats of learning of the eighteenth century, felt the force of the storm. Jena, the popular and democratic university of little Thuringia, took front rank. Here the exponents of the new doctrine were collected — Reinhold its first apostle, Schiller its practical interpreter. Here Fichte found favorable soil for his impassioned radicalism, and continued to exert an important influence until finally he was driven out by the conservatives in the controversy regarding atheism (1799). Schelling and Hegel, the Schwabian hot-heads, came also to Jena and lived there during their productive years. In the political world of that time some new phenomenon showed itself to old Europe every year. And, similarly, in the philosophical world a new system of thought made its appearance. To turn the world upside down at that time seemed to require nothing more than a strong and decided will.

The political constitutions that grew out of the French Revolution show a family resemblance, and so do also the philosophical systems that owe their origin to the critical philosophy. I mention here the marks that are characteristic. (1) Kant's transcendental idealism is the

[1] Page 234.

presupposition common to them all. The physical world is appearance. On the one hand, it is conditioned by the subject that constructs it by means of the synthetic forms of its perception and thought; on the other, it points to an absolute reality, the intelligible world. (2) They all are seeking to attain the same goal — to reach this intelligible world by means of thought. If the world is intelligible, as Kant says, it must lie open to thought. All that is necessary is the courage to pass on from epistemological to metaphysical idealism, which is after all really Kant's view. (3) Common to them all is the method, the *a priori* construction of reality in thought. If the world is an objective thought content, then one must be able, through the immanent development of thought determinations, to outline the entire basal plan of reality. (4) They all alike make the claim that in their philosophy knowledge has reached its final goal, that in it is to be found at once both absolute reality and the meaning of things. A philosophy of nature that explains the ideas in nature, or a philosophy of history that traces the *logos* in history, affords complete and absolute knowledge. The positive sciences do not give us knowledge of this kind. The natural sciences present us with formulæ according to which we calculate the appearance of phenomena; historical investigation yields particular facts, with here and there something of causal connection. And just for these reasons they do not afford real knowledge. Speculative philosophy alone is knowledge in the real sense, the comprehension of the reason that is in things.

In Hegel's system speculative philosophy attains its complete development. This philosophy aims at nothing less than the re-creation of the world in thought. In very truth the process of creation itself here first reaches its goal. Up to this time the world was a merely blind, though potentially rational, fact. In the speculative philosophy, an understanding of its own nature at last breaks over it. It comes to know itself as it really is, a unitary existing system of thoughts. In this self-comprehension of the idea in the form of a concept, the entire evolution of the world has reached its goal. God or the intelligible world thinks itself in the complete philosophy.

With this position the development of the movement has reached its end. The philosophy that started from Kant, going further and further in the path of the *a priori* speculation to which he had shown the way, finally came to deny its own starting point. The gulf between thought and being, subject and object, is completely transcended, thought and reality, logic and metaphysics, are identical. In the place of the critical philosophy, with its injunctions to modesty, with its recognition of the independence both of science and of faith, there has come the logical autocracy in the name of which Hegel demands that science and religion shall submit themselves to the dialectical formula. Never did philosophy assume such a lofty tone, and never were its royal honors so fully recognized and secured as about the year 1830.

But with a kind of rare irony, Hegel's philosophy is forced to see in its own fate a confirmation of its doctrine of the dialectical transformation into the opposite. The generation of absolute philosophy in the first third of the century, was followed in the second third by a generation of absolute non-philosophy. Excessive faith in thought was followed by an excess of mistrust and dislike. Science and religion, the two spiritual forces that felt themselves humbled by the absolute philosophy, again raised their heads and brought its sovereignty to an end.

Religion could not endure the sympathetic condescension with which absolute rationalism conceded that it possessed truth, but of course only in the lower form of the pictorial image, not in the form of the concept. Faith, for which it is just the concrete that is essential, and religious feeling, which attaches itself to the symbol, rebelled against the arrogance of the logical formula that declares its identity with the reality itself.   This feeling was strong in Frederick William IV.; and with his accession to the throne the attitude of the government towards the Hegelian philosophy changed to that of opposition.   This philosophy was stigmatized as an empty, hollow, logical abstraction that promoted discursive reasoning, but was destructive of respect for what is positive, and ruined the youth by means of sophistical arts.

In the same way, scientific investigation also rebelled against the yoke of a philosophy that assumed to be able to derive all essential truths by means of *a priori* deduction, and to determine their nature entirely by its own powers. A new generation of young men repaid to speculative philosophy the scorn that it formerly bestowed upon experience.   A real craving for facts, for mere blind facts, sprang up.   This was the reaction against the extravagance of logical reasoning which had so long prevailed.   The generation of dialectic was followed by that of exact knowledge.   This was characterized by an aversion to the ideas of the recent philosophical systems, indeed, by a dislike of universal ideas in general.   This tendency was equally dominant in the natural and the historical sciences.   There was to be no philosophy of nature and no philosophy of history, but in both fields exact investigation of the particular facts.

In the domain of philosophical literature, this period is marked by a tendency towards the philological investigation of the past systems of philosophy.   In the same way, instruction in the universities confined itself to the history of philosophy.   For the great public, a popularized natural science with a materialistic dress took the place of philosophy.   The strong opposition to the new-fashioned orthodoxy, to the old superstitions and the political reaction, and the open conflict with speculative philosophy gained for this at the time a widespread influence.   Men became accustomed to regard philosophy as secretly allied with reactionary theology, and as an enemy to free science.

In the last third of the century, philosophy has experienced a gradual restoration. Its relation to science has improved; the conviction has again grown up that there are questions beyond the domain of the special sciences that can and must be answered. From scientific work itself epistemological, metaphysical, psychological, and ethical problems have arisen, and demanded an answer from the natural scientists and the historians. And, at the present time, we everywhere see these investigators busied with their solution. The new biology brings the investigator to the ultimate problems of life and being, and its influence upon the historical sciences forces problems of methodology and of the philosophy of history upon the historian and the anthropologist. Even political science and jurisprudence are touched by this influence, and the pressing practical problems that are embraced under the term " the social question " drive one on to investigations in ethics and the philosophy of law. Even theology shows unmistakably an inclination to give up its dogmatic isolation, and to secure its foundations by means of philosophical and epistemological investigations.

Now with this movement the revival of the Kantian philosophy is connected. Since the sixties there has everywhere been manifest in philosophical literature an effort to return to Kant. A new Kant literature, something like a new Kant philology, has arisen. F. A. Lange's *History of Materialism* marks the turning point. Its point of view depends wholly upon Kant's philosophy, and it has contributed not a little to bringing philosophical study back to Kant. Schopenhauer's philosophy, which has come into great prominence since 1860, the year of his death, has exerted an influence in the same direction ; for it too constantly points back to Kant as the necessary starting point of all true philosophy.

Even scientific investigation seeks to connect itself with Kant's philosophy. Mathematics and physics find useful ideas regarding their own presuppositions foreshadowed in his works. Psychology is attracted by his phenomenalistic interpretation of the concepts of body and soul, — without any soul substance. And, on the other hand, theological dogmatics and the philosophy of religion find in Kant indispensable epistemological support for their notions. Every one, too, finds in him sincere respect for all honest work and all honest conviction. Not as an imperious mistress, but as a modest helper and an open-minded arbiter does the critical philosophy offer them its good services.

Thus to-day there is a widespread tendency to regard Kant's thoughts as the permanent basis of philosophy. I, too, am convinced that they can afford such a basis. In the system there appears to me not a little that is accidental and erroneous. But the great fundamental thoughts have a permanent value. In conclusion, I shall bring these together in summary.[1]

1. Kant's philosophy has rightly interpreted the nature of knowledge and of faith. It is therefore in harmony with the two great interests of the spiritual life, and is able to establish peace between them. It has thus solved the central problem of modern philosophy, which was set for it in the seventeenth century by the great conflict between religion and science, more particularly between religion and the modern mechanical sciences of nature.

Kant lived in peace with science, of which he himself had an intimate knowledge. He encouraged investigations which have the purpose of subjecting, as far as possible, the phenomenal world to laws. He was always ready to recognize any certain result. It is right for the understanding to seek to explain all natural phenomena, even the processes

---

[1] In my article, "Was uns Kant sein kann" (*Vierteljahresschr. für wiss. Philos.*, 1881), the reader will find some of these points further elaborated.

of life, according to the principles of mechanical connection. He is of the opinion that there is always a remainder that is not and cannot be exhausted in this way. But he is ready to recognize every result as a desirable step in advance. He does not, as Schopenhauer perhaps does, make exceptions in favor of a vital force which his metaphysics finds necessary. He certainly would have been pleased to welcome Darwin's discoveries. In the same way, the understanding has complete freedom critically to investigate all facts of a psychical and historical nature, and to explain them causally on the assumption of strict determinism. To set limits to the investigation of historical facts by means of a statutory ecclesiastical creed, seemed to him as presumptuous as foolish. Truth is the only goal, and scientific investigation is the only means of attaining this in questions of historical fact. Only in the evaluation of facts, and in the interpretation of their meaning which is dependent upon this, does faith play a prominent part.

On the other hand, Kant's view is in harmony with religious faith, so far as the latter seeks to be nothing more than is possible for it to be. And this is a moral certainty that the highest good is possible in the real world; or, in religious phrase, nothing but practical faith in God and in God's kingdom. For such a faith science leaves a place, and to it philosophy is brought by its own presuppositions. Our scientific knowledge is limited in a double sense — both empirically and transcendentally. From an empirical point of view, the known world is an island in the ocean of the unknown. We know a little about the earth, but of that which lies beyond the earth we see only rough outlines. And even on the earth, the unknown lies close to the surface — the explanation of natural forces, the beginning of organism and life. Indeed, one may say that scientific investigation has made the riddle of the world more wonderful, rather than solved it. The deeper cosmology, biology, and physics penetrate, the greater the secrets which they still see beyond them. Everywhere we stand before the unknown. But even if science included and explained everything in heaven and earth, should we then have an absolute knowledge of reality? No, Kant answers. We should then reach the transcendental and absolutely impassable limits of our scientific knowledge. The world as we know it is only an accidental aspect of reality itself, a projection of things upon our sensibility. Only an understanding that creates things, an *intellectus archetypus*, knows them as that which they are in themselves; an understanding to which they are given through sensibility does not get beyond a knowledge of their external side.

When one makes this distinction between the sensible and the intelligible world, one has at the same time secured a place for faith. If the physical world that appears to the senses were reality itself, our view of the world would be defined by physics. But since this world is mere phenomena, there is room for a metaphysical explanation of phenomena through an intelligible world, nature being regarded as an intimation of an ideal world. This is Plato's view: the world of ideas is the real world. This theory gives expression to a belief that is essentially identical with what the human spirit everywhere seeks. The essence of all religion is the explanation of the world from the ideas of the good and the perfect, which express in them a holy and righteous will.

Kant insists that these thoughts do not lie within the field of scientific knowledge in the strict sense. They are matters of thought, and above all of faith. For this very reason they do not belong to the critique of the understanding, since they are not matters of scientific demonstration. Faith has its origin in practical reason, in the volitional side of our nature; and therefore as such it is secure against any attacks of the understanding.

In this way, Kant has provided a basis for the harmony of religion and science. The first condition of this harmony he finds in an absolute demarcation of boundaries. It is true that, according to Kant, incursions have not been wanting on either side. In the name of religion, science has been called upon to retrace its steps, and in the name of science, faith has been declared abolished, — and this takes place even to-day. Nevertheless, for him who has eyes to see, the limits are permanently marked out, as an injunction and a warning to attend to one's own business and respect that of other people. Religion is not a science, and for that very reason it is not possible to establish its truths by means of demonstration. But just because it is not an error, it is not possible to disprove it by demonstration. Dogmas one may destroy by means of criticism, but religion is in its very nature indestructible. It has its permanent roots in the human spirit, and springs up ever anew from that soil.

2. Kant assigned to will the position in the world that properly belongs to it. He put an end to the one-sided intellectualism of the eighteenth century. The over-emphasis of the importance of intellectual culture was common to the whole modern period from the time of the Renaissance. The worth of man was supposed to depend upon his culture; moral development rests upon knowledge. Kant adopted Rousseau's objection to this assumption, and carried it further. The new point of view may be described by means of two propositions: first, the worth of a man does not depend upon his intellect, but solely upon his will; and, second, one's ultimate metaphysics does not rest upon the understanding, but primarily upon the will.

These two propositions also may be accepted as definitive truths. The first yields a standard for properly estimating the value of human personality. This standard, it is true, social and aristocratic blindness seeks constantly to replace. The second proposition furnishes the basis of correct judgment regarding the value and certainty of what we regard as true. The final and highest truths — the truths by which, and for which, a man lives and dies — do not rest upon scientific knowledge, but have their origin in the heart, in the essential principle of will. The sciences, especially mathematics and physics, have technical truths; they subject nature to concepts and rules of art. But no man is satisfied with merely technical truths. He makes assumptions and cherishes convictions of an entirely different nature. He believes in his fellow-men, in himself, and his vocation, in the future and in progress; he believes in the final victory of truth and right and goodness upon the earth. All these are things that cannot be demonstrated; they possess moral, not logical, certainty; without them I could not accomplish anything or live. Of the same nature is the certainty that belongs to religious truth. Religion, conceived generally, consists in the confidence that that purpose with which I identify myself through my deepest will and character will be realized; that God is for me and my cause. This confidence is not the result of proofs, but precedes all processes of proof. Thus the old proposition, *fides præcedit intellectum*, comes again into honor. In the last resort, men always live by faith, not by knowledge. Even the scientific fanatics, who would admit no faith except that in logically demonstrated truths, live themselves by an immediate faith, — faith in the possibility and absolute value of pure knowledge. If they claim to define the highest good and its possibility in this way by means of their beliefs, it would be reasonable to grant others the same right, and not to complain if these know another highest good, more complete than scientific knowledge and methodological discretion, and make other assumptions regarding reality in accordance therewith.[1]

---

[1] This point is excellently worked out by W. James in *The Will to Believe* (1897), German translation by Th. Lorenz (Fromanns Verlag, Stuttgart, 1899). *Cf.* my *Einleitung in die Philosophie*, 5th edition, pp. 323 ff. [English translation by F. Thilly, pp. 313 ff.].

3. Kant gives a correct account of the nature of mind, and assigns to it its proper position in the world. He brought into prominence the creative power of mind: the nature of the mind is freedom, spontaneous activity. It is not a passive receptacle or a dead product, as French sensationalism and materialism taught. In all fields, Kant emphasized the activity and spontaneity of mind. In the sphere of knowledge, he teaches that knowledge is not a collection of impressions upon a sheet of white paper, but a spontaneous activity. Its stages are: The apprehension of sensations, that are themselves the product of the mind, in a unitary simultaneity and succession in space and time; apperception, by means of the activities of the understanding, whose forms are the categories; and, finally, the unifying of the knowledge of the understanding, by means of the speculative ideas, in a unitary world system that is held together by a single principle of reason. In the sphere of the will, likewise, we find that the will is not an aggregate of reflex responses to external stimuli, but a free, self-positing activity. By means of the practical reason, or the rational will, man forms his own character according to innate ideas that he possesses of the good and the perfect. He raises himself above mere nature, and creates freely his inner moral life in independence of foreign or external authority. With the perception of the activity of mind corresponds the concept of its nature. It is pure activity, a self-positing subject, not a given object. The actualistic theory of the soul is given a new basis by Kant. The soul is not a dead substrate, not an unchanging substance, like an atom, but pure energy, spontaneous energy of knowing and willing. These thoughts, too, may be described as permanent acquisitions of philosophy. This actualistic theory of the soul, after being temporarily obscured, has quite recently again become prominent.

These were the great fundamental thoughts of the Kantian

philosophy in which the philosophy of the present day is again beginning to centre.

In conclusion, I return once more to that side of Kant's philosophy that is most foreign to our thought, — the fixed formalistic rationalism of the system. This dominates the form of his epistemology, and through the epistemology his entire mode of thought and exposition.

The aim of the critical epistemology is to demonstrate the possibility of absolute, eternal truths. It affirms, in opposition to Hume's doctrine of relativity, that there are laws of nature and of morality of absolute universality and necessity. I believe that the scientific thought of the present time is more nearly in agreement with Hume than with Kant on this point. The nineteenth century has turned away from the rationalistic mode of thought of the seventeenth and eighteenth centuries, which took mathematics as its model, and has adopted the historico-genetic, and therefore relative, point of view. The Hegelian philosophy set the example in this procedure; the developmental theory, which has become dominant not less in biology and cosmology than in the historical sciences, completed the revolution. I shall attempt to show this by drawing out the discussion a little further.

In modern times three modes of thought have been successively dominant: (1) the theologico-dogmatic; (2) the rationalistico-dogmatic; (3) the genetic and relativist. One may accordingly distinguish the three periods as the *sæculum theologicum, sæculum philosophicum,* and *sæculum historicum.*

1. The dogmatic theological mode of thought was continued in the modern period from the middle ages, and on the whole remained uninterrupted until about the end of the seventeenth century. It was characterized by a belief in the existence of absolute truths that rest upon revelation, and are formulated in the propositions of the creed. The function of science (of theology, the chief science of the

time) was to demonstrate the truth of these propositions, which are already recognized as true. Philosophy and philology, as subsidiary sciences, stand in the service of theology. In addition to theology, there exist ethics and the theory of law. These, too, form systems of absolute truths that in the last resort stand upon the same basis; the ten commandments is their absolute and immovable foundation.

2. Dogmatic rationalism began in the seventeenth century to make headway against theology; and in the eighteenth century, the *sœculum philosophicum*, it became the dominant mode of thought. Its characteristic mark is belief in absolute truths of reason: all essential truths can be deduced from reason as a system of necessary demonstrable propositions. This is true above all of metaphysical truths, for they have their origin in primary and absolutely certain principles of reason. These form the standard by which theological dogmas are to be tried, and according to which they are to be justified. Thus arises rational religion, which is also known as natural religion. Alongside it we have also "natural law," a system of absolute truths developed from reason, which constitute the propositions of a science of "natural rights," and are principles for conduct and for the regulation of social and political institutions.

The point of departure for this way of thinking was mathematics and mathematical physics. Mathematics contains a system of absolutely valid and absolutely certain truths that have been deduced from rational principles. It affords the standard according to which all the sciences are to be judged with regard to form. The mathematical demonstrative method is the method of science. This was the model that Spinoza followed, even in external details, in his attempt to deduce all real science, or a complete philosophy, from rational principles. But it is clear that particular facts cannot be deduced in this way, and just for this reason there is no real science of particular facts.

It is obvious that we have here a way of thinking that is not less dogmatic than theology, only that the dogmas are not imposed by an external authority, but are the products of the human reason. Their binding force for philosophy is, however, equally absolute. The way for this subjective rationalistic dogmatism was prepared by the Reformation. Protestant, like Catholic theology, claimed to be absolute revealed truth. But since it recognized no final earthly authority, and the Scriptures were not in the form of a system of dogmas, it necessarily became subjective, even to the point of absolute caprice, and therefore incapable of compelling the assent of reason, as the old dogma had the power to do.

3. The historical and genetic fashion of thought has given up absolute truths. Outside of logic and mathematics there are only relative, not eternal truths. Reality is in constant flux, and knowledge follows reality. To the eternal and unchangeable character of God there corresponds theological dogmatism; to the fixed substances with which mathematical physics calculates, rational dogmatism is parallel; while the genetic and relativistic mode of thinking corresponds to a world in process of development.

The first presuppositions of this latter mode of thought were contained in the English empiricism that has influenced German thought since the middle of the eighteenth century. This philosophy recognized no absolutely valid truths. Not in science; for the propositions of science rest upon experience, and are valid until they are tested by further experience. Not in moral philosophy; for the propositions of moral philosophy are formulæ that describe the condition of the development of human nature under given circumstances.

Under the influence of these thoughts as they had been finally formulated by Hume, there came about in Germany that great revolution in the humanistic sciences of which

Herder was the leader. In the *sæculum historicum* this revolution made itself felt in every field of historical investigation. Language, religion, and morals and right are not absolutely fixed essences that are reduced to unchanging formulæ by grammar, dogmatics, ethics, and natural right, as the unhistorical dogmatic view of the eighteenth century supposed. They exist only as vital functions of the life of the people, growing up and undergoing constant transformation along with this life. Thus the science of language teaches us to regard language and its forms as vital functions that change with the life of the people, and all its categories as historical and evanescent. In the same way, the historical view of law considers law and the state as forms of life that have grown up spontaneously, not as means purposively designed for the attainment of ends. And, like language and law, ethics and religion have lost their fixed absolute character under the influence of historical and anthropological considerations.

This mode of thought first received its philosophical expression in Hegel's system. The logical evolution of the dialectic made all truths relative. In this respect Hegel's exposition and criticism of the history of philosophy is perhaps most characteristic: every system is in its place the truth, of course, not an absolute, but only a relative truth.

The second half of the nineteenth century has carried over the evolutionary point of view to the investigation of nature, or it has transformed the logical evolutionism of the dialectic into that of natural science. Nature, in all its aspects, has been brought under the historical point of view. The history of man's life has been assigned a place in a more comprehensive historical development of organic life in general. The latter, in turn, forms but one section of the history of the earth's development. The history of the planets is again united with the development of suns, and this with the process of cosmic evolution itself that transcends our knowledge, and even surpasses the powers of our imagination. And in this movement it is seen that, like all forms of life and existence, even the forms of thought themselves are not absolute but only "historical categories."

In trying to describe Kant's relation to this movement, we may say that although his thought contained strong tendencies toward the historical and genetic view of things, yet he never succeeded in freeing himself from the rationalistic and dogmatic point of view. In the middle period of his life, perhaps influenced in part by his developmental cosmology, he seemed to be about to go over to the empirico-genetic point of view. The writings of the sixties show that in epistemology and in moral philosophy he was following the path of the English philosophers. At that time he gave to Herder the influence that determined the direction of the latter's thought. Then, however (in the *Dissertation* of 1770), he suddenly reverted to the rationalistic and dogmatic point of view that he had never entirely renounced, finding in it the only security for philosophy and science. Thus the critical philosophy stands decidedly on the side of the eternal truths. It undertakes to set up, in opposition to relativistic empiricism, a system of eternal truths. These it finds in the theoretical sphere in the pure principles of the understanding, and the moral law affords for the practical sphere a similar system of necessary truths.

On the other side, though belonging so decidedly to the *sæculum philosophicum*, it nevertheless extends a hand to the coming *sæculum historicum*. It is not an accident that the speculative evolutionism of Hegel developed from the critical philosophy. By means of the dynamic theory of matter, Kant destroyed the fixed atom, and by his actualistic theory of the soul he put an end to the doctrine of the unchanging soul substance. With this change reality became, as it were, fluid, and speculative philosophy urged the fluid mass into the movement of the logical and historical process of development.   Thus history has done justice to the youthful Kant, whose work was continued in Herder, as opposed to the dogmatic Kant of the system.   Although his conflict with Kant was most unfortunate, and the spread of the new dogmatism embittered the end of his life, Herder would not, from the standpoint of the present time, look back on the century that has just elapsed with dissatisfaction.   He would see that even he had not lived in vain.

In this respect Kant represents to us the great turning point of thought, and he mediates in many important respects between the two last great periods of modern history.

IMPORTANT DATES IN KANT'S LIFE, AND A CHRONO-
LOGICAL LIST OF HIS WRITINGS, TOGETHER WITH
A LIST OF THE ENGLISH TRANSLATIONS.

1724   Immanuel Kant, born April 22.

        1728   Lambert born.

        1729   Lessing born.

        1729   Mendelssohn born.

        1730   Hamann born.

1732   Kant enters the Fridericianum.

        1735   His Brother, Joh. Heinrich, born.

        1737   His Mother died.

1740   Kant matriculates at the University of Königsberg.

        1740   Accession of Frederick II.

        1740   Feder born.

        1742   Garve born.

        1744   Herder born.

1746   Kant's first Writing : *Gedanken von der wahren Schätzung der lebendigen Kräfte* ("Thoughts on the True Evaluation of Dynamic Forces ").

        1746   Kant's Father died.

        1749   Goethe born.

        1751   M. Knutzen died.

        1754   Chr. Wolff died.

1754   *Untersuchung der Frage : ob die Erde in ihrer Umdrehung um die Axe einige Veränderungen erlitten habe?* ("Examination of the Question whether the Earth has undergone an Alteration of its Axial Rotation.") [Trans. by W. Hastie in *Kant's Cosmogony*, Glasgow, 1900.]
Die Frage : ob die Erde veralte? physicalisch erwogen ("The Question : Whether the Earth grows old? physically considered "). Both this and the above were published in the *Königsberger Nachrichten*.

1755   *Allegemeine Naturgeschichte und Theorie des Himmels* ("Universal Natural History and Theory of the Heavens"). [Trans. by W. Hastie in *Kant's Cosmogony*.]

1755   Kant qualifies with the Treatise *De Igne*, and becomes habilitated
with the Essay *Principiorum primorum cognitionis metaphysicæ
nova dilucidatio*.

  1756–1763   The Seven Years' War.   The Russians in
  Königsberg.

1756   *Disputation über die Abhandlung "Monadologia Physica"* (" Disputation on the Treatise *Monadologia Physica* ").

  Three short Essays in the *Königsberger Nachrichten* on Earth-
quakes (on the occasion of the Lisbon Earthquake of 1775).
[One of these, "Upon the Causes of Earthquakes from which
the Western Parts of Europe suffered toward the End of the
Preceding Year," has been translated by A. F. M. Willich, in
Kant's Essays and Treatises, 2 Vols., London, 1798.]

  Neue Anmerkungen zur Erläuterung der Theorie der Winde
(" New Remarks in Explanation of the Theory of the Winds ").

1757   Entwurf und Ankündigung eines *Collegii* der physischen Geographie, nebst dem Anhange einer kurzen Betrachtung *über die
Frage : ob die Westwinde in unseren Gegenden darum feucht seien,
weil sie über ein grosses Meer streichen ?* (" Outline and Announcement of a Course of Lectures on Physical Geography, together
with a Brief Consideration of the Question : Whether the Mois-
ture of the West-Wind in this Region is due to its Passage over
a great Sea ").

1758   *Neuer Lehrbegriff der Bewegung und Ruhe* (" New Doctrine of
Motion and Rest ").

1759   *Versuch einiger Betrachtungen über den Optimismus* (" Some
Observations on Optimism ").

  1759   Schiller born.
  1762   Fichte born.
  1762   Rousseau's *Émile* and *Contrat social* appeared.

1762   *Die falsche Spitzfindigkeit der vier syllogistischen Figuren erwiesen*
(" The False Subtlety of the Four Syllogistic Figures "). [Trans. :
By A. F. M. Willich in *Kant's Essays and Treatises*, 2 Vols.,
London, 1798 ; by T. K. Abbott in *Kant's Introduction to Logic,
and His Essay on the Mistaken Subtilty of the Four Figures*,
London, 1885.]

1763   *Der einzig mögliche Beweisgrund zu einer Demonstration vom
Dasein Gottes* (" The only Possible Ground for a Demonstration
of the Existence of God "). [Trans. : By Willich in *Kant's
Essays and Treatises*, 1798 ; by J. Richardson (partial trans.
only) in *The Metaphysical Works of Kant*, London, 1836.]

1763 *Untersuchungen über die Deutlichkeit der Grundsätze der natürlichen Theologie und Moral.* (Prize Essay of the Berlin Academy, published in 1764.) ("Inquiry into the Clearness of the Principles of Natural Theology and Morals.") [Trans. by Willich, *Op. cit.*]

Versuch den Begriff der negativen Grössen in die Weltweisheit einzüfühven ("An Attempt to Introduce into Philosophy the Conception of Negative Magnitudes").

    1763 F. A. Schultz died.

1764 *Versuch über die Krankheiten des Kopfes.* Published in the Königsberger Zeitungen. ("Essay on the Diseases of the Head.")

Beobachtungen über das Gefühl des Schönen und Erhabenen ("Observations on the Feeling of the Beautiful and the Sublime"). [Trans. by Willich, *Op. cit.*]

1765 *Nachricht von der Einrichtung seiner Vorlesungen* ("Announcement of Lectures").

1766 *Träume eines Geistersehers, erläutert durch Träume der Metaphysik* ("The Dreams of a Ghost-Seer Explained through the Dreams of Metaphysics"). [Trans. by E. F. Goerwitz, London and New York, 1900.]

    1766 Gottsched died.

1768 *Von dem ersten Grunde des Unterschieds der Gegenden im Raum.* Published in the *Königsberger Nachrichten.* ("On the Primary Ground of Distinguishing Spatial Positions.")

1770 Kant appointed Ordinary Professor of Logic and Metaphysics.

Disputatio de mundi sensibilis atque intelligibilis forma et principiis ("Dissertation Concerning the Form and Principles of the Sensible and Intelligible Worlds"). [Trans. by W. J. Eckoff in *Kant's Inaugural-Dissertation of 1770,* New York, 1894.]

    1770 Holbach's *Système de la nature.*

1775 *Von den verschiedenen Racen des Menschen* ("On the Various Races of Mankind"). Announcement of Lectures on Physical Geography.

1776 *Ueber das Dessauer Philanthropin.* Published in the Königsberger Zeitungen. ("On the Dessau Experiment in Philanthropy.")

    1776 The North American Declaration of Independence.

    1776 Hume died.

    1778 Voltaire died.

    1778 Rousseau died.

    1780 The Accession of Joseph II.

    1781 Lessing died.

1781   *Die Kritik der reinen Vernunft* ("The Critique of Pure Reason").
       [Trans. : By J. Haywood, London, 1838 and 1848; by M. D.
       Meiklejohn, London, 1855; by Max Müller, London, 1881,
       revised edition, London and New York, 1896 ; by J. P. Mahaffy
       (not literally) in *Kant's Critical Philosophy for English Readers,*
       new edition, London, 1889.   Partial trans. : By J. H. Stirling in
       Text-Book to Kant, Edinburgh, 1881; by J. Watson in *The
       Philosophy of Kant in Extracts,* New York, 1892, new edition,
       Glasgow, 1895.]

1783   *Prolegomena zu einer jeden künftigen Metaphysik, die als Wissen-
       schaft wird auftreten können* ("Prolegomena to Every Future
       Metaphysic that can Appear as Science"). [Trans. : By J.
       Richardson in *The Metaphysical Works of Kant,* first edition,
       London, 1818, last edition, London, 1836; by J. P. Mahaffy in
       Kant's Critical Philosophy for English Readers, London, 1872,
       revised edition by Mahaffy and J. H. Bernard, London, 1889;
       by E. B. Bax in *Kant's Prolegomena and Metaphysical Founda-
       tions of Natural Science,* London, 1883; by T. Wirgman, free
       reproduction in the article " Metaphysic" in the "Encyclopædia
       Londinensis ; " also by Willich in the " Enc. Metrop."]

1784   *Idee zu einer allgemeinen Geschichte in weltbürgerlicher Absicht*
       ("Idea of a Universal History from a Cosmopolitan Stand-
       point"). [Trans.: By Willich, *Op. cit. ;* by De Quincey, Vol.
       XIII. of his Collective Works ;[1] by W. Hastie in *Kant's Prin-
       ciples of Politics,* Edinburgh, 1891.]
       Beautwortung der Frage : Was ist Aufklärung ? Both this and the
       above appeared in the *Berliner Monatsschrift.* (" Answer to the
       Question : What is Illumination ?") [Trans. by Willich, *Op. cit.*]

1785   *Rezensionen von Herders Ideen zur Philosophie der Geschichte.*
       Published in the *Jenaische Litteratur-Zeitung.* (" Review of
       Herder's Ideas toward a Philosophy of History.")
       Ueber die Vulkane im Mond ("On Volcanoes in the Moon").
       [Trans. by Willich, *Op. cit.*]
       Von der Unrechtmässigkeit des Büchernachdrucks ("Upon the
       Injustice of Publishers' Piracies"). [Trans. by Willich, *Op. cit.*)
       Bestimmung des Begriffs einer Menschenrace (" Determination of
       the Concept of a Race of Men "). The last three essays ap-
       peared in the *Berliner Monatsschrift.*
       Grundlegung zur Metaphysik der Sitten (" Fundamental Princi-

---

[1] Among De Quincey's Miscellaneous Essays also are found some translated
extracts from several of Kant's minor writings.

ples of the Metaphysic of Morals "). [Trans.: By Willich, *Op. cit.*; by J. W. Semple in *Kant's Metaphysic of Ethics*, Edinburgh, 1836, last edition by Calderwood, 4th edition 1886; by T. K. Abbott in *Kant's Critique of Practical Reason*, etc., 4th edition, London, 1889 (also separately, 1895). Partial trans. by J. Watson, *Op. cit.*]

1786 *Mutmasslicher Anfang der Menschengeschichte.* Published in the *Berliner Monatsschrift* (" The Presumptive Beginning of Human History "). [Trans.: By Willich, *Op. cit.*; by J. E. Cabot in Hedge's *Prose Writers of Germany*, Boston, 1856.]

Was heisst sich im Denken orientieren ? Published in the *Berliner Monatsschrift.* (" What does it Signify to Orient oneself in Thought ?") [Trans. by Willich, *Op. cit.*]

Metaphysische Anfangsgründe der Naturwissenschaften ("Metaphysical Elements of Natural Science "). [Trans. by E. B. Bax in *Kant's Prolegomena and Metaphysical Foundations of Natural Science*, London, 1883.]

    1786 Frederick the Great died, Frederick William II. succeeded.

    1788 Wöllner's Religious Edict.

1788 *Ueber den Gebrauch teleologischer Prinzipien in der Philosophie.* Appeared in the *Deutsche Merkur.* (" On the Use of Teleological Principles in Philosophy.)

Kritik der praktischen Vernunft (" The Critique of Practical Reason "). [Trans.: (Partial) by J. W. Semple in *Kant's Metaphysic of Ethics*, Edinburgh, 1836, later editions by Calderwood; by J. Watson, *Op. cit.* . . . Complete trans. by T. K. Abbott, 4th edition, London, 1889.]

    1789 The French Revolution.

1790 *Kritik der Urtheilskraft* (" The Critique of Judgment "). [Trans. by J. H. Bernard, London, 1892. Partial trans. : a short extract in Hedge's and Cabot's *Prose Writers of Germany*, pp. 63–71, Boston, 1856 ; more copious extracts by J. Watson, *Op. cit.*]

Ueber Philosophie überhaupt. First Introduction to the *Critique of Judgment.* (" On Philosophy in General.")

Ueber eine Entdeckung, nach der alle neue Kritik der reinen Vernunft durch eine ältere entbehrlich gemacht werden soll. Directed against Eberhard. (" On a Discovery by means of which all New Critiques are to be Replaced by an Older One.")

Ueber Schwärmerei und die Mittel dagegen (" On Sentimentality and its Remedy ").

1791 *Ueber das Misslingen aller philosophischen Versuche in der Theodicee.* Published in the *Berliner Monatsschrift.* ("On the Failure of all Philosophical Attempts at a Theodicy.") [Trans. by
Willich, *Op. cit.*]

1792 *Vom radikalen Bösen in der Menschennatur.* Published in the
Berliner Monatsschrift. (" On the Radical Evil in Human
Nature.") [Trans.: By Willich, *Op. cit. ;* by J. W. Semple in
Kant's Theory of Religion, London, 1838, 2d edition, 1848; by
T. K. Abbott (Part I. only), *Op. cit.*]
Prohibition of the continuation of these articles by the Berlin
Censorship.

1793 *Religion innerhalb der Grenzen der blossen Vernunft* (" Religion
within the Bounds of Pure Reason "). [Trans.: By Willich, *Op.
cit. ;* by Semple, *Op. cit. ;* by Abbott (Part I.), *Op. cit.*]
*Ueber den Gemeinspruch : Das mag in der Theorie richtig sein,
taugt aber nicht für die Praxis.* Published in the *Berliner
Monatsschrift.* (" On the Common Saying : That may be correct in Theory, but does not hold in Practice.") [Trans. : By
Willich, *Op. cit. :* Parts II. and III. by W. Hastie in *Kant's
Principles of Politics*, Edinburgh, 1891.]

1794 *Etwas über den Einfluss des Mondes auf die Witterung.* (*Berliner Monatsschrift.*) (" Remarks on the Influence of the Moon
on the Weather.") [Trans. by Willich, *Op. cit.*]
Das Ende aller Dinge. (*Berliner Monatsschrift.*) (" On the
End of All Things.") [Trans. by Willich, *Op. cit.*]
1794 Cabinet Order of the King and Kant's promise not to
write any more on Religion.
    1795 The Peace of Basle.

1795 *Zum ewigen Frieden* (" On Everlasting Peace "). [Trans. : By
Willich, *Op. cit. ;* by W. Hastie in *Kant's Principles of Politics ;*
by B. F. Trueblood, Boston, The American Peace Society, 1897.
Some Extracts by J. E. Cabot, *Op. cit.*, pp. 71–74.]

1796 Kant discontinues his lectures.
*Von einem neuerdings erhobenen, vornehmen Ton in der Philoso-
phie.* (*Berliner Monatsschrift.*) (" Upon a certain Genteel
Tone which has recently appeared in Philosophy.") [Trans. by
Willich, *Op. cit.*]
*Verkündigung des nahen Abschlusses eines Traktats zum ewigen
Frieden in der Philosophie.* (*Berliner Monatsschrift.*) (" An-
nouncement of the near Conclusion of a Tractate on Everlasting
Peace in Philosophy.")

1797 *Metaphysische Anfangsgründe der Rechtslehre* (" Metaphysical Principles of Law "). [Trans. by W. Hastie, in *Kant's Philosophy of Law*, Edinburgh, 1887.]

Metaphysische Anfangsgründe der Tugendlehre (" Metaphysical Principles of the Doctrine of Virtue "). [Trans. by Semple in *Kant's Metaphysic of Ethics*. The Preface and Introduction are translated also by Abbott, *Op. cit.*]

[The above two works form respectively Part I. and II. of *Die Metaphysik der Sitten* (" The Metaphysic of Morals "). The General Introduction to the Entire Work is translated by Abbott and by Semple, *Op. cit.*]

Ueber ein vermeintes Recht aus Menschenliebe zu lügen (" On an Alleged Right to Lie from Altruistic Motives "). [Trans. : By A. E. Kroeger in *Am. Jour. of Speculative Phil.*, Vol. VII., St. Louis, 1873 ; by Abbott, *Op. cit.*]

1797 Frederick William II. died, Frederick William III. succeeds. Wöllner dismissed.

1798 *Ueber die Buchmacherei. Zwei Briefe an Herrn Fr. Nicolai* (" On Bookmaking. Two letters to Herr F. Nicolai ").

Der Streit des Fakultäten (" The Controversy of Faculties ").

Anthropologie in pragmatischer Hinsicht (" Anthropology from a Pragmatical Point of View "). [Trans. of Book I. by A. E. Kroeger in the *Am. Jour. of Speculative Phil.*, Vols. 9 f., St. Louis, 1875 f.]

1800 *Logik* (" Logic "). Edited by Jäsche. [Trans. : By J. Richardson in *Kant's Metaphysical Works*, London, 1836 and 1848 ; the Introduction by Abbott in *Kant's Introduction to Logic*, etc.]

1802 *Physische Geographie* (" Physical Geography "). Edited by Rink.

1803 *Pädagogik* (" Pedagogy "). Edited by Rink. [Trans. by Annette Churton in *Kant on Education*, Boston, 1900.]

1804 *Ueber die Preisfrage der Berliner Akademie : Welches sind die wirklichen Fortschritte, die die Metaphysik seit Leibniz's und Wolf's Zeiten in Deutschland gemacht hat ?* (" On the Prize Question of the Berlin Academy: What Real Progress has Metaphysics Made in Germany since the Days of Leibniz and Wolff? ") Edited by Rink.

1804 Kant died on the 12th of February.

SELECTED READING

ADAMSON, Robert, . . . *On the Philosophy of Kant,* Edinburgh, D. Douglas, 1879

ARDLEY, Gavin W., *Aquinas and Kant: The Foundations of the Modern Sciences,* N. Y., Longmans, 1950

BECK, Lewis W., *Commentary on Kant's Critique of Practical Reason,* Chicago, Univ. of Chicago Press, 1960

BOWNE, Borden P., *Kant and Spencer; A Critical Exposition,* Boston, Houghton, 1912

CAIRD, Edward, *The Critical Philosophy of Immanuel Kant,* 2nd ed., Glasgow, J. Maciehouse, 1909

CASSIRER, Ernst, *Rousseau, Kant, Goethe: Two Essays . . .* Hamden, Conn., Archon Books, 1961

CASSIRER, Heinrich W., *Kant's First Critique; an Appraisal of the Permanent Significance of Kant's Critique of Pure Reason,* London, Allen & Unwin, N. Y., Macmillan, 1954

CHAMBERLAIN, Houston S., *Immanuel Kant; A Study and a Comparison with Goethe, Leonardo da Vinci, Bruno, Plato, and Descartes,* London, John Lane, N. Y., John Lane, 1914

CLARK, Norman, *An Introduction to Kant's Philosophy,* London, Methuen, 1925

ENGLAND, Frederick Ernest, *Kant's Conception of God; A Critical Exposition of Its Metaphysical Development, . . .* London, Allen & Unwin, 1929

EWING, Alfred Cyril, *Kant's Treatment of Causality,* London, Paul, Trench, Trubner & Co., 1924

GARNETT, Christopher Browne, *The Kantian Philosophy of Space,* N. Y., Columbia Univ. Press, 1939

GAULTIER, Jules de, *From Kant to Nietzsche* (trans. by Gerald M. Spring), N. Y., Philosophical Library, 1961

GREENE, Theodore Meyer, *Moral, Aesthetic, and Religious Insight,* New Brunswick, N. J., Rutgers Univ. Press, 1957

HEIDEGGER, Martin, *Kant and the Problem of Metaphysics* (trans. by James S. Churchill), Bloomington, Ind., Indiana Univ. Press, 1962

HENDEL, Charles Wm., *The Philosophy of Kant and Our Modern World,* . . . N. Y., Liberal Arts Press, 1957

JONES, William Thomas, *Morality and Freedom in the Philosophy of Immanuel Kant,* London, Oxford Univ. Press, 1940

JOSEPH, Horace W. B., *A Comparison of Kant's Idealism With That of Berkeley,* London, H. Milford, 1929

KLINKE, Willibald, *Kant for Everyone* (tr. from German by Michael Ballock), London, Routledge & K. Paul, 1951

KNOX, Israel, *The Aesthetic Theories of Kant, Hegel and Schopenhauer,* N. Y., Columbia Univ. Press, 1936

KÖRNER, Stephen, *Kant,* Hammondsworth, Middlesex, Penguin Books, 1960

KRONER, Richard, *Kant's Weltanschauung,* Chicago, Univ. of Chicago Press, 1956

LINDSAY, Alexander Dunlop, *Kant,* London, E. Benn, 1934

MAIER, Josef, *On Hegel's Critique of Kant,* N. Y., Columbia Univ. Press, 1939

MARTIN, Gottfried, *Kant's Metaphysics and Theory of Science,* New York, Barnes & Noble, 1955

MEIKLEJOHN, Alexander, *Inclinations and Obligations,* Berkeley, Calif., Univ. of Calif. Press, 1948, pp. 203-223

MILLER, Oscar W., *The Kantian Thing-in-itself; or The Creative Mind,* N. Y. Philosophical Library, 1956

MILMED, Bella K., *Kant and Current Philosophical Issues;* . . . N. Y., N. Y. Univ. Press, 1961

PATON, Herbert James, *The Categorical Imperative; a Study in Kant's Moral Philosophy,* Chicago, Univ. of Chicago Press, 1948

SCHLIPP, Paul Arthur, *Kant's Pre-critical Ethics,* 2nd ed., Evanston, Ill., Northwestern Univ. Press, 1960

SMITH, Alice Halford, *A Treatise on Knowledge,* Oxford, Clarendon Press, 1943

SMITH, Norman Kemp, *A Compendium to Kant's "Critique of Pure Reason,"* 2nd ed., rev. and enl., N. Y., Humanities Press, 1950

TEALE, A. E., *Kantian Ethics,* London, Oxford Univ. Press, 1951

TEMMER, Mark J., *Time in Rousseau and Kant,* New York, Gregory Lounz, 1959

VAIHINGER, Hans, *Philosophy of As If,* 2nd ed. (trans. by C. K. Ogden), New York, Barnes & Noble, 1935

WEBB, Clement C. J., *Kant's Philosophy of Religion,* Oxford, Clarendon Press, 1926

WELDON, Thomas D., *Introduction to Kant's Critique of Pure Reason,* Oxford, Clarendon Press, 1945

WELLEK, Rene, *Immanuel Kant in England, 1793-1838,* Princeton, N. J., Princeton Univ. Press, 1931

WHITNEY, Geo. T., *The Heritage of Kant,* Princeton, N. J., Princeton Univ. Press, 1939

WILM, Emil C. et al., *Immanuel Kant, 1724-1924,* New Haven, Conn., Yale Univ. Press, 1925

INDEX

"I wish especially that the spirit of his practical idealism, his lofty ideas of human dignity, right and freedom might again exert an influence in this age of 'realism,' of belief in might and money."

With this hope, Friedrich Paulsen undertook in this book to present more fully the constructive and idealistic elements of the great philosopher's work. As Professor of Philosophy at the University of Berlin, Paulsen was in the midst of the furor between conservatives who deplored Kant as agnostic, and modernists who hailed him as *Alles-zertrümmerer,* "the All-Shatterer" of what they considered outworn belief. Paulsen rejected both views as one-sided; here he aimed at refuting the traditionalists' image of Kant as an undiluted skeptic. Besides analyzing the famous Critiques, his book covers lesser-known papers on metaphysics which take a more positive approach. By treating the philosophy as a whole, this study offers modern readers a provocative "minority report" on Kantian thought.

The book is organized to provide a background of understanding for the